In Sullivan's Shadow

AIMEE EDMONDSON

In Sullivan's Shadow

The Use and Abuse of Libel Law during
the Long Civil Rights Struggle

University of Massachusetts Press
Amherst and Boston

Copyright © 2019 by University of Massachusetts Press
All rights reserved
Printed in the United States of America

ISBN 978-1-62534-409-0 (paper); 408-3 (hardcover)

Designed by Sally Nichols
Set in Linotype Centennial
Printed and bound by Maple Press, Inc.

Cover design by Kristina Kachele Design, llc
Cover art by Kristina Kachele, adapted from *The Children's March*, sculpture by Ronald S. McDowell, c. 1995, Birmingham, Alabama.

Library of Congress Cataloging-in-Publication Data

Names: Edmondson, Aimee, author.
Title: In Sullivan's shadow : the use and abuse of libel during the civil
 rights struggle / Aimee Edmondson.
Description: Amherst : University of Massachusetts, 2019. | Includes
 bibliographical references and index. |
Identifiers: LCCN 2018051547 (print) | LCCN 2018051759 (ebook) | ISBN
 9781613766569 (ebook) | ISBN 9781613766576 (ebook) | ISBN 9781625344083
 (hardcover) | ISBN 9781625344090 (pbk.)
Subjects: LCSH: Libel and slander—United States—History. | Freedom of the
 press—United States—History. | Sullivan, L. B. —Trials, litigation, etc.
 | New York Times Company—Trials, litigation, etc.
Classification: LCC KF1266 (ebook) | LCC KF1266 .E36 2019 (print) | DDC
 346.7303/4—dc23
LC record available at https://lccn.loc.gov/2018051547

British Library Cataloguing-in-Publication Data
A catalog record for this book is available from the British Library.

Portions of the introduction were revised from Aimee Edmondson, "In Sullivan's Shadow: The Use and Abuse of Libel Law Arising from the Civil Rights Movement, 1960–1989," *Journalism History* 37, no. 1 (April 2011): 27–38. © 2019 History Division of the AEJMC. Portions of chapters 1, 3, and 4 were revised from Aimee Edmondson, "A Pulitzer from the North, a Libel Suit from the South: Southern Editors' Civil Rights Writings, 1954–1968," *First Amendment Law Review*, 12 (Winter 2014). Portions of chapter 5 and the conclusion were revised from Aimee Edmondson, "Rearticulating *New York Times v. Sullivan* as a Social Duty to Journalists," *Journalism Studies*, 18, no. 1 (2017): 86–101, DOI: 10.1080/1461670X.2016.1215255.

For Matt

CONTENTS

Preface: An Awakening ix

INTRODUCTION 1

CHAPTER 1
Before *New York Times v. Sullivan* 17

CHAPTER 2
"Heed Their Rising Voices," the *Sullivan* Case, and Turmoil for the *Times* 78

CHAPTER 3
While *Sullivan* Is on Appeal . . . 129

CHAPTER 4
. . . The SLAPPs Keep Coming 163

CHAPTER 5
"Wanted for Murder" 214

CHAPTER 6
Sullivan Sinks In 255

CONCLUSION
The Writing on the Courtroom Wall 296

Notes 305
Index 345

PREFACE

An Awakening

This book is the product of thirty years of ruminations on race and journalism, especially in the American South. I grew up in a small farming community in northeast Louisiana. It was a patriarchal society, no doubt. Girls didn't hunt or fish much, and we didn't drive tractors on our fathers' farms. That was for the boys. In the 1970s and 1980s when I lived there, the white people I knew owned the land and the black people worked for them. My father's main farm hand, Shot, quiet and lanky, a cigarette dangling from his lips, spent endless days folded into a green John Deere tractor in the cotton and soybean fields around our rambling, old farmhouse. His wife, Annie, scrubbed our floors, washed our clothes, and mothered me the way black maids in the South had mothered white children for generations.

Everybody I knew went to the all-white private school that had opened in 1969 when, fifteen years after *Brown v. Board of Education* should have finally settled the question, the white leaders in my town gave up the school desegregation fight. Our school mascot was the Rebels, as in Colonel Reb, and I cheered at many a football and basketball game for an all-white team that waved the Confederate flag. In the 1980s, we were taught never to go into the poverty-plagued "bad" part of town—black, of course—with its juke joints and shotgun shacks.

My home parish of East Carroll tucks into the upper right-hand corner of the state, touching Arkansas on the north and the Mississippi River on the east. The town of Lake Providence is wedged between the river and an eight-mile, bow-shaped body of water that was once part of the Mississippi but is now cut off from the original channel, which snakes across the flat Delta farmland on its way down to New Orleans. When I was a kid, the dirt levee loomed up from the town of just a few thousand residents, mostly black since before the Civil War. In our Louisiana-history class at school, we learned all about Pierre Le Moyne d'Iberville, founder of the French colony of Louisiana, and about his younger brother, Bienville. But I remember learning nothing about the civil rights movement. In these classes, we never reached the 1950s and 1960s—it's as if we ran out of time at the end of the school year or historical time stopped before 1954, the year of *Brown*.

I didn't question the way things were. When I arrived at Louisiana State University (LSU) in Baton Rouge as a freshman in 1986, I landed in a place where the student enrollment was six times larger than the population of my entire parish back home. College was a four-hour drive and what felt like a world away from the farm. That crisp fall across the LSU quad, I spotted a letterman's jacket from my hometown's public school, the Lake Providence High School Panthers, worn by a tall black student who used to bag our groceries at the only market in town. I recalled that once when he was loading up our grocery sacks, I saw an algebra book next to him on the checkout counter. He was probably trying to get in a bit of homework between customers. We were both high school seniors by then, but that was the algebra book I had used as a freshman. I realized later that it was just one of a million exhibits illustrating that in education, separate certainly did not guarantee equality between the all-black and the all-white schools of my youth.

So back at LSU in a flash of recognition and homesickness, I rushed toward his navy blue-and-white letterman jacket and told him we were from the same town! Only, I didn't go to the public school, I informed. He shook his head and said, "No shit." He wasn't rude, just matter of fact. Everybody knew schools were still self-segregated in East Carroll Parish in the 1980s. My dad wore that Panthers letterman jacket as a high school football star in the 1950s, but he would not send his three daughters there in the 1970s and 1980s. This episode, perhaps, was the beginning of my true awakening to issues of race and racism in my world.

Years later, when I was a newspaper reporter in Memphis and working for the metro daily *Commercial Appeal*, I became immersed in the problems of race and racism in the town where Martin Luther King Jr. was assassinated. I covered the public education beat, where race was woven into most issues and stories about the school system. I covered a Ku Klux Klan rally in downtown Memphis as late as 2004—shocked that this kind of racist affront was still happening in civil society—while acrimonious debate raged around the removal of the monuments to Confederate luminaries Jefferson Davis and Nathan Bedford Forrest. I spent five weeks dispatching Hurricane Katrina stories from south Louisiana to my editors in Memphis during that sweltering, life-changing August and September of 2005. The poor, mostly black population I covered there suffered untold horrors, left behind to watch the waters rise. Of course, most people with means and a car had fled north.

But it wasn't until graduate school at the University of Missouri that I dug deeply into the history of the long civil rights struggle. And it was a history that appealed to me in several ways. It's a hell of a story. The quest for equal rights, for human rights, through nonviolent means inspired the journalist in me. Much of that history happened close to my home, where blacks and whites still feel the effects of slavery a century and a half later. In the 1960s, one of our three television channels, WLBT in Jackson, Mississippi, used to put up a "technical difficulties" sign when its parent network, NBC in New York, had the gall to broadcast news, documentaries, or anything that might be objective or even sympathetic about the civil rights movement or disrupt the racial status quo in the region. I was ignorant of this practice until graduate school, when I began seriously studying the history of the American media.

My mother told me years later that she saw no television and very little newspaper coverage of civil rights issues in the 1950s and 1960s. She said she didn't pay attention because she was busy raising babies and running a household. But raising kids, hosting the garden club, and putting up sweet corn in the freezer weren't the only things that kept her away from events of the day. I came to learn that most of the mainstream media in the South ignored the civil rights story for years, and many southerners expressed outrage at northern or national media invading Dixie to cover this emerging race beat. No wonder mom hadn't heard or read much about the seismic events and changes shaking the racial foundation of the segregated South in the 1960s and 1970s.

In graduate school, I also came across a book, *Witness to the Truth: My Struggle for Human Rights in Louisiana,* by John H. Scott and Cleo Scott Brown.[1] Scott was an African American Baptist preacher in Lake Providence terrorized and nearly murdered for trying to register to vote in East Carroll Parish in 1962, just six years before I was born. I knew the family names of most, if not all, of the whites living in the parish and included in the book, but the names of blacks were entirely new to me. There was the story of successful black farmer Francis Joseph Atlas, who suffered a full economic boycott by whites for testifying about voting irregularities in the parish in U.S. District Court seventy miles down the road in Monroe, Louisiana.[2]

No one would buy his cotton or soybeans or sell him feed for his livestock. Well known in the community, he had lived in East Carroll all his life, served as PTA president, sent his children to college, and volunteered as a church superintendent for twenty years. His prosperity, in addition to his testimony, threatened to upset the racial status quo and splashed a huge target on his back. He owned about 175 acres and twenty-five head of cattle, wealth unusual for a black man in the 1950s Deep South. He voted for the first time at age fifty-nine in 1962, and he tearfully told *Jet* magazine about white reprisals three years after he cast that vote, while my hometown newspaper, the *Banner Democrat,* ignored the story altogether.[3]

My mentor, Dr. Earnest L. Perry Jr., at the Missouri School of Journalism, inspired me to study the broader history of civil rights and pointed me to his University of Missouri colleague Dr. Carol Anderson, whose enthusiasm for the work encouraged me to research and write this book. Anderson, who moved on to Emory University, pointed me to the legal history of Charles Hamilton Houston, dean of the Howard Law School and the first special counsel to the National Association for the Advancement of Colored People (NAACP). Houston trained most of the lawyers, including Thurgood Marshall, who dismantled Jim Crow in the nation's schools state by state and case by case starting at the college level. I situated my own research on First Amendment law, specifically libel law and the landmark *New York Times v. Sullivan* case, into this civil rights history. It was critical to place this libel case in the social and cultural context of its day, specifically Montgomery, Alabama, in the early 1960s. Thus began my study of libel cases filed by southern public officials relating to news coverage of the massive civil rights upheaval, also known as the Second Reconstruction, that captured the nation's attention thanks in large part to the national news media.

Anthony Lewis's book, *Make No Law: The Sullivan Case and the First Amendment,* also helped start me on this journey. Lewis covered *Sullivan* for the *New York Times* when it was argued before the U.S. Supreme Court in 1964, and he crafts a powerful narrative placing the case in the context of the social turmoil of the time. My study is an expansion of Lewis's work, exploring little-known lawsuits adjudicated in the shadow of this famous case.[4] Most were filed by small, defiant towns—many like the one where I grew up—that bristled at the new world order and refused to acknowledge *Sullivan*'s crushing blow in southern courts. Significantly, the great names of the civil rights movement, such as Martin Luther King Jr., Fred Shuttlesworth, James Farmer, and others, were forced to defend themselves against waves of libel suits, mostly behind the scenes, as they marched against segregation across the South.

Dozens of cases in the area of libel, litigated out of the spotlight that nation-altering cases such as *Sullivan* attracted, have gone unexplored by scholars. The layers of history found at the intersection of race, libel law, and journalism are much deeper and more complex than historians and legal scholars generally assume. In a broader sense, this research might help remind them that major social change is rarely the product of one incident but rather emerges from many actors and actions whose power and significance become apparent over time.

As I write this preface, I return to Carol Anderson's powerful work, *White Rage: The Unspoken Truth of Our Racial Divide*, about the long history of white people's pushing back against black progress. Published in 2016 after the upheaval in Ferguson, Missouri, the book came out of her remarkable op-ed for the *Washington Post*, the most-shared piece on social media published by the newspaper that year, and its message is more relevant than ever with the election of Donald Trump to the U.S. presidency.[5] I pondered inauguration weekend in January 2017 as a milestone in my profession. Angered by what he saw as reports that deliberately understated the size of his inauguration crowd, the president called journalists "among the most dishonest human beings on earth." The attack was part of his ongoing, decades-old criticism of the Fourth Estate. As a lifelong journalist and now a journalism professor, I am troubled by this rhetoric, like so many others in my field.

With the rise of the "fake news" phenomenon during the 2016 election, Trump appropriated the term and applied it to the mainstream media's political coverage of him, threatening to sue those outlets whose coverage he despised. This takes me back to my newsroom days at the *Commercial Appeal* and a tradition called Error Court, which was instituted by the intimidating yet beloved editor Angus McEachran, who put our journalistic credibility above all else. If a reporter wrote a story that contained an error, the newspaper would run a correction the next day—followed by the reporter's attendance at Error Court on Thursday afternoon to explain to Angus how that mistake got into the newspaper. Then a demerit was placed in the reporter's personnel file. The grilling was frightening. It was said that grown men cried in Error Court after a tongue-lashing from Angus. I think I had to go three times between 1998 and 2002 during his tenure, human error being what it is.

Angus, who reminded me of the Warner Brothers cartoon character the Tasmanian Devil, had a famously short temper. Back in the day when he ran the metro desk, legend had it that when he got mad, his face would turn red, his neck veins would bulge, and he would tear the bulky Memphis telephone book in half—and not by the binder, that would be too easy. Everybody respected Angus, though. As metro editor in 1968, he oversaw the coverage of King's assassination. Later, he directed the coverage of Elvis Presley's death, including the revelations of the music legend's drug abuse.

When he became the top editor at the *Commercial Appeal* and instituted Error Court, Angus wanted to track the number and kinds of mistakes his reporters were making. He thought that if we knew where our mistakes were coming from and how they happened, we could cut down on the number getting into the newspaper. If we lost our credibility, we had nothing, he believed. At the end of every day, I printed out my stories to take home. Those printouts stayed by my bedside at night so when I woke up in the middle of the night sweating about whether I misspelled a name or wrote something down wrong, I could double check on that computer printout, calm down, and get a bit more sleep. I believe the traditions of such careful reporting championed by Angus McEachran are still alive and thriving today, especially in mainstream journalism, contrary to Trump's inflammatory rhetoric that we are the "enemy of the people." It has had staying power. Sometimes that brand of journalism seems hard to find amid the noise of all the other media out there today. But everyone works under the same rules of law, such as those governing libel.

The libel cases in this study are stories of local people, their struggles, and their day in court. We Americans live by those court decisions today. In part because cases build on prior decisions, the lawsuits in this narrative are presented roughly in chronological order. However, some groups of cases—or events—dealing with similar issues are presented together. As such, this volume is organized into three major areas: the cases that came before

New York Times v. Sullivan; then *Sullivan* and the lesser-known *Sullivan*-era cases; and, lastly, the post-*Sullivan* decisions.

One final personal thought. I wish I could have ridden with Johnny Popham in his green Buick at least some of the fifty thousand miles a year he drove across the American South in the middle of the last century. Popham was the first northern newspaper correspondent to cover the region in depth and file dispatches for the *New York Times* as the civil rights struggle erupted amid mounting racial turmoil in the 1950s. He had many friends on both sides of the civil rights fight. Born in Virginia, a region of Old South whites unwavering in their racial beliefs, he told his editor: "I can never be angry about the last-ditch fights of some of these people, because I understand what made them. I knew their type and often their families. . . ."[6]

In the socially segregated rural South of the 1970s and 1980s, I knew them too. My dad helped start the private academy my two sisters and I attended—it was one of many that sprouted in those cotton fields throughout the region in the 1960s and it still exists today. He was president of the all-white school board for a time, and while I walked those all-white halls from kindergarten through the twelfth grade, he played a big role in sustaining the school that helped get me ready for college. He was a product of that antiquated southern way of life that in many ways still exists, but I believe he was a wise and honorable man.

We fell on hard times and eventually had to sell our farm in the late 1990s, but my dad was the hardest-working person I've ever known. I realized that when I was almost thirty years old, when I spent a summer at home driving a tractor for him after he had a stroke and before I started graduate school. He was evolving even to the point of accepting that girls could, in fact, drive tractors. Regarding race, things hadn't changed as much as one would think. He told me in 1996, "I'm a racist, but I hate racists." I believe that aptly describes the way a lot of people thought—and still think—especially in the South.

In Sullivan's Shadow

INTRODUCTION

Turner Catledge ran the world's most powerful newspaper, and he was scared. As executive editor, he directed the *New York Times*' coverage of the civil rights revolution of the 1950s and 1960s, and here he was in the middle of it, staring down expensive libel suit after libel suit filed by enraged southern politicians. Catledge was a Mississippi native, his two grandfathers had served in the Confederate Army, and he had sinned against his southern brethren. In 1960, they sought their retribution in the form of a $500,000 libel suit against the *Times* in a case filed by Commissioner Lester B. Sullivan of the Police and Fire Department in Montgomery, Alabama. At the time, the amount was the largest penalty requested by a plaintiff in the state's history and a huge sum anywhere in the United States.

While the *Times*' team of lawyers waged war in court, Catledge admitted, "I'm frightened as hell at this new weapon of intimidation which seems in the making."[1] Libel law was fast becoming a political cudgel to intimidate the press and stop the reporting of racial upheaval of the day. In a letter-writing campaign banged out on his personal typewriter, Catledge warned other editors around the country that they too were in danger of being dragged into southern courts for civil rights coverage should the paper lose its appeal. The case was the first of nine libel actions that Alabama public officials, including Governor James Patterson, would lodge against the newspaper in 1960. All told, the *Times* faced libel actions totaling more than $4.6 million—more than $25 million in current dollars—for publishing an advertisement supporting civil rights as well as an article written by the internationally known correspondent Harrison Salisbury in April 1960. Catledge wasn't sure the newspaper—or journalism in general—could endure the financial hardships from the wave of suits, complaining that the newspaper's bank accounts "were coming out 'cleaned.' This is an expensive business."[2] Catledge fretted to a friend at the Associated Press (AP) that if the U.S. Supreme Court upheld the Alabama judgment, "all of us are out of business, because we will not be able to do our jobs."[3]

Catledge was right to worry. Without the U.S. Supreme Court's landmark decision in *New Times v. Sullivan* in 1964, media coverage of the civil rights struggle, the most significant social movement—along with the abolition of slavery—in the nation's history, would have been sharply curtailed if not squelched altogether. What was overlooked among journalists in the early sixties and what is unacknowledged among historians today, however, is the larger role that libel law played in the African American freedom struggle before and after *Sullivan*. My goal in this book is to highlight the little- or lesser-known cases in which public officials and public figures tried to shut down political dissent by filing libel suits against the media and civil right activists. Taken together, these legal assaults constitute a clear historical pattern showing how white political leaders turned to libel law as a weapon for silencing all critics on the momentous issue of racial justice, not just news coverage by national and local media.

The issue at hand was, among other things, police brutality against the citizenry, a constant concern among civil rights groups. In the *Sullivan* case, activists placed a full-page advertisement in the *Times* in March 1960 criticizing the actions of police and public authorities in southern cities, notably Montgomery, Alabama. The full-page ad, "Heed Their Rising Voices," paid for by the Committee to Defend Martin Luther King Jr. and the Struggle for Freedom in the South, spoke of alleged police violence against demonstrators as part of its plea to help pay for King's mounting legal bills and for general financial assistance to the growing movement. Although he was not named in the ad, Commissioner Sullivan argued that the criticism of him and his police force was based on false statements that defamed him as the individual in charge of law enforcement in Montgomery. He filed suit against the *Times* and five civil rights leaders for the advertisement. His legal action, although the most widely known case, was only one of many libel suits filed by police and public officials in the South for adverse discourse and coverage as detailed in this study. The difference is that the *Sullivan* case reached the U.S. Supreme Court first and ultimately transformed libel law in this country.

Four long years after Catledge embarked on that letter-writing campaign to fellow editors around the country, the nation's highest court reversed the Alabama Supreme Court's decision against the *Times*. In one of the most famous First Amendment cases in American history, *New York Times v. Sullivan,* Justice William Brennan wrote in 1964 that not only is it the right of citizens—it is their duty—to criticize their government and its official representatives— including police officers, state actors who wield enormous power over the citizenry. Brennan eloquently wrote of the "profound national commitment to the principle that debate on public issues should be uninhibited, robust, and wide-open, and that it may well include vehement, caustic and sometimes unpleasantly sharp attacks on government and public officials."[4]

Police brutality against the citizenry—what could be more worthy of public debate? Before this case, a plaintiff in a libel case could recover damages if he was able to prove that what was written or spoken about him was both false and defamatory. Damages were presumed if the content was based on false information. Sullivan had argued successfully before the Alabama Supreme Court that this advertisement amounted to false and defamatory criticism of him. There were indeed minor errors of fact in the ad, but the U.S. Supreme Court saw Commissioner Sullivan's suit as an attempt to resurrect seditious libel and overturned the Alabama Supreme Court's decision. The U.S. high court agreed that the *Times* had been punished for criticizing the government, specifically the actions of government representatives in Montgomery. Justice Brennan said that this was the very type of public speech and governmental tyranny that the First Amendment was intended to protect and to guard against. Justice Hugo Black, an Alabama native, met the issue of race head on in his concurring opinion in *Sullivan,* arguing that libel law was being deployed to beat down the civil rights movement: "One of the acute and highly emotional issues in this country arises out of efforts of many people, even including some public officials, to continue state-commanded segregation of races in the public schools and other public places, despite our several holdings that such a state practice is forbidden by the Fourteenth Amendment."[5]

Sullivan shifted the burden of proof in libel cases from the defendant to the plaintiff and introduced the notion of fault in this context. Under this new actual malice standard, the plaintiff had to show that the defendant published false information with a high degree of fault, that is, knowingly or recklessly. Up to this point, the U.S. Supreme Court had not considered a libel case in the freedom-of-speech context. Libel laws were state laws, and the First Amendment did not previously protect libel or slander within the federal court system.[6] The U.S. Supreme Court's reversal of *Sullivan* marked a fundamental evolution in First Amendment theory, which in turn would help alter the course of the civil rights movement. The Supreme Court ruled that in order to win a suit, a public official such as Sullivan must prove that the publisher, the *Times* in this case, knew the material was false or that it exhibited "reckless disregard for the truth" when it printed the information. Sullivan could not meet that tough new actual malice standard.

This book illustrates that *Sullivan* was just one example of the use and abuse of libel law during the civil rights movement. I tell the stories of the heretofore little-known lawsuits and courtroom dramas—many of them arising from charges of police brutality—that were filed in the long shadow of the famous *Sullivan* case in Alabama in 1960, through its adjudication in 1964 and in its aftermath. This book expands on the evidence and argument that southern officials used existing libel law to craft and apply what amounted to sedition law; their object was to proscribe and quash press coverage of the civil rights struggle.[7]

Their message was simple and suppressive: Criticize our government or our public officials and you will be punished. Had the U.S. Supreme Court failed to overturn *Sullivan*, the Alabama court's impact on the civil rights movement would have been staggering.[8] The *Times*—unarguably the leading newspaper on the race beat down South prior to Sullivan's suit—was effectively shut out of the state of Alabama and forced to rely on too-often-scant wire reports of civil rights demonstrations and related issues until *Sullivan* was overturned. Without the world looking at the South through the lens of the national press, southern officials and other segregationists would have been free to continue squelching activism in their own way. "The last desperate reaction of a clinging regime was to try to suppress the message itself," wrote legal scholar Rodney A. Smolla. "If one could not stop the marches, one might at least keep the marches off television and out of the newspapers."[9]

This book illustrates that the use of libel law became an integral part of the story in the battle for equal rights. In these cases, public-official plaintiffs and other prominent community leaders, angered by the unflattering press, complained that their stories treated them unfairly and reflected negatively on them. I argue that these cases fit the very description of the SLAPP (Strategic Lawsuits Against Public Participation) suit genre identified by scholars George W. Pring and Penelope Canan. These legal actions, or assaults, are intended to discourage and punish those parties who speak out about issues of public concern and whose speech disrupts the status quo.[10] Outside the context of criticism of police brutality, Pring and Canan identify a body of case law they label "intimidation lawsuits," in which plaintiffs might not feel defamed but rather seek to silence any critics and sway public policy or opinion their way. Most of these efforts fail in court, thanks to the *Sullivan* decision, but Pring and Canan estimate that between 1976 and 1996, thousands of people were sued into silence. Through their scholarship, Pring and Canan have popularized the term SLAPP in their 1996 book, but they limit their study primarily to the 1970s and later. They do not focus on issues of civil rights, and they give very limited treatment to cases filed by police officers. This book helps fill that void.

My work is grounded in critical race theory (CRT). This framework in contemporary legal studies focuses on the intersection of society and culture with the legal system and demonstrates the complicity of the law from the municipal to federal levels in upholding white supremacy throughout American history. In the 1970s, the Harvard University law professor Derrick Bell was among the first scholars to repudiate the idea of the colorblindness of modern law with his pathbreaking book, *Race, Racism, and American Law,* and a similarly titled course. My study, a history of libel law within the context of the civil rights movement, reinforces that finding. Critical race theorists have evolved and applied this conceptual framework to critique how the law helped to create, rationalize, and enforce an unjust social order, emerging as a sociohistorical movement in legal academia by the late 1970s. Prominent among the voluminous research by CRT scholars is their work on the administrative and legal foot-dragging in the South's implementation of *Brown v. Board of Education of Topeka,* which outlawed school segregation in 1954.[11]

Indeed, such delays have been widespread across many areas of the law, including voting rights,[12] equal pay,[13] laws forbidding interracial marriage,[14] restrictive housing covenants,[15] and segregated interstate transportation. In the last example, the South's refusal to acknowledge U.S. Supreme Court desegregation rulings brought the Freedom Riders, mostly idealistic college students, to the South in 1962 in a desperate attempt to force southern courts, police, and politicians to acknowledge *Boynton v. Virginia.* This 1960 decision held that racial segregation in public transportation was illegal because it violated the Interstate Commerce Act.[16] I argue that the same delays held true for libel law: intransigent southern judges, lawyers, and plaintiffs clung to the master narrative of white supremacy and segregation well after the U.S.

Supreme Court overturned Sullivan and protected public speech critical of governments and their authorities.

This story of the civil rights movement is told through the court battles initiated by approximately forty plaintiffs, primarily police officers, public officials, and prominent southerners who used SLAPP suits to silence speech about civil rights and punish the speakers and those journalists who wrote about them. Libel suits were filed to attack a wide variety of civil rights actions, including the fight to desegregate schools, and the recruitment of plaintiffs to challenge *Plessy v. Ferguson*, the 1896 case that upheld the constitutionality of racial segregation.[17] But media coverage of civil rights actions and of their often-violent suppression triggered the largest number of libel suits. Among these episodes were the Birmingham bus station beatings during the 1961 Freedom Rides,[18] the University of Mississippi (Ole Miss) riots in 1962 as James Meredith sought to desegregate Mississippi's flagship university,[19] the March on Washington in 1963,[20] and the Freedom Summer murders of three civil rights workers in Philadelphia, Mississippi, in 1964.[21] Still more suits were filed for coverage of Martin Luther King Jr.'s assassination in 1968.[22] The legal battles covered in this book rightfully have not gotten the same attention as bombed churches, beaten and bloody Freedom Riders, or civil rights workers mysteriously disappearing in the night. But this legal history remains a significant piece of the civil rights story as well as an example of the insidious shackling of free-speech rights in the United States.

Libel law, especially *Sullivan,* has been widely studied. Anthony Lewis, who covered the *Sullivan* trial for the *Times,* places the case in the historical, cultural, and social context of the day in his superb book, *Make No Law: The Sullivan Case and the First Amendment.* Kermit L. Hall and Melvin I. Urofsky argue persuasively that *Sullivan,* filed in the cradle of the Confederacy, Montgomery, Alabama, where Jefferson Davis took the oath as its first and only president, was as much a civil rights case as a libel case. They point out that the Supreme Court found Alabama's application of libel law a threat to both the free press and equal rights for African Americans.²³

This book broadens the history and deepens the analysis of southerners' weaponizing of libel against activists and the media, emphasizing how the civil rights revolution helped shape that law in significant ways. Scholars and other media experts agree *Sullivan* stopped what surely would have been an onslaught of libel cases brought in the South. Yet knowledge has been scarce on the suits that actually *were* brought to stop public discourse relating to civil rights issues. One assumes that these cases eventually would have been dismissed after *Sullivan* was overturned in 1964 given that public-official plaintiffs (and later public-figure plaintiffs) were required to meet the newer, tougher actual malice standard. But that does not diminish their historical value in the context of the civil rights movement and southern officials' concerted efforts to sustain white supremacy—cultural, political, and economic—in the face of federal statutes and legal decisions intended to dismantle segregation and protect minority rights. This book shows that libel suits continued to work their way through the courts much longer than media historians and legal scholars have previously noted. Many studies of civil rights history and media begin in the 1950s and end in the 1960s. The last libel case presented here was dismissed in 1989.²⁴

But the intersection of libel, race, and journalism can be traced as far back as 1829 when a slave trader sued the fiery abolitionist and newspaper editor William Lloyd Garrison for his criticism of slavery. Garrison's battle emerged from his "Black List," a catalogue of "Horrible News—Domestic and Foreign" in the Baltimore newspaper, the *Genius of Universal Emancipation,* which he wrote and edited with Benjamin Lundy. Garrison compiled stories of atrocities from public records, correspondence with a wide range of sources, and reports from other newspapers. He published statistics on the thousands of slaves shipped from the Chesapeake area to the Deep South, relayed stories of free blacks in the North who were kidnapped and sold into slavery, and shamed other newspapers for running ads about upcoming slave auctions. He taunted and baited slave merchants and anyone who had anything to do with the slave trade. Labeling them immoral, Garrison scorned all men who mistreated others "for purposes of heaping up wealth." What got him in legal trouble was his attack on a specific ship owner. He reported that the ship *Francis,* owned by a merchant named Francis Todd, had sailed from Baltimore for New Orleans with seventy-five slaves onboard. Garrison wrote that any man who participated in this wicked trade should be "sentenced to solitary confinement for life" and that he was no better than "highway robbers and murderers."[25]

A Baltimore grand jury indicted Garrison and Lundy in February 1830 under a rarely used criminal statute against publishing "a gross and malicious libel," in this case against the merchant and ship owner Todd. In addition to jail time, the editors faced a $5,000 civil defamation suit filed by Todd's attorneys for damages to their client's reputation. Always in a precarious financial situation, the editors worried that this legal trouble would put them out of business for good. In his biography of Garrison, historian Henry Mayer characterized Maryland's decision to prosecute the abolitionists as politically inspired. The *Genius* had repeatedly attacked prominent merchants and well-connected slave traders, and, in Mayer's words, "the local authorities had decided to silence them." Charles Mitchell, an established Baltimore lawyer with abolitionist sympathies, volunteered to take on Garrison's defense pro bono. He had Lundy's case severed from Garrison's because Lundy was out of town when the offending material was published and ultimately avoided prosecution. Mitchell believed Garrison's case would be an easy win: Todd owned the ship, which had in fact carried slaves. The published report was true, he argued in the Maryland state court, so it could not be libelous. He also argued that Garrison should not be punished for expressing a specific moral view about slavery.[26]

Mitchell expounded eloquently that the law of libel was "the last and most successful engine of tyranny" and had done "more to perpetuate public abuses, and to check the march of reform than any other agent." It took the jury fifteen minutes to come back with a guilty verdict. Garrison's legal appeal failed, and the judge sentenced him to six months in jail or a fine of fifty dollars plus court costs. Garrison could not pay the fine, and he walked into the Baltimore jail on April 17, 1830, embracing his martyrdom in the cause of abolition.[27]

Lundy continued to publish the *Genius* and observed almost a month into Garrison's imprisonment that other newspaper editors were afraid to comment on his partner's case or touch on issues relating to free speech. "The press is now muzzled," Lundy wrote. Yet those were busy days for Garrison. From his jail cell, he penned letters to friends and supporters about the righteousness of his cause. He sent written greetings to Todd, exhorting him, "Consult your bible and your heart." Lundy published Garrison's account of his confinement, arguing for the principles of a free press and asserting that the Baltimore court had coordinated "a burlesque upon the Constitution."[28] These articles got the attention of New York philanthropist Arthur Tappan, who promptly paid Garrison's fine. In the end, the fiery editor had spent forty-nine days in jail.

Garrison was still not in the clear. In October of that year, a jury of merchants found Garrison guilty in Todd's civil libel suit and ordered him to pay $1,000 in damages. The sum was enormous at the time, particularly in the case of the journeyman editor, who sometimes survived on water and stale bread, which he got from a nearby bakery. By then, however, Garrison had moved to Boston and was preparing to launch the *Liberator*, which would become the most famous dissident press in the history of American journalism. The paper would publish weekly without interruption for thirty-five years, ceasing operation only when its mission was accomplished with the ratification of the Thirteenth Amendment, which constitutionally abolished slavery in 1865. Garrison ignored the civil libel verdict and, now relocated to Boston, was beyond the Maryland court's jurisdiction. He neither paid the fine nor went to jail.[29]

The first black newspaper sued for libel was the *Colored American*, started in New York City in 1837 and edited by Samuel

Cornish. In its second year of operation, Cornish had run a letter identifying a ship's captain as having kidnapped three Africans from Gambia and mistreating them on a ship bound for New York. In his defense, the editor claimed that the letter was surreptitiously typeset for printing without his knowledge and plead innocent to the libel charge. The local court found Cornish guilty and fined him nearly $600 in damages and court costs. With attorneys' fees the amount came to a hefty $1,500 (the equivalent of almost $38,000 in 2018), a great deal of money for a new publication such as the *Colored American*. The newspaper started a successful drive for funds to help pay the costs, and the paper published into 1842.[30]

Although informed by this early history, my focus remains on the twentieth-century context of the civil rights fight. I trace the use of SLAPP suits beginning in 1925, when *California Eagle* editor Charlotta Bass, a bold leader of the western black press and a civil rights icon, became a target of the Ku Klux Klan in Los Angeles. Similarly, South Carolina civil rights leader Rev. Joseph A. DeLaine faced a libel suit in January 1950 after he insisted that black schools and their white administrators in Clarendon County were far inferior to white institutions and their leaders, just as the white majority had designed. Members of the white school board bankrolled a libel suit against DeLaine. In another case, black journalist and activist John Henry McCray served hard time on a South Carolina chain gang in 1952 after questioning the guilt of a black man sentenced to die for raping a white girl.

Catledge at the *New York Times* wasn't the only white southerner assailed by segregationists. They would attack whites in their own communities. In 1954, Hazel Brannon Smith, the editor of the *Lexington Advertiser* in Mississippi and later a Pulitzer Prize winner, was sued by the local sheriff for her editorial criticizing his violent harassment of black citizens and calling for his resignation after he accidentally shot one person in the leg.[31]

Still, the libel suits kept coming. Birmingham leaders—most notably police commissioner Eugene "Bull" Connor of Birmingham, Alabama—sued the *New York Times* and one of its reporters,

Harrison Salisbury, for a story, "Fear and Hatred Grip Birmingham," that ran in April 1960, two weeks after the "Heed Their Rising Voices" advertisement appeared. Salisbury, a Pulitzer Prize winner and a former *Times* Moscow correspondent, wrote of Birmingham, "Every inch of middle ground has been fragmented by the emotional dynamite of racism, reinforced by the whip, the razor, the gun, the bomb, the torch, the club, the knife, the mob, the police and many branches of the state's apparatus." Published on the front page, the article infuriated the city's white establishment. Connor and other Birmingham officials sought damages for Salisbury's story in court.[32]

What is too often missing from writings about these libel cases is their historical and legal context within the civil rights movement. For example, the libel plaintiffs Sullivan and Connor were the police officers who, in 1961, gave mobs of Klansmen time to waylay Freedom Riders at the Montgomery and Birmingham bus stations before they instructed their officers to haul the wounded demonstrators off to jail.[33] Connor, along with other city officials, also sued CBS over Howard K. Smith's documentary, "Who Speaks for Birmingham?" in 1961. In addition, Smith's broadcasts on the Klan beatings of Freedom Riders had thrown a blinding and damning spotlight on the city.[34] As legal historian Lawrence M. Friedman asserts, the law is an integral part of our culture, the product of social forces working in society, "a mirror held up against life."[35] State law across the South reflected systems of racial segregation enforced with the threat of violence and, if necessary, actual violence. Battles fought by journalists against libel suits in state and federal courts were a critical and little-known front in the civil rights movement that challenged and dismantled de jure racial segregation in the South.

As previously noted, the Ole Miss riot in the fall of 1962 triggered a flurry of libel litigation, most notably from the conservative personality and retired U.S. Army general Edwin A. Walker. The case, *Associated Press v. Walker*, extended *Sullivan*'s actual malice standard to public figures, thus continuing the Supreme Court's rewriting of libel law through civil rights–related suits.[36]

Walker filed scores of suits against the individual newspapers that ran an AP story that described him helping lead the charge against federal marshals deployed to keep the peace as James Meredith desegregated the University of Mississippi by federal court order. Among Walker's many suits was a case filed against the venerable *Atlanta Constitution* editor, Ralph McGill, for a syndicated column about Walker's involvement in the riots. Hodding Carter Jr. of the Greenville, Mississippi, *Delta Democrat-Times* also faced Walker in a slander case based on remarks the famous editor made about him at the University of New Hampshire's Distinguished Lecture Series in October 1962.[37]

Still more libel suits that have received little scholarly attention were filed by Sheriff Lawrence A. Rainey of Neshoba County, Mississippi, against several media outlets that covered the story about the three murdered civil rights workers during the Freedom Summer of 1964.[38] Rainey was suspected of involvement in the deaths of Andrew Goodman, Michael Schwerner, and James Chaney. All three had disappeared while investigating the burning of a black church that was also a voter's registration site. All told, Rainey filed six separate suits against the media—refusing to yield years after the *Sullivan* verdict made it incredibly difficult for him to recover damages. As late as 1989, Rainey sued Orion Pictures and movie producer Fred Zollo for $8 million, arguing that fictionalized accounts in the movie *Mississippi Burning* unfairly portrayed him as a malevolent villain. "They have sure done some terrible harm," Rainey said. "Everybody all over the South knows the one they have playing the sheriff is referring to me."[39]

A trio of cases from the New York City area in 1964 and 1965 further highlight the fact that police officers were turning to libel to silence their critics despite the *Sullivan* decision's raising the legal standard for proof of actual malice in court. These three cases also illustrate that northern lawmen joined their southern counterparts in seeking to muzzle criticism of their official actions. On July 16, 1964, Lieutenant Thomas Gilligan, an off-duty New York City policeman, shot and killed James Powell, a fifteen-year-old African American, after he spotted the youth running from an apartment building with a knife. The incident triggered a three-day riot during which more than two hundred stores were damaged and 122 people arrested. The Harlem Defense Council published a poster, "Wanted for Murder," that included a photograph of Gilligan in his police uniform and identified him as "Gilligan, the cop." Exonerated by a grand jury and internal police investigations, he filed a $5.25 million libel suit alleging he had been falsely accused of murder by numerous civil rights leaders, including James Farmer and Martin Luther King Jr.

Two other police shootings brought publicity to brutal police tactics and sparked libel suits. Almost a year to the day later, rookie patrolman Sheldon Liebowitz shot an African American man in Brooklyn, prompting civil rights marches to police headquarters in Manhattan. The Harlem Defense Council again published a "Wanted for Murder" poster, this time running a photograph of Liebowitz in his police uniform. Seeking $2.5 million in damages, Liebowitz's attorney used the language of the *Sullivan* decision, asserting that the poster was published with actual malice toward his client, with reason to believe it false, and with the intent of exposing him to "hatred, contempt, ridicule and aversion and [to] injure and dishonor him" as a police officer.[40] In a third case that same year, a police officer shot and killed an African American man in Newark, New Jersey. Civil rights leaders criticized Officer Henry Martinez for murder and again were slapped with a libel suit.

Libel suits issued even from men of disrepute. For instance, James Earl Ray, Martin Luther King's confessed assassin, was quite litigious. While sitting in his prison cell, he sued *Time* magazine, among others, for coverage of the shooting, the resulting manhunt, and his murder trial.[41] This suit was among the first cases that helped establish the "libel proof doctrine," which now applies to the notorious and infamous, typically habitual criminals and high-profile murderers. In essence, Ray's reputation was so bad after King's assassination that he was considered libel-proof. No one could write anything that would actually libel him or worsen his reputation, according to the court.[42]

Detective Frank Pape of the Chicago Police Department, dubbed the "Toughest Cop in America," sued *Time* magazine over its report of a critical study published in 1961 by the U.S. Commission on Civil Rights and detailing his abuse of a black man suspected of but never charged with murder. The libel case wound its way through the court system until, finally in 1971, the U.S. Supreme Court relied on *Sullivan*'s actual malice standard to exonerate *Time*.

Modern applications of this study are numerous. In 2016, the Republican presidential candidate Donald Trump weaponized libel law in his campaign. If elected president of the United States, he vowed to "open up" libel laws to make successfully suing the media easier than it was after *Sullivan*. In the process, he sowed anger against all media by what he saw as unfair criticism of him and his policies. This effort to loosen the legal standards of libel would most certainly be a resurrection of seditious libel, a dangerous turn against free speech in this democracy.

In addition, the wave of protests relating to police shootings of black men after the Ferguson, Missouri, incident in 2014 illustrate now more than ever why Americans must maintain the right to engage in robust public discourse surrounding such incidents—without fear of costly and intimidating libel suits. Ferguson, of course, is the St. Louis suburb where the shooting of an unarmed black man, Michael Brown, by Officer Darren Wilson became a national symbol of tension between the police and minorities. As was the case with the trio of police brutality and libel cases in New York City area in 1964 and 1965, demonstrators in 2014 marched with signs proclaiming "Wanted for Murder," along with the image of Officer Wilson, who pulled the trigger.

In 2016, two Baltimore police officers charged in the death of African American Freddie Gray sued State's Attorney Marilyn Mosby for defamation. They said she made false statements about Gray's death at a press conference in 2015. At the time of the suit, Sergeant Alicia White and Officer William Porter were facing charges of involuntary manslaughter after Gray died from spinal injuries that prosecutors said he suffered in the back of a police transport van. Gray's death shook the city and prompted widespread protests about police treatment of minorities.

Today, as more videos of police brutality are posted online, internet companies are noting a major increase in requests from government officials, particularly police officers, for Google to take down content they deem libelous. From 2011 to 2015, for example, government officials asked Google Web Search to remove 15,576 items from various platforms, citing "defamation." A very distant second cause for removal requests, numbering 2,530, was "privacy and security," followed by trademark infringement with 1,132 requests during the same period.[43] While Google's Transparency Reports do not go into great detail about each take down request, one report in early 2011, for example, informed that Google received "a request from a local law enforcement agency to remove videos of police brutality" from YouTube. It refused to do so. In defamation law, truth is the ultimate defense.

Indeed, I argue that the story of libel, race, and journalism is ongoing. So is the urge to silence dissent.

CHAPTER 1

Before *New York Times v. Sullivan*

The terrorists called themselves the California Ku Klux Klan. They dressed in long white robes and hoods with masks and paraded through the streets, spewing hate against African Americans, Catholics, and Jews and championing white supremacy. And they tried to scare the local editor the best they could. They telephoned her newspaper and house at all hours of the night and day: "Is this that nigger newspaper?" and "Is this that nigger woman who owns that dirty rag called the Eagle?" They painted huge KKK letters on the sidewalk in front of her Los Angeles newspaper office. And they sued her for libel in 1925, even though there was little chance any of their white friends had even heard of this African American newspaper, much less read it. When the trumped-up libel charges didn't silence her, the terrorists came to her office when she was working alone one night. Eight men in ghostly sheets stared at her through the wide plate-glass windows of the *California Eagle* office. They pulled at the door handle and demanded she let them in. But she kept a gun in her desk drawer and whipped it out, glaring down the barrel at the men. "This was really a joke," she later said, for she had never handled a gun before and wasn't quite sure which end to point at the intruders. But the Klansmen didn't know that and "beat a hasty retreat." Her husband later told her, "Mrs. Bass, one of these days you're going to get me killed." She answered back, "Mr. Bass, it will be in a good cause."[1]

The editor was Charlotta Spears Bass, and for forty years, she ran the oldest black newspaper on the West Coast. From 1912 to 1951, she campaigned to achieve equal rights for African Americans on every Jim Crow front imaginable. She even crusaded against the release of D. W. Griffith's 1914 film, *Birth of a Nation*, which celebrated Ku Klux Klan violence and helped bring about the rise of the Klan in California before World War I. She took on restrictive covenants in housing and land use that kept black and white residents in distinctly separate neighborhoods. She battled discriminatory hiring practices, encouraged the boycott of white businesses that refused to hire blacks, and protested their exclusion from jobs ranging from streetcar conductors to nurses to telephone operators. She campaigned against police brutality and segregated schools in Los Angeles. Her criticism of all forms of government-sponsored racism got the attention of postal officials, who threatened to revoke her mailing privileges.

This chapter will detail eight key court battles waged between 1925 and 1956. Along with Bass, black journalist-activists faced libel suits filed by public officials in Kentucky, South Carolina, and Florida. A white editor in Mississippi and a white newspaper in Georgia were the target of suits initiated by law enforcement officers outraged by coverage of police brutality against black citizenry. Some of these defendants won; most lost. Either way, all defendants suffered profound stress and paid big legal fees. In the words of legal scholars George W. Pring and Penelope Canan, they were "getting sued for speaking out."[2] In today's terms, these libel suits meet the very definition of SLAPP, Strategic Lawsuits Against Public Participation, and are prime examples of the stifling of public speech about civil matters of grave concern by government authorities in a pre-*Sullivan* legal system.

The summer of 1925 was particularly stressful for Bass, worse than most. Klan leaders had taken notice of her blend of journalism and civil rights activism, a combination that had made her a leading black voice in the city. Incensed at her coverage of Klan activities, they sued Bass in local court, a new civil rights battlefield for her. The *Eagle* had obtained and published a secret letter reportedly penned by Klan leaders and outlining a strategy to manipulate the black vote in Watts, a railroad town south of Los Angeles. Among other things, the letter discussed ways to drive out or neutralize three of the most influential black citizens in the city. The *Eagle* reported that the letter, which had found its way to the local police department and then was leaked to the newspaper, detailed a plot to involve the black leaders in a traffic accident in Watts and frame them for drunk driving. The plotter stated, among other things: "We could plant a bottle of booze in the enemy's car."[3] The letter lamented the large black population in Watts and the sizeable Catholic vote but advised, "Nevertheless you can use these aliens to forward the ideals of Americanism and can consequently relegate them to the rear." The letter spoke of two spies working in the black community to undermine its efforts. "Neither of these Negroes have any racial pride and very little brains," it read. The letter also referred to black leaders who might not cooperate with the Klan program, focusing on an individual called the "Negro Knox":

> The influence of Negro Knox is waning, and will be easily killed if we can bring proper pressure to bear. Negro Buford is wavering and might be bought over, though it will take much work to do so.
> Watch out for Oscar, Knox and Buford. They are much alive as yet. Knox uses the churches, but we are starting a fight against him in his own church and [to] break his influence. We can trap Knox and Buford and break their influence. But great care must be used. This information must not be given out at any cost.
> We could plant a bottle of booze in an enemy's car and have on hand enough of the faithful to get a conviction before Judge Hunter or Wilson or some other of our fellow Klansmen who are pledged to give justice. And if these tactics fail, we can fall back on the old method of "a woman."
> The best way to get rid of our unprincipled antagonists is to make them leave Watts in disgrace. They will never come back.

The letter, signed by G. W. Price, Imperial Representative, Realm of California, Ku Klux Klan in Los Angeles, closed: "The white people in Watts are tired of being run by people who are not 100% Americans. So it will only be necessary to corral the Negro vote."

After a story about the Klan conspiracy ran in the *Eagle*, however, Imperial Representative Price insisted that the letter was a fake, that he had neither written it nor seen it before. In the next issue of the newspaper, Bass gave Price many column inches to deny that he wrote the letter under the headline, "Editor Visits Klan Chie[f]tain in His Lair." Bass responded with her typical style, in the first-person plural, ever transparent to her readers. She described seeing Price at his office after he placed an "urgent call" to her about the letter published under his name in the April 10, 1925, edition. She wrote: "We must say, however, that he greeted us in a most cordial manner, and free from any anger or resentment in any manner whatever, discussed the Watts situation with us." Price told her he "regretted very much that there was a misunderstanding as to the Klan's attitude toward the Colored people. He stated instead of thwarting us it was their desire to work together with us for a better Americanism." Bass replied that *Eagle* editors "have no doubt that he is sincere." Price had tried to convince them to publish an article in the next edition of the paper stating that the original letter was a fraud. She and her husband refused to do so.[4] The niceties were over.

Bass blamed all Klan leaders for the letter and its sentiments: "The fact that they countenance robes and disguise and that we have daily demonstrations through all sections of the movement to curtail members of our group from their rights under the constitution makes us leary [sic] and at variance, emphatically so, against any program of accomplishment by the Ku Klux Klan." As was typical of Bass, the article provided some back story about the newspaper and the community's reaction to the Klan's letter, trumpeting brisk *Eagle* sales amid the controversy. Bass wrote: "Quite a furore [sic] was evident as a result of the exposure in last week's *Eagle* among all classes in Watts. A grand rush was made for copies and early in the week all extra copies had been purchased and copies were at a premium."[5]

On May 8, weeks after the *Eagle* published the article, Bass shared with readers her summons to the county prosecutor's office for an interview about her decision to publish the letter.[6] The city prosecutor told her the article "was clearly libelous." Criminal libel statutes permitted state prosecution, although journalists were almost never prosecuted under them. Again, in a front-page article, Bass defended the newspaper's decision to run the letter: "We did so without any malice toward any individual, as a matter of fact, we had no individual in mind, but we always have in mind the mob-like spirit of the Ku Klux Klan. Whenever we learn of the diabolical propositions they are pulling off we cannot refrain from giving the same pitiless publicity. If we are to be in jail by the City Prosecutor for this policy, he just as well keep on filing complaints for we promise that whenever such information as this comes to our hand just that often do we intend to publish the same."[7]

The next week the *Eagle* reported that the Basses had been arrested for criminal libel and defamation of character, arraigned before a judge, and released on their own recognizance to appear the following Saturday in municipal court for trial.[8] They faced a $5,000 fine or one-year in jail, or both. In *Garrison v. Louisiana* some forty years later, the U.S. Supreme Court would rule that state criminal libel statutes allowing prosecution for the publication of truthful information and publication without actual malice violate the First Amendment.[9] Prior to this ruling, public figures and private individuals with significant political power or with friends in high places could target—with the backing of county prosecutors—journalists who wrote critically or disparagingly about them. Virtually all libel cases are civil cases today, though some states still have unused criminal libel laws on the books. From her editorial office, Bass wrote: "Now the big chief of the Klan strikes out to throttle the press. We opine that it will be interesting to see how far he gets on his mission."[10]

Bass seemed to relish the fight. Born in Sumter, South Carolina, in October 1880, Charlotta Spears was the sixth of eleven children, the third of four girls. She moved to Providence, Rhode Island, when she was twenty years old. Living with her oldest brother, Ellis, she worked as an "office girl and solicitor" for the local newspaper, the *Providence Watchman*. In 1910, on the brink of exhaustion after ten years at the paper, she moved to Los

Figure 1. Charlotta Bass, editor and publisher of the *California Eagle* from 1912 to 1951, suffered harassment and even death threats during her long journalism career.
—The Charlotta Bass/California Eagle Photograph Collection, Southern California Library, Los Angeles.

Angeles on her doctor's advice to get plenty of sunshine and rest. Although from a privileged family, Bass was not wealthy. "After a few months, due to the high cost of living, I found it necessary to come out of the sunshine and earn at least part of my expenses," she wrote in her unpublished memoir. So Bass began soliciting subscriptions for the *Eagle* and collecting money for renewals, earning $5 a week.[11]

Founded by John Neimore in 1879, the *Eagle* had staked its claim as the first black newspaper on the West Coast. Neimore had grown up in Texas and moved to Los Angeles with only a dime in his pocket and one suit of clothes. He envisioned the *Eagle* as "an agency to attract Negroes to California, where they would enjoy a greater portion of freedom and human rights than in their former slave environs."[12] In 1912, Spears promised Neimore on his deathbed that she would keep the *Eagle* alive, a tall order given that the paper had long limped by on a shoestring budget.

After his death, Bass became owner, editor, and publisher of the ailing newspaper, which inhabited a little shack on Central Avenue, the heart of the Los Angeles black community. The *Eagle* had $10 in cash and $150 in unpaid bills. Like Neimore, Bass believed the *Eagle* was a new underground railroad, the vehicle through which she could raise the social and political consciousness of African Americans in Los Angeles. In those early years, she lived on milk and crackers many days. Two years later, she hired Joseph B. Bass, one of the founders of the *Topeka Plaindealer,* as editor of the *Eagle*. They soon married, and he became editor and she managing editor. They were life partners who never took time for "romancing"; they had no children. Instead, they nurtured the *Eagle,* a mouthpiece for African American civil rights and social justice.

On the portly side, rather like a schoolmarm with her wire-framed spectacles, Charlotta Bass looked more like a mother than a pioneering activist and editor. Ink smudged her hands and face and her loose fitting floral dresses. Within the *Eagle*'s news pages, Bass was often front and center, a character in the action, with her husband taking more of a behind-the-scenes role. Along with the *Eagle,* she promoted herself and her causes with gusto. In the 1920s, she still endorsed the notion of uplifting oneself, but over the years, her racial politics had evolved to embrace the radical position of W. E. B. Du Bois, a founder of the National Association for the Advancement of Colored People (NAACP).

Black newspapers such as the *Eagle* were indispensible to their communities in part because there was no other place for their members to receive news about themselves. White newspapers ignored African Americans unless they were outstanding sports figures, famous entertainers, or notorious criminals.[13] Black editors clearly had an agenda—to advocate and advance civil rights—which would find no champions among white editors of the mainstream press. With customary bravado, she boasted that by 1914 the *Eagle* "had won the reputation of being a people's paper, fighting on all fronts for the rights of the Negro People and other minorities to enjoy complete civil liberties."[14] For example, in the area of employment, the city's forty thousand blacks were shoehorned into only a handful of jobs considered suitable for them. Women were domestic servants while men were janitors, elevator operators, held menial jobs and too often unemployed. So in 1918, Bass cut a deal with County General Hospital administrators: If she could find women to clean the hospital, they might later qualify for training as nurses. The *Eagle* office became an employment office of sorts for the county hospital, with Bass agreeing to screen and recommend women to hire. The hospital relied on her and took her recommendations.

Like other leading black newspapers, the *Eagle* circulated widely, even beyond Los Angeles, and encouraged southern blacks to migrate to parts of the United States outside the segregated South. The *Eagle*'s circulation reached far beyond California with a high of about 60,000 copies by 1924, though never rivaling the more famous *Chicago Defender*'s circulation of more than 100,000 or the *Pittsburgh Courier*'s 250,000 in the 1930s.[15] And her fight with the Klan was long-lived. Bass railed against KKK graffiti around town and complained to the police chief and city council when the Klan burned the houses of black families in Watts. Her battle with the KKK peaked with the libel suit in 1925.

After the Basses were arrested, the *Eagle* offered extensive coverage of the court case and trial. The newspaper published a letter submitted by John Alexander Somerville, a dentist and NAACP leader in California, who beseeched readers to donate money to help pay for the Bass's legal fight: "Everyone admires the stand taken by Mr. and Mrs. Bass of the California Eagle in their outspoken defense of Justice and Fair Play. . . . They should not be left alone as martyrs while we stand by with only sympathy. Every thoughtful Negro in Los Angeles should render every possible assistance and subscribe to a fund to be used in their defense."[16] Alongside Somerville's appeal, Bass explained that the Klan's lawsuit was an attempt to frighten the press from covering issues of race and discrimination in Los Angeles: "It is said that the Ku Klux Klan seeks to put fear in the heart of the smaller publications and a criminal prosecution has been resorted to with that end in view against the editors of this publication. Therefore the result of this case promises to be far reaching indeed. We are in need of the fullest support of all forces which are opposed to the Ku Klux Klan."[17] Bass was correct. Libel would become a powerful weapon against the demands of civil rights activists in the 1950s and 1960s.

Bass kept stories about the case on the front page, even when there was nothing new to report. In the June 12 issue of the *Eagle*, she reminded readers that the case would be heard later that week. With her usual flair for drama, she wrote: "The case promises to be hotly contested as the powerful Ku Klux Klan organization will leave no stone unturned to secure our conviction. On the other hand we will put up the very best defense possible to maintain that we are within our rights when we publish letters which have been received and passed to the police department for its investigation."[18]

Her coverage of the trial itself was thorough. The crowded courtroom filled up mostly with members of the black community, and the *Eagle* pointed out: "We rejoice to state that most of the attendants at this service were of the Colored race—they came en masse [to oppose the] nefarious organization known as the Ku Klux Klan."[19] The first witness was G. W. Price, who testified that he had nothing to do with the letter published in the *Eagle* on April 10. His assumption was that the Watts Division of the Klan, not his own Los Angeles group, had sent it. The Bass's attorney,

Hugh E. Macbeth, called on Price to produce the names of the Watts Klan members. Price said he had no records of names and could only remember one name, Bowers, identifying him as the exalted cyclops and an attorney in Watts.

At the end of the day-long trial, Macbeth argued for the defense that the very nature of the Klan's activities and the organization itself "constitutes one of the blackest pages in America's history and no one who was at the head of it could be defamed." This line was an early argument for the libel-proof doctrine, which declares an individual's reputation already so tarnished that nothing written can further damage his or her reputation. Judge J. S. Chambers promised to render his decision within the week. The *Eagle* hoped that "the people" would be protected by a favorable decision, editorializing, "For if they succeed in throttling the press, you take away from them one of their greatest weapons for defense and offense."[20]

Judge Chambers ruled in favor of the newspaper the next week, concluding that the letter handed over to police and then to the *Eagle* was privileged. This common law defense protects journalists who accurately and in good faith report issues of public concern with no evidence of malice. In the July 26 issue, *Eagle* editors celebrated their win. Praising the judge, they trumpeted the victory: "Truly the supposed Klan has judges trembling upon the bench, prosecutors doing their will, but Judge Chambers reads the law and applies the same [to] all alike and in this situation, the Ku Klux Klan as represented by its Imperial Head in the person of G. W. Price met its doom. Heretofore Price had met all the forces against him and won his battles; it remained for the Eagle Editors representing the Colored group of our citizenship to lay him low." Emboldened by the court's decision, the *Eagle* criticized larger newspapers for failing to take a stand against racism: "The big daily papers discreetly sidestep any more mention of the Klan. Economic pressure brought this about. The cancellation of large advertising contracts stare them in the face."[21]

On July 3, the *Eagle* ran a final round of letters about the lawsuit from readers across the state. A. A. Burleigh from Hermosa

Beach, California, wrote: "Your present fight is an incident never known before in Negro journalism. Who ever heard of a white man in this country making the pretensions of G. W. Price, suing a Negro newspaper for libel?"[22] Other letters of congratulations came from Iowa, Massachusetts, Alabama, Florida, and even the Virgin Islands. Bass wrote in the last of her coverage of the libel suit: "And thus ended the effort of the Imperial Wizard of the Ku Klux Klan to strike terror to the hearts of the humble weekly press and to wrench from the hands of the people their only weapon of defense."[23] Bass later wrote, however, that the "sweeping victory" was short-lived as the Klan continued to terrorize black citizens and dominate local politics. Still, she fought back. The "asinine phone calls," she wrote in her memoir, "were the daily bread of this editor. She learned through this episode of Klan terror that those gentlemen who cover their heads and faces with sheets and hoods, are cowards of an indiscriminate and blasphemous type."[24]

After a lengthy illness that left him bedridden, Joseph Bass died in 1934, leaving Charlotta to run both the business affairs and the editorial side of the *Eagle*. Her stature continued to grow among California civil rights leaders over the next two decades. She appeared at various political- and civil rights–related events across the state and country, often including details of her exploits in the pages of the *Eagle*. By the 1940s, Bass's politics were even more radical, and she united with the leftist Progressive Party, which challenged aspects of the free-market capitalist system and became controversial even among black leaders in Los Angeles.

One catalyst for her radicalism might have been the death of her nephew, her sister's son, who was killed in 1945 in the Battle of the Bulge in Germany. She had been grooming the youngster, John Kinloch, to take over the *Eagle* after she retired. Before he left for the war, he had served as the *Eagle*'s managing editor for a time. Like many black editors during World War II, Bass participated in the Double V for Victory campaign, signifying the fight for victory over fascism abroad and the struggle for civil rights at home. During the war, she also faced threats from the Federal

Bureau of Investigation (FBI) to shut down the newspaper if she continued to equate the fight against Nazism with that for civil rights at home.[25]

Her life remained controversial and storied. In 1943, she was the first African American to sit on a Los Angeles grand jury. Two years later, she made an unsuccessful bid for the Los Angeles City Council. The Klan threatened to kill her if she did not drop out of the race, but she held fast until election day. In 1952, the then sixty-two-year-old militant ran as the vice-presidential candidate for the Progressive Party, with the ticket receiving less than 1 percent of the vote.[26] Making history again, she was the first woman of African descent to seek national office.[27] There were many accusations during these years that Bass was a communist, something she always denied. This allegation turned off her readers, though, and Eagle circulation dipped. However, she did travel to the Soviet Union and write articles for *Soviet Russia Today* and the American Communist Party newspaper, heaping praise on the progressive racial attitudes of the Soviets.[28]

The Central Intelligence Agency (CIA) followed Bass abroad, describing her in FBI documents as "short, elderly, negro, female, gray hair, fat, wearing glasses, waddling walk."[29] In the early 1950s, Bass sold the *Eagle* to Loren Miller, who wrote for the newspaper in the 1930s before moving to the *Sentinel*, another black paper in Los Angeles. Miller was a noted civil rights lawyer and city court judge when he bought the newspaper. Bass remained active in civil rights issues until she suffered a stroke in 1966. She died in a Los Angeles nursing home at the age of ninety-five in 1969.

The Klan's libel case against the leading black voice in Los Angeles serves as a relevant antecedent to the flurry of later suits relating to discourse on and coverage of civil rights in the United States. It is notable that the Basses' case had an outcome different than the early cases of the 1950s and 1960s. For instance, this case was decided at the trial level in favor of the media and without appeal. It was resolved within months, ending in an acquittal for Charlotta and Joseph Bass. Many libel cases from the 1960s would remain in the court system for years, cost media outlets a great deal of time and money. Their appeals languished in the appellate courts before the high courts overturned lower-court decisions and brought about the rewriting of libel law in the United States.

If more whites had read or been more aware of the crusading black press, there likely would have been more libel cases like the Bass case. It was a brave thing in 1925 for a prominent black editor to dub the Ku Klux Klan a "nefarious crowd of hooded cowards" in the newspaper, but Bass did just that—and lived to tell the story.[30]

Critical race theory posits that law mirrors society, that the racism of any period is reflected in the prejudices of the judges and attorneys who populate the legal system. The rule of law, according to critical race theorists, is a false promise of principled government, of a principled court system.[31] Judge Chambers, based in California rather than the Deep South, may provide exception to this theory.

"The White People Are Waiting Patiently for a Neck-Breaking Party"

Two years after Bass's libel trial, two more black editors faced criminal libel indictments in Louisville, Kentucky, for their coverage of a case in which three black men were charged with the rape of a white woman. William Warley of the *Louisville News* and I. Willis Cole of the *Louisville Leader* were indicted for the criminal libel of a circuit court judge. The charges stemmed from their coverage and commentary relating to the highly publicized conviction of two of the men in Madisonville, Kentucky, about 150 miles southwest of Louisville in April 1926. Before the reported rape and in response to what it saw as a recent crime wave, the Hopkins County KKK had paraded through the streets of Madisonville in support of law and order, stopping at all of the white churches in town to kneel and pray. The previous year, there had been another case in which a white woman accused a black man of rape but that had gone unsolved. The KKK warned that if the police could not control the blacks, then it would.[32] Then a white woman, Nell Catherine Breithaupt, came forward with her own rape accusations. The rape case garnered headlines in both white and black newspapers for weeks, with Warley and Cole watching the case closely from Louisville.

William Warley founded the *Louisville News* in 1913, using it as his primary instrument for speaking out for black voting rights and against school inequality and segregated streetcars. After graduating from high school in Louisville, he had earned his living as a clerk at the Louisville post office while attending college and, for several years, after graduating from State University's Law School.[33] Editing a black newspaper typically was not a profitable enterprise.

Like Charlotta Bass, Warley did more than write about inequality. In 1914, he led a successful black boycott of a local theater's policy restricting blacks to the gallery and back entrance. Yet he is best known for his involvement in a case that was not related to libel, one that would rise all the way to the U.S. Supreme Court. In 1917, he and several liberal white allies challenged the legality of a city ordinance mandating segregated housing in Louisville. A white real-estate agent named Charles H. Buchanan sold Warley a house on the corner of Thirty-Seventh Avenue and Pflanz Street in the white section of Louisville. Under Louisville's ordinance, Warley would not have been allowed to live there, and the two men secretly agreed before the deal that Warley would back out at the last minute.

Buchanan would then sue Warley for payment as a way to challenge the Jim Crow ordinance that both despised. In this case, they figured the court would note a violation of the civil rights of a white citizen more than those of a black one given that Buchanan brought the suit and asserted that he was harmed by Warley's backing out of the contract.[34] In *Buchanan v. Warley*, the U.S. Supreme Court struck down the ordinance that prohibited blacks from living on a block where the majority of residents were white. In its ruling, the court cited post–Civil War or Reconstruction-era federal laws, the Civil Rights Act of 1866 and the Fourteenth Amendment, which provided African Americans, particularly freed slaves, full citizenship and equal protection guaranteed due process under the law.[35] *Warley* remains a landmark case in the black struggle for equal housing.

Willis Cole, also a well-known civil rights leader in Kentucky during the first half of the twentieth century, ran the largest black newspaper in the region. He grew up in Memphis and graduated from LeMoyne Junior College before moving to Louisville in the summer of 1915 to work as a Bible salesman. He liked the river town and settled in to stay, starting the weekly *Louisville Leader* in 1917 with fifty dollars. Like Warley, he was steadfast in his call for desegregation and voting rights for blacks.

And like Warley, his outspoken activism often put him at odds with the traditional black elite in Louisville. Cole's paper flourished in the 1930s, and a number of his employees became publishers and printers elsewhere. He employed twenty people at the paper's height, and the *Leader* had a reported circulation of about twenty thousand. Cole, like Charlotta Bass, tried to break into politics, running unsuccessfully for the Kentucky Senate in 1922 as a member of the Lincoln Independent Party, which had broken away from the Republican Party. Warley and Cole also were part of a group of young African American leaders who believed the Republican Party, the party of Lincoln that represented the end of slavery, no longer served their needs. Nor did the Democratic Party, they complained. They felt less dependent on whites than the generation before them and were more outspoken than the older black leaders in Louisville.[36]

Both Warley and Cole were also members of the fledgling NAACP, formed in 1909 by W. E. B. Du Bois and some thirty other black professionals with white progressives in New York City. The organization moved to counter Booker T. Washington's more conservative racial stance, using its monthly publication, *The Crisis*, to publicize and spread its message demanding the federal enforcement of African American civil rights. Warley served as president of the Louisville chapter of the NAACP at the time of the libel suit detailed here. Unsuccessful at politics, Cole continued to put his considerable energy into his own NAACP leadership duties and as the recording secretary of the National Negro Press Association.

By the 1920s, both editors became ever more aggressive in their quest for equal justice, and their dogged coverage and criticism of inequalities in the justice system drew the ire of white Madisonville lawyers and judges during the rape trial there in 1926. In this case, Nell Catherine Breithaupt alleged that three black men raped her while she and her boyfriend were parked on a lover's lane in Louisville. Police arrested one man, Columbus Hollis, who in return for a promise of a light punishment, implicated Bunyan Fleming and Nathan Bard in the crime. Police had heard that all three black men had previously engaged in sex with white prostitutes. According to historian George C. Wright, white authorities reasoned that the men would try satisfying their "animal lust" by assaulting other white women.[37]

Five hundred guardsmen were deployed to deter mob violence as crowds of thousands descended on Madisonville for the trial. Local white newspapers treated the arrests as if the crime was already solved, even referring to Fleming as a "monkey man."[38] But Warley and Cole saw scant evidence of guilt, labeling the trial a "legal lynching" of epic proportions. The editors were quick to point out that the woman was unable to definitively identify the two men in court. As part of their general coverage and criticism of the justice system, both editors pointed to previous Kentucky cases in which a "colored" man was hanged for an alleged assault on a white woman and, within a few weeks, a white man was declared insane for an assault on a young "colored" girl.[39]

The *Louisville Leader* carried the headline, "Justice Mocked Again. . . . Mother Cries, 'My God Is There No Justice in America?'"[40] The next week, another *Leader* headline called out, "Madisonville Sets Stage for Speedy Trial and Hanging of Negroes."[41] The article sarcastically boasted that Kentucky was outdoing Mississippi, Georgia, and other southern states in the legalized murder of blacks accused of crimes. The angry headlines in the

Louisville Leader screamed, "Legal Lynching Coming!" "Madisonville Men Apparently Being Rushed To Gallows by Farcical Trial," and "Is Kentucky to Have Another Legal Lynching? That Is the Question on Each Colored Person's Lip in Kentucky."[42] Despite a lack of evidence, the all-white jury took just minutes to find Fleming and Bard guilty.[43]

A flurry of letters ensued between New York–based NAACP secretary James Weldon Johnson and Fleming's mother, Martha Summers, who lived in Encorse, Michigan. Desperate to save her son, she wrote in a scrawling, shaky hand: "I have spent all the money that I have trying to get him a new trial in the cort [sic] of appeals which have just convened in Frankford [sic]. But they have refused to grant a new trial. Therefore I most humbly beg the murcey [sic] and aid from your organization acknowledging that no girl nor boy has identified them as the men who committed the crime."[44] Nudging the NAACP to take interest in the case, she said that she was not a member of the NAACP but her other children were. Her efforts failed to yield results.

Dated December 1, 1926, a Western Union telegram from Warley to Johnson at the NAACP stated in all capital letters: "KENTUCKY COURT OF APPEALS HAS DECIDED THAT FLEMING AND BARD MUST DIE." The Sixth Circuit had affirmed the verdict against the men, and NAACP leaders brainstormed with Warley and Cole about what else might be done to save them. Warley, discouraged but not ready to give up, sought advice from a prominent white lawyer, Matt O'Doherty, in Louisville. After reviewing the case, O'Doherty recommended that lawyers for Fleming and Bard appeal to the governor of Kentucky for executive clemency and ask for life in prison rather than execution. From his jail cell, Fleming admitted to G. P. Hughes, president of the Louisville branch of the NAACP, that he and Bard were doomed. He wrote, "We haven't had a dog's chance for our lives and as God is my judge, I am innocent and I don't know anything about the crime." Though Fleming had given up hope, he expressed relief that support seemed to come from both races: "I had several sound minded white people who believe in the right thing to come here at my cell door and tell me they didn't like the evidence we were convicted on at all. I had one White man tell me if the Court of Appeal[s] did turn me down, to take the case to the U.S. Suppreme [sic] Court. I told him I was not able. So you can see there are some White people who believe we are innocent."[45]

After exhausting all appeals, the men were hung on November 25, 1927, for a crime that probably never occurred. The case was another example, in scholar Mark Robert Schneider's words, of "how race hatred deformed the justice system throughout the era of white supremacy."[46] The local white newspaper, the *Daily Messenger*, put out an extra edition on the execution with the bold headline, "XTRA: 2 RAPISTS HANG." The front page included a big photo of Nell Catherine Breithaupt, the "beautiful daughter of Mr. and Mrs. Leo Breithaupt."

Fleming and Bard had been dispatched, so authorities now turned their enmity to the messengers. As part of the criminal libel indictments, local officials charged that the editors "unlawfully, willfully, maliciously, and falsely imputed dishonesty, misconduct in office, and corruption" to Judge Ruby Laffoon, who had presided over the trial—"all of which was done for the malicious purpose and intent to injure his good name and fame as a public officer." Kentucky's seditious libel law made it a crime to criticize a public official. The statute stated, "Charging that a judge is conducting a farcical trial, or that the trial is mob law, or that he had not given a thought to the presumption of innocence that the law throws about the accused, is certainly a charge of want of integrity on the part of the judge, and it is therefore libelous."[47]

It did not matter that neither newspaper named Judge Laffoon in the stories. He was nonetheless identified, according to the court. It also rejected Warley's and Cole's contention that under the First Amendment, they were "applying to those invested with the power of government for redress of grievances." Black newspapers across the country were quick to defend the Louisville editors. The *Afro-American* in Baltimore declared, "Whatever criticism there was made by the editors in these cases . . . was against the system rather than the individual judge in the case."[48]

NAACP leaders saw the libel charges as yet another threat to their work toward equal rights. A press release informed the public that the organization had sent a $500 check from its Legal Defense Fund in New York to cover lawyers' fees for the defense. According to the news release, NAACP leaders said it took some time for Madisonville authorities to figure out how to silence the two editors: "The County Attorney at Madisonville did not like what was said by Messrs. Warley and Cole, and first brought indictment against them for creating race friction and race hatred. Finding that this charge did not hold good, an attempt was made to charge them with contempt of court. The Grand Jury finally brought an indictment against them for libel."

The NAACP believed that the implications of the Warley-Cole case were potentially calamitous for civil rights journalism and advocacy. Secretary Johnson said: "The case of these editors is one of the most important and far-reaching the N.A.A.C.P. has taken part in. It involves the freedom of the press, the freedom of colored editors to speak their honest opinions on racial injustices even in the South, unmuzzled by threat of imprisonment. The outcome of this trial will be vital to the colored press and the colored people."[49] Indeed, this language sounds a great deal like the that used by journalists and civil rights leaders concerned about SLAPP suits in the 1950s and 1960s. These same arguments were deployed by lawyers for the *New York Times* when they defended the newspaper in court against Commissioner Lester B. Sullivan in Montgomery, Alabama.

Warley and Cole were found guilty of libeling Judge Laffoon of the Circuit Court, and each was fined $250 in December 1926.[50] The *Western American* in Oakland, California, seeing the significance of this case, opined: "We wonder if the case was directed wholly against Worley and Cole or against the public press, especially the Afro-American press."[51] Warley, however, saw a different picture: Two men, falsely accused of rape, had died from hanging as a result of an unjust legal system. He was concerned more about Fleming and Bard than about his own fate in the libel case. In a letter to Johnson in New York, Warley wrote: "Frankly the Court of Appeal's opinion in this case has hurt us and discouraged us more than our own cases because we cannot see by what stretch of imagination the Court of Appeals can say these men had a fair trial."[52] The NAACP paid the editors' fines, the equivalent of about $7,000 in 2018, drawing precious resources away from ongoing desegregation cases in the civil rights fight.

Like Charlotta Bass, the activist Louisville editors sported huge targets on their backs. Whites did not read black newspapers, but the white leaders were undoubtedly aware of them along with the editors' stature and work as civil rights leaders in the community and state. Warley and Cole had long complained in their news pages that justice was doled out differently to defendants depending on whether they were black or white. And African Americans, such as Fleming and Bard, were penalized for their color and suffered injustice far too often. The libel suit was an attempt to silence that criticism—or truth.

The smaller of the two black newspapers in town, Warley's *Louisville News,* closed during World War II. As a result of his activism, Warley had been dismissed from his post office job, and over the years he became bitter that his fellow African Americans did not appreciate his sacrifices for their cause. "In many ways Warley lived a tragic life," writes historian George C. Wright. The editor, a difficult man to work with, had a hard time keeping competent employees and was often left to produce his paper alone. He had a drinking problem that grew worse in the stressful days of the 1930s and 1940s and that left him virtually bankrupt.[53] Both men died in their early sixties, Warley in 1946 and Cole in 1950. They never got to witness the full force of the civil rights movement that would blossom in the 1950s.

Teaching the North a Lesson

The bullet-riddled body of a young black sharecropper, Jesse James Payne, lay in a ditch in rural Madison County, Florida, in October 1945. He had escaped from the unguarded county jail, where he was awaiting trial for a shocking crime, the rape of a five-year-old white girl. Payne had insisted the charges were fabricated by the girl's father, his landlord, who wanted to run him off the farm and steal his tobacco, cotton, peanut, and corn crops.[54]

Payne's murder garnered attention from newspapers across the country amid a resurgence of calls for federal anti-lynching legislation, but Florida governor Millard F. Caldwell sought to squelch what he saw as negative publicity about law enforcement officials in his state, issuing a statement that an investigation into Payne's death found "stupid inefficiency of the sheriff and not from his abetting or participation" in the killing.[55] He did not want this one incident to trigger more calls for a federal anti-lynching law and instead insisted the crime was simply a murder, one that lacked key elements of a lynching, such as a mob killing under the pretext of justice.

Governor Caldwell scolded the media for printing "negative" editorials about the incident in Madison, which lay in the center of the Florida panhandle with its northern border touching the state of Georgia. He also blamed the press for having "smeared the state with the sole lynching in the U.S."[56] Reported lynchings had been common before World War II, but American fighting forces—many of whom were black—had returned home after defeating Nazism and fascism in the name of freedom. The reaction on the part of the press to Payne's murder was swift and condemnatory. Yet Caldwell believed southerners best understood their own social problems, including race relations, and resented any outside intervention or criticism of him and his state.

Caldwell, who was also an attorney, told the AP that he worried about bringing the rape victim into open court and subjecting her to a cross-examination by the defense. It could cause an injury as devastating as the original crime, he said. *Collier's* denounced Caldwell for refusing to admit Payne had been lynched and editorialized that the governor "went on to opine that the mob had saved courts, etc., considerable trouble."[57] In response, Caldwell sued the New York magazine for $500,000 in U.S. District Court in Tallahassee, Florida, in March 1946, announcing that he would donate any damage award to the Florida Agriculture and Mechanical College, the state's black college in the state capital.[58]

This case bounced up and down in the court system for two years before finally coming to trial in Tallahassee in 1948. Caldwell's attorneys focused on the damage *Collier's* editorial had done to the governor's race-relations efforts in the state, claiming that black Floridians no longer trusted him and did not want to work with him. "I found it difficult to deal with the negroes of this state on regional education and educational matters," Caldwell testified.[59] For their part, *Collier's* attorneys focused on whether Governor Caldwell truly felt defamed, pointing out that within a couple of months after the editorial ran, he was named chairman of the National Governor's Association. The country's governors clearly regarded him highly enough to name him to the organization's leading office. Caldwell's testimony must have given them some satisfaction: "That's right," he testified. "Governors are not guided too greatly by what appears in some magazine."[60]

Collier's also argued the content in the editorial amounted to fair comment and criticism of a public official and that the editorial writer offered a reasonable interpretation of the governor's words. Caldwell's attorneys, however, painted the magazine as a northern agitator attacking the integrity of the state of Florida, its leader, and its citizens. Agreeing with that interpretation, the jury awarded Caldwell $237,000, at the time the largest sum for damages ever awarded in a libel case tried in the United States. In modern-day dollars, that's well over $2 million in damages.

The U.S. Circuit Court of Appeals for the Fifth Circuit in New Orleans reversed the decision and remanded it for retrial, holding that the original trial judge had failed to instruct the jury correctly on various elements of libel law.[61] At the second trial in Gainesville, Florida, in June 1949, a jury again returned a verdict in favor of the governor, this time awarding him $100,000. Initially, *Collier's* promised to appeal but, weary of the court battle and racking up even more attorneys' fees, agreed to a settlement of half the verdict, giving $25,000 to Caldwell and $25,000 to his lawyers. After three and a half years, the fight was over, and Caldwell donated the money to the historically black university in Tallahassee as promised.[62] The Tallahassee *Daily Democrat* opined after the settlement that the South had taught the North "a lesson of tolerance and unbiased contemplation of the views of others."[63]

John Henry McCray Faces Hard Labor on a South Carolina Chain Gang

In rural South Carolina during the first half of the twentieth century, businesses routinely posted Jim Crow signs reminding the public that no persons of color were allowed inside. Their hate turned away a significant volume of business given that blacks made up a large percentage of the state's population. "No negro or ape allowed in building," blustered a large sign at a one-pump gas station in rural Calhoun County. Above the wooden front door, another handwritten sign advised in bold capital letters: "Negros not wanted in the North or South. Send them back to Africa Where God Almighty put them to begin with [*sic*] that is their home." A poster of Jesus and a "Closed on Sunday" placard rounded out the signage in this remote filling station between the state capital of Columbia and coastal Charleston.[64] In the late 1930s and 1940s, journalist John Henry McCray risked his life in this hostile environment to jumpstart the civil rights fight in the state of South Carolina, which fired the opening shot of the Civil War in 1861.

Like Bass, Warley, and Cole, this African American journalist in the Palmetto State became as much a civil rights leader as a newspaperman. It is important to note that the principles of objectivity and detachment had been woven into the profession of journalism by the 1920s. Journalism education came into being with courses offered at several midwestern schools including the University of Missouri. In part payment for his past sins for the yellow journalism published in his newspapers during the Gilded

Age, newspaper mogul Joseph Pulitzer gave the money that would launch Columbia University's journalism school in 1912. The professional organization, Sigma Delta Chi, later called the Society of Professional Journalists, was established at DePauw University in Indiana in 1909. As mainstream journalists carried out their work in a more neutral or objective manner, the black press made no secret of its agenda, the advocacy of civil rights for African Americans and of an end to racial segregation.

John Henry McCray remained on a mission to destroy the racial caste system of Jim Crow in the South. He was born in 1910 and grew up in Lincolnville, an all-black community some twenty miles inland from Charleston, that had been founded during Reconstruction. His father served as Lincolnville's part-time chief of police and the assistant pastor at Ebenezer African Methodist Episcopal Church. His mother was a member of the city council, active in civic groups in town and in the local NAACP. It was a rare thing, this kind of black leadership in the South, but all seemed normal for McCray, the oldest of five brothers and three sisters. His formative years in such an unusual town likely explain why he became widely known among blacks in South Carolina as a fearless flamethrower in the battle for equal rights and a major antagonist to the white establishment. He simply grew up believing that blacks were equal to whites, shocked by discrimination he later faced outside Lincolnville.

McCray served as editor of his high school paper and developed his activist journalistic style while studying at Talladega College in Alabama. He wrote columns in the school newspaper, the *Mule's Ear,* full of passionate appeals to his fellow students to become more politically active. And he brought that passion back home to South Carolina after graduation in 1935, resuscitating the dormant NAACP, rallying black political engagement, and sounding the militant call for confrontation with the white power structure. As editor of the *Lighthouse and Informer,* the state's leading black newspaper that he created with other black civil rights leaders in 1941, McCray challenged the accommodationist doctrine and culture of Booker T. Washington, bringing the state's black population into the modern civil rights era.[65] The *Lighthouse and Informer* operated in the heart of the black business district in Columbia, publishing fiery editorials that took on salary disparities between black and white teachers and the Democratic Party's all-white primary. The newspaper was distributed statewide and enjoyed a circulation as high as fourteen thousand copies within a decade, although historians estimate that readership was much higher as people passed along their papers to friends and neighbors after reading them.[66]

Early black and white photos show McCray sporting a sharp three-piece suit, a pencil-thin mustache over an earnest smile, his long forehead leading up to closely trimmed hair. With his editor's pen, McCray helped build support for the legal challenge to school segregation, working hand in hand with the NAACP, its membership starting to tick up in the 1940s. The organization launched *Briggs v. Elliott,* a case that became one of five under the umbrella of *Brown v. Board of Education of Topeka,* the landmark Supreme Court ruling outlawing school segregation in 1954. McCray and other local leaders such as Reverend J. A. DeLaine were charged by the NAACP with finding plaintiffs to challenge school segregation, settling on Harry Briggs as one of twenty plaintiffs in the local suit in Clarendon County. The *Briggs* case was the only one of the five later consolidated under the *Brown* suit that was originally filed in a state below the Mason Dixon Line.

But before *Brown* shattered the separate-but-equal precedent and rocked the South, the court case that brought McCray a surprising amount of grief and expense turned out to be one of libel. On October 1, 1949, he published an account of a rape case involving a sixteen-year-old white girl from the point of view of the accused, a black man named Willie Tolbert, who said they had consensual sex. The twenty-four-year-old Tolbert, virtually illiterate, refused to take the stand on his own behalf and was convicted and sentenced to death in a highly publicized whirlwind of events. Tolbert's voice only came out because of McCray's death-row interview. The editor wrote the story without using the teenage girl's name, telling Tolbert's side of events: the girl had offered to have sex with him, charging rape only when the encounter was discovered.[67]

The Greenwood County solicitor, Hugh Beasley, turned out to be the girl's father and charged McCray with criminal libel for publishing Tolbert's side of the story. He insisted that McCray had published false and libelous statements that defamed the character of the young woman. White AP reporter Deling Booth also wrote a story about the Tolbert case and was charged with criminal libel, but that charge would eventually be dropped by the prosecutor.[68]

McCray's reporting had violated the sacred tenant of white supremacy: a white woman would never have consensual sex with a black man. The black male was an oversexed and a dangerous predator that victimized chaste white women, so the dominant narrative went.[69] The local white newspaper, the *Greenwood Index-Journal,* had covered the events from the white point of view, reporting the young woman's side of the story as told in court. She and her boyfriend spent the evening of August 8 at the movies and then stopped off at a favorite hangout for a bite to eat. They were parking on a country road when an unknown negro man approached them. She said she jumped out of the car and ran, but he forced her back into the Buick where he raped her in the back seat. Both she and her boyfriend, seventeen-year-old Sammy Cassels, testified that Tolbert put his hand around her throat and threatened to kill her if Cassels tried to stop him. In the tense courtroom, she testified that Tolbert kissed her and boasted, "Now, don't say you've never been kissed by a Negro in South Carolina." She said the assailant then hopped in the driver's seat and sped off with the young couple to neighboring Laurens County and raped her again. He threatened to wreck the car and kill them if they tried to get away, stopping twice for gas and cigarettes. The girl said she wrote the word "Help" in lipstick outside the car, but none of the gas station attendants saw it. He then drove the pair back to the original spot where he found them earlier and took off on foot.[70]

The young woman had sketched the face of her assailant, describing him as a husky, strongly built black man, and the police search centered on Tolbert, who had a history of small-time criminal activity. He was 5 feet 9 inches tall and 150 pounds. Married with one child, Tolbert worked for the city of Greenwood garbage pick-up at the time of the incident. He had served time for snatching a white woman's purse and again for petty larceny and receiving stolen goods.[71]

An intense manhunt in Greenwood and Laurens Counties ensued, with nearly a thousand private citizens, including armed women and children, forming a posse to help with the hunt.[72] A pack of bloodhounds and three airplanes aided the hundred police officers on the ground. After three days Tolbert snuck back home, and his wife turned him in. A sheriff's deputy had suggested to her that his surrender was the only way to save his life. When the police arrived, Tolbert gave himself up and was taken to the State Penitentiary in Columbia for "safekeeping." Sheriff Cal White announced to the press that Tolbert had confessed to the crime, refusing to let journalists interview the prisoner. The trial was set for the next month, the mid-September term of court.[73]

Then McCray stepped in. He traveled some eighty miles west to Greenwood to investigate the case after blacks there insisted that Tolbert was innocent and had been tortured in jail. McCray's bylined story ran under the headline "IS WILLIE TOLBERT JR. GUILTY?" in the largest typeface the pressroom owned. In the story, McCray puzzled over why the young woman's escort "sat quietly on the front seat" of the car and allowed the rape to occur. Tolbert's version of events, relayed to McCray through his attorney, offered a story that night: On August 8, he and some friends went out drinking, and when their money ran out, they bought a bottle of rubbing alcohol and mixed it with spring water. After the party, he was walking home at about 9:30 p.m. when he came across the parked Buick. He asked the couple for a match to light a cigarette, which he received, and Cassels asked where they might find some whiskey. Tolbert said the young man asked him to chauffeur the car to find some. They drove to nearby Laurens County but couldn't find an open store that carried liquor.⁷⁴

The next part of McCray's story undoubtedly enraged the white establishment, including solicitor Hugh Beasley, father of the victim. The article explained:

> Tolbert said that enroute home the young man asked him to pull to the side of the road and stop; this he did. Tolbert said he sat on the front seat and was aware that the couple was having relations but didn't move nor look around. When this was over, he said, the young man came to the front sat [sic] and asked if he wanted a relation. He said "I said 'yessir thank you.'" Questioned severely at this point, Tolbert said there was no protest of any sort from the young woman. He later resumed his place at the wheel and drove the car to within a hundred yards of his house, said good night and left them. Later, he said, he discovered considerable activity in his community by law enforcement officers, became suspicious and fled. The rest of his story, the search by an armed posse and his surrender, has been told.⁷⁵

Tolbert said he got in the car in the first place because he figured he'd get cash for helping the couple find some whiskey. In graphic terms for the time, McCray also challenged traditional mores regarding sexual encounters between the races: "How much of Tolbert's story to believe is conjecture, but employees around hotels and pleasure spots where Negroes are servants agree that there is nothing fantastic about his having been offered relations. It is a daily occurrence, these employees say, oftimes coming from white women themselves who offer their bodies in return for 'business' from the employees."⁷⁶ McCray, ever the crusading editor, challenged the white myth that all white women were pure and all black men animal rapists.

The jury, all white males, took only ten minutes to find Tolbert guilty of rape, and the judge sentenced him to death by electrocution. AP reporter Deling Booth interviewed Tolbert in jail after the verdict was rendered, and the *Anderson Independent* picked up the story. Booth reported that Tolbert swore his innocence but refused to testify on his own behalf because Sheriff White warned him not to talk. Tolbert believed his life would be spared if he stayed silent.⁷⁷ Sheriff White denied those charges in the

Greenwood Index-Journal that afternoon, and Tolbert died in the electric chair that night, October 28, 1949.[78] After Tolbert's punishment was carried out, it was time to punish the journalists.

The Greenwood County Grand Jury indicted McCray and Booth in January 1950, using the language in both cases: the newsmen "did willfully and with malicious intent originate, utter, compose, circulate, and cause to be published . . . a certain false statement about and concerning the said Martha Beasley."[79] It was widely known that Hugh Beasley was behind the indictments, Booth's widow said years later.[80] Neither reporter had named Martha Beasley in their stories. Both had said the victim was from a prominent Greenwood family.

White coverage of the libel indictments was mixed and light, but the major black newspapers across the country reacted angrily and came to McCray's defense. The *Baltimore Afro-American* asserted in a front page story: "Everyone in the State is convinced that the real target is the Lighthouse and Informer, which is expected to round up about 200,000 primary election voters."[81] In an accompanying editorial, the *Afro-American* noted that, even in a state like South Carolina, the libel case was surprising, admitting that this "latest wrinkle has caught us off guard." Yet McCray remained steadfast: "I have no apologies nor regrets for the story we published because it was the last words of a man put to death for an alleged offense around which there appears to be some extenuating circumstances. It wasn't my story we published. It was Willie Tolbert's."[82]

Facing down the libel suit, McCray made a plan to ask three hundred friends for $25 to help pay the estimated $7,500 cost of his defense. Like most black newspapers of the era, the *Lighthouse and Informer* had long operated on a shoestring budget, and McCray sometimes had to operate the press himself to print the paper. His form letters read: "I write to you as a friend I believe interested in the full rights of all citizens, and one who should know that never before have I asked anybody to aid me in making any of the fights in which we have engaged. And, but for the pressure of my friends now, I would much prefer to take any punishment which might be handed me than to write this letter."[83]

He didn't have to fight this battle by himself. The Negro Newspaper Publishers Association (NNPA) helped fund the defense and appealed to the U.S. Justice Department to investigate the McCray libel case, arguing that the indictment was an assault on press freedom everywhere. John Sengstacke, editor and publisher of the *Chicago Defender,* and C. A. Scott of the *Atlanta Daily World,* served on a committee of prominent black publishers appointed by the NNPA to fight McCray's and Booth's indictments.[84] The editors also complained in their editorial pages, repeatedly coming to McCray's defense. The *Chicago Defender* argued: "The racial atmosphere of the South Carolina county has obviously influenced the action taken against the newsmen. Their right to publish vital news, which incidentally did not violate the libel laws of South Carolina which prohibits the printing of the name of a rape victim, cannot be abridged by a group of prejudiced persons who want to take the Constitution into their own hands."[85]

McCray enjoyed a groundswell of support from the local people in South Carolina, African Americans who followed his celebrity and subscribed to his activist newspaper. Handwritten letters with words of prayer and encouragement poured into the newspaper office, along with crumpled, hard-earned dollar bills to help him mount his legal defense and keep the paper going. Black churches in little hamlets like Bishopsville passed the collection plate to support "Brother McCray," sending him $10 checks and $5 money orders to support his defense. The Marion County Progressive Democrats declared Sunday, May 21, 1950, "John H. McCray Day" to publicize the editor's plight and raise money on his behalf. In one such letter, a minister named W. T. Murray wrote: "I do wish to have you to know that I am praying that Divine hands will at the needy time, enjoin its works of Satan, leaving him in Perfect defeat. While the truth which is being crushed to the Earth will rise up with J. H. McCray standing with his head unbowed. God Bless you. The Church is at prayer. . . . Trust God! And keep up the good work."[86]

Although juggling a heavy load of civil rights cases around the country, big-time NAACP lawyers from New York took McCray's libel case. They included future U.S. Supreme Court justice Thurgood Marshall and Jack Greenberg of the NAACP Legal Defense Fund (LDF). Greenberg would succeed the famous Marshall as head of the LDF from 1961 to 1984 and later teach at the law schools of Columbia, Harvard, and Yale as another icon on the front lines of the legal fight for equal rights. It became customary for the NAACP lawyers to team up with local civil rights lawyers on the ground, and in the McCray case, that lawyer was Harold Boulware, who had defended Willie Tolbert in his rape trial and had given McCray details on that trial.

The legal team advised McCray to find a white lawyer to represent him in court, hoping that such legal counsel might help sway an all-white jury. McCray appealed to several white lawyers, and finally one did agree to help with the defense in secret, meeting him only at night. McCray had a solid defense, and his lawyers got the trial moved to nearby Newberry County to escape the taint of such heavy publicity from local newspapers. But his attorneys decided that he wouldn't get a fair trial anywhere in the state, that he was a notorious black "agitator," and that pleading guilty would at least keep him out of jail and allow him to continue publishing the newspaper.[87]

McCray had wanted to see the case through and was willing to risk going to prison, but he finally agreed to make a deal. He reasoned that he could stay out of jail to continue fighting for his people and publishing the newspaper.[88] On June 19, 1950, he pleaded guilty before Circuit Judge Steve Griffith, receiving a reduced fine of $3,000 (rather than the initial $5,000) and three years' probation.[89] He also had to admit is guilt on the front page of his *Lighthouse and Informer*. Perhaps, too, McCray knew what life could be like on a South Carolina chain gang, where African Americans were often beaten and sometimes killed. In 1949, McCray wrote about the state of New York's reluctance to approve the extradition of a black South Carolina chain-gang escapee: "It is better to die and go to hell than to live and get in jail in South Carolina."[90]

McCray had one month to pay the fine, a massive sum for him. By the first week of July, he had borrowed $633 to pay some of the attorney and court fees and had to figure out how to find the money to pay $3,000 to the court. If he could not pay in time, he faced one year on the Newberry County chain gang and the full fine of $5,000, the equivalent of more than $52,000 in 2018 dollars. The black publishers' group, the NNPA, put out a call for help, creating the Lighthouse Defense Fund. *Defender* editor and publisher Sengstacke headed up the group from Chicago and promised McCray $2,200 by the deadline. "I sincerely hope that this will help you win the fight you are making," the venerable editor wrote McCray.[91] Money continued to trickle in from county chapters of the NAACP and other groups, including the Colored Funeral Directors & Embalmers Association of South Carolina, which mailed him a $25 check from its Rock Hill, South Carolina, headquarters in early July.[92] Churches across the state passed the collection plate for Brother McCray, mailing him nickels, quarters, and crumpled dollar bills. Groups such as the Progressive Democrat Institute held rallies to raise money for McCray's defense, and one event in Columbia on May 12 raised an impressive $207. Members of the faculty of Holmes School in Florence took up a collection and sent him $63.[93]

Other scholars have seen this libel case as an attempt to silence a relentless black agitator. Although John W. White does not use the term SLAPP in referring to the suit, he holds the case up as an example of intimidation directed toward civil rights activists: "McCray's brush with the legal system was an important indication of the degree to which whites controlled the state's bureaucracy and utilized official state agencies to subdue 'troublesome' blacks." He continues, "The conviction was an obvious attempt to discourage McCray from engaging in political activism and a reminder to middle class African Americans that their relative prosperity was dependent on staying in the good graces of the white power structure."[94]

McCray paid his fine and continued his political activism while filing monthly reports to his probation officer, Roy D. Stutts, at the Newberry County Courthouse. For example, in October 1952, he reported to Stutts that he worked twenty-eight days, earned $240, and attended church twice during the month of September.[95] On top of the stress caused by the libel case and resulting financial hardships, McCray and his first wife were in the process of getting a divorce. She had been fighting for custody of their children, and her lawyers brought to the attention of the parole board (unbeknownst to her) that McCray had left the state twice over several months, a violation of his probation. He had traveled to Illinois to deliver the keynote address at a function for Congressman William L. Dawson in Chicago, believing he had permission to leave the state. McCray had also given the Negro Achievement Week address for the Omega Psi Phi fraternity in Durham, North Carolina.

McCray was arrested and convicted of violating his probation. During the hearing, Stutts was a hostile witness and was allowed to give only "yes" or "no" answers. McCray later said he had mentioned his frequent out-of-state trips to Stutts, and the officer approved as long as McCray did not change his permanent residence to an address outside the state. According to McCray, when Stutts was asked whether he had given McCray specific written permission to leave the state on the trips in question, the officer said "no."[96] Judge Griffith sentenced McCray to five weeks on a chain gang in November and December of 1951. The state Supreme Court rejected his appeal for reversal of the sentence.[97]

Again, the black press rallied to his defense. The *Afro-American* in Baltimore opined: "From where we sit, this last chapter in the McCray case has all the earmarks of a not too thinly disguised attempt on the part of the irritated South Carolina officials to silence this man's thunderous voice."[98] The *Pittsburgh Courier* argued that McCray's ongoing work on the Clarendon County school desegregation cases had brought this next round of punishment: "It is apparent that Editor McCray is a marked man, because of his crusading tactics."[99]

While he served on the Newberry County chain gang, McCray's younger brother kept the *Lighthouse and Informer* going with the help of several other civil rights activists. More than three dozen people, including a seventy-four-year-old church elder, volunteered to serve for McCray on the chain gang, but South Carolina law prohibited such proxies. A committee was formed to handle the high volume of correspondence pouring into the newspaper office expressing support for the editor. Black ministers across South Carolina honored him from their pulpits during Sunday services.[100]

He served thirty-seven days of his sixty-day sentence. McCray said later that he believed South Carolina governor James F. Byrnes, furious about black civil rights activism in the state, ordered the arrest.[101] In an editorial headlined "How to Make a Martyr," the *Chicago Defender* pointed out: "McCray has long been a stinging political gadfly constantly irritating the governor and the embattled dixiecrats [sic] in the carrying out of their white supremacy policies." Certainly, McCray worked hard to find brave black families willing to sue for equal school facilities. And he headed up the state's Progressive Democratic Party, which would make him the leader of a significant voting bloc as conservatives began to fear any black political power. In 1950, McCray had launched a voter registration drive in a push to get two hundred thousand African American voters on the roles in time to vote in the 1950 Senate primary, trumpeting the lofty goal in a front-page editorial in the *Lighthouse and Informer*.[102] The *Defender* also complained that justice was doled out by "the color of a man's skin." While McCray toiled on the chain gang, the white AP reporter was "free and pursuing his duties as a newsman."[103]

Ultimately, the cash-strapped *Lighthouse and Informer* couldn't withstand McCray's legal troubles and folded in 1954, the same year the U.S. Supreme Court decided the *Brown* case. But McCray's career as a journalist and activist went on, and in the 1950s, he reported on the South Carolina civil rights fight for several black newspapers, including the *Afro-American* and *Pittsburgh Courier*. In 1962, he left his beloved South Carolina to take a job as public relations director at his alma mater, Talladega College, where he worked until his death in 1987.[104]

Charles Franklin Beall Jr., who studied Willie Tolbert's case and McCray's involvement as part of his thesis at the University of Virginia, raises probing questions about Tolbert's guilt. He writes, "Could an unarmed man really take two people and a car hostage? Why did they not attempt to escape or seek help when they stopped at the filling stations? Why would Tolbert take them back to a spot less than one hundred yards from his house? . . . Just three people knew what really happened that evening in August of 1949—and one of them was dead within three months."[105] Historian Kari Frederickson has also studied the Tolbert case, questioning his guilt and characterizing Martha Beasley's "scripted" testimony as disturbing. Beasley characterized Tolbert's act as one of sexual desire, not one of power, violence, humiliation, or rage; he was willing to risk everything because he desired her. Frederickson concludes: "Her testimony closely resembled southern whites' collective fantasies and fears about African American men. Having been raised in the South, the girl must have known that such an account would play well to a small-town jury."[106]

In what had become glaringly obvious, McCray spelled out what critical race theorists would posit years later. In a letter to *The State*, the daily newspaper in Columbia, he asserted in 1959: "The Greenwood case was an example of how often happens in South Carolina that in order to inflict reprisals upon those Negroes who strike out for Constitutional rights for their people, the instrument called South Carolina Law and Order is turned against them in an effort to reduce or nullify any effectiveness they may attain."[107]

"The Terrorist Treachery" against Reverend DeLaine

It all started with a school bus. Black children slogged to school on foot while white children sat warm and dry in comfortable school buses funded by the all-white school board. But the inequality was much bigger than that. White schools in South Carolina had indoor plumbing; black schools did not. White schools were modern; black school buildings were mostly rickety, tumbledown structures. The average white teacher earned two-thirds more than the average black teacher.[108] More than 6,000 black children, compared to 2,000 whites, attended school in Clarendon County, South Carolina, yet the state allocated $100,000 more to pay for the white schools in the late 1940s.[109]

In 1947, Reverend Joseph Armstrong DeLaine of Summerton lived with his wife Mattie and their three children across the street from Scott's Branch School where she taught. DeLaine, a well-known and respected black minister in Clarendon County, served as principal and taught at a three-room elementary school out in the country, and he believed that the only way for blacks to rise up from poverty was to educate themselves. He had earned his bachelor's and divinity degrees from Allen University in the state capital of Columbia in 1931. Filling his days preaching and teaching, DeLaine was a product of his day. Born in 1898, he had been raised at a time when South Carolina blacks asked the white power structure for more funding for their schools rather than challenge the separate-but-equal doctrine rendered by the U.S. Supreme Court in *Plessy v. Ferguson* dating back to 1896. But he became interested in the NAACP in the summer of 1942 as the organization kept up the fight for the equalization of teachers' salaries, a campaign led by John McCray and others in Columbia. Inspired by their grit and courage, DeLaine created an underground NAACP branch down the road in rural Clarendon County, calling it the Citizen's Committee and using only plain envelopes for correspondence in order to remain undetected by the whites, particularly county authorities, planters, and others. This was the heart of South Carolina's black belt—so named for the fertile soil that supported cotton plantations—where African Americans comprised more than 70 percent of the county's population in 1950, the highest percentage in the state.[110]

But DeLaine got the attention of the white power structure when at the behest of blacks in the county appealed to the white superintendent, L. B. McCord, for a school bus. McCord explained to him that because blacks did not pay as much in taxes as whites, it was not fair to ask whites to absorb that extra financial burden. So when asking nicely didn't work, local NAACP leaders turned to DeLaine to find a plaintiff to sue. The reverend's behind-the-scenes work yielded *Pearson v. County Board of Education* in 1948, with a brave black farmer named Levi Pearson stepping forward to take on the school board for equal facilities. The case was a bit of a false start, though, when that it was thrown out of the local court on a technicality.[111]

Lawyers for the school board discovered that most of Pearson's land straddled a different school district, so he was suing in the wrong jurisdiction. "I think that's when my hair turned white," recalled DeLaine, slender and clean cut, typically dressed in a well-worn black suit accented with his white preacher's collar.[112] He appeared to crumble a bit under the strain of working to disrupt the racial status quo in South Carolina. Along with suffering from pleurisy, a painful inflammation of the membrane surrounding the lungs, he suffered mentally from the strain of his civil rights work. "In 1934–35 I broke down and couldn't do any work for more than a year," he wrote to his friend John Henry McCray. "Then in 1943–45 I again broke down to the extent that I did not preach a time for 18 months."[113] Yet again and again, he would be called on by other NAACP members to step into the void of leadership in Clarendon County when he would have preferred leading a quiet life. "My work with the Church, School and effort to work the folks up to want full citizenship was more than I could take under the war strain and privation."[114]

After the Pearson case fell through, the school board replaced the Scott's Branch principal, the beloved A. Maceo Anderson, who had served there eighteen years, with a less-educated man, I. S. Benson, who had a long history of doing the white man's bidding. This act was widely seen as retribution for the school bus case and symbolized the powerlessness of black parents when it came to educating their children. Parents suspected that Benson was stealing from the school as money from school fundraisers began to mysteriously disappear. The new principal started charging various student fees, and if students didn't pay, he threatened to withhold their diplomas.[115]

Historian Richard Kluger writes of the new principal: "In short, he was a bully, a thief, and a malingerer in the eyes of the black community, and probably a traitor to his race: they suspected he had funneled much of the ill-got money to white officials who let him keep the rest."[116] Members of the black community were furious. They had put a substantial amount of their own money into Scott's Branch because white school officials had refused to do so. Scott's Branch served as the hub of civic life in Summerton, and parents had felt locked out of the decision-making processes governing their children's education.[117] In a heated mass meeting, parents and teachers selected DeLaine to lead a small grievance committee in an appeal to Superintendent McCord and the school board to replace the new principal, but his request to discuss the matter was ignored for months. As spring turned into summer, written requests for a public hearing, sent by registered mail, were returned to DeLaine—unopened. Morale had dropped, so DeLaine mailed out a flyer to parents and teachers in early fall to rally the community: "Money paid to a school should be used for the benefit of the CHILDREN of that school, and the parents should know how it is spent. . . . A Principal who receives his SALARY from monies appropriated for PUBLIC INSTRUCTION should be glad to let the PARENTS know what is being done with the moneys they pay or give, unless it is going in the 'RAT HOLE' or the 'PRIVATE SINKING FUND.'" Superintendent McCord finally agreed to a hearing in late September 1949, where the accused principal had no answers for the complaints against him. He was fired and left town two days later, and Mattie DeLaine took over as acting principal. Her husband, however, was advised that his teaching and administrative duties in the school system would not be needed the following year.[118]

But now the fledgling fight had some momentum. The NAACP had been working to convince DeLaine to find still more plaintiffs who would sue for equal funding for buses, buildings, and teachers. This time, however, the organization needed a large group of reliable plaintiffs, not just one courageous soul. It took him and other civil rights leaders, including John McCray, only a short time to find twenty names to deliver to NAACP attorney Thurgood Marshall to challenge the school system. Harry Briggs was the first name on the complaint, and white reprisal was swift and crippling. Briggs, a U.S. Navy veteran with five children, worked at a gas station, and his wife, Liza, cleaned rooms at a motel. They and other petitioners were fired from their jobs, as was DeLaine and his wife. The reverend's niece and sisters were also dismissed from their teaching jobs. DeLaine received hate mail signed by the KKK threatening "to take him for a ride if he didn't shut his mouth." He was almost run off the road while driving in his car. Afraid for his life and his family, he posted armed guards at his home and warned "innocent persons" not to approach his home at night lest he inadvertently shoot them. Then, in early 1950, he was named in a $20,000 libel suit by the ex-principal of Scott's Branch School, I. S. Benson, who'd been fired by the county school board the previous October.[119]

At the trial, Superintendent McCord sided with the ex-principal, testifying that DeLaine had made up the complaints and turned the black community against Benson. It was the white superintendent's word against DeLaine's, and the all-white jury awarded Benson $2,700.[120] One of the men who testified against DeLaine was Roderick W. Elliott, a local sawmill owner and school board chairman who would be the defendant in the famous *Briggs v. Elliott* case, which would join with four other cases decided under *Brown v. Board of Education of Topeka* in 1954. DeLaine couldn't pay the libel damages even if he wanted to, later calling the suit "terrorist treachery." Historian Richard Kluger calls the entire affair "a kangaroo court" built on "trumped-up charges."[121]

Meanwhile, the AME Church bishop transferred DeLaine to St. James Church in Lake City, about thirty-five miles northeast of Summerton in 1951 in an effort to help keep the DeLaine family safe. Then their home back in Summerton, which still held most of their furnishing and possessions, mysteriously burned to the ground. Local firefighters later explained that DeLaine's house was twenty feet outside the city limits so they couldn't fight the blaze.[122] DeLaine's insurance company refused to pay his claim after the fire, giving the money to settle the $2,700 libel judgment instead.[123]

In October 1955, the year after the U.S. Supreme Court ruled in *Brown* that separate schools were inherently unequal, a group characterized by DeLaine as "Night-Riding Thugs" began to occasionally shoot bullets into his home, the church parsonage in Lake City.[124] After each of the shootings, DeLaine gave the license plate numbers to the police. The officers refused to investigate, telling him, "Preacher, get yourself another pair of eyeglasses." Then he started shooting back. DeLaine fired two shots at a car on the night of October 10, later saying he was only answering gunfire from a car outside his parsonage.[125]

A warrant was issued for his arrest. His wife hid at a neighbor's house, and friends smuggled her to Columbia in the trunk of a car the next day. She met her husband in nearby Florence, and they fled the state. He hid under blankets on the floor of the backseat as they crossed the state line into North Carolina. "God delivered me and my wife that night out of a gun parade," DeLaine later wrote.[126] "I shot back because I wanted to mark that car. I believed the people in that car were the ones who sent me a threatening letter, who threw bricks through my window and who burned my church. I thought if I marked the car the police would have the honor to break open the case," DeLaine told the *New York Post* after he had safely reached New York City. "When I fired those shots I felt as though a great burden had been lifted."[127]

DeLaine founded a new church with sixty members the next year in Buffalo, New York. It was later named the DeLaine-Waring AME Church in honor of the exiled preacher and the South Carolina judge Waties Waring, a white southerner who worked to whittle away at the Jim Crow infrastructure of the Palmetto State and who, declared a traitor to his race and threatened by the KKK, also moved to New York. DeLaine later settled at Calvary AME Church in Brooklyn, reflecting back on the libel case in a letter to McCray in 1961: "When I think of the six white men who witnessed falsely against me in a frame up lawsuit trying to rob me out of $20,000; all the three trustees are dead: Mr. George Kennedy, Mr. Deno Carson and Mr. R. M. Elliott are gone. The other three school officials may be alive but I don't think they are any more happy than I am. They are Mr. McCord, Mr. Betchman and Mr. Mills. I want to live until they see the folly of their evil doings in denying innocent children of their rights and thinking to rob me behind legal pretense would make them more happy."[128] He lived in exile the rest of his life, dying of cancer in 1974 at the age of seventy-six in Charlotte, North Carolina. Toward the end of DeLaine's life, South Carolina officials said they would not arrest him if he came home. DeLaine didn't chance it.

"He Wanted the Money. We Paid Him."

More than a year after the U.S. Supreme Court overturned *Plessy*'s separate-but-equal doctrine in *Brown,* NAACP leaders in Sumter County, South Carolina, pushed for desegregation of the two small school districts there. Local NAACP leaders of course were eager to see *Brown* enforced. "Negroes are not asking any favors or special privileges or treatment, we want to be treated as any other American citizen, and [ask] that the 'Supreme Law' of the land be obeyed and carried out," the twelve members of the NAACP executive committee informed the community in a letter to the editor of the *Sumter Daily Item,* the only newspaper in the rural county. Sumter adjoins Clarendon County in the central Piedmont region of the state, an ideal climate for cotton in the loamy soil that stretches between the tropical, marshy low country of the coast and the rugged mountains that make up the Appalachian foothills to the west. Sumter had two white school districts. Eighty black residents signed a petition to enroll their children in one district while forty signed to enroll theirs in the other. In their published letter, which was big news of the day, the NAACP Executive Committee members in Sumter County informed in the newspaper that the petitions were drawn up by their attorneys, presented at a mass meeting, then circulated throughout the black community with a full explanation of the petition's intent.[129]

All twelve members of the board, mostly ministers, steeled themselves for a showdown as the white establishment dug in to maintain segregation. The school board released the names of those who signed the petitions, and the names were published in the newspaper. Now those signees faced a wide range of economic reprisals from the white power structure. The school board had hired prominent white attorney Shepard K. "Shep" Nash to handle the uprising, and he later said several signers came to his office to withdraw their names from the petitions. He also gave the names of the petition signers to other newspapers in the state, which had been watching the drama unfold with much interest.[130]

Nash reported that a black man named Roland E. Blanding visited his law office on September 9, 1955, with a letter that stated: "I read the petition which was presented to me very carefully and it did not request integration of the two races. The petition I signed requested the leaders from both races to talk over the problems which have arisen in an attempt to find a resolution." Nash said he witnessed Blanding sign the letter before he released it to the *Sumter Daily Item*, which printed it verbatim. Desperate to hold together the petition drive, the NAACP Executive Committee responded with the lengthy letter published in the paper on September 13, 1955.[131]

The letter responded to the school board's charge that the NAACP had used improper tactics to secure some signatories to the desegregation petition filed with the board. The authors argued: "Those eligible to sign were asked to do so of their own free will. There was no coercion, persuasion or pressure by any [NAACP] member. . . . Signees who are being pressured by certain employers as economic reprisals for signing the petition cannot truthfully say he did not know what he or she was signing. No one was forced to do so." In the case of Blanding, the letter declared: "He not only signed after reading the petition, but on one occasion directed others how to sign them." But he couldn't take the pressure. In its letter, the NAACP Executive Board appealed for whites to stop punishing black signers of the petition with economic reprisals. "Both groups suffer from the un-Christian procedure," the board wrote.

Nash took exception to one sentence relating to reports that Blanding had asked for the removal of his name from the petition. The letter stated, "Either [Nash] is double-talking or the officials who released his statements to the press are wording these retroactions to fit the Citizen's Committees." In other words, Nash took this statement to mean that the NAACP was accusing him, as the school board's attorney of inducing Blanding to lie in the service of the local chapter of the Citizens' Council, a white supremacist group quickly sprouting across the South after the *Brown* decision came down. The council sought to squelch the petitions. In October 1955, Nash, a former state senator, sued the twelve leaders of the Sumter chapter of the NAACP in the Court of Common Pleas in Sumter County Court. Asking for $120,000, he insisted that the group intended to damage his reputation as a practicing attorney.

In his motion to dismiss, NAACP attorney Lincoln C. Jenkins Jr. of Columbia said there was nothing libelous in the letter. It didn't mention Nash by name, and he didn't show specifically how the letter had damaged him. Jenkins said the letter was directed toward a political group and had nothing to do with Nash's work as an attorney. Judge William H. Grimball overruled that motion in January 1956, and Jenkins prepared an appeal to the South Carolina Supreme Court. NAACP assistant counsel Jack Greenberg helped out from his office in New York. In the appeal, they stopped short of calling the letter political speech, although this undoubtedly is what it was. They explained: "In this age of widely disseminated news and great public interest in public affairs all parties to issues of public interest seek to win its favor. . . . The language, the timing, the balance, are all designed to present a point of view."

But the state Supreme Court affirmed Judge Grimball's ruling.

Although Nash was not mentioned by name, the court declared, he was obviously identified as the school board's attorney dealing with the petitions for desegregation and releasing related information to the press. The court disagreed with the NAACP that the words were not libelous per se, that is, libelous on their face: "We think that the inference is plain that [the] plaintiff dishonestly worded the retractions." To call an attorney dishonest is defamatory, the court wrote in its unanimous affirmation.[132]

NAACP attorneys prepared for trial in Sumter. Greenberg consulted with Thurgood Marshall and the rest of the New York legal staff about how best to present the case. They decided that only local counsel should appear in the courtroom, and Greenberg, who was white, advised Jenkins that "it would be extremely inadvisable for me to be present at that trial. Thurgood says that my presence—as a New York lawyer, could only serve to further prejudice the jury."[133]

NAACP lawyers argued that Nash was not identified in the letter published in the local newspaper and that he had not shown that he suffered any harm, either personally or in his professional standing as a lawyer. They insisted that the letter was privileged, that it was fair comment on an important political and public issue of the day.[134]

But they knew they'd find no sympathy from the all-white jury. After one day of testimony in October of 1956 before Judge Steve C. Griffith of Newberry, both sides agreed to settle out of court for $10,000. Greenberg admitted, "The settlement was the best way out of an extremely difficult situation, but the defendants now have the difficult problem of raising the ten thousand dollars." Behind the scenes, Jenkins had learned from the jury foreman that the all-white group was ready to bring back a verdict of $50,000 and would only agree to the lesser sum if the national NAACP promised not to help pay the settlement.[135]

Local white officials wanted their black citizens to suffer. "The suit was not brought for money alone, but, rather for the purpose of killing the NAACP in Sumter," Jenkins said later. "It is rumored that the Citizens Council gave Nash 'hell' for letting us off the hook so easy." Jenkins wrote Greenberg after the settlement: "We did the best we could under the circumstances. We didn't stand a chance before the jury, which was packed with members of the Citizens [sic] Council." Time was rushed, however, because the NAACP and Nash made the deal on October 5 and had only until November 17, 1956, to pay the settlement.[136]

One of the local NAACP defendants was a Presbyterian minister. A representative from the church's national office reached out to help. This offer inspired Greenberg and other NAACP leaders in New York to brainstorm about what other organizations might be willing to help: perhaps a medical association since one of the defendants was a doctor, they mused.[137] Fearful of phone-tapping by state authorities, Greenberg asked the president of the South Carolina NAACP to talk to the defendants in person about other possible sources of revenue. The NAACP and churches across the state raised $7,200 in less than three weeks. The black-owned *Carolina Times* in Durham, North Carolina, marveled at the "unprecedented display of unity" in the NAACP fundraising efforts: "Starting from scratch, the organization and churches of all denominations sent out appeals less than a month ago and the money began pouring in from 25 cents up."[138]

It reported that an unidentified "white northern church denomination" sent the Sumter NAACP chapter a blank check with instructions to fill in any amount up to the necessary $10,000. The NAACP only used $3,000 of it. Before a packed audience at First Baptist Church in Sumter, Reverend H. P. Sharper, the pastor and local NAACP president, laid more than $7,200 on the collection table. He said an additional $3,000 would come from an anonymous donor. NAACP leaders delivered the check to Nash in mid-November of 1956. Reverend Hinton, president of the South Carolina Conference of the NAACP, praised members across the state for this extraordinary fundraising campaign, which he called "their greatest effort."

Nash said, "Tell your people I'll never spend a penny of this money on myself."

He put the check in his bank account and said he would return it "to Negro people who had contributed" if the NAACP would provide a list of the donors and would not file any school integration suits in Sumter County in the next ten years. He set a six-month deadline on his offer, expiring May 20, 1957. But the NAACP leaders, still determined to desegregate South Carolina public schools, rejected Nash's proposal, issuing a statement to the press: "He wanted the money. We paid him. We don't want it back, nor do we need it. We still want schools integrated in Sumter County." Nash later said he would spend half the settlement to pay his lawyers in the libel suit and give the other half of the money to the Shriner's Hospital for Crippled Children in Greenville, South Carolina, and to the all-white Sumter First Presbyterian Church.[139]

Rather than demolishing the NAACP, the libel suit and resulting fundraiser seemed to boost the morale of the local chapter in Sumter and indeed statewide organization. The *Afro-American* in Baltimore quoted an anonymous NAACP member in Sumter: "I saw people there that I never knew were supporting us. I saw hundreds of our best citizens publicly contributing to the cause."[140] The NAACP did not mention the national church's gift to Nash when it settled, and it was later reported in newspapers across the state that the Philadelphia-based Presbyterian Church USA gave the NAACP $10,000 to pay the settlement—although the actual sum was only the $3,000 balance.[141]

The Columbia, South Carolina, KKK, publicized the support of the white church denomination in a prepared statement directed toward white Columbia. The outraged Robert E. Hodges, the kligrap (secretary) of the supremacist group, griped at this act of racial treason: "Few Americans and fewer Presbyterians ever thought they would see the day when the Presbyterian Church would sink so low in the mire of social gospel politics as to raise funds for the race-mixing activities of the Communist-dominated National Association for the Advancement of Colored People."[142] The church and the KKK were on poor terms anyway. Presbyterian leaders had criticized the Klan at their annual assembly of the southern branch of the church in Birmingham earlier that week in May 1957, censuring the KKK as an organization "whose purpose is to gain its point by intimidating, reprisal and violence."[143]

In 1963, the local NAACP chapter filed suit a second time to desegregate Sumter County's public schools, with Jenkins and Greenberg once again taking on Shep Nash in court. Representing thirteen black children, the NAACP demanded that the county reorganize the school district on a "nonracial basis," assigning students to schools based on where they lived and not on their race. Ten years after the *Brown* decision, South Carolina still required school districts to maintain segregated schools. But these children's parents served in the American military and lived on Shaw Air Force Base, a federal installation, so they figured Sumter County was a good place to retrench and push for the enforcement of *Brown*. For their part, Nash and other attorneys representing the Sumter School Board argued that the "ethnic, cultural, racial, intellectual, anthropological and physical differences" between the races offered a "sufficient rational basis" to continue segregation in Sumter County. The U.S. District Court in Columbia disagreed, ordering in August 1964 that the Sumter School District must desegregate the following 1965–1966 academic year.[144]

Much CRT scholarship recognizes that race is a legal construction. At minimum, race is a social construction partly fashioned by law. Ian F. Haney Lopez argues that legal actors—attorneys and judges—are both conscious and unwitting participants in the legal construction of race. By advancing an argument that the races should be separated because of their "ethnic, cultural, racial, intellectual, anthropological and physical differences," Nash and other attorneys in Sumter County sought to uphold within the law the white belief in material differences between the white and black races. In this constructed reality, racial dominance and subordination become part of the socioeconomic fabric of society and the law. Lopez explains, "As laws and legal decision-makers transform racial ideas into a lived reality of material inequality, the ensuing reality becomes further justification for the ideas of race."¹⁴⁵ In other words, with unequal funding for buildings and textbooks and with disparities in teacher salaries, black and white schools were destined to remain unequal, and each passing year would make it more difficult for a black student to receive the same education as a white student. Ten years after *Brown*, a federal court in South Carolina was putting a stop to such arguments. But this case was just one in countless courtrooms across the South, where NAACP lawyers continued the desegregation drive years after *Brown*. White defiance and legal foot dragging persisted into the late 1960s as whites began creating exclusive private schools for their white children.

Shep Nash had served in the state House of Representatives for two years in the early 1930s and state Senate for twelve years afterward. He was a deacon at the First Presbyterian Church in Sumter. He served on the school board and chaired the Sumter Democratic Party for eighteen years. The University of South Carolina honored him after his death in 1980: "Shep Nash was a kindly man who loved his fellow man. He was a trial attorney without peer who championed his client's cause."¹⁴⁶

"I Ain't No Lady. I'm a Newspaper Woman."

Hazel Brannon rolled into Holmes County, Mississippi, in 1936 in her Cadillac convertible. Fresh from the University of Alabama's journalism school, she had borrowed $3,000 to buy her own newspaper, the struggling weekly *Durant News*, with a circulation of six hundred copies.¹⁴⁷ Brannon, a journalist since she graduated from high school in Gadsden, Alabama, in 1930, paid off her *Durant News* loan in four years and bought the more established *Lexington Advertiser*, the Holmes County seat's eighteen-hundred-copy weekly, in 1943. Brannon's newspapers prospered with their small-town recording of births, deaths, weddings, and anniversaries for the area's white readers. Her column, "Through Hazel Eyes," initially supported the racial

Figure 2. Hazel Brannon Smith stood out in a crowd with her Lily Dache hats, colorful dresses, and vivacious personality. Here the young editor holds court at a convention of the Mississippi Press Association.
—Hazel Brannon Smith, Mississippi Press Association Records, Manuscripts Division, Special Collections Department, Mississippi State University Libraries.

status quo, imagining a Jim Crow world where whites and blacks lived happily, peacefully, and separately—and knew their place.[148]

Yet she was a crusader from the start. A southern Baptist, Brannon took on illegal bootlegging and gambling and for months, her editorials hounded local law enforcement to clean up the county. In early 1946, she even challenged Sheriff Walter L. Murtagh to enforce the law or resign.[149] After the sheriff executed search warrants and began confiscating cases of liquor, Brannon continued her prodding under the headline: "What about the Slot Machines?"[150] Later that spring, a grand jury returned fifty-two indictments for gambling and prohibition violations. Brannon felt triumphant, writing in her column: "The bootlegger is definitely on the run."[151] She reported that the public health department wanted to set up a clinic to treat sexually transmitted disease among the poor, and her use of the words "venereal disease" in the newspaper shocked one of her Saturday night dates, a young man from among the "better" families in the county. He told her, "Ladies just don't talk about venereal disease." She then informed him: "I ain't no lady. I'm a newspaper woman."[152]

After the U.S. Supreme Court's *Brown* ruling in 1954, Hazel Smith (her named changed when she married Walter "Smitty" Smith in 1950 whom she met on an around-the-world cruise) defended racial segregation in her column but declared that the court was "morally right": separate schools are inherently unequal.[153] Although Smith had grown up in a southern culture built on maintaining distinct racial identities and enforcing segregation, she began to form a new sense of right and wrong. In Indianola, less than fifty miles from Lexington, the first White Citizens' Council was created in response to *Brown* and chapters began springing up around the state. These white-supremacist groups billed themselves as law-abiding citizens who opposed segregation, but Smith eyed them warily, editorializing in 1954, "They appeal to prejudice and to ignorance–and their religion is the doctrine of hatred and greed implemented by the weapons of fear and distrust."[154]

Smith was no longer in lockstep with her community on the issue of race, most notably regarding fair and equal treatment under the law. And for that left turn, she became a political lightening rod, antagonizing a community now bent on ruining her. Smith later traced a run-in with the local sheriff over his mistreatment of blacks—and his resulting libel suit against her—as the turning point in her newspaper career. Although she was able to buy two more newspapers, the Banner County *Outlook* in Flora in 1955 and the *Northside Reporter* in Jackson in 1956, a steady barrage of legal harassment and economic boycotts by whites would cripple her financially for decades, make her a legend in national newspaper circles, and leave her virtually friendless in her own community.[155]

The libel suit stemmed from a front-page story, "Negro Man Shot in Leg Saturday in Tchula; Witness Reports He Was Told to 'Get Goin' by Holmes County Sheriff."[156] Smith reported in July 1954 that Sheriff Richard F. Byrd

> came driving up where a group of Negroes were congregated and asked one of them what he meant by "whooping." When the Negro replied that he had not whooped, Sheriff Byrd was reported to have cursed and struck the Negro on the head. When the Negro raised his hand to ward off further blows Sheriff Byrd was reported to have pulled out his gun and told the Negro to "get goin" whereupon the man started running. At this time, Sheriff Byrd was reported to have fired his gun several times, one of the bullets entering the left thigh of the victim from the rear and passing through the leg to the front.... No charges have yet been filed against Sheriff Byrd in the shooting.[157]

In an editorial the next week titled "The Law Should Be for All," Smith called for Byrd's resignation for this brutal, unwarranted act, his overall brutality of black citizens, and "shocking reports too numerous to ignore."[158] Furthermore, Smith wrote: "In our opinion, Mr. Byrd as Sheriff has violated every concept of justice, decency and right in his treatment of some people in Holmes County. He has shown us without question that he is not fit to occupy that high office."[159] She was defending a black man over a white—an editorial stance virtually unheard of in a white newspaper at the time. It had long been established that justice was dispensed differently to white and black races. Smith defended the wounded black man, twenty-seven-year-old Henry Randle: "He had not violated any law—the Sheriff was not trying to arrest him for any offense. He just made the one mistake of being around when the Sheriff drove up."[160]

Denying that he shot the man, Byrd sued Smith for $57,500 in damages in Holmes County Circuit Court. Smith replied in print: "This newspaper has in the past, and will continue in the future to print the truth as we know it to be.... No damage suit can shut us up so easily."[161] Byrd won $10,000 at the trial in October 1954, and Smith appealed to the Mississippi Supreme Court.[162]

She argued that the libel verdict was "punishment for daring to criticize a white man for abusing a Negro."[163] In October 1955, the state's high court reversed and rebuked Byrd in an opinion written by Justice Percy Lee: "Under the facts of this record, there was no justification whatever for hitting the Negro with the blackjack or shooting him. . . . It follows that the Negro was unlawfully assaulted in both instances."[164] The court held that "proof of the substantial truth of a publication, made with good motives and for justifiable ends, is defense to an action of libel" under Mississippi law.[165] The court also praised Smith's work, pointing out that she had tried to reach Byrd multiple times before running the story and that several witnesses said Byrd fired the shots: "As a newspaper woman, she conceived that it was her duty, through her papers, to give the public the news, and this she did in the utmost good faith. After the news item was published and the Sheriff made no complaint about it, she assumed that it accorded with his version of the facts, and she thereafter made the editorial comment on July 15." Addressing the issue of First Amendment rights, Justice Lee wrote that "the freedom of speech and of the press shall be held sacred . . . and if it shall appear to the jury that the matter charged as libelous is true, and was published with good motives and for justifiable ends, the party shall be acquitted."[166]

Like Smith, Lee was ahead of his time, defending press rights in a civil rights–related case almost ten years before the Supreme Court would do so in *New York Times v. Sullivan*. In November 1955, Smith commented on her libel case in an editorial headlined "Freedom's Safeguard." The piece essentially presaged what Justice Brennan would say in the *Sullivan* ruling: "The real point at issue was the right of an editor to criticize a public official in the performance of his official duties. If that right is abridged, the opportunity for people to know and to understand the actions of public officeholders will be seriously weakened, for it is the alert newspaper and the courageous editor who keeps the people informed."[167] Her statement was a direct challenge to public authorities in the Deep South desperate to defend decades of racial segregation and keep blacks in their place as second-class citizens.

Holmes County residents were unimpressed, and their retaliation came kudzu-quick. Smith had long agitated the establishment with her controversial editorials, and after the libel decision, the fight became even more damaging financially. Smith's husband was fired as administrator of the local hospital, advertisers stopped buying ads in her newspapers, and her printing business shrank.[168]

"Sometimes I feel like just going on and selling out . . . but if I did I feel that I would be compromising everything I have ever stood for and believed in and I can't do it," Smith wrote her friend, Hodding Carter Jr., the famous southern editor of the *Delta Democrat News* in Greenville, Mississippi.[169] As Smith's debts began piling up, Carter and several other mostly moderate southern editors organized a committee to raise money to help keep her businesses afloat.[170] "The gal is too courageous to be destroyed," Carter wrote Norman Isaacs of the *Louisville Times*.[171] They appealed to virtually every editor in the country, and thousands of dollars poured in from scores of newspapermen ranging from the media baron Roy Howard to editors from the *Chicago Tribune, Boston Herald,* and *St. Petersburg Times,* and even the *Honolulu Advertiser.* Smith was to use the money to pay for ad space at $164 a page, and editors could pick and promote a nonprofit organization such as the American Heart Association. Carter also cosigned on a loan from a Greenville bank.[172] The National Council of Churches contributed $3,000, earmarking the money for lawyers' fees related to the sheriff's libel suit.[173]

Failing to run her out of business, a group of community leaders started the *Holmes County Herald* in 1958 with Citizens' Council backers who included public officials, lawyers, and prominent Lexington businessmen. Smith challenged them in an editorial: "There is not enough business in Lexington for two newspapers. . . . Somebody is going broke."[174] While Smith picked up state and national journalism awards, the harassment and intimidation was unabated at home. Undeterred by the threats, she used her column to cajole advertisers to come back to her newspapers, pointing out in July 1961 that the *Herald* was late getting its edition on the streets for the fifth week in a row and lamenting that the crusade against her was a "continuing campaign that has been waged without letup since Richard Byrd filed a libel suit against me in July of 1954—seven long years ago."[175]

In October 1963, law enforcement officers sued her again for libel. This time, two Lexington policemen, W. M. McNeer and Frank Davis, sought $50,000 each in actual and punitive damages for a news story and editorial in the June 13 editions of the *Advertiser* and *Durant News*. The officers had shot and killed thirty-eight-year-old Alfred Brown, an African American World War II veteran who had recently been released from a veterans' hospital where he was a mental patient.[176] The officers said they tried to arrest him for public intoxication, and they hit him over the head with a blackjack when Brown pulled a knife. Davis suffered a deep cut on his neck and Brown was shot twice. Using eyewitness reports, Smith's story, "Negro Veteran Killed by Officers," ran in all her papers. In an accompanying editorial, she wrote: "From all accounts of reliable eyewitnesses the killing was senseless and could have been avoided. . . . If we are to continue to have racial peace here the present situation needs a great deal of improvement from the standpoint of law enforcement–and spirit and attitude as well." Echoing her statements about Sheriff Byrd, which prompted the earlier libel suit, Smith suggested that the city order Lexington police officers to treat both blacks and whites with respect or fire them.[177]

At the trial in Holmes County Circuit Court, Smith's attorney, Robert H. Weaver, said the officers never complained to Smith about the story or said it contained errors. Judge Arthur Clark Jr. ruled that Smith should publish a statement by the officers, giving them a chance to refute the story. The police officers' reply in her newspaper tried to debunk her story line by line.[178] Smith said in an accompanying article that the "written statement of the police officers was much different than witnesses to the scene."[179] But, surprisingly, she seemed to back down. She published a retraction to any "erroneous portions" of the story: "It was not our intention to impugn either their character or reputation, or to imply they were guilty of unlawful acts."[180] The case ended as a win for Smith, though, with the judge ruling against the plaintiffs for failure to establish a case. The officers reinstituted their libel suits in January 1964, but the actions languished in court on routine continuances until they were dismissed at the cost of the plaintiffs in 1967.[181]

For her editorials condemning the White Citizens' Council, Smith won the Pulitzer Prize in 1964, the first woman to do so. Her *Northside Reporter* was bombed that year, and her competition, the *Holmes County Herald,* had more than a foothold in the circulation war in the county. By 1968, some fourteen years after Sheriff Byrd's libel suit, Smith said she had fallen more than $200,000 in debt but still promised not to quit.[182] "When are they (the white people) going to find out that what I am trying to do is help ALL PEOPLE, white and black, so that we may work together and try to understand each other in order to build a better community and county?"[183] The bank foreclosed on her home, Hazelwood, and its accompanying 135 acres in 1985.[184]

Smith had long insisted that her coverage of race relations and her criticism of elected officials were protected speech under the First Amendment. Mississippi justices agreed with her, even though her stance was extremely unpopular among whites at the time. The favorable ruling does not change the fact, however, that journalists like Smith still had much to fear from being hauled into court in an expensive libel case. In his *Sullivan* opinion, Justice Brennan would worry about this "chilling effect" that could stifle public dialogue on issues of public interest. And as was the case in the *Sullivan* suit, Smith was analyzing and criticizing the behavior of police officers in their official duties. The Supreme Court later would leave no doubt that this is the kind of speech the First Amendment was designed to protect and enable.

"For Those Who Could Not Fight for Themselves"

The same year attorney Shep Nash sued in Sumter, South Carolina, 1955, another white lawyer and state legislator in Florida sued the NAACP leader in Fort Lauderdale, Florida, for criticism of his job as a state lawmaker. Representative Prentice Pruitt introduced a bill to abolish Florida public schools rather than desegregate them in compliance with the *Brown* decision. Dr. Von Mizell, a black surgeon and founder of the NAACP in Broward County, fired off a lengthy and indignant telegram to Representative Pruitt, who represented Jefferson County in the Florida panhandle. Mizell wrote that the bill should "come as a shock to all good thinking people of the state of Florida." He also told Pruitt, "With 63 percent of the population of your county being negroes, you are not a true representative of the people, but assume dictatorial power over the majority by force." At the height of the Red Scare, whites had often accused NAACP members of being involved with or infiltrated by communists as a tactic to undermine the organization. However, Mizell powerfully turned that accusation back on Pruitt, an ardent segregationist. Mizell's telegram continued: "You may not be a communist, but the aid and comfort you give the communist cause by your philosophy and tactics do them more good than any card carrying member can do in these parts. . . . The people of this great state deserve something better."[185]

Mizell also wrote to Florida representative A. J. Musselman, who supported Pruitt's bill and had suggested an amendment to the U.S. Constitution to circumvent the *Brown* decision. In the letter, Mizell asked him to cease such efforts: "For you who represent the finest part of the finest people in the State of Florida to join ranks with the hoodlums of West Florida, at whose action of this type we are not surprised, is more than we can understand. . . . We are hoping that you will rectify your good name by withdrawing any effort on your part to even suggest any such vile and unjust legislature [sic] to our Federal Government. We expect Ex-Governor Johns, Rep. Pruitt and their kind to carry on this red communistic tactics against our citizens."[186]

Pruitt sued Mizell for $500,0000 in Leon County Circuit Court in Tallahassee, asserting that he had been libeled in the telegram and letter. His suit specified: "The foregoing was meant and intended to convey that plaintiff is a 'hoodlum'; [sic] was and is guilty of Un-American racial prejudice against persons of negroid origin and guilty of conduct unbecoming a public officer; was and is guilty of committing a crime; was and is guilty of violating his statutory oath." As a result of Mizell's communications, Pruitt said he had been held up to "scorn, contempt and ridicule," that he had been shunned by his friends and neighbors, and that he had been held "in contempt in the eyes of his clients that he represents in a professional capacity."[187]

Von Delany Mizell clearly knew how to make waves. He created the first NAACP chapter in South Florida, staged protests and sit-ins, boycotted Fort Lauderdale's "Colored School," helped create a hospital for black residents, and successfully sued the Broward County Medical Association for admission. He even led "wade ins" to gain African Americans access to public beaches starting in 1946. Risking threats of assassination, he carried on his leadership of the black community as his father had before him. The Mizell family had settled in Fort Lauderdale in 1908, when Isadore Mizell, the son of an ex-slave from Georgia, bought farmland and started growing tomatoes for commercial sale. During the Great Depression, he fed many black families for free with produce from his farm.[188]

When commercial farming failed to be profitable, Isadore took up carpentry and built the first black school in the area. One of his fourteen children, Von Mizell graduated from medical school and worked at his own clinic. He was the first practicing black surgeon in Florida and cofounder of Provident Hospital, Fort Lauderdale's first medical facility for blacks. (James Sistrunk, the first black medical doctor in Florida, was a qualified surgeon, but he was not allowed to practice surgery in white hospitals in Florida.) For Mizell's high-profile civil rights activism, the KKK burned a cross in his front yard and threatened to assassinate him. "He had to have people come to his office at night to surround him, walk him to his car and ride shotgun. [Klansmen] were coming almost every night looking to kill him," said his nephew Don Mizell. "He was rich, owned lots of property and with fair skin and blue eyes he could cross over to the white side whenever he felt like it. In

Figure 3. Dr. Von Mizell, founder of the NAACP in Broward County, Florida, could have "passed" as white and led a peaceful life. Instead, he chose to lead his people in the fight for equal rights, holding "wade ins" to desegregate public beaches and risking threats of assassination.
—Photo provided by Don Mizell, Esq.

fact, he was encouraged to do so. Yet he still fought for those who could not fight for themselves."[189]

Von Mizell used his own money to challenge Jim Crow laws, which had become commonplace in Florida by the 1920s. But his cash reserves weren't endless, so he appealed to the NAACP executive secretary, Roy Wilkins, in New York for help in his libel defense. "I am willing to spend what money I can spare, but I am unable to meet the large fees required by the local white attorneys who would consider the case," Mizell wrote. "If this case can be won it will be a moral victory for all the Negroes of Florida."[190]

It is unclear how much support the New York office was able to lend, although its staff did keep close tabs on the case. Mizell's chief counsel, Francisco Rodriquez of Tampa, unsuccessfully argued that because the telegram and the letter were not circulated beyond Representatives Pruitt and Musselman, they did not defame the public officials. His motion to dismiss was denied, and he and Mizell prepared to go to trial in the spring of 1956. In the end, Mizell lost his case and was ordered to pay a total of $15,000 to Pruitt. The NAACP lawyers in New York City saw this result as inevitable, thanking Rodriguez for his hard work on the case. From New York, Bill Taylor wrote Rodriguez: "We were distressed although not really surprised to read of the verdict against Dr. Mizell. It was a hopeless situation in the trial court and you must have done well to hold the verdict down to $15,000."[191] Mizell agreed to pay the money, saying it would be useless to fight the case in Florida courts.[192]

"Not as Beasts to Be Shot Down Unmercifully"

The year before Montgomery commissioner L. B. Sullivan would sue the *New York Times,* a Georgia police officer challenged the *Savannah News Press* for criticizing his actions on the job after he shot and killed a black teen he suspected of robbery. In 1959, Patrolman J. R. Harley, a white police officer, sued the *Press* after a letter to the editor accused him of murder. Harley had been suspended from duty and charged with shooting another "not in his own defense" under Georgia law. However, a local Savannah court absolved Officer Harley of any criminal responsibility in shooting thirteen-year-old Claud Sutton.

Harley and his partner were on patrol when they came across

what they believed to be a burglary in progress in the cab of a large tractor-truck parked at the corner of Bay and Montgomery streets in Savannah, Georgia. According to court documents, Harley and his partner "hastened to apprehend the trespassers, whereupon the offenders quit the truck cab and began to run and make their escape." The officers said the fleeing suspects ignored their shouts to "halt," so Harley fired his revolver at one of the suspects to stop him in his tracks. Harley said he aimed at Sutton's feet but the bullet entered his side at the hip as the teen was fleeing.[193]

Under the headline "Church Labels Shooting as Murderous," the *Savannah News Press* ran a letter from leaders of the black Bethlehem Baptist Church addressed to Mayor Walter Lee Mingledorff and condemning the shooting. The ministers wrote: "We feel that it is one of the most disgraceful things a law enforcement officer could do in the light of circumstances given. We do not condone crime and believe that all criminals should be punished, including Patrolman J. R. Harley, for his unjustifiable shooting of this boy, but we do feel that law violators should be treated as human beings, and not as beasts to be shot down unmercifully."[194] The letter was signed by L. Scott Stell Jr., minister; J. H. Bennett, church clerk; and E. Cooper, chairman of the Board of Deacons. The letter also questioned the Savannah Police Department's handling of the shooting and why it sealed the records of the case: "The withholding of the full report is most baffling. Why is there so much secrecy about it? We are desirous of knowing the future status of the patrolman involved, and our police department. Can the city of Savannah be proud of a department that will condone such practices as this?" The letter also asked how the officer could not tell the victim was a youngster and questioned the officer's training. "Is it a fact that we would employ one so poorly trained that he would aim at the feet to halt a minor violator, and hit him in the chest and ending his life?"[195]

Harley took issue with the word "murderous," which appeared in the letter. In his lawsuit against the *Savannah News Press*, he said the word "imputed to him the carnal sin of breaking the

Sixth Commandment." Because he had not been convicted of murder in a court of law, Harley said the letter was false and unfair. The trial court found for Harley in the libel suit, but a sympathetic Court of Appeals of Georgia reversed the lower court's decision in September 1959.[196] The court said that it was unclear exactly what the two men were doing in the cab of the truck and that they may have been committing a felony or even the misdemeanor crime of trespassing—"if they were engaged in any crime at all."[197]

The Court of Appeals pointed out that Harley had the right to arrest the men in the cab in order to stop a felony from being committed. But he had no right, "merely to prevent an escape, to shoot a misdemeanor suspect who is fleeing from him." The court then turned to *Webster's New International Dictionary* to define the words *murderous* and *criminal*, the two words Harley took issue with in the letter. It also looked at the local magistrate's decision not to find Harley guilty of murder. But the Georgia Court of Appeals wasn't so sure about that finding: "It appears that the statements contained in the alleged libelous article are true." The court said Harley had no cause of action against the ministers because true statements cannot be considered libelous, thus delivering a major victory to the newspaper.

In the civil rights–related libel suits filed before *Sullivan* then, it is apparent that civil rights activists and journalists could get a fair trial–on occasion. Bass won her case in California, Smith prevailed in Mississippi, and the *Savannah News Press* was victorious in Georgia. But the governor of Florida prevailed in his suit against *Collier's*. Warley and Cole in Kentucky, McCray and DeLaine in South Carolina, and Mizell in Florida lost their cases, thus illustrating that the SLAPP suit had been established as a form of legal intimidation. These black journalists and activists were considered agitators by the white establishment and punished for their speech in the fight for civil rights. It would take the landmark *Sullivan* decision to finally protect them.

CHAPTER 2
"Heed Their Rising Voices," the *Sullivan* Case, and Turmoil for the *Times*

When Montgomery, Alabama, police commissioner Lester Bruce Sullivan sued the *New York Times* for libel in 1960, he had long been accustomed to reading newspapers run by editors who thought like he did.[1] In his mind, African Americans had their place below and separate from whites in society, and white authorities and citizens should deploy all means of prevention if they ever tried to step out of it. A majority of white southerners agreed. In the 1950s and 1960s, newspapers across the South often wrote glowing editorials about the activities of their city's White Citizens' Council chapter, a socially acceptable version of the KKK. Editors gushed over the "civic" group, which almost always included "the finest white citizenry" such as bankers, lawyers, businessmen, and farmers, the latter being akin to the antebellum planter class.[2] The *Meridian Star* in Mississippi encouraged readers to join the local council. The *News and Courier* in Charleston, South Carolina, urged its local chapter to "be strong" to protect the state during the crisis imposed by the school desegregation decision, *Brown v. Board of Education*, in 1954. And the *Jackson Daily News* in Mississippi offered support under such headlines as "Citizens' Council Gets Credit."[3] With the Citizens' Council chapters sprouting up across the South, members stirred up white hysteria after the court decision, widely calling the day the high court issued the *Brown* "Black Monday," a dark day for the country.

But northern journalists had begun swooping into Alabama in the 1950s to write about race. They reported the story of the civil rights movement as it unfolded and told it from the African Americans' point of view—which was unheard of in the South and throughout much of the United States. Commissioner Sullivan would become just one of many government officials and police officers using libel law to shut down public speech critical of his official actions, speech he found threatening to his office and reputation. But long before this, government officials' silencing of unpopular speech with libel law had found a comfortable place in American society and history.

The ink was still drying on the First Amendment when Congress passed its first sedition law in 1798.[4] This law stopped speech critical of government officials, in this case, President John Adams and the U.S. Congress, which his Federalist Party dominated. Tensions with France and fear that the upheaval of the French Revolution might spread to the United States helped prompt the Federalist-controlled Congress to look for ways to silence agitators and critics.[5] As paranoia and fighting through party newspapers increased, President Adams' Federalists attempted to muzzle enemies and dissenters with the Alien and Sedition Acts of 1798. Congress voted on the acts along party lines on July 4, ironically, and set an expiration date of 1801, when Adams' term as president would expire.[6] This would protect Adams from criticism and leave the next president, possibly a Republican, to fend for himself. The Sedition Act criminalized writing, publishing, or speaking in "a false, scandalous and malicious" manner about the government—Congress or the president—"with the intent to defame" them or arouse "the hatred of the good people of the United States." It was widely considered a blatant attempt to hush administration critics and the Republican newspapers that supported Thomas Jefferson. Anyone convicted of a violation faced two years in jail and a fine of up to $2,000.[7] America's colonial courts had long relied on English common law, in which criticism of government officials was automatically considered seditious. It was assumed that such criticism was false, scandalous, and malicious and that such unrestrained expression would likely provoke public unrest. Truth was not a defense. The act or case was actually worse for the speaker or writer when the words were true because truth could be more damaging than a falsehood. The jury's job was to decide whether the speaker said or published the words, while the judge's role was to decide whether the speech was seditious.[8]

One early libel case in British colonial America served as an anomaly but provides a glimpse of what would eventually be. The German immigrant John Peter Zenger, publisher of the *New York Weekly Journal,* was charged with seditious libel in 1734, although he was really printing the words of his boss, James Alexander. In an unprecedented move, the jury disregarded English common law, finding Zenger not guilty of seditious libel for his newspaper's criticism of the unpopular New York governor, William Cosby. The eloquence of Zenger's lawyer, Andrew Hamilton, was and has been widely credited for the jury's radical departure from tradition. Admitting outright that Zenger printed the material, Hamilton convinced the jury that it was a citizen's right to truthfully criticize his elected officials.[9] But this case deviated from the norm at the time, and the law did not change. When the Bill of Rights was adopted in 1791, federal common law and state laws were already in place to criminalize speech critical of the government and punish violators with jail terms and fines. But the outcome of the case did plant the seed, that the utterance of words critical of the government should not be a crime. Truth as a libel defense was an American invention, starting with the 1798 Alien and Sedition Acts. Adams and his fellow Federalists even tried to spin the passage of these repressive laws as a good thing for the press: Truth would defend them.[10] But that so-called principle carried no legal weight in court. Most judges were Federalists, and they required defendants to prove the truth of every word they had written or spoken, no matter how trivial or minute. The standard of proof was impossible to meet.

All ten convictions under the Sedition Act were of Republicans, and eight of those were editors of the country's most influential Republican newspapers. Still in its infancy then, the U.S. government had become quite successful in silencing its critics.[11] The Alien and Sedition Acts, which contributed to Adams's defeat in the presidential election of 1800, expired when Jefferson took office. No test case of their constitutionality reached the U.S. Supreme Court, but Jefferson pardoned those individuals convicted under the Sedition Act, and Congress later agreed to return their fines. In Anthony Lewis's words, "as a political tactic, the Sedition Act was a disaster. . . . But the act did make an inadvertent contribution, an important one, to the American system of government. It made large numbers of Americans appreciate the importance of free speech and freedom of the press in a democracy."[12]

This chapter reviews the details of the *Sullivan* suit along with cases filed by Bull Connor and other public officials in Birmingham and the bedroom community of Bessemer, Alabama. In addition to the *New York Times*, CBS News got caught in the crosshairs for its coverage of Freedom Rider beatings on Mother's Day in 1961 and for coverage of voter-registration efforts in Montgomery. This chapter also details an obscure case from Oklahoma City, yet another libel suit filed by a police officer against local civil rights leaders and the local black newspaper that criticized him after he shot a black man in his own front yard.

"Seditious Libel and White Supremacy"

Along with stopping the demonstrations sweeping across the South in the 1950s and 1960s, southern whites sought to prevent outsiders from revealing the state of the South to the outside world. It made sense that they would turn to the courts. And it goes without saying that the cult of whiteness had long oozed into the justice system. The legal history of black as racial otherness in the United States is as old as America itself, critical race theory has long posited. For example, the three-fifths compromise between northern and southern states in the U.S. Constitution, which established the apportionment for the House of Representatives, counted slaves as "three-fifths of all other persons."[13] The most famous libel case, of course, the one that would reach the U.S. Supreme Court first, was about race, that of the Montgomery police commissioner Lester Bruce Sullivan. After a *New York Times* advertisement called "Heed Their Rising Voices" ran on March 29, 1960, Sullivan sued the *Times* and four African-American ministers for libel. The ad claimed that unnamed public officials used violent and often illegal measures to stop and disrupt civil rights protests in the South. The ministers named in the suit were well-known leaders, often lightning rods, in their Alabama communities: Ralph Abernathy and S. S. Seay, both of Montgomery; J. E. Lowery of Mobile; and Fred Shuttlesworth of Birmingham. They knew nothing about the ad before it was published, much less agreed to have their names included at the bottom of the page.[14]

The New York–based Committee to Defend Martin Luther King and the Struggle for Freedom in the South placed the full-page advertisement to raise money for King's mounting legal bills in Alabama. Officials there had charged him with felony tax evasion and perjury in the filing of his state income-tax returns, the first such charge in the state's history, when he was pastor at Montgomery's Dexter Avenue Baptist Church. The Alabama attorney general John Patterson (who would later be governor and a plaintiff in the *Sullivan* case) engineered the case against King, charging that he diverted church and civil rights contributions to his personal bank account without declaring them on his tax return.[15]

Audited by the state of Alabama and the Internal Revenue Service, King paid back taxes totaling more than $2,000. After a citizen paid back taxes, he or she likely would not even face misdemeanor tax-evasion charges, but in this case, the state of Alabama charged King with a then-unheard-of felony. Even more unusual was that Attorney General Patterson had King arrested in Atlanta, where he was then living, and extradited from Georgia.[16] The charges against King came just days after he had endorsed the sit-in movement that started at a Woolworth's lunch counter in Greensboro, North Carolina, and that swept across the South. The ad in the *Times* quoted an editorial printed in the same newspaper a week before: "The growing movement of peaceful mass demonstrations by Negroes is something new in the South. . . . Let Congress heed their rising voices, for they will be heard." The ad reported that demonstrators were "being met by an unprecedented wave of terror." It said students were expelled from the all-black Alabama State College for singing "My Country, 'Tis of Thee" on the capitol steps in Montgomery. It said "truckloads of police armed with shotguns and tear-gas ringed the [campus]" and "their dining hall was padlocked in an attempt to starve them into submission."[17]

The ad didn't list any names but referred to "Southern Violators of the Constitution" who were "determined to destroy the one man, who, more than any other, symbolizes the new spirit now sweeping the South—the Rev. Dr. Martin Luther King Jr." The ad said "the Southern Violators" had bombed King's home and had "arrested him seven times for such petty offenses as speeding and loitering." Further, the ad read, "Obviously their real purpose is to remove him physically as the leader to whom the students and millions of others look for guidance and support. . . ." The signatures of such significant public figures and celebrities as Eleanor Roosevelt, Jackie Robinson, Sidney Poitier, Marlon Brando, and Harry Belafonte were atop names of sixty other supporters, including twenty black ministers from the South.[18]

Montgomery officials probably would never have seen the ad if not for Ray Jenkins, editor of the local afternoon newspaper, the *Alabama Journal*. He came across the ad while flipping through the *Times* on his lunch break and immediately noted the local angle.[19] He wrote a short story that detailed the ad's content and that, in turn, got the attention of Grover Hall Jr., the editor of the dominant newspaper in town, the *Montgomery Advertiser*. Hall's father was a crusading editor who had won a Pulitzer Prize in 1926 for editorials criticizing the Ku Klux Klan. But the conservative son was furious about the ad in the *Times*. He editorialized that it was full of "lies, lies, lies . . . and possibly willful ones" on the part of "abolitionist hellmouths."[20] The next day, Sullivan wrote the *Times* to demand a retraction, insisting the ad charged him of "grave misconduct" and that it was "false and defamatory." He sent the same letter to the four Alabama ministers, who said they were unaware that their names were included in any advertisement.[21]

Sullivan was a well-known figure in state and local politics from the early 1950s until his death in 1977. A Kentucky native and the son of a sheriff, he headed the Alabama State Police during the 1950s and, like many southern lawmen, was reported to have close ties to the Klan.[22] He was described by those who knew him well as "smooth, polished, relatively sophisticated for Montgomery. He had read a few books."[23] With the title of former state director of public safety behind his name, Sullivan was elected to a similar position in Montgomery after the bus boycott on a pledge to bring new business to the state capital.[24]

The New York law firm representing the *Times* responded to Sullivan on April 15, informing him that it was investigating the matter, but it also asked Sullivan to explain how the ad reflected on him since he was never named. Sullivan didn't respond. Instead, he filed his libel suit against the *Times* and the four ministers in the Circuit Court of Montgomery County, seeking $500,000 in damages. Three weeks before the ad ran in the *Times*, he had lauded the cooperation between a hoard of five thousand whites and the police, who successfully halted black demonstrators marching to the state capitol building. Sullivan told the *Montgomery Advertiser* that demonstrators who continued to march and conduct sit-ins would face police discipline for "flaunting their arrogance and defiance by congregating at the Capitol." The marchers were protesting the expulsion of Alabama State students who previously had requested service at the capitol building's basement cafeteria as similar sit-ins spread across the South.[25]

John Patterson, the former attorney general who became governor, ordered the Alabama State University president, H. Councill Trenholm, to expel the students who had requested food service at the capitol, and faced with losing state funding, Trenholm told reporters he had no choice but to do so.[26] Sullivan had been incensed by the students' demonstrations. Appearing on television, his face red with eyes bulging, he declared, "I want to assure the citizens of Montgomery that we are prepared to take whatever actions that might be necessary to maintain and preserve the time-honored traditions and customs of the South."[27]

As money poured into King's defense fund in response to the *Times* ad, State Attorney General MacDonald Gallion announced that Governor Patterson had asked him to study how he might sue the *Times* and the ad's sponsors for libeling Alabama officials.[28] It was not long after Sullivan filed his suit that a white jury found King not guilty in the perjury case, and as Roberts and Klibanoff put it in their Pulitzer Prize–winning book, *The Race Beat,* "Now the governor decided on a different strategy against King." His new legal weapon was the libel suit.[29] Three weeks after Sullivan filed suit, Governor Patterson demanded that the *Times* run a retraction for the "Heed Their Rising Voices" ad, complaining that he was accused of "grave misconduct" as head of the state of Alabama. State law required that public officials ask for a retraction before filing a libel suit. If no retraction was made, they were empowered to recover damages—typically a higher dollar amount than actual damages—meant to punish a defendant for illegal behavior. In response, the *Times* ran an apology in a story under the headline, "*Times* Retracts Statement in Ad."[30] Patterson filed suit anyway. It was identical to Sullivan's complaint, naming the newspaper and the four ministers and demanding a total of $1 million in damages. One exception, however, was that Patterson named King in the suit, and by naming the Alabama ministers, he and Commissioner Sullivan had insured that an Alabama Court would hear the case. Otherwise, the *Times* might have been able to move the case to a federal court and likely received a more sympathetic hearing.[31]

Patterson also had a long history of fighting desegregation in court. As state attorney general, he had secured a court order in 1956 barring NAACP activities in Alabama and fining the organization $100,000 for failing to turn over its membership roster and contribution list.³² Patterson had brought that suit as part of the white retribution surrounding the 1955 Montgomery Bus Boycott launched after Rosa Parks refused to give up her seat to a white man. The NAACP shut down its offices in Birmingham and relocated to Atlanta. Seven years later, the U.S. Supreme Court would rule against the state in *NAACP v. Alabama*, finding that it had violated the Fourteenth Amendment.³³

For his part, Patterson had become well known as Alabama's crime-fighting attorney general in 1954 after he finished cleaning up Phenix City, an army-base town that sat next door to Fort Benning and was known for its corruption. His father, as the local district attorney in Phenix City, had started that campaign and had been murdered for attacking the gambling and prostitution rackets there. Patterson forged a bond with Sullivan, then director of Public Safety for Alabama, and Walter B. Jones, the judge on the *Sullivan* case, when they worked together on several Phenix City cases. With an eye toward the governor's race in 1958, he had met with other southern attorneys general to plan a "massive resistance" legal strategy to fight desegregation.³⁴ Following Sullivan and Patterson, three more Montgomery officials filed libel suits of their own. Mayor Earl James, Commissioner Frank Parks, and former commissioner Clyde Sellers each sued the *Times* and the four Alabama ministers for $500,000.³⁵ The total damages sought by the five white plaintiffs for the "Heed Their Rising Voices" ad was $3 million.

On to Trial

The Sullivan trial started November 1, 1960, in Montgomery, the first capital of the Confederate States of America, as the Kennedy-Nixon presidential campaign was coming to a close.

Things looked bad for the defendants from the very beginning. Judge Jones, an avowed white supremacist and segregationist, presided with a Confederate flag displayed behind him. He was the son of a Civil War hero, Thomas Goode Jones, who became a two-term Alabama governor in the 1890s. The judge founded a law school in Montgomery in 1928 and named it after his father. Starting in 1924, Jones wrote a regular column, "Off the Bench," that ran in the *Montgomery Advertiser*. Judge Jones called the Civil War "the War for Southern Independence" and condemned to "the nine long, tragic years when the South was forced to undergo the horrors of Reconstruction."[36] He complained in his column about Congress' move to wipe out the poll tax, which five southern states, Alabama, Arkansas, Mississippi, Texas, and Virginia, still enforced in 1962. He groused that "extreme liberal people" were seeking to eliminate poll taxes for purely political reasons—"to get the Negro vote."[37] And perhaps most tellingly, he railed against the "unjust" assault of "radical newspapers and magazines, communists and the federal judiciary" on southern society and traditions.[38] He wrote further: "Columnists and photographers have been sent to the South to take back to the people of the North untrue and slanted tales about the South. Truly a massive campaign of super-brainwashing propaganda is now being directed against the white race, particularly by those who envy its glory and greatness." In yet another column, he reflected on a handsome Confederate monument he saw while visiting Columbia, South Carolina, with its "touching and ennobling inscription." He delighted in reporting that a Junior Citizen's Council Club at a Clanton, Alabama, elementary school had asked him to write "A Confederate Creed" that its members could recite during their weekly gatherings. Judge Jones included a couple of stanzas at the end of his column in December 1959: "I see in the Stars and Bar [sic], the glorious banner of the Confederacy as it waves in the Southern breeze, a symbol of freedom and devotion to constitutional rights, and emblem of honor and character. I believe the veneration for the ideals held dear by the Confederacy will make us a better people and a stronger state."[39]

Bringing this southern white background to the Alabama bench, Judge Jones unsurprisingly had a history of ruling against civil rights progress. He was the justice who had decided that the

NAACP must turn over its membership list to the state, although the U.S. Supreme Court would overturn that decision. He also issued an injunction to force a local bus company to comply with Alabama's segregation laws in 1956. With his round, bald head and wire-framed spectacles, Judge Jones was a local media darling in Montgomery. In 1958 the press honored him with a citation by the National Association of Press Photographers. He smiled broadly from a *Montgomery Advertiser* photo in which he is pictured with journalists from the *Advertiser* and *Birmingham News*. The caption spoke of the mutual respect local journalists and Judge Jones had for each other, and, ironically, "the judge expounded on the merits of a free press."[40] *New York Times* reporter Harrison Salisbury, who would also face a wave of libel suits in Birmingham, later said that Jones was involved in the initial plan to counterattack the northern media by using defamation law. "Gossip in the Montgomery courthouse had it," Salisbury wrote, "that Jones sat in with the Montgomery citizens who masterminded the 'libel suit' strategy."[41]

Louis Loeb, the general counsel for the *Times*, spent weeks searching for local counsel in Alabama to help with the defense. Establishment law firms politely declined before Loeb's partner, Tom Daly, had an inspired thought. Daly had defended *Reader's Digest* in Birmingham against a libel suit brought by the former governor Jim Folsom and had been impressed with Roderick Beddow of Beddow, Embry and Beddow, a large criminal-law practice that represented many black clients. Of the firm, the colorful southern liberal Cecil Roberts said, "They were the kind of lawyers who took black clients and got them life sentences instead of the death penalty."[42] Loeb recalled later that Beddow and T. Eric Embry jumped into the case with vigor and imagination: "They worked like beavers, and their judgment and advice was [sic] sound."[43] Embry grew up in Pell City, Alabama, the fourth generation of his family to study law, and he would go on to be elected to the state Supreme Court in 1974. But he took on unpopular causes in his early days.[44]

Embry, as well as the lawyers for the black ministers, objected to the use of the word "nigger" in opening statements of the Sullivan trial, but Judge Jones overruled them because the use of the word for *Negro* was the customary in Alabama.[45] Sullivan's attorneys also refused to address one of the ministers' lawyers, Fred Gray, as "Mr." and instead insisted on calling him "Attorney Gray." Gray, an African American lawyer, was King's long-time attorney and had represented Rosa Parks when she refused to give up her seat on the bus and sparked the 381-day boycott. *Times* lawyers were also astonished that half the jurors appeared in Confederate uniforms as part of the celebration of the centennial of the Confederacy. There were parades and ceremonies every day.

As it turned out, there were minor mistakes in the ad. And Sullivan's attorneys pounced on them as evidence of falsity and defamation. If the ad carried false statements, it contained false criticism of him, his lawyers argued. King had been arrested four times, not seven, in Alabama. The students had sung at the capitol "The Star-Spangled Banner," not "My Country 'Tis of Thee," which the ad claimed. Police did not "ring" the Alabama State University campus but rather amassed along one side of it, armed with carbines, submachine guns, tear gas, and drawn rifles. Also, nine Alabama State University students were expelled for demanding service at the lunch counter at the Montgomery County Courthouse, not for leading the demonstration at the capitol building. The campus dining hall had not been padlocked by the university administration or public authorities, and nobody tried to starve the students into submission. It was found at the trial that students who had protested were not allowed to register for the next semester, so they lacked access to the cafeteria between semesters. During this "week of grace," registered students were issued temporary meal tickets to tide them over.[46] During the protests, state and Montgomery police did stand by while baseball-bat-wielding Klansmen waded into a group of black students from Alabama State. This incident helped form the basis for the "reign of terror" charge in the *Times* ad.[47]

These errors were bad news for the *Times*. If Sullivan could show that there were errors, however insubstantial, in the ad, he could win the libel case. Truth is an absolute defense in a libel suit, long established in common law and through various state statutes. A series of witnesses for Sullivan testified that the ad reflected badly on him. They included *Montgomery Advertiser* editor Hall, who had previously ranted in an editorial that the *Times* ad contained "lies, lies, lies."[48]

On cross-examination, Embry tried to coax witnesses into saying the ad made Sullivan even more popular in the community rather than damaging his reputation. All six witnesses said they believed the ad was false, and none thought any less of him because of it. Two witnesses also said they had not seen the ad until Sullivan's attorney showed it to them. On the stand, Sullivan admitted that he had not been shunned or ostracized after the ad ran, that no one had suggested his removal from office, and that he had lost no compensation.[49] Embry set out to show that Sullivan suffered no animosity in his community, that his reputation did not suffer, and therefore that he could not prove defamation. Yet, at the end of the three-day trial, the jury awarded Sullivan exactly what he asked for—$500,000 in damages. The Alabama Supreme Court later affirmed the decision.[50]

The court agreed that the ad referred to Sullivan and that two paragraphs in question were libelous per se. Under Alabama law at the time, this meant that the words tended to injure a person's reputation, trade, or business, or charged him with an indictable offense or brought him into public contempt. While the case worked its way through appeal, authorities seized Shuttlesworth's late-model Plymouth, which brought $400 at auction, to help pay the judgment. They also sold off land owned by the three other ministers, bringing $4,350 at auction. Historian Kermit L. Hall notes, "The large damage judgments were meant to do with the Southern Leadership Conference what had already been done with the NAACP—drive it and its leaders from the state."[51] Mayor James's libel trial came next, in February 1961. *Jet* magazine reported that the beards that James and five jury members wore were in preparation for the upcoming Civil War centennial event commemorating the Confederacy.[52] Judge Jones, also presiding over the James trial, was to administer the oath of office to a Jefferson Davis re-enactor at the event honoring the Confederate States of America. In keeping with tradition, Jones continued to strictly enforce racial segregation in the courtroom. He had also issued a state injunction barring the Freedom Riders from the state, although demonstrators ignored it.[53]

To the Supreme Court

Up to this point, the U.S. Supreme Court had not considered a libel case in the freedom-of-speech context. Libel law was a matter for state court, and the First Amendment did not protect libelous or slanderous statements.[54] Scholars have suggested that the circumstances surrounding *Sullivan* were so blatantly racist, so over the top, the Supreme Court was compelled to take the case. Legal scholar Louis G. Forer sums up what many analysts of *Sullivan* have concluded: "The lawsuit was preposterous, and the verdict outrageous."[55] This case amounted to unjust punishment of persons critical of government officials and their policies. Justices on the federal court also figured that, if they did not quash *Sullivan,* Alabama segregationists would simply devise another case to harass agitators and critics.[56] Lewis, the *Times* reporter who covered the *Sullivan* case during arguments before the Supreme Court, wrote that in *Sullivan,* "the sense of unfairness was intensified by the context of racial hostility."[57] Not only would the *Sullivan* case transform libel law and protect government critics, but it would go on to change the way the United States looked at, thought about, and discussed the issue of race.

In the U.S. Supreme Court's reversal of *Sullivan* in March 1964, it established the landmark actual malice standard, marking not only a fundamental change in the law but setting a path for First Amendment theory that would help alter the course of the civil rights movement. The Supreme Court ruled that in order to win a libel suit, a public official such as Sullivan must prove that the *Times* knew the material was false or that it exhibited "reckless disregard for the truth" when it printed the information. In his famous opinion, Justice William Brennan Jr. wrote that some errors are inevitable in an open debate of public issues and that freedom of expression needs "breathing space" to survive. Some false and defamatory statements should therefore be protected.[58] In a case against a public official relating to his official conduct, merely allowing for truth as a defense does not protect speech as it should because it does not take into account self-censorship, the nation's high court reasoned. People will be less likely to speak if they fear they later will have to prove the truth of every utterance in court. Brennan referenced John Milton and John Stuart Mill on the important role false statements play in a hearty debate. Quoting Mill, Brennan wrote, "There is a 'clearer perception and livelier impression of truth, produced by its collision with error.'"[59] The nation's high court agreed that the defendants were being punished for criticizing the government. Consequently, seditious libel had been resurrected. Brennan also drew from James Madison's "central meaning" of the First Amendment: The people, not the government, are sovereign. The justice wrote that "the great controversy over the Sedition Act of 1798 . . . first crystallized a national awareness of the central meaning of the First Amendment."[60] In his analysis of *Sullivan*, legal scholar Wat Hopkins sees Brennan's heavy footprints through the social responsibility theory.[61] It is each citizen's duty—not right alone—to question and even criticize the government. Furthermore, Brennan drew on the work of Justice Oliver Wendell Holmes Jr. in applying the marketplace of ideas theory relating to sedition law: When given an opportunity, truth will win out over falsity.[62]

Sullivan shifted the burden of proof in libel cases from the defendant to the plaintiff and introduced the notion of fault. Since *Sullivan,* the plaintiff has had to show that the defendant published the false information with a high degree of fault, that is, knowingly or recklessly. With the *Sullivan* decision, the court allowed for honest mistakes in writing and speaking about a public official and his public conduct. The court also ordered Sullivan to pay $13,000 of the *Times*' court costs. *Sullivan* nullified the case of Mayor Earl James, whom the Alabama court also awarded $500,000. The other suits never came to trial.

It is important to note that not all the cases filed in the shadow of *Sullivan* automatically went away for the defendants after the U.S. Supreme Court's surprising reversal of the Alabama decision. For example, a similar libel case filed against the *Times* in Birmingham by the notorious commissioner of public safety Bull Connor dragged on for two years after *Sullivan,* spending a total of six years in the court system. Other officials continued to try the same legal tactic, but now with the added burden of proving actual malice. Some plaintiffs pursued their libel cases in southern courts for years after the *Sullivan* ruling. Southern plaintiffs and their attorneys did not appear to see the actual malice standard as insurmountable, with some merely adding the new "actual malice" language to their original complaints already in the court system and plowing forward with punitive libel actions.

Fear and Hatred Grip Birmingham

Just weeks after the advertisement, "Heed their Rising Voices," ran in March 1960, the *Times* managed to stir up another hornet's nest ninety miles north in Birmingham, Alabama, the fiefdom of the legendary segregationist Theophilus Eugene "Bull" Connor. *Times* editors had realized their lead civil rights reporter, Claude Sitton, needed more help as protests spread across the South in early 1960. National News Editor Harold Faber sent in more reporters, including the venerable Harrison Salisbury, who had won a Pulitzer Prize for international reporting and had witnessed untold atrocities covering war in Europe. In April, he was dispatched to the South for a few days. He would gather information for a "situation" piece by parachuting into several communities and studying the conditions and atmosphere as well as the attitudes of the people. Most mainstream media coverage of the civil rights movement up to this point was about something happening, spot news such as a demonstration, for example.

Salisbury, the author of several books including a bestseller on juvenile delinquency, had covered wartime London and the Russian front for United Press before moving to the *Times*. Five years in Moscow yielded a sweeping series of articles that won him the Pulitzer, and as a correspondent, he knew how to drop into a town, size up the conditions, and craft beautifully written situation pieces. In April of 1960 then, he popped into several southern cities before bouncing from Baton Rouge to Birmingham, where he settled in at the luxurious Tutwiler Hotel downtown to capture the mood of the city. In one story, he compared the atmosphere in Birmingham to that of Stalin's Moscow, although that analogy was later edited out as too inflammatory. In his memoir, Salisbury wrote that Birmingham was not a run-of-the-mill story: "I quickly compiled a list of horrors—beatings, police raids, floggings, cross burnings, assaults, bombings (dynamite seemed to be as common as six-packs), attacks on synagogues, terror, wiretapping, mail interception, suspicion of even worse. . . . I soon realized that I had stumbled into a part of the United States where I had to apply the conspiratorial rules of reporting I had practiced for years in the Soviet Union."[63] One source told him: "Be careful of what you say and who you mention. Lives are at stake."[64]

Salisbury drafted his story on the long night flight back to New York, and the *Times* ran it on page one of the April 12, 1960, issue under the headline, "Fear and Hatred Grip Birmingham." He wrote: "No New Yorker can readily measure the climate of Birmingham today. . . . Ball parks and taxicabs are segregated. So are libraries. A book featuring black rabbits and white rabbits was banned. A drive is on to forbid 'Negro music' on 'white' radio stations."[65] Salisbury also wrote of black men standing guard at night over black churches that were likely bomb targets because the police would not help. His assessment was chilling and disturbing: "Every channel of communication, every medium of mutual interest, every reasoned approach, every inch of middle ground has been fragmented by the emotional dynamite of racism, reinforced by the whip, the razor, the gun, the bomb, the torch, the club, the knife, the mob, the police in many branches of the state's apparatus." He also spoke of authorities' surreptitious surveillance as they worked to stop progress on civil rights: "Telephones are tapped, or there is fear of tapping. Mail has been intercepted and opened. Sometimes it does not reach its destination. The eavesdropper, the informer, the spies have become a fact of life." He quoted anonymous sources, both black and white, who said they were afraid they would be killed if they spoke out. He quoted "an educator," the president of a local college, as saying: "I'm ashamed to have to talk to you off the record. . . . These are not ordinary times. The dangers are very real and people up North must realize that." Salisbury also wrote that in seeking election, Commissioner Bull Connor of the Birmingham Police "ran on a platform of race hate." The journalist quoted an anonymous businessman who said, "Bull is the law in Birmingham, like it or not."[66] Salisbury said he telephoned Connor several times but failed to reach him. Despite (or because of) the snubbing, he couldn't resist Connor's infamous and sometimes confused declarations: "Damn, the law—down here we make our own law"; and "we're not goin' to have white folks and nigras segregatin' together in this man's town."[67]

Response to Salisbury's article was swift and furious in Alabama, starting with the local media in Birmingham. The *Birmingham News* reprinted Salisbury's story two days later under the page-one headline: "*New York Times* Slanders Our City—Can This Be Birmingham?" An accompanying editorial groused that Salisbury's story offered up "another journalistic and literary libel against the South" and complained that it was "an amazing recital of untruths and semi-truths."[68] The next day, the *News* printed another story about Salisbury under the headline, "All the News That's Fit to Print?—*N.Y. Times* Continues Attack." The *News* complained that the *Times* story was "maliciously bigoted, noxiously false, viciously distorted." Conservative columnist John Temple Graves II of the *Birmingham Post-Herald* said Salisbury's stories represented "almost a total lie" and pointed out that Salisbury was from Minnesota, "the most South-hating of the states." "The Times must have known this," he growled. "Only in malice could it have picked him." Had the story been confined to the *New York Times*, it likely would not have gotten as much attention in Birmingham. Connor complained that the *Times* told only one side of the story and that Salisbury did not try to verify facts or contact him. He demanded a retraction after the story ran, so the newspaper printed his letter and an editor's note recognizing that the *Times* failed to "stress the obvious fact that an overwhelming percentage of the citizens of that city lead happy and peaceful lives in a growing and prosperous community . . . [and] that this substantial element of the citizenry deplores any lawlessness that may exist in their city."[69] The newspaper also ran a rebuttal by the Birmingham Chamber of Commerce.[70] Connor and other city leaders, commissioners J. T. "Jabo" Waggoner and James Morgan filed identical $500,000 libel suits against the newspaper.[71] Not long after the first three suits were filed, a Birmingham city detective named Joe Lindsey sued, also seeking $150,000, bringing the total up to $1.65 million.[72]

A communiqué between Waggoner and his lawyer, James A. Simpson, casts some doubt on whether Waggoner felt defamed personally. Simpson told Waggoner the suit would help deter newspapers such as the *Times* from committing "ruthless attacks on this region and its people. I am sure this is the primary motive which has prompted you to embark upon this troublesome litigation."[73] This letter illustrates that defamation wasn't the issue. The object was to punish and muzzle the *Times*.

Jim Simpson, a corporate lawyer and former Alabama state senator who presided over the country club set in Birmingham, represented Connor and city officials against this latest northern assault on the South. He had molded blue-collar Connor from small-time, cornball sports-radio personality to the emperor of Birmingham City Hall. Simpson famously said of Connor, "He may be a son of a bitch, but he's my son of a bitch."[74] Then three city commissioners from the nearby industrial community of Bessemer filed identical $500,000 libel suits, bringing the total up to $3.1 million.[75] Salisbury had written of a lawless atmosphere where the police there acted like hoodlums, beating civil rights protesters and sympathizers in the nearby enclave of belching steel mills: "If fear and terror are common in the streets of Birmingham, the atmosphere in Bessemer, the adjacent steel suburb, is even worse."[76] Writing about the "flogging" of a nineteen-year-old white woman named Barbara Espy, he reported: "She was seized by four or five men, dragged into a car, beaten until she signed a confession that she had been 'dating' Negroes. She has since sworn out warrants charging that she was abducted and beaten by a sheriff's deputy, an alderman and three other persons. The sheriff repeatedly refused to entertain charges against his deputy. The Federal Bureau of Investigation has been asked to look into the case for possible violations of civil rights. . . . The list of beatings, intimidations and violence could be continued almost indefinitely."[77]

In addition to the civil suits, a Bessemer grand jury indicted Salisbury on forty-two counts of criminal libel. No one could remember such a case in the previous quarter-century, and legal researchers on the case could find no direct precedent.[78] Salisbury faced $21,000 in fines and twenty-one years in jail on the criminal counts.[79] Lawyers for the Birmingham commissioners had demanded a list of everyone Salisbury had talked to when he was researching his story, and when he refused, they subpoenaed the telephone records of the Tutwiler Hotel. In Bessemer, the grand jury had heard from a parade of Salisbury's sources from that same phone list. Salisbury later said: "My careless use of the phone brought tribulation to a dozen people who had had the courage to talk with me. Birmingham newsmen who had met me found themselves in jeopardy of [losing] their jobs. Blacks got threats of arrest—or worse. Educators encountered difficulty with their trustees, clergy with their vestrymen."[80]

One white minister, Robert Hughes, who had been working quietly to address racial strife in Birmingham, had met Salisbury behind drawn curtains. Hughes had documented cases of intimidation, police beatings, and other violence as part of his work on the biracial Alabama Council on Human Relations. He refused to bring his records before the Bessemer grand jury in the Salisbury inquiry; the result was that he spent four days in jail for contempt of court. Hughes couldn't find a lawyer to defend him and was temporarily suspended from his church. It was evident, Salisbury later said, that southern leaders had major objectives in filing the slew of libel suits against him and the *Times:* "to keep reporters out of the South, to 'chill' their reporting of Civil Rights cases, to make a newspaper or a TV network or a news magazine question the usefulness of sending a reporter into a southern state to cover a Rights controversy and make them think twice about reporting the facts, harsh and raw as they often were."[81]

Grover Hall's *Montgomery Advertiser* discussed the same trend in a story about the rash of libel cases, including the *Sullivan* case. The subtitle on one article was "State Finds Formidable Legal Club to Swing at Out-of-State Press." Hall concluded, "The recent checkmating of the *Times* in Alabama will impose a restraint upon other publications."[82] General counsel Loeb was shocked by the onslaught against the *Times*: "In all the years I have practiced law nothing had ever arisen that was more worrisome. Nothing scared me more than this litigation."[83] Indeed, lawyers for the *Times* advised reporters to steer clear of Alabama for fear of bringing more libel suits or for risk of being served with a subpoena. Claude Sitton, the *Times*' most noted civil rights reporter, later told Salisbury: "Boy did I cuss you out. Your damn stories kept me out of Alabama for over a year."[84]

But Sitton's coverage of the movement was curtailed for much longer than twelve months. On the advice of their lawyers, *Times* editors killed a Sunday story Sitton wrote in late 1962 about a change in the Birmingham city government that might "depose Commissioner Eugene (Bull) Connor, whom Negroes regard as one of the South's toughest police bosses."[85] *Times* lawyer Tom Daly advised editors that the story "might indicate malice" in the Sullivan suit pending before the Alabama Supreme Court.[86] Indeed, it did appear, as journalists Roberts and Klibanoff have asserted, that "public officials had achieved their objective, [and] Jim Crow could return to its good old days, operating with virtually no scrutiny."[87]

Bull Connor and the Freedom Rides

On a Wednesday in May 1961, exactly seven years since the *Brown vs. Board of Education* desegregation case shook the South, ten Freedom Riders rolled south on a bus from Nashville, Tennessee, to Birmingham, hoping to draw attention to yet another unenforced federal court ruling, this one mandating the desegregation of interstate travel.[88] Birmingham police commissioner Bull Connor ordered his officers to pull the bus over as it reached the outskirts of his city. Connor boarded at the front and saw two Freedom Riders, one black and one white, sitting together in the seat directly behind the driver. He told Paul Brooks and Jim Zwerg to separate, but the pair stayed put. The smiling Connor, whom journalist-historian David Halberstam later labeled "the most powerful racist in Alabama," said they were breaking Alabama law and ordered his officers arrest them.[89]

Connor had been a local baseball broadcaster and got his nickname for his uncanny ability to shoot the bull on the radio during periods of inactivity on the field. "Bull" also seemed to fit his reputation as the swaggering cop that elite Birmingham whites, industry captains and business leaders called the "Big Mules," relied on to browbeat and intimidate blacks who stepped out of their place.[90] Connor had ties to the Ku Klux Klan and a reputation of only halfheartedly investigating the many racial bombings across his city, now nicknamed "Bombingham." Rather than integrate Birmingham's sixty-eight public parks, thirty-eight swimming pools, and four golf courses, for example, the all-white Birmingham City Commission followed Connor's recommendation to shut them down.[91]

By May 1961, Connor had known about the Freedom Rides for more than a month. The FBI kept the Birmingham Police Department updated on the Riders' plans with the idea that local law enforcement could help protect the demonstrators from angry whites. However, keeping Birmingham's law enforcement in the loop had the opposite effect. Connor could not afford direct and blatant association with the Klan, but his police sergeant,

Tom Cook, was an enthusiastic Klan supporter who shared the Riders' itinerary with the white-supremacist group and helped prepare "a rude welcome for the invading 'niggers' and 'nigger-lovers' who were about to violate the timeworn customs and laws of the sovereign state of Alabama." Martin Luther King Jr. had been warned that the Freedom Riders were heading for serious trouble when they crossed into the state, and he, in turn, warned them before they reached the Deep South.[92]

Anything but subtle, Connor remained confident that he could maintain the racial status quo, and he rode with the Freedom Riders into the Birmingham station on the bus he boarded that day. Once in the terminal, he ordered his officers to cover the bus windows with newspaper and tape so members of the press could not see in. Inside the darkened bus, officers inspected each bus ticket, and used their billy clubs on anyone trying to head for the door.[93] Freedom Rider John Lewis, later a U.S. congressman from Georgia, had been badly beaten in the Greyhound terminal in Rock Hill, South Carolina, a few days before. The battered college student was relieved when he saw reporters in Birmingham as the bus pulled into the terminal. He remained optimistic since the demonstrations were finally getting the attention of the national media. "There was no purpose in offering yourself up to your sworn enemies if no one was watching," pointed out David Halberstam, then a reporter for the *Tennessean* in Nashville, who covered the protests.[94] After about two hours in the dark bus, Connor had the demonstrators arrested and hauled to jail, what veteran civil rights protestors called "Connor's Chapel for Freedom."[95]

Just as Connor covered the windows to shut out the media's view that day at the bus station, he sought to shut out the world's view of his brand of law and order in Birmingham—to end coverage of the race story being broadcast around the country night after night. In so doing, Connor and other southern officials turned to the court system and libel law in their quest to compel northern newspapers to go back home and mind their own communities. By 1964, when the U.S. Supreme Court heard the first such libel case, *Sullivan,* government officials had filed at least $300 million in libel actions against newspapers, news magazines, television networks, and civil rights leaders.[96]

It took six years for the Birmingham cases stemming from Salisbury's articles in the *Times* to wind through the courts, starting on Connor's home turf before an Alabama jury.[97] One big difference, though, compared to *Sullivan,* was the robed man sitting on the bench. Kentucky-born Harlan Hobart Grooms had earned his law degree from the University of Kentucky in 1926 and worked in private practice in Birmingham until 1953, when President Dwight D. Eisenhower nominated him to the federal bench, the U.S. District Court for the Northern District of Alabama. Grooms is perhaps best known for ordering the University of Alabama to accept African American students in a famous showdown with Governor George Wallace, who stood at the school entrance in 1963. NAACP lawyer Constance Baker Motley later called Grooms "a fearless and responsible judge," who didn't hesitate to order Alabama's dean of admissions to allow Autherine Lucy to enroll for classes.[98]

A moderate Republican, Grooms first heard the school desegregation case just months after his appointment to the court, when NAACP lawyers were still figuring out who exactly they should sue at the university. Initially, they named the dean of admissions and the members of the Board of Trustees of the University of Alabama. Grooms granted the trustees' motions to dismiss but not that of the dean of admissions. To the amazement of the NAACP lawyers, he directed Motley to amend the NAACP's complaint to name only those officers or administrators who enforced the state's policy to exclude blacks from the institution or who operated the key to the door. "Bring me the man with the keys," Judge Grooms instructed her. The Fifth Circuit affirmed Judge Grooms's order to admit Lucy in 1955, and the U.S. Supreme Court refused to hear the university's appeal, thus letting his decision stand. She enrolled but was soon suspended from classes after growing student unrest unsettled the campus and supposedly for her own protection, a thinly veiled reason to keep the state's flagship university all white. Again in 1962, Grooms ordered the university to admit Vivian Malone and James Hood, prompting Governor Wallace's nationally televised stand in the door of a university building to block the students' way. After a brief confrontation at that doorway, Wallace stepped aside to allow the first black students to enroll at the Tuscaloosa campus of the University of Alabama.[99]

Judge Grooms's decisions helped reshape Alabama history, but he has been relegated to the role of a supporting actor in the vast civil rights litigation literature. Much of what is known about him comes from the local daily newspapers of the day, including local society news pages. A member of the First Baptist Church of Birmingham for forty-three years, he taught a men's Bible class for much of that time and served on the Board of Deacons. Tall and spectacled, with closely shaved hair on his balding head, Grooms was active on the hospital board and other civic committees. But he and his family suffered because of his even-handedness on the bench. Angie Grooms Proctor, his youngest daughter, who also served on the Birmingham City Council in the 1970s, remembered the stress at home in the 1950s and early 1960s, especially. She recalled "people telephoning threats. Sending letters saying they hoped my father would die. But do you know he wasn't setting an example for anyone—he was just affirming his belief in the law."[100] In 1961, Grooms also ruled that segregation of Birmingham's public parks was unconstitutional, prompting Bull Connor to shut them down. That particular lawsuit forcing desegregation of the city's sixty-seven parks, swimming pools, and golf courses, had been filed by the fearless local civil rights leader Fred Shuttlesworth, who was facing down another libel suit as part of the "Heed Their Rising Voices" ad, which he never actually signed. Grooms had long considered himself "a good conservative, but not so conservative that I can't see what the law is."[101]

The Birmingham cases came to trial in fall of 1964, six months after the U.S. Supreme Court overturned *Sullivan*. These SLAPP-like cases were not automatically—or magically—thrown out after *Sullivan*. Salisbury feared that he would be arrested when he returned to Alabama because of the criminal indictments in Bessemer, so Embry and other attorneys on the case worked out a deal to provide him with immunity while he sat in federal court for the Connor, Waggoner, and Morgan cases, which were to be tried simultaneously in Birmingham. There were moments of high drama. "Suddenly word came to Judge Grooms that sheriff's deputies from Bessemer were on their way to arrest me," Salisbury said later. "Grooms ordered federal marshals to surround the courtroom and advised the Bessemer district attorney that he would hold him in contempt if there was any interference.... Reluctantly the Bessemer deputies turned back." Attorneys Loeb and Daly stayed by Salisbury's side day and night in Birmingham, sticking to him like glue, he later learned, to protect him.[102]

On September 16, 1964, plaintiffs' attorney Jim Simpson kicked off the trial with opening comments about the city and its leaders, telling the jury: "These statements about the way the City of Birmingham was run reflected upon these men as individuals in the sense that had they been honorable men, honest men, men of integrity and character, and law abiding men, they having the power to run the City of Birmingham, would not have permitted Birmingham to be governed in that manner." Simpson and Connor ruled Birmingham City Hall together, so no doubt the lawyer saw himself as fighting for his own honor. In his opening statements, Simpson adopted the language the U.S. Supreme Court had used to overturn *Sullivan*, referencing the new actual malice standard, promising to prove that Salisbury "either knew what he put in this article was not true, or he put it in there, and the newspaper published it with reckless disregard as to whether or not it was true."[103]

Embry then stepped up to deliver his own opening statement, also focusing on *Sullivan*'s new actual malice standard, pointing out that the *Times* sent Salisbury to Alabama specifically because he had no experience covering civil rights issues in the South. The *Times* had wanted a fresh look at the emerging situation from a reporter with no agenda. Embry stated: "He [Salisbury] had no animosity toward Mr. Connor or Mr. Morgan or Mr. Waggoner. He didn't even know who they were before he arrived in Birmingham, never had heard of them, that he was not reckless because he made an investigation over a period of three days and he talked to many people and he observed many things. And on this basis and honest belief that what he wrote was true, he wrote it." Salisbury had exercised no malice toward the three plaintiffs or the city of Birmingham.[104]

After opening statements, Simpson called the director of the Birmingham Public Library, Fant H. Thornley, to testify that *The Rabbits' Wedding,* a children's book about the marriage of white and black rabbits published in 1958, was not banned. Connor, as public safety commissioner, appointed the Birmingham Library Board, which had complete charge of the library. Embry's cross-examination of Thornley revealed that the library was segregated at the time but that the book had been banned in Montgomery, not in Birmingham. When pressed, however, Thornley admitted that *The Rabbits' Wedding* had been removed from the list of available reading materials from the Alabama Public Library Service and thus was difficult to locate in any public library in the state.[105]

Next on the stand was John R. Chadwick, a newspaper reporter with twenty years of experience in Tennessee and Alabama, who then worked as a stringer for the *Times*. Chadwick testified that he compiled a list of about twenty names, a cross-section of the community, at the request of Salisbury, who would contact them on reaching Birmingham. This list included a few clergymen such as Fred Shuttlesworth, along with the head of the steelworkers' union, the president of the Chamber of Commerce, local college presidents, and various Birmingham business leaders. Chadwick also drove Salisbury around town, providing a guided tour of the city and putting fifty-two miles on a Hertz rental car. Indicating his anti-Semitism, perhaps for the benefit of an anti-Semitic jury, Simpson asked Chadwick whether Salisbury was "particularly interested in any particular segment of our population."

EMBRY: "We object to that as leading and suggestive."
THE COURT: "Overrule."

CHADWICK: "Whether it was during the course of that conversation, I do not know for certain, sir, but at one point in our conversation during my association with Mr. Salisbury here, he did indicate that he wanted to talk with some members of the Jewish community explaining—because of the *New York Times*, as he described it, [had] considerable Jewish leadership."

SIMPSON: "Do you remember whether you gave him any—any members of the Jewish race except the Rabbi Mesh and Rabbi Grafman?"

CHADWICK: "I can't be positive, sir. I think I gave him the name of Mervin Sterne, I cannot be positive."[106]

Witness by witness, Simpson set out to prove the falsity and Embry, the truth of each detail in Salisbury's story. Embry pointed to a TV and radio critic's column, "Thame's Line," in the *Birmingham News* as evidence of a drive to limit "Negro" music on white stations. While Salisbury was in town, the column included a series of letters raging against disc jockeys playing of "Negro" music on the radio. "More power to you," wrote one reader. "Leave the Negro records to the Negroes. We need more like you and Bull. The John Does of Birmingham." Mrs. L. G. E. Fairfield, another contributor to the critic's column, remonstrated: "If you want to hear Negro music, turn to their station. Let all of the stations give us our own music." Still another Birmingham reader, F. A. Vines, wrote: "I have quit listening to the radio except for news. When I try to listen it is cluttered up with this trash."[107]

Simpson set out to prove the falsity of Salisbury's premise that Birmingham was erupting in racial strife. Fred Taylor, a journalist for twenty-five years, mostly in Birmingham, testified on behalf of the plaintiff that there was no racial unrest in Alabama. "I don't think we have had any strife among the races," he claimed. "You have had agitators come here. You have clashes between the police and certain agitators, certain demonstrators. . . ." Taylor was city editor at the *Birmingham News* when Salisbury came to town to research his story, but he had left the news business to work in advertising and public relations. Taylor also testified that Connor had enforced the law fairly and that he had not run on a platform of "race hate." Under Simpson's gentle questioning, Taylor said that, in his view, the controversial article was about the city's elected governing body, the three-man commission of Morgan, Waggoner, and Connor. On cross-examination, Embry pointed out that Taylor handled the advertising and public relations in Connor's political campaign for the Alabama Public Service Commission. And he remarked that both Taylor and Simpson, Connor's attorney, politically supported the police commissioner.[108]

"I am certainly not ashamed of it," Simpson fired back from his seat during Embry's questioning. The *Times* lawyer then pointed out as evidence that the article did not damage Connor's reputation in his community: "Mr. Connor was re-elected after the publication of this article over three opponents to the Public Safety Commission by a clear majority of nine thousand votes. . . . A month after this article was published of which he complains it injured his reputation and damaged him, he received twenty-five thousand and one hundred four votes . . . ." Embry continued to breakdown the vote count, showing Connor handily beat the other three candidates with 61 percent of the vote.[109]

Simpson and his clients had taken issue with Salisbury's report that Connor had run on a platform of race hate. So Embry asked Taylor, "Have you ever heard the statement attributed to him that white and Negro are not to segregate together?" Taylor responded, "Yes, I have heard that, that became a matter of comment down in the legislature once."[110]

Embry also maneuvered to contradict Taylor's testimony that he had seen "no manifestations of fear, force or terror" in Birmingham. He pointed to a story about the castration of a black man named Judge Aaron, which occurred on September 4, 1957. To Taylor, Embry fired: "Would you undertake to tell the jury that you would give your opinion, honest opinion, from that witness stand that after he had been castrated by a band of men with a razor blade, that he had not felt any fear, had not been subjected to any terror." Embry pressed the witness: "Can you give that honest opinion to this jury?" Simpson objected: "How would this man know about the fear of one individual?" But Embry countered:

"We are talking about a state of mind. We are not talking about a person. We are talking about a community, things, events...."[111]

Judge Grooms allowed Embry to flood Taylor with exhibits, even copies of his own *Birmingham News* filled with local and regional wire stories of terror against civil rights demonstrators. Embry hammered his witness with fifty-one news stories, page after page, story after story. Articles relating to acts of violence, bombings, and beatings were read into the record; Embry convincingly illustrated that a climate of fear ruled Birmingham, particularly its African American community—all over Simpson's repeated objections. Embry entered the white-supremacist terror into the federal court record. He pointed to articles about sit-ins at downtown department-store lunch counters spreading across the city in the spring of 1960 and the late-night arrest of two ministers, one white and one black, who were working to help improve race relations.

EMBRY: "Would you say, Mr. Taylor, that a person who was dragged out of their home at night in their bathrobe and pajamas, and taken from their residence to the jail and only vaguely informed with what they are charged with, and held there without being permitted to communicate with anyone until the following day, would be apt to feel fear or feel terror or be subjected to force?"[112]

Judge Grooms certainly had his work cut out for him during the often-hostile back-and-forth of the two Birmingham attorneys. Throughout Embry's questioning of Taylor, Simpson peppered objections and asked for copies of the local-news articles Embry was relying on.

EMBRY: "No. They cost too much."
SIMPSON: "I am sorry the New York Times is hard pushed."
EMBRY: "We object to that."
THE COURT: "Sustained. That is excluded."
SIMPSON: "Will you exclude they cost too much?"
THE COURT: "That is excluded too. Colloquy of counsel is not evidence in the case."[113]

Still, Embry kept to his rhythm, reciting evidence of white attacks on blacks and of black resilience in the face of the terror. "The reaction to the sit-in demonstrations has been new manifestations of fear, force and terror punctuated by striking acts of courage," he told the court. Then Embry pointed to stories in the *Birmingham News* about an attack on African American singer Nat King Cole on April 11, 1956, in the city auditorium in Birmingham; attacks in the black neighborhood of Fountain Heights, which had been dubbed "Dynamite Hill"; two police officers beating a black man in jail; and threats to bomb Phillips High School after Shuttlesworth sought his children's admission there by court order. He pointed to a story, published on April 20, 1959, about three black musicians who had been forced off the road and beaten by a gang of whites.[114] Again, Embry came out swinging after an afternoon recess. He reminded Taylor: "The Birmingham News offered a reward for information leading to the arrest and conviction of persons guilty of bombing or attempted bombing. This particular incident was concerning the bombing of a North Birmingham Negro Church, that's what we are talking about in Exhibit 35, right?" Taylor said he didn't recall many of the stories because in the late 1950s, the years leading up to Salisbury's story from Birmingham, he had worked the political beat out of the state capital, Montgomery. Embry was relentless.

> EMBRY: "Now these reports that you do have a recollection about, now that you have seen these reports of incidents from 1956, '57, '58, now that you have seen those reports of mob violence and recall attacks on a Negro singer, bombing of Negro homes, more bombing of Negro homes, threats of bombing of Phillips High School, attempts to bomb Temple Bethel here in Birmingham, bombings of a North Birmingham Negro Church and North Birmingham Negro homes in Fountain Heights which you will recall referring to as dynamite hill, do you still say, Mr. Taylor, there were no manifestations of fear or terror or force in Birmingham? Is that still your opinion?"
>
> TAYLOR: "My opinion, as I stated, was that I didn't feel there was any general feeling of fear between the races here as such, as I recall what I said. I was trying to remember."[115]

On redirect, Simpson asked his witness to recall "who precipitated" the events at Phillips High School and the beatings at the bus station. "A Negro minister," Taylor answered. "Was it not Fred L. Shuttlesworth?" Simpson asked over Embry's objections. "Isn't it a fact Fred L. Shuttlesworth was a man who aroused and caused several of these incidents?"[116]

Simpson appeared to blame the most prominent civil rights leader in Birmingham for the violence and fear described in Salisbury's story. Connor had also complained the *Times* libeled him by reporting that Shuttlesworth was a frequent target of police harassment. Shuttlesworth had told Salisbury that he was arrested three times in a seventy-two-hour period, that his telephone was tapped, and that he had several civil rights–related cases on appeal.[117] Judge Grooms responded somewhat wryly, "A random glance at [court records] indicates that Rev. Shuttlesworth has indeed been involved in extensive appellate litigation."[118] A sampling of Shuttlesworth's arrests, for example, included parading without a permit, failure to obey an officer, vagrancy, conspiring to commit a breach of the peace, disorderly conduct, criminal contempt for statements made at a press conference, and violating Birmingham's segregated bus ordinance.[119]

SIMPSON: "The only point I am making is certain individuals ran all the way through this trouble, and they are not going to make anybody afraid or excite anybody except themselves, and he has a lot of incidents tied to one man. . . . Isn't it a fact Fred L. Shuttlesworth was a man who aroused and caused several of these incidents?"

EMBRY: "That is the most flagrant violation of the rules of evidence I have ever heard of a man practicing law 50 years to make in open court."

SIMPSON: "Make it 52 and let's go ahead."[120]

Judge Grooms sustained Embry's objection.

During the second day of testimony, Simpson called witnesses both black and white to talk about the atmosphere in Birmingham in the late 1950s. All said they did not see the lines of communication shut down between the races. All said they assumed the articles were about how the three elected commissioners ran the city. Embry objected repeatedly, trying to hammer home the points made in *Sullivan,* that criticism of public officials in their public work had been declared a right protected under the First Amendment. "You can't libel government," he said. "You can't libel government or community."[121]

James W. Morgan, mayor when the Salisbury article was published, stepped up to the stand before lunch on the second day of the trial. The seventy-three-year-old politician had lived in Birmingham his entire life except during World War II and for three summers when he played minor league baseball. He testified that after the war, he went to work for Wholesale Grocery and Produce Company and then entered into business for himself for ten years. Morgan was elected commissioner of public improvements in 1937 and spent twenty-four years in public office, serving continuously as a commissioner or mayor until 1961, when he retired. Under this system of government, there were a mayor and three city commissioners, each having equal authority and control of the city. He had long complained about the South suffering a "hostile press" arrayed against it, pledged himself to fighting any attempts to alter the racial status quo, and declared that blacks must remain second-class citizens. In 1957, he wrote, "We simply cannot accept them as our equals, particularly socially, and expect to perpetuate anglo-saxon [sic] race."[122] Morgan testified that the city comptroller, Mr. Armstrong, subscribed to the *Times*. Of his exposure to the Salisbury piece, Morgan stated: "No telling how many others showed me the article. But I recall most vividly in the Birmingham News, the reprint of it."

SIMPSON: "After that article appeared, did you as—did you receive letters from people?"

MORGAN: "Oh, Lord, abuse from all over the world, United States, telephone, people, I was ashamed to walk down the street, people would look at you. I quit going to my civic clubs. Some would openly be—ask questions 'what's the matter, can't you people down there handle the situation?' And all of those things. You were looked on with a question mark. I even stopped going to church for quite a while, then I took sick. And I couldn't sleep, I had headaches, my wife was very nervous. We went through an ordeal that I hope no one else will ever have to go through with such as followed that article."[123]

Morgan said he had never seen evidence of strife between the races. "We have always gotten along good, and when the problems broke out, there were two or three leaders that took over and made capital of it and misled a lot of our people." He complained of Salisbury's characterization of the industrial smog of Birmingham: "The haze of acid fog belched from the stacks of the Tennessee Coal and Iron Company." The description was located in the second paragraph, Morgan remembered. "You could tell he was hostile at the very outset." Embry interjected: "We object to that. It is not libelous to describe conditions of weather." Judge Grooms agreed.[124]

During questioning, Morgan called the sit-in demonstrations "agitating occurrences." He testified: "That wasn't coming from our colored people. It was coming from a few leaders who were capitalizing financially and otherwise on that." He complained about coverage of Birmingham in general, even beyond the reporting of the *New York Times:* "And the impression was, through a hostile press, through commentators not really honestly knowing, I think so many of them knew absolutely nothing, but had that conception of Birmingham." Simpson entered into evidence an article from *Ebony* magazine published in June 1960. The piece pictures Morgan with prominent black business leader A. G. Gaston and his wife at the dedication of their new motel in Birmingham. Morgan said he made the principal speech in front of ten thousand people at that dedication, trying to illustrate the good relationship between white and black community leaders in Birmingham.[125] Simpson then steered Morgan back to Salisbury's article.

SIMPSON: "Who did the article refer to?"
MORGAN: "The city governing body."

SIMPSON: "Who was that at that time?"

MORGAN: "That was the three commissioners, Waggoner, Connor and myself."[126]

UNDER EMBRY'S CROSS-EXAMINATION, MORGAN SAID: "We lost industry, millions and millions and millions of dollars. The story went all over the world. It hurt us and it hurt me personally, and it hurt Birmingham, and we haven't recovered yet because it was so nasty."[127]

Embry pushed Morgan on the issue of truth, as Simpson had done, on the state of race relations in the city. The lawyer painted a dark picture: "Mr. Morgan, you said the relations between the races was very good before 1960 in April. While you were in office, you remember the bombings of Negro homes and bombings of Negro churches, and acts of violence committed against the persons of Negro citizens of the community, don't you?"

MORGAN: "Yes."

EMBRY: "Do you consider that an expression or manifestation of good relations between the parties involved in those instances?"

MORGAN:: "I want to say this. Every city has its share of thugs, and we were no exception. . . . A few leaders that agitated things, caused those thugs to come in, and that is all they were, thugs. Anybody that throws a bomb is a thug of the lowest order, and the people of Birmingham felt that way about it. We all deplored those incidences."

EMBRY: "But they did happen, did they not?"

MORGAN: "They did happen, and they happen everywhere else."[128]

Embry pointed out that in the eleven years before the 1960 Salisbury article, there had been twenty-two reported bombings of black churches and homes in the city. He did not mention the Sixteenth Street Church bombing in 1963, which killed four little girls, probably because the atrocity occurred after Salisbury's article ran. For his part, Simpson put witness after witness on the stand to testify that they did not feel fear in the three or four years leading up to April 1960, when Salisbury's article was published.

Next on the stand was Morgan Smith, a former reporter on the *Birmingham Post* and *Birmingham News*, who had since moved into public relations work. He managed Connor's successful city commission campaigns in 1957 and 1961. Smith said he was a cub reporter on the police beat when he met Connor and had been friends with him ever since. Simpson asked whether Connor ran on a platform of race hate, using Salisbury's words, verbatim. Smith replied:

> On the contrary. It was obvious Mr. Connor had not brought race hate in his campaign because I would have advised him against it, in the first place. And in the second place, he had no reason to bring in any racial issue because everybody knew where Mr. Connor stood on that question, and there was no reason for him to bestir any part of it. . . . Mr. Connor's attitude toward segregation has been one of firmness. He has believed in it. He has never equivocated on that matter. He has never dodged the issue. I think Birmingham and the whole state realizes his position, and I don't think there is any question about it.[129]

Smith also said Connor did not hate black people: "I have known that Mr. Connor has friends among the colored race, and many respect his straightforward attitude.[130]

Under cross-examination, Embry pointed to an interracial group that had been meeting to work out problems prior to 1960 as "a channel of communication," also using Salisbury's words. The Jefferson County Coordinating Council and other groups dissolved because of deterioration in race relations. As evidence of racial strife in early 1960, Embry pointed to an article in the March 7 issue of the *Birmingham News* reporting that Connor had begun beefing up the police department response to the spreading civil rights demonstrations, requiring seventy-five firefighters to attend classes on riot control so they could help the police. Embry pointed to another article in the *Birmingham News*, working to illustrate that Connor ran his campaign and his office "on a platform of race hate," again employing Salisbury's language. He quoted the item: "Mr. Connor will close schools before mixing them." And the *Times* lawyer read Connor's own declaration quoted in the newspaper: "'Before I will be party to seeing our park facilities and golf courses integrated, I will order every one of them closed.'" Connor was also concerned that blacks might be elected to offices in local government and "'that Negroes want supremacy, not equality.'"[131]

Next on the stand came plaintiff James Thomas "J.T." Waggoner. The fifty-seven-year-old Birmingham native had held a variety of blue-collar jobs before being elected commissioner three times, starting in 1956. He had been a prison guard, worked at automobile service stations, and driven trucks for the city of Birmingham. He testified that he first read the *Times* article in his office after his secretary brought it to him. He said the article referred to "me and Jimmy Morgan and Bull Connor in particular, talking about every decent person in the City of Birmingham in general." Waggoner insisted there was no racial strife in Birmingham: "I had four hundred fifty Negro employees in my department that I talked with daily. . . ." He was unapologetic and unsympathetic about neighborhood bombings: "It was a blockbusting effort being made to ruin a white neighborhood. Buy a house in the middle of the block, and ruin the value of the houses around it, and do that in the next block and ruin the value of houses surrounding it. Yes, sir, that effort was being made." But he said this white resistance did not "disturb race relations."[132]

In a heated exchange, Embry asked Waggoner to point out where he had been named or identified in the article. Waggoner read Salisbury's article from the witness stand: "Yes, sir. 'From Red Mountain, where a cast-iron Vulcan looks down 500 feet to the sprawling city, Birmingham seems veiled in the poisonous fumes of distant battles.'"

EMBRY: "Is your name mentioned in that paragraph?"
WAGGONER: "Yes, sir, it certainly is. He pictured me—"
EMBRY: "Is that the paragraph you have just read?"
WAGGONER: "Judge will you please let me answer this question?"
THE COURT: "Well—"
EMBRY: "I asked him to point out where his name was mentioned."[133]

AFTER A TESTY BACK AND FORTH WITH EMBRY, WAGGONER SAID: "Since the cleanliness, the anti-pollution of our air was a part of my responsibility, along with the ordinances that were set up by the City Commission, the enforcement of them was my responsibility and when a man says that the air was polluted with an acid fog in this city on a fine April day, that it was only an acid fog belched from the stacks of the Tennessee Coal and Iron Company from Fairfield and Ensley Works that lies over the city, that man told a direct lie about me. . . ." Embry reiterated his question: "I asked you how it refers to you, please, sir?" An irritated Waggoner responded, "About me and my responsibility to the people of Birmingham as an official." Embry: "All right. Go on to the next paragraph."

WAGGONER: "But more than a few citizens, both white and Negro, harbor growing fear that the hour will strike when the smoke of civil strife will mingle with that of the hearths and forges."[134]

His temper finally exploding, Waggoner launched into a diatribe, reading Salisbury's story line by line and insisting it referred to him as an individual and as a member of the city's governing commission. Embry seemed to be allowing Waggoner to hang himself on the stand. The testimony offered a vivid window into the commissioner's frustration with the *Times* article, indeed any article written by a reporter from the North. Waggoner insisted: "He is referring to me as to the kind of indecent person I am to allow that sort of thing, as a church member or as a member of the Y.M.C.A. Board, and particularly as a member of the City Commission." Judge Grooms attempted to control the plaintiff from the bench: "Mr. Waggoner, you can take this thing up sentence by sentence and we can spend an hour, two hours on it. Just go down there and if you see any place that you think that it has reference to you, then mention that and let's refrain, if we can, as much as possible from making speeches." Embry's grilling had frustrated and enraged Waggoner. Anything disparagingly written about Birmingham, he explained to the court, reflected badly on him as a city commissioner, "a member of the human race," and a "decent person." Yielding the floor, Embry said, "Thank you, sir." And the court took a fifteen-minute recess.[135]

Then Bull Connor took the stand. He testified that he did not hold people charged with vagrancy incommunicado for three days, as Salisbury reported. Defending the conduct of his office, Connor told the court, "That statement is not true, gentlemen." Responding to Simpson's question about running on a platform of race hate, Connor said: "That is not true. I hate nobody." Simpson queried the police commissioner about his views on segregation.

SIMPSON: "In all your public life have you advocated the doctrine of segregation of the races?"

CONNOR: "Yes, sir, I have. . . . I am still for segregation of the races. I think it is best for both races."

SIMPSON: "Did you ever tell anybody, damn the law, down here we make our own law?"

CONNOR: "No sir."

SIMPSON: "I believe someone asked whether or not after newspapers or someone had said about you that you had said whites and Negroes are not to segregate together, what was the occasion of that statement?"

CONNOR: "Mr. Simpson, I don't remember ever making that statement. I think some newspaper man might have took advantage of what little education I have and just wrote that."

THE COURT: "It is a classic statement?"

CONNOR: "Yes, sir, I have to agree with you, judge."[136]

Simpson also walked Connor through his process of insuring that suspects were not held longer than needed for questioning at the city jail. Contrary to Salisbury's article, Connor insisted, he had put systems in place to either charge individuals or let them go quickly.[137]

Questioning and testimony turned to the impact of the *Times* article on Connor and his wife. After the article ran, Connor explained, "I received lots of letters, lots of phone calls at home. I would have to take my phone off the hook and notify headquarters to send and get me if anything happened on account of the phone calls after I got in bed. They would call my wife and talk terrible to her when I wasn't in the home in the daytime. We got letters from all over the world, I did, letters, and the other commissioners said they got letters, but you would feel it. You would walk down the street, and you would feel a lot of people that usually would stop and talk with you, they looked like they were trying to dodge you or something. It was bad." Simpson followed up: "How many would you say you received of such letters of abuse and so forth, in the course of a month, say, after the article appeared?" Connor replied, "I would say over a hundred letters from all over this country."[138]

Simpson offered into evidence four letters to serve as examples, reading them into the record. "Mr. Connor," one letter read, "I am not an expert on faces, but even an amateur can tell from the scowl on your face that you are a dirty dog. You have Hitler in your heart and Mussolini in your soul. You are the devil incarnate. You are a vicious Fascist." The letter, according to Simpson, was from "Max Nimkoff, 101 West 23rd Street, New York, New York." Another letter, this one posted from Plainville, New Jersey, Madline H. Squier, read: "Dear Sir: I have been reading about your escapades in the New York Times. So, you are a law unto yourself. In other words, an outlaw. You look like the disgusting character you are." Simpson was undoubtedly playing to regional pride in the southern jury and cultivating old prejudices against mean, contemptible, and ignorant Yankees.[139]

It took years for *Sullivan* to be felt on the ground—for southern officials and their attorneys to understand what the U.S. Supreme Court meant by "actual malice." But it is clear that Judge Grooms understood the legal concept and standard in this case. He questioned whether Connor was actually harmed by the article. From the bench, before releasing the jury for deliberation, he instructed its members that when they considered whether Connor suffered damage from the article, they also might consider whether "instead of being damaged, Mr. Connor's political, social and financial prestige has likely been enhanced by *The New York Times* publication in Alabama. . . ." Indeed, Grooms charged the jury with several tasks that seemed extraordinary and indicated that the judge clearly understood the suit within the context of the civil rights movement. From the bench, he all but called the case a SLAPP suit, an effort to silence criticism of the city commissioners and mire the speaker in costly litigation.[140]

Among the twenty-two separate instructions to the jury, he started with two astounding declarations, directing it to find in favor of the *Times:* "I charge you, gentlemen of the jury, that under the evidence in this case you may not return a verdict in favor of plaintiff and against defendant. I charge you, gentlemen of the jury, that the language of the article complained of, which mentions the plaintiff by name, is not libelous." In his third instruction, Judge Grooms informed the jury that Connor could not win by "simply establishing that the language complained of was critical of the Police Department, the City or people of Birmingham or conditions therein." Grooms addressed Connor's history as a white supremacist in his fourth instruction: "I charge you, gentlemen of the jury, that if you find that the plaintiff ran for office on a platform of white supremacy that he cannot be libeled by the statement that he ran on a platform of race hate and therefore [the] plaintiff cannot recover because of such a statement."[141]

Grooms also said that if the *Times* made an error, it still might win the case against a public official. He instructed, "I charge you, gentlemen of the jury, that if you find the article in question to have been inaccurate in some respect as it concerned the plaintiff, that the article was based upon information derived by the defendant from sources it believed to be reliable, and that [the] defendant honestly believed that the statements in the article which refer to the plaintiff were true, then you must return a verdict in favor of the defendant. . . ." The judge also undertook a significant part of his instructions to the jury to clarify the new actual malice standard and how it differed from mere negligence.[142] Grooms explained that the law now obligated Connor to prove that the *Times* and Salisbury published the information with knowledge of falsity or reckless disregard for the truth. The new libel standard allowed for some false information to reach print, as long as the publisher did not know it was false at the time. "I charge you, gentlemen of the jury," the judge declared, "as a matter of law that The New York Times in criticizing the official conduct of Mr. Connor is not compelled, or under a duty to guarantee the truth of the factual assertions of the article." In other words, there could be honest mistakes in the story. Grooms also ordered that, in considering possible damages, the jury must take into account the fact that only 365 copies of the *Times* were sold in Alabama and that "by far the greater amount of notoriety came as a result of the reprinting of the article in local newspapers." Finally, the judge delivered an astonishing charge from the bench: "There is no evidence in this case that the plaintiff has sustained any actual damage, and I further charge you that in the event you find the issues in favor of the plaintiff, your verdict may be for nominal damages only."[143] Judge Grooms had obviously seen through the real purpose of this libel case brought by the three Birmingham city authorities—to impose a news blackout over the suppression of civil rights protests in the Deep South.

Most certainly Judge Grooms signaled that the use of libel should be curtailed and such SLAPP suits summarily rejected by the court. But the jury did not follow his instructions. After almost nine hours of deliberations, the Birmingham jury found that the *Times* acted with actual malice and awarded Connor $40,000 in compensatory damages rather than the $400,000 in compensatory and punitive damages he had requested. Connor told reporters he was pleased with the amount. "I appreciate it," he told reporters from the courthouse steps.[144] This was September 24, 1964, six months after the Supreme Court reversed the *Sullivan* case. The two other libel suits filed by Mayor Morgan and Commissioner Waggoner came to trial with Connor's suit, but Grooms dismissed them because, unlike Connor, neither of their names were mentioned in Salisbury's story.[145]

The *Times* appealed Connor's case, and the Fifth Circuit Court of Appeals reversed the verdict under the *Sullivan* rule in August 1966. The court held that Connor could not recover damages because he failed to show that the *Times* acted with actual malice—that Salisbury wrote the article knowing it was false or should have known it was false.[146] It also ordered Connor to pay $2,617.50 in court costs.[147] In its reversal, the court praised the *Times'* coverage: "They have exhibited a high standard of reporting practices. Salisbury did contact persons representing different viewpoints and made a conscientious effort to interview Connor and others. . . . There is no evidence that he misquoted his sources or gave the information acquired from them a different slant than intended. . . . Clearly these are not the actions of a sensation-seeking publication or of careless and shoddy reporting."[148] After referencing the actual malice standard established in *Sullivan,* the court said that a reporter may rely on statements made by a source—even though they show only one side of the story—without fear of libel suits filed by public officials. The famous journalist Edward R. Murrow, however, found grave defects in Salisbury's reporting. After Murrow worked on his own stories from Birmingham in 1961, he said the situation was much worse than Salisbury had reported. He had never seen such an atmosphere except in Hitler's Berlin just before World War II.[149]

CBS in the Crosshairs

A year after the suits were filed against Salisbury and the *Times,* Connor once again turned to libel law when faced with coverage of the civil rights demonstrations in Birmingham. But this time, he aimed his wrath at CBS reporter Howard K. Smith, who had made his mark as a correspondent during World War II. He was one of "Murrow's Boys" dominating television news in the early days of broadcasting. From network headquarters in New York, Smith traveled down to Birmingham to check out Salisbury's *Times* reports and found that the reporter had not exaggerated.[150] Many of his black sources were afraid to go on the air or be identified, yet Smith believed his documentary would be in good shape to air after a week of editing and refining back in New York. He decided to delay his trip home after receiving a Klansman's tip that something big was going to happen at the bus terminal the next day, which also happened to be Mother's Day, as the Freedom Riders made their way into the Deep South on May 14, 1961.

Staked out at the Greyhound station before their bus arrived, Smith noticed police activity that would become their modus operandi during demonstrations: Connor's men melted away, refusing to keep order or protect demonstrators. Hundreds of whites milled around the terminal, which was across the street from police headquarters and Connor's office. The only national newsman on the scene, Smith later wrote: "All at once, in midafternoon, policemen began moving from the street into the basement of the Police HQ. . . . Within five minutes there were no police to be seen anywhere."[151]

When the bus pulled in, the melee soon became a bloodbath, Smith reported. He later wrote: "The riders were being dragged from the bus into the station. In a corridor I entered they were being beaten with bicycle chains and blackjacks and steel knucks. When they fell they were kicked mercilessly, the scrotum being the favored target, and pounded with baseball bats."[152] Smith then saw a white man look at his watch and shout to the others that it was time to leave. The police arrived moments after the whites fled in cars and on foot. Smith broadcast hourly from Birmingham for the remainder of the day, and the *Times*, still steering clear of Alabama, published his eyewitness accounts directly from the CBS broadcasts.[153] The reporter received so many death threats over the next few days that he had to hire bodyguards. After seeing Smith's CBS reporting, the mayor of his hometown, Monroe, Louisiana, sent him a telegram asking, "When are you going to do something we can be proud of?"[154] Smith's producer, David Lowe, had warned him that the response to CBS coverage was going to be convulsive in the South, telling him before the broadcast: "You know how this report is going to turn out. However balanced we try to keep it, the Establishment is going to look awful because its position is awful."[155]

After the bus station beatings, the local Birmingham press, usually silent on civil rights issues or critical of the demonstrators and out-of-town troublemakers, actually began to cover the news with some semblance of balance. The headline of an editorial published in the *Birmingham News* asked, "'Where Were the Police?'"[156] The *News* accused Connor of knowing that the white "hoodlums" were waiting to waylay the Freedom Riders and that he sat in his office at city hall and did nothing about it: "The Birmingham Police Department under Mr. Connor did not do what could have been done Sunday." In the same piece, Connor defended his department's performance by pointing out that he had let many officers off for Mother's Day. And he showed his disdain for the unwelcome invaders of his city: "I have said for the last 20 years that these out-of-town meddlers were going to cause bloodshed if they kept meddling in the South's business."[157]

Smith's documentary aired to a national audience at 9 p.m. (EST) on May 18, 1961.[158] He gave time to both black and white citizens in a long series of interviews. In one interview, *Birmingham Post-Herald* columnist John Temple Graves insisted that Salisbury's reports were incorrect, that there was no "reign of terror." Birmingham attorney William S. Pritchard blamed "northern agitators" for wreaking havoc in his city, causing "Negroes" to "believe that they are the equal to the white man in every respect and should be just taken from savagery and put on the same plane with the white man in every respect. That's not true. He [the Negro] shouldn't be." Pritchard continued his racist diatribe on the air, insisting that "even the dumbest farmer in the world knows that if he has white chickens and black chickens, that the black chickens do better if they're kept in one yard to themselves." Shuttlesworth, one of the defendants in the *Sullivan* case, was among the few civil rights leaders willing to go on the air.[159] He talked of the beatings, of the attempts to bomb his church and home, including a blast on Christmas in 1956 that blew him out of his bed. He was amazingly unharmed. The minister explained to Smith: "I have to have somebody guard my home at night. . . . The police won't do it. . . . Life is a struggle here in Birmingham, but it's a glorious struggle."[160]

At the end of the hour-long documentary, after recounting the latest beatings of the Freedom Riders at the bus terminal, Smith quoted a May 16 *Birmingham News* editorial agreeing with Salisbury's story: "Fear and hatred did stalk Birmingham's streets yesterday."[161] Yet, back in New York, CBS executives were running scared; they were critical of Smith's civil rights coverage, insisting he should have been more balanced. Simpson, the attorney for Connor and two other Birmingham officials, wrote CBS to demand a retraction. The letter insisted that Commissioner Connor, Mayor Morgan, and Commissioner Waggoner were embarrassed both personally and as public officials and that the broadcast falsely accused them of dereliction of duty. Simpson also argued that Smith falsely reported his clients were "guilty of or encouraged or condoned ethnic, racial or religious intolerance." Connor denied that he "aided, abetted, encouraged or approved delay in the arrival of police" to the scene of the Mother's Day assault at the bus station.[162]

After receiving the letter, CBS attorneys flew from New York to Birmingham to meet with Simpson. During the long meeting, almost three hours, CBS representatives tried with little success to convince Simpson that the broadcast was truthful and presented both sides of the story.[163] In a letter to his clients, Simpson discussed the issue of balanced reporting and encouraged them to proceed with the suit: "You cannot cure a libel after you have once stated it by showing that someone else disagrees with you or takes a different view."[164] CBS retracted the story in the *Birmingham News* on November 30, 1961, and broadcast a retraction on the local station, WBRC-TV.[165] CBS also suspended the venerable reporter, Howard K. Smith, long a household name. CBS executives were deeply concerned with the network's image in the South. Smith remembered CBS founder William S. Paley once complaining: "While you boys are attending awards ceremonies for your latest bold thrust, it is left to me to look after the source of your livelihood, the offended Southern station owners who threaten a mass disaffiliation. You give me a stomachache."[166] CBS officials then fired Smith and prepared for a court battle with Connor and his cohorts.[167]

In November 1961, CBS also faced libel suits from George Penton and Samuella Willis, the registrars of voters in Montgomery County, Alabama, for reporting that they were working to prevent or at least delay the registration of black citizens. The U.S. Justice Department had sued for an injunction against Penton and Willis for their discrimination against blacks registering to vote under the 1957 and 1960 Civil Rights Acts.[168] In the libel suit, Penton and Willis both sought $100,000 for a CBS News story on a voter-registration school, insisting that there were false statements in the program, "Douglas Edwards with the News." The story in part focused on Erna Dungee, a Montgomery native who helped voter applicants prepare to register. She was also named in the suit because she warned prospective applicants that the registrars would give them certain information "only to mislead" them and make it more difficult to register.[169] Penton and Willis said they were libeled by their depiction as resorting to underhanded methods to prevent blacks from registering. Weary from the libel assault, CBS settled the case for an undisclosed sum in December 1963, issuing an on-air apology to Penton and Willis as well as in a press release distributed to other media outlets. Bull Connor, they had decided, was enough of a worry.

When the Freedom Riders moved on from Birmingham to Montgomery, federal officials realized too late that Sullivan was in cahoots with Connor.[170] Sullivan also gave a mob of Klansmen time to confront the Freedom Riders at the bus station before bringing in security.[171] *New York Times* reporter David Halberstam reported later: "The local cops had agreed to give the Klan fifteen minutes to welcome them and work them over, and then, the damage done, the cops were to arrive. Fifteen minutes to have their pleasure."[172] After the riot, Sullivan told reporters in the terminal parking lot: "I really don't know what happened. When I got here, all I saw were three men lying in the street. There was two niggers and a white man."[173] But it became apparent that he and other city leaders were getting worried about how the lawless beatings would look in press reports. He said later that afternoon: "We all sincerely regret that this happened here in Montgomery. . . . It could have been avoided had outside agitators left us alone. Providing police protection for agitators is not our policy, but we would have been ready if we had had definite and positive information they were coming."[174] A Klansman was later overheard heralding Sullivan for working with his organization. "Sully kept his word," the man boasted. "He said he'd give us half an hour to beat up those God-damned sons of bitches and he did."[175]

"The Lynchers of Albert E. Scott Did Not Wear White Robes"

Pierce v. Moon was filed the same year as *Sullivan*. A white police officer sued the *Black Dispatch* and leaders of the NAACP in Oklahoma City for critical comments about his official actions. The officer, D. D. Pierce, had shot to death an African American man in his front yard on February 12, 1960, when the policeman and his partner went to the man's house to investigate a minor traffic accident. A reporter arrived on the scene minutes after the incident and quoted the officer as saying that he saw the man, Albert E. Scott, holding a shotgun. However, the official police report later said Scott was sighting down the barrel of the shotgun when he was killed.[176] Rather than holding the gun at his side, the official report claimed, Scott held up the gun barrel as if he was going to shoot.

Six NAACP leaders, including local chapter president E. C. Moon Jr., a dentist, sent a letter to Chief of Police Roy Bergman and several media outlets, calling for further investigation after the county attorney dismissed the matter as justifiable homicide. The African American leaders called the shooting a "lynching" in the published letter: "The State of Oklahoma has placed its seal of approval upon this revolting act of lawlessness. The lynchers of Albert E. Scott did not wear white robes. . . . Rather they were and are now members of the Police Department of Oklahoma City. They wore uniforms of that department of the city, and they were shielded with the badge of its authority." Officer Pierce fired the shot that killed Scott, but he and his partner had backup of between eight to twelve officers, who arrived at the scene after the shot was fired.

The letter further complained: "There is no suggestion and no showing that either police officers present ever ordered him to surrender to arrest, that he in any manner resisted arrest, that he was sighting the shotgun at or towards any of the officers or anyone else, or that he intended to sight it at any one of them, or that he had any criminal intent or purpose in any of his actions." In 1960, it must have been shocking to the white officers to see a black man holding a gun in his yard, but NAACP leaders asked readers to consider a role reversal. What if the officers had been black and had come upon a white man holding a gun in his own yard? Would shots have been fired then? Would there be no punishment of or at least serious investigation of the black officer's actions? The letter concluded: "Herein lies the ugliness of this whole unconscionable happening. . . . If this lawlessness is allowed to prevail, let never a voice be raised in this community against the atrocities committed in Hitler's Germany, or Stalin's Russia."[177]

Initially, Moon and other local civil rights leaders tried to get *Black Dispatch* editor Roscoe Dunjee to run the letter as an editorial, but he refused, preferring the front-page treatment of the letter signed by all local NAACP leaders. Dunjee had founded the paper in 1914 and crusaded through its news page for more than forty years. Long active in the NAACP, he helped develop more than eight local NAACP branches in Oklahoma, and in 1932, he pulled the chapters together to start the state NAACP, serving as its president for sixteen years. He chided whites for their "Negrophobia" and called for "black power" at the ballot box long before that phrase was popularized in the 1960s and 1970s. He urged blacks to be proud of their skin color, and the *Dispatch*'s masthead displayed a black angel holding a horn and proclaiming to be the "Mouthpiece for All Better Thinking Colored People."[178]

It was probably only a matter of time before he faced a libel suit given his high-profile activism in Oklahoma. Editing the paper with a shotgun next to his desk, Dunjee focused on the coverage of lynchings in the region, and he fought against voter-registration laws that included literacy tests. He also helped fund several cases where black residents were trying to integrate neighborhoods not zoned for blacks. An Oklahoma judge relied on *Buchanan v. Warley* (1917) to rule the state law unconstitutional. But this latest lynching, the police shooting, needed a united battle by the growing NAACP in Oklahoma City. After months of working on the legal defense with local attorneys, NAACP president Moon and others wrote to the organization's lawyers in the New York office for financial help with the libel suit. "Our boycott and sit-in activities here have drained our treasury, so we are asking the National Office to send us enough money to cover these expenses," Moon informed attorney Robert L. Carter with the NAACP Legal Defense Fund in New York. Moon also advised that supporters were mounting fund drives to raise money for the defense and that local leaders were working hard to secure a big-name entertainer to appear at a fundraiser.[179]

A flurry of letters between Oklahoma City NAACP leaders and the national office ensued. Carter and the legal team resisted underwriting the entire case, weighted down with their own court cases and other libel actions. Carter sent $250, but the sum wasn't near enough. Oklahoma City attorney E. Melvin Porter, who helped with the defense, reported expenses of $3,800 by January 1961; he was still occupied with the pleading stage of the case. This amount included $500 for a private investigator and $200 for depositions and a court reporter in addition to $3,000 in attorney's fees. Porter, recently elected president of the local NAACP Branch, asked that Carter and the national office send more money quickly. "As you perhaps know, a case of this nature involves a tremendous amount of time and research and certainly so where several points of law will have to be argued," Porter explained.[180] Carter replied that the national officers were sympathetic but could not underwrite the entire case, asking him to try to keep costs down. Another defendant in the suit, local NAACP officer James E. Stewart, told Carter that by March 1961, more than a year after the shooting and resulting protests, the Oklahoma City branch of the NAACP had raised $1,000 for the libel-suit defense. He also told Carter that the *Black Dispatch* was an "innocent bystander and should get out of this situation at our expense."[181]

Carter foreshadowed the fact that more libel cases were surely coming, and he worried about how to keep local NAACP members protected from the wave of punishing suits. He also knew he couldn't handle every single case that local branches were facing, but he advised and coached where he could. Writing to Stewart, Carter advised: "I think this case has to be handled in such a manner the people involved can get off with as few scars as possible. It is a dangerous and ticklish case, and it has to be handled with that in mind rather than the attitude 'damn the torpedoes, full speed ahead.'"[182]

By fall of 1963, six months before the U.S. Supreme Court would overturn the *Sullivan* case in favor of the *Times*, NAACP leaders in Oklahoma City had had enough. They settled the case with Officer Pierce for $5,000, funded primarily by the national office in New York. Carter was concerned about the big picture, especially the toll these libel suits were taking on the bank accounts of the organization. He pondered how he could stop them and repeatedly reminded branch officers to be more careful when speaking about civil rights issues, especially in the local press. "Unless the officers of our branches become more cognizant of the fact that we are subject to actions for libel and slander when we make charges which we cannot prove," Carter cautioned, "we are going to be in for a great deal of trouble."[183]

CHAPTER 3

While *Sullivan* Is on Appeal...

Benjamin Elton Cox understood the meaning of the word *segregation* at the age of four. Born in Whitesville, Tennessee, in the early 1930s, he wondered about reciting the Pledge of Allegiance in kindergarten. The words "liberty and justice for all" puzzled him. "I knew the Pledge, but I knew that it didn't mean what it said because we had to get off the sidewalks when a white person came by and had to hike up extra stairs and sit in the worst seats in the theaters."[1] Cox's interest in civil rights issues carried into high school in Kankakee, Illinois, when he and two friends felt offended when they saw a school-sponsored minstrel show, which they insisted degraded the race. He and others protested to the principal of the school, who, in turn, stopped the shows. "That served as a catalyst to me in terms of civil rights," he said. Protest leads to action. Protest leads to results.

Cox would make history as one of the thirteen original Freedom Riders in 1961, serving as a Congress of Racial Equality (CORE) field secretary in the 1950s and 1960s, fighting for civil rights in thirty-seven states. By his own tally, he went to jail seventeen times for his civil rights work. He later recalled: "My life has been threatened eighty-seven times in writing. I've been shot at trying to get people to register to vote." In 1961, he wrote out his will and left it with his parents when he hopped on the bus to challenge segregated interstate transportation with a group of idealistic college students, both black and white. It was said toward the end of his career that he had an FBI file almost as thick as Martin Luther King Jr.'s. Like King and so many other civil rights leaders, Cox served as an ordained minister, having finished his theological studies in 1957 at the Howard University School of Religion.[2] Cox is best known, though, for his civil rights work in Baton Rouge, Louisiana, and a resulting free-expression case, *Cox v. Louisiana,* relating to picketing and public demonstrations.

This chapter focuses on libel cases filed while *Sullivan* worked its way through the appeals process. Along with a case against Cox, public officials went after NAACP leader Aaron Henry in Clarksdale, Mississippi, after seemingly benign comments he made to a reporter. At the same time, scores of newspapers faced the wrath of retired U.S. Army general Edwin Walker from coverage of events related to the Ole Miss riots in fall of 1962. Walker would ensnare newspapers that ran an Associated Press report about his conduct at Ole Miss, specifically in his leading the charge against U.S. marshals dispatched to keep order in Oxford while James Meredith enrolled in the university. The Walker case against the Associated Press would represent another landmark ruling, which extended *Sullivan*'s actual malice standard to public figures in 1967.

But in the shadow of *Sullivan* and in the shadow of perhaps better-known civil rights leaders, Elton Cox led local people in peaceful protests across the South. Events leading up to his libel case started the winter after the Freedom Rides. On the morning of December 15, 1961, Cox led about two thousand Southern University students on a four-mile march from the school in the suburban black enclave of Scotlandville to the courthouse in Baton Rouge. As CORE field secretary for North Carolina and Louisiana, Cox, along with other CORE leaders, came to town to help the fledgling student chapter at Southern University launch a new wave of sit-ins. CORE workers had readied themselves for direct action, distributing leaflets calling for a boycott of downtown stores, conducting workshops on nonviolence, and lining up bail money for the arrests that would inevitably come. Twenty-three students had already been arrested and were sitting in jail when Cox started the march. The event was heavily publicized beforehand, and the Baton Rouge mayor instructed the police to provide protection for the demonstrators as long as they were orderly and peaceful. Chief Wingate White brought in sixty off-duty police officers to help maintain order and talked to Cox about what the demonstrators were planning as they embarked. Cox said they would congregate for seven minutes at the courthouse, where the parish jail was located, sing two songs, hear a four-minute speech, then walk back to Southern University.

As the demonstrators neared the state capitol, police became wary when more than three hundred whites gathered on the other side of the street to heckle the black demonstrators. Officers instructed the crowd to disperse, but Cox refused, asking his followers to hold fast. The police officers acquiesced with reluctance, and when protesters reached the courthouse two blocks away, Chief White instructed Cox to keep demonstrators on the sidewalk about one hundred feet from the courthouse steps. In the pouring rain, students swayed together. Five people deep on the sidewalk, they sang "God Bless America" followed by "We Shall Overcome," with cheers erupting as they heard singing echo down from the courthouse jail cells. Cox then invited students to try eating lunch at the twelve downtown stores targeted by CORE, instructing them to sit at the whites-only lunch counters for one hour if they were refused service.[3] The whites across the street began to mutter and grumble at Cox's instructions to the students.

Police ordered the crowd to go home, then panicked at Cox's defiance. One police officer set off a canister of tear gas and sheriff's deputies shoved some of the students, according to multiple eyewitnesses. Officers waded into the crowd with German shepherds, and a dozen more tear gas canisters exploded among the fleeing throngs. Police arrested Cox and forty-nine students the day after the melee, and Southern University closed four days early for the holiday break as the students spent Christmas in jail.

In early January, Judge E. Gordon West of the U.S. District Court issued a temporary restraining order that banned CORE from holding future demonstrations and any other protests in Baton Rouge.

Police charged Cox with four offenses under Louisiana law: criminal conspiracy, disturbing the peace, obstructing public passageways, and picketing a courthouse. Typically Cox wore a "Freedom Ride" pin on the lapel of his black blazer with his minister's black shirt and white color underneath. His Baton Rouge Sheriff's Office mug shot, inmate 55241, showed him in a denim shirt. His longish hair, typically oiled carefully into place, was disheveled around his serious, mustachioed face. In the end, Cox was acquitted of criminal conspiracy and convicted under the other three offenses. Judge Fred S. LeBlanc of the Nineteenth Judicial District in East Baton Rouge Parish said it was inherently a breach of the peace for that many "Negroes" to demonstrate downtown and that, by "their mere numbers," they created a disturbance.[4] He sentenced Cox to twenty-one months in prison. The state Supreme Court affirmed, holding that Cox's "inflammatory speech" had morphed the demonstration into a "disorderly and seething mob" that had "intended to storm the courthouse."[5] While he was in jail, Cox said he heard rumors that Louisiana District Court judge Fred A. Blanche Jr. and District Attorney Sargent Pitcher Jr. had shared bribes. Pitcher was a charter member of the White Citizens' Councils of Louisiana and legendary among civil rights leaders for harassing black activists throughout the 1960s.[6]

While he was out of jail on appeal, Cox said in a mass meeting that Pitcher and Blanche took money from some black protesters, who wanted to avoid going to jail themselves. It is unclear how this got back to the judge, but Cox and Reverend Arthur L. Jelks, president of the Baton Rouge NAACP, were arrested under Louisiana's criminal libel statute in October 1962. The statute outlawed all speech that "tends to expose any person to hatred, contempt or ridicule or to deprive him of the benefit of public confidence or social intercourse." Historian Adam Fairclough argues that such an accusation would not have been unusual in Louisiana politics, but the criminal libel statute was handy for silencing black militants: "If it were to be enforced, half the population of Louisiana, including every politician in the state, would face indictment."[7]

At the libel trial the next month, Cox's attorney made a motion to desegregate the courtroom, which was denied by Circuit Judge LeBlanc. Reverend Jelks, whose libel case was eventually dismissed, also kept trying to desegregate the courtroom. He tried twice to sit in the white section and was ordered to move. Three young women, all NAACP members, were fined $100 or ten days in jail for contempt of court for sitting on the white side of the courtroom.[8] Cox argued that the criminal libel statute violated his First Amendment right to free expression, but after the two-day trial, he was found guilty of defaming Judge Blanche and District Attorney Pitcher and sentenced to the maximum penalty under the law, a $3,000 fine and a year in prison.[9]

On appeal to the Louisiana Supreme Court, Cox continued to argue that the criminal libel statute violated his First Amendment right to free expression, but now he had another weapon, *New York Times v. Sullivan*, which had been decided three months earlier. He argued that he had a right to criticize a public official, particularly his or her actions in a public office. On June 8, 1964, the state Supreme Court set aside the conviction and ordered a new trial. In its lengthy opinion, the court pondered Cox's allegations delivered at the NAACP meeting. In the court's words, he said "that it was common knowledge that the oppressed Negroes who appeared in Judge Blanche's court had to pay a fee which inured to Judge Blanche's benefit to keep from going to the penitentiary."[10]

There was a separate trial for his alleged defamation of the district attorney, but the two cases were decided and appealed together. The court refused to set aside Louisiana's criminal libel statute, asserting that the law was fully in accord with the *Sullivan* case—that when a comment is made with reasonable belief of its truth (regarding a person in public affairs), the speaker already has qualified privilege. "Our criminal statutory requirements for proving actual malice are in accord with those set out by the New York Times case for civil libel," the court explained.¹¹ The court also asserted that the privilege to criticize "public men" was not absolute: "Public affairs could not be conducted by men of honor, with a view to the welfare of the country, if attacks upon them could be made at will, destructive of their honor and character and made wholly without foundation. Our statute sufficiently protects those honestly criticizing their public officials as to their official conduct to satisfy the First Amendment, but it properly forbids unjustified malicious attacks upon them."¹²

What interested the court, however, was the timing of the district attorney's recusal from prosecuting the libel cases. The court frowned on the fact that Pitcher had prosecuted a case in which he was the plaintiff. The district attorney and his staff had argued against the various motions made by Cox's attorneys, including a request for a change of venue, a motion to desegregate the courtroom and courthouse, and a motion to dismiss the case. After the court had ruled on all of these motions and only two days before the actual trial, Pitcher finally recused himself, the court noted with disapproval. And even after that recusal, members of his staff continued to work the case. The justices on the Louisiana Supreme Court, however, were careful not to offend Pitcher. In fact, they salved his bruised honor before slapping his wrist: "A sincere and conscientious public official like District Attorney Pitcher would naturally be outraged by the alleged defamatory statements, as would any person having his good reputation. He would naturally feel that a conviction of the accused would be a public vindication of the wrong done him, and he would have a great personal interest in seeing that the accused was convicted. He appeared at certain stages of this prosecution as a prosecutor and appeared later as a prosecuting witness with a personal interest. The two roles are incompatible."¹³ This violated Cox's right to a fair trial, so the state Supreme Court set aside the conviction and sent the case back down for a new trial.

In addition to the libel suit, Baton Rouge officials figured out another way to shut down the protests. Chief White and Mayor John Christian sued CORE for violation of the Fourteenth Amendment rights of the people of Baton Rouge. The diversion of all available police to maintain order during the downtown protest in December 1961 deprived citizens across the city of police protection. And because the police and demonstrators blocked certain public streets, the citizens of Baton Rouge could not exercise their "right to freely use the public streets and ways without interference and hindrance." In January 1962, the local court issued a sweeping permanent injunction restraining CORE from "financing, sponsoring, encouraging or engaging in meetings or any other activities whereby violations are suggested, advocated or encouraged."

But in its September 1963 reversal, the Fifth Circuit Court of Appeals seemed incredulous that the white establishment of Baton Rouge would use a Reconstruction-era amendment meant to protect African Americans from KKK and police terror and violence as an instrument to stop civil rights demonstrations. "This case presents new twists in civil rights litigation," the court commented somewhat wryly. Judge John Minor Wisdom wrote in the opinion that the practice of reducing police protection in one part of the city to strengthen it in other areas or neighborhoods was common in Louisiana, pointing to the revelry of the annual Mardi Gras parades as an example. "The contention has the earmarks of a bad pun," he said. The court denied Baton Rouge officials' request for a rehearing.[14]

The other case against Cox, the right-of-assembly case, had worked its way up to the U.S. Supreme Court, which heard arguments for both sides in October 1964 and released its decision in January 1965. A key piece of evidence was a film of the protest. The footage countered the state's claim that the demonstration had turned into a riot before the police brought in the dogs and tear gas. The justices closely watched the film, which clearly showed the protest was peaceful until the police panicked. The court overturned all three convictions on First Amendment grounds, finding that the demonstrations had been orderly and the Baton Rouge Police had permitted them to take place in the first place.[15]

Still determined to punish the troublemaker, District Attorney Pitcher brought charges against Cox yet again, this time seeking to prosecute him for "attempting" to obstruct justice. In 1965, the Fifth Circuit in New Orleans seemed to have lost patience, throwing out the Baton Rouge conviction. "The district attorney's transparent purpose is to harass and punish the petitioner for his leadership in the civil rights movement," the court declared, "and to deter him and others from exercising rights of free speech and assembly in Louisiana—in this instance, by advocating integration of public accommodations."[16]

Pitcher then dropped defamation charges against Cox. But the damage was done. CORE's momentum had faltered under the waves of injunctions and prosecutions, and Cox had served a total of 107 days in jail. *Cox v. Louisiana,* however, had lasting implications for the movement. In 1965, when the U.S. Supreme Court struck down the state law under which he was convicted, it opened the door even wider for civil rights demonstrators to gather in public spaces. They would take advantage of the new opportunities the judicial ruling opened to them.

Aaron Henry and the "Diabolical Plot"

Mississippi's NAACP president Aaron Henry was driving about thirty miles south of his home in Clarksdale in March 1962 when he picked up a white hitchhiker. After the teenager, Sterling Lee Eilert, settled in the front seat and the pair was back on the road, Henry asked the Memphis youth if he could find him a white woman. When Eilert refused, Henry said he could stand in as a substitute and reached for the eighteen-year-old's crotch. Eilert then jumped from the slow moving car and ran, noting the make and model of Henry's vehicle and the last few digits of his license plate number.[17] This is the story that Clarksdale police chief Ben Collins spread around anyway. He arrested Henry on a general charge of misconduct the same day and jailed him overnight. At a hearing with a justice of the peace two days later, the hitchhiker testified that the Clarksdale pharmacist had picked him up, then propositioned him for sex.[18]

Henry said he had never seen Eilert before and accused Collins and Coahoma County district attorney Thomas H. (Babe) Pearson of setting him up to make everyone believe he was homosexual. Henry said Collins and Pearson must have enlisted the teenager to make the charges against him. The NAACP leader was fined $500 and sentenced to six months in jail on a charge of disorderly conduct.[19] He said the usual accusation that NAACP leaders were communists or communist sympathizers was not doing enough to discredit civil rights leaders, so this was what Collins and Pearson must have come up with instead. "There's not a soul involved in this except that goddamn Ben Collins and that chickenshit Babe Pearson," Henry said to some friends, later wishing he had not been so vocal in public. But he worried that charges of homosexuality would scare away would-be participants in the movement and figured Collins and Pearson would do anything to discredit him.[20]

Vera Pigee, a civil rights activist who worked regularly with Henry, told him a few days later of an anonymous phone call she had received. The caller whispered to her that Henry was lucky to be alive. The caller said he had agreed to hang Henry in the jail the night he was charged but decided not to go through with it. The plot was that police would explain the next day that Henry committed suicide in disgrace over the morals charge.[21] Henry's friend Medgar Evers encouraged him to tell U.S. Justice Department official John Doar about the incident, and they made a late-night appointment to meet while Doar was in Jackson. United Press International (UPI) reporter John Herbers saw Henry leaving the federal building after midnight and called him the next day to ask what was going on. "I told him everything that had happened and almost everything I suspected," Henry later wrote in his memoir.[22] Henry didn't remember using the words "diabolical plot." He thought later that Herbers suggested the descriptive label, and he agreed. Regardless, Herbers quoted him as saying there was "a diabolical plot cooked up" by Pearson and Collins to discredit him.²³ Further, Henry said he asked the Justice Department to investigate his Saturday-night arrest and said he had "unimpeachable witnesses to prove" he had not left Clarksdale over the weekend.²⁴

Clarksdale officials were outraged by the impudence of one of their second-class citizens. Henry recalled: "Babe Pearson phoned me and said, 'Look here, nigger, I just got through reading the paper where you have been talking about me. Listen goddammit, I'm gonna stop you from talking about me.'"²⁵ Pearson filed a $25,000 libel suit against Henry several days later based on the UPI story and the "diabolical plot" quotation attributed to Henry.²⁶ Collins also filed suit, this one for $15,000, for the same story.²⁷ Henry, Pearson, and Collins had already experienced a long history as leaders of the black and white communities of Clarksdale, a Mississippi Delta hamlet about seventy-five miles south of Memphis. Henry worked for equal rights; Pearson and Collins had long worked against him.

Pearson and Collins targeted the civil rights leader rather than the media outlet distributing the message. Clearly, in their efforts to keep whiteness supreme, southern officials had become interested in punishing both the disenfranchised speaker and the media messenger. Henry had grown up in Clarksdale, and prior to World War II, whites did not consider him a threat. But Henry served as a staff sergeant in an all-black trucking unit during the conflict and returned to Mississippi with an eagerness to change society, as did so many other African American soldiers. Blacks had fought Nazism and fascism overseas in a war to preserve Western democracy, and the time had come to insist on exercising their individual and political rights back home. In 1946, when Henry returned home to Clarksdale, he became the first black to register to vote in Coahoma County. He faced no opposition from whites. A handful of other black men, mostly World War II veterans, saw that Henry was not harassed for registering so they followed suit, all voting in the next Democratic primary.

There was no pharmacy school for African Americans in Mississippi, so he attended Xavier University in New Orleans on the

GI Bill, graduating in 1950 with a bachelor's degree in politics and government, as well as pharmacy. With his new wife, Noelle, he opened a drugstore in Clarksdale. The Fourth Street Pharmacy became the unofficial headquarters for civil rights workers during the next three decades. Two years after he moved home, Henry led the push to establish an NAACP chapter in Clarksdale when two white men raped two black teenagers and went free. He was elected president of the local chapter at the organizational meeting in 1952. Originally, the idea was to get NAACP legal help when court cases arose, but national NAACP representatives such as attorney Thurgood Marshall visited Clarksdale from time to time and promised astonishing things. The desegregation of Ole Miss was one. Medgar Evers became one of the first members of Clarksdale's chapter, and he would become its best-known figure.

In 1956, the state legislature established the Mississippi Sovereignty Commission to fight the enforcement of school desegregation, suffrage, and other civil rights, dumping $250,000 of taxpayer funds into its operation. Along with conducting a massive public relations campaign, the Sovereignty Commission funneled state dollars to the local Citizens' Councils and set up an intricate spy network to undermine civil rights efforts. Clearly Mississippi segregationists were concerned with the image of the state and combating what they saw as negative publicity. Governor James Coleman appointed Hall C. DeCell, editor of the weekly *Deer Creek Pilot* in the small Delta town of Rolling Fork, as public relations director. He was expected to fight "the animosities against the state . . . generated by vicious and slanderous misrepresentations and falsehoods appearing in national publications at the behest of . . . antagonistic pressure groups," including the NAACP.[28] The commission, which existed for seventeen years, employed investigators and paid informers to watch the troublemakers. Sovereignty Commission records detail the close tabs segregationists kept on Henry, showing an eagerness to follow his actions closely and discredit him if need be.[29] In 1957, Clarksdale's white leaders told Sovereignty Commission investigators they would rather have Henry lead the local chapter of the NAACP because they knew him. DeCell reported: "He acts in the open and makes it easier to keep up with the activities of the Negros in [the] area. About all that Henry and his crowd have done is to talk. . . ."³⁰ They noted that Henry planned to run for the state NAACP presidency and that he appeared to have enough support to be elected. White leaders "found him to be lesser a radical than the current group of state officials."³¹

Henry was elected NAACP state president in 1959. It was customary for a state officer to resign his local post, but no one wanted to take the Clarksdale leadership position for fear of white reprisal, so Henry kept that position. Reprisals would come, however, as Clarksdale whites began to worry about Henry's growing influence. The Citizens' Council plotted to neutralize him. In a 1959 memo sent to the director of the Sovereignty Commission in January 1959, investigator Zack Van Landingham, a former FBI agent who was at one time an administrative assistant to Director J. Edgar Hoover, wrote: "The Citizens' Council in Clarksdale is giving thought to measures of bringing pressure against Henry for the purpose of having him move away from Clarksdale. It is believed that if Henry leaves this area, the NAACP will die as he is the main one and keeps it alive."³²

With Henry's growing notoriety as a civil rights leader, pharmaceutical companies were refusing to sell him their products, so he had to drive north to Memphis, where he could replenish his stock. Business was down, however, because he was forced to pass on the extra cost to his customers. White leaders also discussed how to get Henry's wife fired from her teaching job in the Coahoma County school system. Several members of the Citizens' Council had accused the school superintendent L. L. Bryson of "playing politics" in his refusal to fire Henry's wife and the wives of other NAACP members.³³ Because of Bryson's refusal, whites began actively campaigning against his reelection as superintendent. It was clear that whites were seriously alarmed about the possibility of Clarksdale's black community gaining any political power. About seven hundred black citizens were on the voting roles and about four hundred actively voted by 1959.³⁴ Bryson lost reelection, and white leaders expected the new superintendent "to get rid of" Noelle Henry.[35]

Clarksdale's state legislators were gleeful when they thought they had evidence of Henry's violating state tax laws in 1960.[36] According to the local tax commissioner, Henry reported that he had sold several hundred dollars of school supplies to the county, claiming that the materials were tax exempt when they were not. State legislator Kenneth Williams "was very anxious that Aaron Henry be criminally prosecuted for this violation rather than have him pay a penalty and back taxes. Williams said that [local attorney] John Stone had told him they had never used the criminal provisions to put anyone in jail under this particular tax law, but when Williams told Stone that Henry was President of the NAACP in Clarksdale, Stone said that this might put a different light on the situation."[37] State tax commissioner Noel Monoghan agreed to send an investigator to Clarksdale to look into the matter within ten days. A Sovereignty Commission memo also noted: "Mr. Monoghan said that Kenneth Williams has tried every way possible to 'get' Aaron Henry. He had tried to get Henry in handling dope and liquor, but Henry has always been too smart to fall for such."[38]

Henry became even more notorious as a troublemaker for complaining about brutality inflicted on blacks by Clarksdale police officers and the Mississippi State Patrol.[39] The Sovereignty Commission noted that whites were angry about blacks addressing them by their first names in retaliation for whites' refusal to properly address them as "Mr." and "Mrs." They blamed Henry and the NAACP for the social and political fracas threatening to disrupt the racial status quo. In May 1960, Landingham reported, "The Citizens' Council are [sic] trying every way possible to deflate Aaron Henry in the eyes of the negroes of the community so they will realize he can't do them any good."[40]

After blacks were excluded from Clarksdale's annual Christmas parade, Henry and the NAACP called for a boycott of area stores. Their slogan was "If we can't parade downtown, we won't trade downtown." Clarksdale businesses immediately began hurting since more than half the city population was black. In response, county attorney Pearson charged seven black leaders with restraint of trade for conspiring to boycott.[41] Five of the so-called conspirators, including Henry, were tried and convicted, fined $500, and sentenced to six months in jail. All appealed the verdict. "The five Negroes convicted in this case are five of the most vicious agitators in Mississippi," wrote Sovereignty Commission investigator Tom Scarbrough. "I do not know what this group will do next, but they are not going to remain quiet for long. Most of this group are school teachers or housewives teaching in Coahoma County. Steps should be taken by those in authority to cut off as much of this gang's income as possible. This was discussed at the December 28 meeting in the Mayor's office."[42]

Whites attacked Aaron Henry through his wife, Noelle, whose teaching contract with Coahoma County Schools was not renewed for the 1962–1963 school year. At that time, teachers were required to provide a list of all organizations they belonged to. Noelle listed the NAACP; she was the only teacher in the state to do so.[43] A public school teacher for eleven years, she appealed to the school board for an explanation of her firing, but it refused to talk about the decision. She filed suit in 1962, charging that she was being penalized because she was a member of the NAACP and her husband was state president. At trial, school representatives said they did not renew her contract because her husband had been convicted on the morals charge. They also pointed to the libel suit working its way through the courts, denying that her NAACP membership had anything to do with her firing. The U.S. District Court for the Northern District of Mississippi refused to issue an injunction requiring the re-employment of Noelle Henry by the school district, and the Fifth Circuit Court of Appeals affirmed. The appeals court said the superintendent had broad discretion to recommend teachers for employment and that Henry had failed to prove that her husband's civil rights activism had anything to do with her termination.[44]

Meanwhile, Aaron Henry continued to fight the morals charge. After he was found guilty at the justice-of-the-peace trial, Henry made an unsuccessful appeal to the circuit court. He and six other witnesses testified that he was in Clarksdale when the hitchhiker said Henry picked him up. Henry also made sure to tell the court that he was not homosexual.[45] The Mississippi Supreme Court reversed the circuit court conviction on a technicality, agreeing that Collins had searched Henry's car illegally.[46] However, the court reversed itself a few weeks later, holding that while the search was illegal, defense attorney Jack Young lost the right to object to it because he had failed to do so during the trial.[47] Attorney General Joe Patterson of Mississippi issued a statement commenting on the high court's reversal, praising the "judicial courage and the legal talent exhibited by [the court]." He gushed, "It is indeed indicative of the high caliber of justices making up our court."[48]

To Patterson, also a plaintiff in a *Sullivan* companion suit, one threat to the southern way of life had been neutralized. Here was institutional racism at its highest level in Mississippi, and at the same time, the libel suit against Henry proceeded. A jury in Coahoma County Circuit Court agreed that Henry had libeled Pearson and Collins, awarding both officials their requested amount, $25,000 and $15,000 respectively.[49] Pearson's lawyer, Charlie Sullivan, who later ran unsuccessfully for governor, told the all-white jury that Henry had made false statements about the county attorney with the intention of defaming him. He said Pearson was afraid he would not be reelected because of Henry's "diabolical plot" comment. If he lost the next election, Pearson would lose his salary, which amounted to $16,800 over a four-year term. On cross-examination, however, Pearson said he had received neither calls nor criticism since the article ran.[50]

On the witness stand under Sullivan's hostile questioning, a frazzled Henry testified that he did not remember using the word "diabolical" and denied using the word "plot."[51] Henry said: "I am saying the words 'diabolical plot' were developed during the conversation." However, Sullivan produced a letter that was written by Henry the day before the news story came out and in which Henry used the words "diabolical plot" in complaining about Pearson's and Collins' harassment.⁵² Along with talking to the UPI reporter, Henry had given an interview to AP reporter Van Savell, who testified at the trial that Henry employed "diabolical plot" during their conversation.⁵³ In his closing argument, Pearson's attorney told the jury, "If Aaron Henry had accused this man of being a dirty crook, there was a time when there would have been a killing that night." Pearson was merely asking for $25,000 instead.⁵⁴ The attorney made a similar statement at Collins's libel trial the next week. The juries awarded Pearson and Collins full damages, and the Mississippi Supreme Court affirmed that decision in 1963, holding that the evidence "showed positively that no one had framed the defendant or cooked up any plot, diabolical or otherwise, to have him arrested."⁵⁵

This was the same year in which more than seventy-eight thousand disfranchised voters cast ballots in a mock election called the Freedom Vote in Mississippi. Both Democratic and Republican tickets ran on segregationist platforms. Henry ran at the top of the Freedom Vote ticket with Edwin King, a white minister from Jackson. The vote was held over a three-day period in two hundred communities, in churches, schools, poolrooms, and "votemobiles."⁵⁶ This was also the year that Henry's home was bombed. Up to this time, physical threats against Henry and his family had been nominal, limited to harassing phone calls and intimidation on the street. But on Easter weekend in 1963, while the family was asleep, two firebombs were thrown into their house. Michigan congressman Charles Diggs was a guest in the home at the time, and news of the bombing was published in newspapers around the country. The local fire department took almost thirty minutes to arrive; Henry and Diggs had most of the fire extinguished by the time the firemen got there. The following morning, Chief Collins said that there was supposed to be a third bomb, which Henry had better find. Two white men were eventually charged with the crime. At the trial, however, the first was found not guilty by an all-white jury, and the charges against the second man were dropped. After the bombing, Henry put a huge sign in his front window that read, "Father Forgive Them, For

Figure 4. The civil rights fight was front and center at the pharmacy owned by Aaron Henry in Clarksdale, Mississippi. The pharmacist's Fourth Street Drug Store served as a gathering place for civil rights activists until it burned down in 1963. His home was also firebombed. Henry filled the store with posters, photographs, and signs reflecting the critical issues and current events of the day.
—Mississippi Valley Collection, Special Collections, University of Memphis Libraries, Tennessee.

they know not what they do." In May 1963, an explosion ripped a hole in the drugstore. No charges were ever filed in that incident.[57]

In 1965, the U.S. Supreme Court agreed to hear Henry's appeal of the Collins and Pearson libel suits.[58] It was one year after the *Sullivan* ruling, and the high court held that Henry's remarks amounted to fair criticism of public officials. The court's reversal held that the Mississippi high court's decision violated the First Amendment since this was merely a criticism of public officials' performance of their duties. Not long after the case was decided, Henry bumped into Ben Collins at the jail, where he was posting bond for a friend. Henry recalled, "Ben stopped me and said, 'Say, fellow, when you gonna pay me?' . . . 'When am I gonna pay you?' I said. 'Ain't you heard what the court said? You are gonna have to pay me.' Ben looked perplexed for a second and then said, 'Is that right. Well, I sure ain't got it.'" After that, the pair bantered back and forth about the case when they saw each other at civil rights demonstrations. "About this time, the question of my life insurance became a joke with Ben, and I never really minded," Henry said.[59] Henry, who had been jailed more than thirty times for his civil rights work, was elected to the Mississippi House of Representatives in 1979.

The Ole Miss Riots and "Those Bastards"

The bucolic images of the South's magnolias and mint juleps continued to crumble under the powerful work of photojournalists such as Charles Moore in the 1960s. With camera in hand, he spent years on the front lines of the civil rights conflict. And when Air Force veteran James Meredith desegregated the University of Mississippi by court order in 1962, Moore was the only photographer trapped inside the Lyceum, the campus' administration building, with scores of U.S. marshals dispatched by President Kennedy to keep order. In his photographs, the officers looked like invading aliens in their gas masks and white-domed helmets.[60]

o white southerners, the marshals might as well have been evil, malevolent invaders. They descended on Oxford, Mississippi, to dismantle a way of life, white supremacy, which had enjoyed decades of cultivation, entrenchment, and enforcement. Moore's pictures showed rows of bandaged and bloodied federal officers after the riot. Earlier in the day, he had gone all over town with his camera, capturing images of jeering Ole Miss students and other locals sitting on one another's shoulders and waving Confederate flags the size of bed sheets.

The South looked bad in the national media, and Colonel T. B. Birdsong, commander of the Mississippi Highway Patrol, hated the way it portrayed his troopers. These journalists were taking over some of the tools—newspapers and magazines—that white southerners had long utilized to help them maintain in stark opposition the traditional binary of blackness and whiteness. The conventional southern image of the black animal rapist, aptly described by historian Grace Elizabeth Hale, was thrown out the window by James Meredith. Clean-cut and wearing a necktie, he appeared civilized and upstanding, while the white protestors were the crazed, snarling animals, according to media images broadcast around the world. That role reversal represented a direct threat to the race making—the construction of racial stereotypes and hierarchy and the institution of racial segregation—that had formed the bedrock of southern society for decades.[61]

Stinging from the coverage in the days following the riot, Birdsong was particularly angry about a story in the *Saturday Evening Post* titled "What Next in Mississippi?" and authored by Robert Massie, a freelancer living in New York, who witnessed the Oxford riots on September 30, 1962.[62] Like the scores of other reporters on the scene, Massie portrayed the white protestors as the armed aggressors and the marshals as overwhelmed peacekeepers. Segregationist governor Ross Barnett had whipped the protestors into a frenzy. On statewide television and radio, he declared that Mississippi, a sovereign state, would not obey the court's desegregation order. Racial mixing, according to Barnett, was unthinkable and would lead to the pollution and demise of the white race. "NEVER!" he railed on television and radio. "We will not drink from the cup of genocide!"[63]

Birdsong filed a $220 million class-action suit for Massie's article, which said that his state troopers had failed to help federal marshals rein in the mob that night.[64] He and his men, argued the colonel, were libeled in these two sentences about the riots, which killed two people and wounded more than a hundred others: "A sizable portion of the blame must go to the gray-uniformed men of the Mississippi Highway Patrol. Those bastards just walked off and left us," said one top official of the Department of Justice.[65] Birdsong took exception to the expression "those bastards"— "obscene and fighting words" that reflected on the reputation of him and his officers.[66] Yet the work of other reporters lent credence to Massie's veracity in the *Post* article. For example, Karl Fleming of *Newsweek* saw Mississippi state troopers doing little to control the riot, and he overheard one officer scornfully dub the marshals "Kennedy's Coon Clan."[67] With another *Newsweek* reporter, Fleming had darted into an adjacent building and watched the battle from the windows of a science-lab classroom. He wrote, "The badly outnumbered and outgunned marshals were fighting for their lives."[68] Fleming said that during the riots, he was stunned to see the patrolmen driving away from the scene in a long line of patrol cars. He recalled: "I counted sixty-eight cars in all—past [sic] our window and out of the campus, leaving the marshals on their own. The front entrance to the campus was now unguarded, and more rioters poured in, armed with .22 squirrel guns, high-powered rifles, shotguns, knives, clubs, and blackjacks."[69]

The U.S. Marshals Service's investigation backed up Fleming's observations. Of the 127 marshals deployed to the scene 79 were wounded by the end of the night—28 by gunfire.[70] As part of his investigation into the Ole Miss riots, Chief U.S. Marshal James McShane directed his deputies to report their experiences of the melee that night, particularly the behavior of the crowd, their efforts to control it, and the actions of the Mississippi Highway Patrol.[71] The Ole Miss battle had appalled northerners and southerners alike, although for different reasons, and Chief Marshal McShane undoubtedly needed all possible information to protect the U.S. Marshals Service from criticism that would surely come from multiple directions. Indeed, deputy marshals deployed to the scene at Ole Miss overwhelmingly criticized the Mississippi Highway Patrol for escalating the violence, encouraging the rioters, and vacating the scene at the height of the mayhem.

The bitterness of many deputy marshals was palpable in their descriptions of Birdsong's officers in the upheaval. Walter E. Bryan of Missouri complained: "I personally feel that the responsibility of the riot should be placed on the shoulders of the Mississippi State Police. They were laughing and jeering with the crowd, and could have gotten the crowd to do anything that they asked." "DISGUSTING" was the adjective flung at the state patrol by James T. Hearell of Danville, Illinois. Gordon D. Coen of West Virginia concurred: "The local law was a disgrace to law enforcement." Deputy Marshal John R. Alexander of Texas wrote: "The local law enforcement officers made no effort to control the mob and actually seemed to enjoy seeing us made the target for the obscene insults and flying objects."[72]

Beyond the highway patrol's passivity during the riot, some deputy marshals charged the state force with complicity in the attacks. Coen was astonished to see "one State Trooper" thrust "a newspaper reporter" backward "into the mob," which engulfed and battered him and "demolished" his camera. Although he held the crowd back "for a long time," Delmer E. Anglin of Louisiana described the state police shining "a spotlight" on his position "so the mob," growing in size and ferocity, could target him. Especially damning was the recollection of Edward T. Bartholomew of Virginia, who recalled the malevolence of one Mississippi patrolman in particular. As "bricks, rocks and other debris" began sailing into the marshals' line, the officer declared, "'You marshals are going to hurt some of these students, and I'm going to take this magnum (revolver worn in his holster in plain view) and kill every GOD DAMN ONE OF YOU.'"[73] The loyalty of the state patrolmen at Ole Miss was to the white rioters and legal segregation, not to federal law and the U.S. marshals, whom they viewed as unwelcome invaders of Mississippi soil and unwanted disruptors of racial customs.

What probably stuck in Birdsong's craw most of all was the charge that the Mississippi Highway Patrol abandoned the marshals to violent assault by an enraged white mob. In the eyes of federal marshals, the state police behaved like disinterested spectators. "All the patrol cars were doing as I saw," growled Deputy Marshal Ernest S. Mike of Kentucky, "were just driving by and receiving cheers from the crowd." When the campus disorder reached a violent pitch, Bennie E. Brake of South Carolina explained, "The Mississippi Highway Patrol jumped into their cars and sped off." Deputy Marshal Alexander recalled, "As soon as the first gas was thrown, the local law officers left the scene, and did not come back."[74] Friendliness and assistance to rioters and sudden retreat suggested to the Marshals Service that the Highway Patrol was complicit in the violent upheaval on the Ole Miss campus.

Birdsong's official police report of the riot painted a completely different picture of his state troopers' actions that night. Birdsong, code named "Unit A," faulted the marshals for starting the riot and characterized them as overtly hostile to his police force.[75] Birdsong wrote that before the riot started, several of his officers saw an unprovoked marshal strike a student with his billy club. "Students came to his rescue and Highway Patrolmen stepped in and sent the crowd back across the street. . . . The marshals were told by the Patrolmen that they had come close to causing a riot and that their cooperation was necessary to prevent one getting started. . . . The crowd was complying excellently with the Patrolmen's directions." Birdsong continued: "Suddenly . . . someone shouted 'Gas,' and the marshals began firing immediately. . . . There was no incident or provocation that prompted the firing of gas."[76]

Birdsong said the marshals fired their gas guns point-blank at his troopers' backs instead of shooting them at the feet of the crowd, the customary tactic. One trooper, Birdsong wrote, was even knocked unconscious and hospitalized by a canister blow. After they retrieved their gas masks from their cars, the troopers returned to their posts, according to the report. The gas was so overwhelming, however, that "Unit A" ordered the men to regroup on Highway 6 and await further instructions. Birdsong said that he met with the federal officers inside the Lyceum administration building, and they agreed the state troopers should move out of town to set up roadblocks against any additional rioters arriving on campus. He said his officers held their posts "throughout the night without sleep and no relief." At dawn, Birdsong said, a detachment of the 503rd Military Police Battalion confronted his troopers at the roadblock on Rebel Drive and Fraternity Row. The MPs had fixed bayonets and marched the state troopers to the shoulder of the road before releasing them a couple of hours later.[77]

Stories of what happened and when incidents occurred are bound to differ amid and after such massive chaos. Historian Taylor Branch confirms some of Birdsong's version of events. There were a "few remaining highway patrolmen struggling against the mob." They received "a dose of gas from behind," and a casing knocked one patrolman unconscious, the gas nearly killing him."[78] FBI agents said they heard Birdsong's withdrawal order on the Mississippi State Patrol's radio frequency at about 7:25 p.m. Birdsong's report recorded the time at "2100 hours," or 9 p.m. Branch wrote that by 7:40 p.m., "it was generally established that most of the highway patrolmen had vanished."[79]

Stories such as Massie's report for the *Post* graphically painted the Mississippi officers in a bad light. He wrote that a state patrolman laughed as white protesters slashed the tires of an army truck. He also said a state trooper stood by while a mob beat up a news photographer. "An Oxford woman rushed over to the state trooper. 'Aren't you going to stop them?' she cried. The patrolman grinned at her. 'I don't see nothin', lady, do you?'"[80] This description of the willfully negligent trooper was the antithesis of the gallant, law-abiding southern gentleman, the image cultivated by the South since before the Civil War. Birdsong demanded a retraction; *Post* editors refused.

Although the riot occurred in Mississippi and all plaintiffs were residents of that state, Birdsong sought $220 million in a class-action suit filed in U.S. District Court in Birmingham, Alabama, before Judge Harlan Grooms. Birdsong said the *Post* libeled all 220 officers in the Mississippi Highway Patrol, but lawyers for Curtis Publishing argued that a class-action suit, by its very definition as a large group of plaintiffs, could be a libel action.[81] The individuals in such a case were not identifiable.[82] In June 1964, with the *Sullivan* case decided, Curtis's lawyers continued to wage their case in court, arguing that Massie's article merely quoted "an impersonal criticism of governmental operations."[83] The court ruled that the case could be heard in Alabama. Curtis Publishing appealed to the Fifth Circuit on the grounds that Alabama courts had no jurisdiction in Mississippi. The riot did not occur in Alabama. The writer did not even pass through Alabama while working on the story, and none of the parties involved in the case had any connection to Alabama.[84]

Before the Fifth Circuit Court of Appeals, Curtis Publishing argued successfully that the actual malice doctrine applied in this case because the alleged libel concerned criticism of public officials in the performance of their official duties. The appeals court reversed the lower court's decision.[85] But it did not even reference the *Sullivan* ruling, by then almost two years old. There was no discussion about the need to prove actual malice when writing about a public official. Instead, the appeals court focused on jurisdictional problems and the use of the words "those bastards." The appeals court understood why Birdsong sought an Alabama court, which had proven that its "long-arm" jurisdiction statute was more generous than that of Mississippi. Alabama courts had become notorious for ruling that northern publications should have to answer to Alabama citizens for adverse or unflattering coverage of the civil rights movement, as illustrated by cases filed by Sullivan, Connor, and others.

The Fifth Circuit also agreed with Curtis Publishing that the word "bastards" did not defame Birdsong or his men: "It is not entirely clear whether the plaintiffs are alleging that by the use of the phrase 'those bastards' the allegedly libelous article questioned the legitimacy of their birth."[86] The court held that no reasonable person would believe that the reporter accused every patrolman on duty at Ole Miss "of having been born out of wedlock." The court said that the words "reflect more on the character of the user" than on the person or persons to whom they are referring.[87] So the court side-stepped the *Sullivan* ruling in finding for Curtis's *Saturday Evening Post,* but this northern media company would be hauled into court yet again over its coverage of civil rights issues.

General Walker's Libel War

Within the legal history of libel, the Ole Miss riots are best known among legal scholars for the U.S. Supreme Court case that extended Sullivan's actual malice rule to public figures, *Associated Press v. Walker.*[88] With this case, the court left no doubt that reporting on the movement—and the national conversation about it—were protected by the First Amendment. Former army general Edwin A. Walker, a Texan, had been highly decorated in World War II and the Korean War. President Dwight D. Eisenhower assigned him to command federal troops at Little Rock's Central High School in 1957 during federally mandated desegregation efforts there. Four years later, the army disciplined General Walker for distributing extremist right-wing literature to troops under his command in peacetime Europe. In response, he resigned his commission, admitting that he had despised Eisenhower's intervention to desegregate Central High. Now an influential face of American conservativism and anticommunism, he ran unsuccessfully for Texas governor in the Democratic primary in early 1962. Months later, the unchastened Walker turned up at Ole Miss, a hotspot in the civil rights struggle to integrate southern universities. Journalists and federal authorities at the university widely reported that Walker unofficially led the white-supremacist forces during the violent resistance to desegregation.[89]

Over a Shreveport, Louisiana, radio station and with the integration of the university days away, Walker issued a call to arms at Ole Miss, exhorting white southerners to join Governor Barnett in fighting James Meredith's enrollment.[90] During the broadcast, he called the Supreme Court "the anti-Christ" and urged "ten thousand strong . . . to bring your flags, your tents and your skillets!"[91] The next day, he renewed the call during a television interview in Dallas. The day after that, he rallied listeners on a New Orleans radio station. At a press conference in Oxford, Mississippi, on September 30, 1962, he again urged whites to stand by defiant Governor Barnett. Meanwhile, President Kennedy urged peace and calm as Meredith was escorted on campus by Chief U.S. Marshal James McShane and others.

Journalists on the scene reported that when the melee commenced that night, Walker was front and center, egging on the protesters. *Newsweek*'s Fleming later said Walker hopped onto a Confederate statue to encourage the crowd. "This time I'm on the right side," he shouted, waving his signature Stetson. "Don't let up now. You may lose this battle, but you will have to be heard. You must be prepared for possible death. If you are not, go home now."[92] AP cub reporter Van Savell wrote in his dispatch that he was standing less than six feet from Walker when the former general rallied his impromptu battalion. The twenty-one-year-old Savell, who dressed like a college student, fit in with the mob unnoticed. He also was a Mississippi native and former reporter for the segregationist Jackson *Clarion-Ledger*. His report, a spot-news story, was also a scene setter told partially in the first person:

> Walker first appeared in the riot area at 8:45 p.m., Sunday near the University Avenue entrance about 300 yards from the Ole Miss Administration Building. He was nattily dressed in a black suit, tie and shoes and wore a light tan hat.
> The crowd welcomed Walker, although this was the man who commanded the 101st Airborne Division during the 1957 school integration riots at Little Rock, Arkansas. One unidentified man queried Walker as he approached the group. "General, will you lead us to the steps?"
> I observed Walker as he loosened his tie and shirt and nodded

"Yes" without speaking. He then conferred with a group of about 15 persons who appeared to be the riot leaders.

The crowd took full advantage of the near-by construction work. They broke new bricks into several pieces, took survey sticks and broken soft drink bottles. Walker assumed command of the crowd, which I estimated at 1,000. . . .[93]

The next morning as the riot subsided, federal marshals arrested Walker and charged him with sedition and insurrection. He was held by federal officials on a $100,000 bond and sent to a Springfield, Missouri, psychiatric facility for examination.[94] Doctors pronounced him sane, but a grand jury in Oxford later refused to indict him.[95] The all-white grand jury made up mostly of "middle-aged farmers" did indict Marshal McShane, however, for ordering tear gas fired into the crowd. According to the indictment, "such conduct lead to a breach of the peace and did incite a riot."[96] McShane, a former New York City police officer, flew back to Oxford in late November and surrendered to the Lafayette County sheriff in Oxford. Almost two years later, U.S. District Judge Claude F. Clayton ruled that McShane had acted appropriately, that the chief marshal "had reasonable cause to believe that drastic action was necessary to carry out his duties, and that he had reasonable cause to believe the use of tear gas was a proper measure to be taken."[97]

Meanwhile, Walker sued the Associated Press and Savell for the stories about his actions in the Ole Miss riots, denying categorically that he had any part in charging the marshals, as had been widely reported on the news wires. He said he had counseled restraint and peaceful protest.[98] And he filed other virtually identical libel suits against fifteen additional media outlets for more than $33 million in damages.[99] Walker said he had been libeled with the report that he "led a charge of students against federal marshals on the Ole Miss campus" and with the words "Walker assumed command of the crowd."[100]

Walker's first case came to trial in post-*Sullivan* 1964. Since Walker was not a public official, he did not have to prove that the AP acted with actual malice. A particularly generous Shreveport, Louisiana, jury awarded him $3 million even though he had only asked for $2.25 million.[101] He also found early success when a

Texas jury awarded him $500,000 in compensatory damages and $300,000 in punitive damages.[102] But the U.S. Supreme Court found this ruling ridiculous. In its 1967 reversal, the court extended the *Sullivan* rule to public figures. It reasoned that "public men" are often in a position to exert an enormous amount of influence on society with their words and actions. They often speak about issues that are of public interest, the court said, pointing to Walker's media blitz leading up to the riot. And, like public officials, public figures can counter stories about them through ready access to the media, so they have plenty of opportunities to give their side of the story or counter any inadvertent mistakes the press might make.[103]

Holding that the AP did not publish the story with actual malice, that is "with knowledge of falsity or reckless disregard for the truth," the Supreme Court bought the argument as sold by the AP's attorneys—that Walker "willfully, aggressively and defiantly thrust himself into the vortex of the controversy" at Ole Miss, a controversy "of profound political and social importance and national public interest." And because of Walker's stature, he was "in a position to significantly influence the resolution" of the "Oxford confrontation," a showdown "which arrested the attention of the entire nation, and which has become a milestone in the century-long battle for racial equality."[104] Attorneys for the AP also pointed to what they saw as an obvious attempt by southern officials to stop coverage of the civil rights movement: "These cases were for the most part filed in forums in Southern or border states where it could reasonably be anticipated that juries would share the belief, widely held in the South, that the South's position in the segregation controversy had been grossly falsified and maliciously reported by the national news media, and might therefore be influenced, in determining the issues of liability and damages, by the widespread regional feeling that 'irresponsible outsiders' should be taught a lesson."[105]

In reversing the judgment, the Supreme Court said there was no evidence that the reporter had "personal prejudice" against Walker. Savell's reporting was accurate given that witnesses for both the plaintiff and the defendant testified that Walker assumed command of the crowd and led a charge. The court also said the nature of Savell's work, rapid dissemination of wire reports as events unfolded, should allow for innocent mistakes and there "was not the slightest hint of a severe departure from accepted publishing standards."[106] But Walker's many suits disrupted the news flow as members of the media across the country found themselves in years-long court battles.

Hodding Carter Jr. and the "Seditious Psychopath"

Hodding Carter Jr. was a thorn in the side of white supremacists in Greenville, Mississippi, long before the modern civil rights movement took off. In his *Delta Democrat-Times*, he had run photos of Jesse Owens, winner of four gold medals in the Olympics in Berlin in 1936, a time when no southern newspaper ran *any* photos of blacks, much less one whose athletic feats shattered Aryan claims of racial superiority.[107] Since African Americans did not exist in mainstream newspapers in the South unless they committed a crime, Carter challenged the norm of a parallel but invisible society living and working under the white man. Carter was a moderate, a dirty word among southerners at the time. But that moderation came later in life. A native of Hammond, Louisiana, the young Carter had bought into the cult of whiteness that society was so thoroughly steeped in. As a seventeen-year-old, he shocked his classmates with his racism at Bowdoin College in Brunswick, Maine, refusing to speak to the only black student at the school. Both of his grandfathers had fought for the Confederacy, one riding with General Nathan Bedford Forrest, later a founder of the KKK. But as the stamps on his passport multiplied—he traveled to Egypt and India as a public relations officer for the U.S. Army in the 1940s—he became more open-minded. And the more he traveled, the less prejudiced he became.[108]

The cultural climate of Greenville, a river town with a significant Syrian and Chinese population, was more progressive than that of

Figure 5. Hodding Carter in his office at the *Delta Democrat-Times* in Greenville, Mississippi. He pushed hard for racial equality at a time when most Mississippi newspapers worked to maintain the status quo of white supremacy.
—Hodding Carter, Hodding and Betty Werlein Carter Papers, Manuscripts Division, Special Collections Department, Mississippi State University Libraries.

most southern cities. By the 1930s, it had become somewhat of a gathering spot for the state's best-known writers. The cultural paragon of Greenville was William Alexander Percy, a cotton planter, lawyer, and banker, who enjoyed a national reputation after publishing four books of poetry. Percy became a magnet for visitors such as Carl Sandburg, William Faulkner, and Shelby Foote. The country club even had a Jewish president when clubs in other towns refused to admit Jews. But African Americans remained in their customary place, the lowest class. They were poorly paid and worked mostly as manual laborers or as maids.[109]

In his editorials, Carter regularly ridiculed the Klan and tackled issues of race and prejudice head on. He spent his summers in Maine, writing novels, such as *Where Main Street Meets the River*, that were for the most part widely acclaimed.[110] And he earned thousands of dollars writing for national magazines such as *Life* and *Look*. As Carter became more famous, not just in Greenville or in Mississippi, his calendar filled up as requests for public lectures poured in from the North. He spoke progressively about race but also became a noted defender of the South and the importance of slow change in his home state. Some city leaders tried to get merchants to stop advertising in his paper, but business owners resisted and circulation held steady. In 1950, a third of the newspaper's twelve thousand subscribers were black.[111] The Carters also were bombarded with insulting letters and telephone calls. He hid an iron bar under the front-office counter after some particularly vile threats. Another time, Carter huddled in the bushes in his driveway with a shotgun, waiting for a man who had threatened to kill him.[112]

Carter's troubles with General Walker came after he gave a talk as part of the University of New Hampshire's Distinguished Lecture Series in October 1962. As was customary for him, Carter attempted to explain the causes of the Mississippi mindset, both defending and criticizing the state in his lecture, "The Why of Mississippi," delivered to about fifteen hundred students, faculty, and guests.[113] Carter had originally planned to discuss President Andrew Johnson as "a moderate and defier of the bigots and extremists of his own time," but the Ole Miss riots were still fresh and stinging. Carter said: "The University of Mississippi has suffered a cruel and undeserved blow. There were but a minority of students who took part in the rioting. The troublemakers were mostly hoodlums, crackpots, and racists from the outside." He also told the audience that "we can be comforted and reassured" by certain "evident truths." Among them, "General Edwin Walker, who personally led the insurrectionists on the Ole Miss campus, has been exposed once and for all for what he is: A seditious psychopath."[114]

The *Union Leader* in Manchester covered Carter's speech, although that article did not include his remarks about Walker.[115] However, the university's student newspaper, the *New Hampshire*, printed much of Carter's talk verbatim, including the section referring to Walker.[116] Thus, Carter joined the multitude of journalists in libel actions lodged by the Texas general. Walker filed the slander suit in Washington County Circuit Court in Greenville, seeking $2 million in damages.[117] Carter's attorney interviewed a wide range of audience members in New Hampshire, trying to build an argument that they were already aware of Walker's role in the Ole Miss riots and his resulting arrest thanks to widespread news reports.[118] Lawyers around the country who were fighting libel suits from the General formed the "Walker Suit Club" and included Carter's counsel along with those for *Newsweek*, the *Associated Press*, *St. Louis Post-Dispatch*, *Denver Post*, *Louisville Courier Journal*, *Atlanta Constitution*, and *Fort Worth Star-Telegram*, among others. They agreed to share information that might help in their defenses. Attorneys' fees weren't cheap, but Carter maintained a sense of humor, quipping to a friend: "It is very flattering to be sued for two million dollars when the *Times Picayune* has been asked for only three million."[119]

Timing helped Carter in this particular instance. A Washington County circuit judge dismissed the case in December 1967, citing *Sullivan* and a case decided earlier in the year (Walker's own suit against the AP) extending the actual malice standard to public figures.[120] The judge pointed out that when Carter made his statements, Walker was under arrest for charges of sedition and had been taken to a hospital to determine if he was mentally capable of standing trial. Also, his actions at Ole Miss—that he personally led a charge of students against federal marshals—had been widely reported. Most notably, the judge said Carter did not act with actual malice. His statements "were made with a reasonable belief in their truth," and there was a legitimate public interest in the issue being discussed.[121]

Another Moderate Editor, Another Big Libel Target

Like Hodding Carter, Atlanta's Ralph McGill also faced vilification for his stance on the race issue. And like other moderate editors, such as Mississippi's Hazel Brannon Smith of the *Lexington*

Advertiser and Buford Boone of the *Tuscaloosa News* in Alabama, McGill won the Pulitzer for editorial writing. His long-awaited win came in 1959. Unlike the other three editors, however, McGill excluded any mention of libel from his personal papers, which are housed at Emory University. Historian Leonard Ray Teel does not include a mention of Walker or the libel suit in his biography of McGill, but Teel does give a revealing behind-the-scenes look at how upset the editor was over another libel suit in 1947. Teel writes that McGill was distraught the day Rev. Frank Norris of Atlanta filed a libel suit for an editorial about Norris's sermons against traitorous newspaper editors who had urged compliance with the Supreme Court's school desegregation orders.

McGill wrote that Norris "told the crowd they'd nail the hides of newspaper editors to the fence; assured them they must defend their heritages. . . . Dr. Norris denies any pro-KKK connection."[122] Visitors to McGill's office on May 20, 1947, were embarrassed by his behavior. "Mr. McGill had for many years been somebody special to us," wrote former student Calvin Kytle, "and to see him as he was this afternoon was like watching a fine old race horse agonizing over a broken leg." McGill was "rocking in his swivel chair, running his fingers through his hair, his speech sometimes faltered . . . he looked terribly tired, almost to the point of hysteria, and his body looked to be sagging under the weight of the world."[123]

From the 1940s through the 1960s, McGill had been a leading voice for racial and ethnic tolerance in Georgia, challenging the demagogues who railed against equality under the law. McGill's newspaper career began in 1920 when he was a student at Vanderbilt University in Nashville, and he knew controversy back then after he was suspended from school for writing editorials that angered school officials. He worked as a part-time copy boy with the *Nashville Banner*, climbing his way up to sports editor before he left to take the position of assistant sports editor on the *Atlanta Constitution* in 1929. Ten years later, he was an editorial writer and executive editor, and then became editor of the growing newspaper.[124]

When Walker sued the *Constitution* for the AP wire stories, he named McGill in an accompanying suit for his column about Walker's role in the Ole Miss riots published by the newspaper on October 2, 1962. McGill told the court that he relied on newspaper, radio, and television accounts when writing the column, which was syndicated by the Cox chain, after it bought the *Constitution* in 1950.[125] In his column, McGill outlined the wire reports and opined that Walker was "an alarming figure, albeit a pathetic one. . . . He appears now as an aging man, willing to inflame young college students and hoodlums against the laws of the country he once served with honor."[126] A year later, McGill defended himself in court documents in the libel suit: "I had no intention of writing any untruthful statements concerning General Walker. He was, in my opinion, a man in whose public conduct society and the press had a legitimate and substantial interest."[127] In his complaint filed in U.S. District Court in Atlanta, Walker took exception to McGill's calling him "mentally deranged" and "an alarming figure inflaming young college students and hoodlums to riot."[128] Walker sought $5 million in general damages and $5 million in punitive damages.[129] The legal wrangling in the Walker-McGill suit continued until its dismissal in April 1968, four months after the U.S. Supreme Court overturned *Associated Press v. Walker* and established the actual malice rule as applicable to public figures. The First Amendment once again trumped the cult of whiteness. McGill and Carter had become big targets in the South, ostracized by their communities and region, threatened with death, and sued for libel by white supremacists. Still they published. Those white supremacists were starting to run out of ideas and options.

CHAPTER 4

...The SLAPPs Keep Coming

Abraham Williams and his wife, Eloise, drove down from Brooklyn, New York, to Darlington, South Carolina, in their sleek, new Chevrolet Impala with its New York plates on Saturday, December 23, 1961, to visit their parents, cousins, aunts, and uncles during the Christmas holidays. They had grown up in the small town of Darlington, a tobacco-growing community in the northwestern part of the state and, like many African Americans, had moved north in search of a better life in the big city. At about 11 p.m. on Christmas Eve, Abraham was driving from the Log Cabin restaurant about a mile outside of the Darlington city limits when he passed a police squad car cruising back into town.

He noticed in his rearview mirror that the squad car had turned around and followed him. As he drove toward house of his wife's parents, the patrol car followed but police did not flip on the siren or make any effort to stop him. Nervous, he kept his speed at about thirty miles per hour, pulling into his in-laws' yard at 539 West Broad Street and turning off the ignition. He hopped out of the car after locking its doors. That's when he saw the police cruiser stop and an officer start walking toward the house.

"Come here, boy," the officer called to him. Williams said he was "a man, not a boy." A second officer got out of the police car, opened the rear door, and told him to get in. Williams asked if he was under arrest. "You're one of those smart New York niggers,"

Officer C. W. Haynes said. Williams told him he was not smart and offered to show the officers his driver's license. Another officer in plainclothes then got out of the car and joined the other two, and the three men surrounded Williams as he stood on the sidewalk in front of the house. Williams later said in an affidavit that the plainclothes officer "struck me a violent blow in the face" and another threw him into the back of the police car. The officers pinned his arms behind him and began beating him about the head and face, especially aiming for his eyes. Williams asked again why he was being arrested. "I was unarmed and made no effort whatever to resist the three officers," Williams later said. His wife and her parents heard the commotion and rushed out into the front yard in time to see officers holding him down and putting handcuffs on him. The police threw him on the floor of the back seat and two officers got in the back with him.

"Abraham told them that he would go with them without being handcuffed," said his mother-in-law, Aleen Fleming. "As the car drove off I could hear Abraham hollering as officers were beating him." The police drove him to the station and threw him in a cell. He was bleeding so profusely that the officers decided to take him to the town doctor's office, leaving him to wait in the car. Dr. Wilson looked at him but gave him no treatment, and the officers hauled him back to the city jail. They finally booked Williams just after midnight on charges of driving under the influence, disorderly conduct, and resisting arrest.[1]

This chapter details even more SLAPP suits involving police brutality charges in South Carolina and Alabama. Along with a South Carolina case arising from Abraham Williams' run-in with police, the chapter covers a libel suit arising from a story by famous playwright Lillian Hellman inspired by the March on Washington in August 1963 and published in *Ladies' Home Journal*. It covers Freedom Summer 1964, and libel suits resulting from coverage of the deaths of three civil rights workers in Philadelphia, Mississippi, at the hands of the KKK with complicity of local law enforcement. It concludes with a libel battle waged between moderate Alabama editor Buford Boone of the

Tuscaloosa News and Robert Shelton, imperial wizard of the United Klans of America, in 1964 and 1965 as southern courts were still coming to grips with the meaning of the *Sullivan* decision.

"Christmas Eve It Was Abraham"

Abraham Williams, beaten and bloody, sat in jail, on Christmas Eve 1961. What had angered the police? Was it his fancy car with the New York plates? Was it his pushback that he was "a man" and not "a boy"? Eloise and her parents, Aleen and James, tried to get him out of jail that night, but police told them to return the following day with bail money. The family returned to the jail Christmas morning. Aleen Fleming said, "I went back to the cell where Abraham was confined and saw him. His face was a mass of blood. He was bleeding from his nose, eyes and face and evidently had received a savage beating. . . . His left eye was completely closed." Later in the day their attorney, Elliott Turnage, brought $300 in bail money to the jail and drove Abraham home. "At no time was I guilty of any of the charges made by these policemen against me," Abraham wrote in his affidavit. "At no time did I resist arrest and the action of the policemen, of violently beating me while holding me helpless in the police car was without cause or provocation." He had to get medical treatment for the beating. "Abraham was not drunk," Aleen Fleming said in her affidavit. "At no time did I see Abraham offer any resistance. . . ."[2]

After learning about the incident, Darlington NAACP president A. W. Stanley tried to rally African Americans in the community by writing a letter and circulating it as part of his protest of the officers' brutality:

> To Whom it may concern,
>
> On Christmas Eve Night, December 24, 1961, Abraham Williams of Brooklyn, New York, the son-in-law of Mr. and Mrs. James Fleming of this city, was brutally beaten by members of the Darlington Police Force. Such unwarrant-

ed action by an organization supported by tax payers is unfounded and is a violation of the laws of the Constitution of the United States, which protects the civil rights of All American citizens.

The Darlington Branch of the N.A.A.C.P. is urging you and all freedom loving peoples to come together and support an effort to put an end to all such un-American and un-Christian practices.

Christmas Eve it was Abraham. Tomorrow it may be one of us or someone dear to our hearts. This kind of action must not be ignored. Being afraid and hoping it won't happen won't stop it nor will waiting for a change of heart . . . stop it. We must stand up as men and women and protest these evils nonviolently, and through the proper courts of justice. A full account of this incident will be made Sunday afternoon, December 31, 1961, at the Community Center. The time will be 4:00 o'clock. We are urging you to come and bring your children so they may learn and benefit from these experiences.

We will expect to see you Sunday afternoon at the meeting.

Yours For Freedom,

A. W. Stanley, President[3]

The letter reached the Darlington Police Department, and Officers C. W. Haynes and Preston Huntley sued Stanley and the local branch of NAACP in the Court of Common Pleas in Darlington County. Calling the letter false, slanderous, and libelous, they sought actual and punitive damages, although neither officer had been named in Stanley's flyer. In four separate cases filed in 1963, the officers sued Stanley and the Darlington NAACP, each charging that Stanley had intended to "hold him up to public ridicule and to degrade and reduce his reputation and to injure him in his vocation." Damages in the four suits totaled $600,000.[4]

The field secretary of the NAACP, I. DeQuincy Newman, sent out another public notice informing African American citizens of the libel suits, warning them that the cases represented the latest assault on the black community and affected everyone. "Your name may not be spelled out as a defendant in the suit, nevertheless, all Negroes who are sensitive about the mutual welfare and the social, economic and political advancement of the Negro will view this suit as an attack upon the entire race." In his letter to the community, Newman pointed out that the suit was brought almost two years after the alleged libel occurred. And it came only after Stanley had been involved in a school desegregation suit in Darlington, which by the early 1960s was one of many popping up across the South after local communities delayed implementing the *Brown* decision.[5]

Newman underscored in his letter that the local white establishment filed the libel suit in an effort to punish Stanley for seeking desegregation through the local court system. He reprinted Stanley's original letter calling for a public meeting and for the defense of Abraham Williams after his beating. Then Newman informed the community that the second public meeting at St. James Methodist Church would be held to discuss the defense against the libel actions. He asked everyone to bring friends and promised that state NAACP leaders would be on hand talk strategy on the night of the meeting. The two police officers took exception to the republication of Stanley's letter and filed two additional $50,000 libel suits against Stanley on December 31, 1965, bringing the total money damages sought up to a whopping $700,000.[6]

This sum was a ridiculous amount of money, an amount beyond anyone's dreams, in hardscrabble rural South Carolina at the time. Darlington's tiny farming community had become famous for stock car racing's oldest asphalt high-speed race, the Southern 500 at the Darlington Raceway. The sport was birthed here, and Officer Preston Huntley was involved in racetrack activities every weekend. The city even bought its police force celebratory Confederate-like uniforms to wear during the 1958 race weekend, and the crimson flags bearing the stars and bars abounded on track signs and souvenir programs.[7]

Such was the environment that Stanley and NAACP leaders found themselves in as they readied their legal defense. In New York and South Carolina, NAACP lawyers prepared themselves for this latest fight. Noted black civil rights attorney Matthew J. Perry, based in Spartanburg, South Carolina, worked with New York–based NAACP general counsel Robert Carter on the defense. Both puzzled in December 1963 how Stanley's statement could be considered libelous when neither officer was named and Stanley spoke about an issue of public concern. Surely this statement, they surmised, was fair comment and criticism of a public official.

"I might say that these statements do not appear defamatory to me at this time," Perry wrote to Carter in December 1963. "However, as you will probably agree we must carefully examine the statements and compare them with statements which the Courts have held to be defamatory." Lawyers for both sides filed a flurry of motions relating to the six suits in the Court of Common Pleas in Darlington over the next year. By then, Perry was fighting civil rights litigation on several fronts. He served as lead counsel in a case to integrate nearby Clemson University and local hospital waiting rooms, just to name two, while juggling the libel defense. Perry filed one particular motion to make the libel complaint "more definite and certain." He asked how the officers were "discredited" in their "vocations" as they had claimed. They provided no evidence of defamation. He also wanted to investigate the beating of Williams and prove that it most certainly occurred and that the officers were guilty of assault, focusing on the affidavits of Abraham Williams, Aleen Fleming, and others. He sent those affidavits to the U.S. Civil Rights Commission in Washington, D.C., along with two graphic photos of the beaten and bloody Williams after he was released from jail.[8]

Feeling the momentum of the civil rights fight, Perry did not press for a hearing in the libel cases, however. He believed that the more time passed, the better their chance to prevail in court, for civil rights demonstrations across the South had picked up steam. In January 1964, he and other NAACP lawyers argued in their pretrial motions to dismiss the cases, that Stanley's statements in his flyer were vague, indefinite, and certainly not actionable, that the plaintiffs, as city employees, were public officials, and that the comments were well within the bounds of a citizen's privilege to fairly and freely criticize the officers. This motion was filed three months before the U.S. Supreme Court decided *Sullivan*, and Perry did not use the argument within a free-speech context in great detail, instead merely stating that citizens had the right to criticize the actions of police. A specifically stated First Amendment right didn't yet exist within the nation's legal system. Then the U.S. Supreme Court reversed *New York Times v. Sullivan* in March, creating the actual malice standard and placing libel law under the purview of the First Amendment. Although Perry and Carter took much notice of the *Sullivan* case, they perhaps did not yet realize its true impact. They made no immediate motion to dismiss after *Sullivan,* and the Darlington cases dragged on. More than a year later in July 1965, Perry again wrote Carter in New York: "I had hoped that the Supreme Court's decision in New York Times v. Sullivan would have convinced our opposition that they should simply drop these cases or allow them to die."[9] Southern lawyers and their clients refused to give up the fight. Perhaps southern judges and plaintiffs would ignore the ruling, put off complying with yet another civil rights rights–related U.S. Supreme Court decision the way they had ignored the *Brown* case and so many others. Benny R. Greer, the lawyer representing the police officers, stopped by Perry's office in July 1965 to let him know they were indeed moving forward with the case, suggesting a compromise settlement of $10,000. Greer told Perry to take the offer post haste because such a "low" figure would be off the table once they went to court.[10] From New York, Carter scoffed at the settlement suggestion in a letter to Perry: "Out of the question. I would doubt that anyone down there could pay it, even if it were thought that it was desirable, and certainly we cannot."[11]

Carter was widely considered a thoughtful legal historian among his colleagues. His well-reasoned argument relating to the evils of school segregation in part became the U.S. Supreme Court's reasoning in its conclusion in *Brown*. Carter had earned his law degree in 1940 from Howard University, the fertile training ground for black civil rights lawyers under the venerable Charles Hamilton Houston, and received a master of laws from Columbia Law School in 1941. Carter had been the lead attorney in the landmark case *Sweat v. Painter,* successfully challenging the University of Texas Law School's refusal to admit a black applicant in 1950. He succeeded Thurgood Marshall as the general counsel of the NAACP in 1956, winning the *NAACP v. Alabama* case, in which the U.S. Supreme Court held that the state of Alabama did not have a right to the organization's membership lists.[12]

As Carter, Perry, and other lawyers in the Stanley libel cases prepared for trial, they pondered a wide range of defenses, poring over precedent and law reviews relating to "fair comment" and "freedom of public discussion." But they kept coming back to the *Sullivan* decision. NAACP assistant counsel Maria L. Marcus wrote Perry: "Nothing could be more in the public interest than a report that a public official was recreant to his trust." She also pondered what surely must have been an obvious point relating to the state of the divided society in South Carolina in the early 1960s: "Certainly, it is hard to imagine that Negro civil rights leaders could affect the reputation of a white police officer in the dominant white community." But she still circled back around to the case law she knew at the time, perhaps not seeing the *Sullivan* case as the salvation in a libel case relating to police brutality against African Americans, a case in which civil rights leaders also had issued a public call for help in addressing the problem, an appeal similar to the "Heed Their Rising Voices" advertisement back in 1960. Marcus mused: Did A. W. Stanley conduct a thorough enough investigation about the beating before he sent out the letter? She suggested: "One could argue that where the harm to the plaintiff is small, the degree of investigation before publication of the charge can be correspondingly small."[13]

Or perhaps, Marcus pondered, if the NAACP counsel could show that that Stanley had a strong basis for believing that the police beat Abraham Williams while he was in custody, the remarks could be privileged. She did not use the words "actual malice," which were introduced in the *Sullivan* case. She then pulled from a *Columbia Law Review* article that the court might find legal value in Stanley's appeal to the community. Marcus quoted the law review in a letter to Perry in August 1965: "'The making of a charge is frequently the only way to prove it, for it can force an investigation, rally others to come forward with bits of proof in their possession or maneuver the plaintiff himself into damaging admissions.'"[14] They also looked at the Aaron Henry libel cases in Clarksdale, Mississippi, arguing the merits of "fair comment" and agreed to include that in Stanley's defense.[15] Henry, a pharmacist and leader of the NAACP, had become a big target in his hometown, facing down libel suits from the local police chief and district attorney.

In January 1966, Perry again argued to the court that Stanley's words were not libelous on their face and that the police officers had failed to claim specifically how they were damaged by them. He also began using the language from Justice Brennan's *Sullivan* decision, although Perry did not cite the case directly. He argued that the two police officers were public officials and public employees, that Stanley had the right to criticize them, and that his words were protected under the First and Fourteenth Amendments. In mid-March 1966, Perry appeared in the Darlington court to argue the NAACP's position on the demurrers, which are objections that the opponent's points are irrelevant or invalid. The judge said he would not consider the constitutional arguments Perry made relating to *Sullivan* or *Henry v. Collins*, that those were issues that could only be considered at trial.[16]

The police officers' attorneys argued in this pretrial appearance that Stanley and the NAACP acted with malice in circulating the letter, obviously picking up the language of the *Sullivan* decision. After the court appearance, the plaintiffs' lawyers told Perry that the police officers would accept considerably less than the original $10,000 settlement offer.[17] It was clear by this time that Perry was stalling, waiting for the *Sullivan* decision to influence the outcome of his case. By March 30, 1966, two full years after the Supreme Court overturned *Sullivan*, NAACP general counsel Carter continued to keep a close eye on the Darlington libel suits, noting the impact such suits could still have on the civil rights fight. He told Perry, "These kinds of civil suits are critical, and we will have to raise all the questions possible if we are to avoid having heavy judgments against us." But he was undoubtedly worried, and he advised Perry to again talk to lawyers for the police officers about a possible settlement.[18]

By February 1968, though, it appeared that the police officers had given up. Their cases were removed from the court calendar. The officers' lawyer had not answered several filings with the court, and Perry had been waiting to hear the judge's ruling on various pretrial motions. All had been at a stand still for more than a year. Perhaps, the plaintiffs wanted in part to bankrupt the defendants through attorney's fees. NAACP lawyers and local civil rights attorneys who worked the cases on the ground were most certainly underpaid when they were paid at all. Perry only charged the NAACP national office $1,684 for his work on the six cases over the five years they slogged through and languished in court. He and his colleagues at the South Carolina law firm of Jenkins, Perry & Pride had spent hundreds of hours on the suits. Although it looked like the cases were dead, Perry remained alert, hoping that the judge would throw out all six rather than merely taking them off the court calendar. He didn't want the officers to reactivate the cases later. On the other hand, Perry told Carter, he felt pretty confident that the First Amendment argument in this post-*Sullivan* world would protect his NAACP clients.[19]

The cases never came to trial, and Perry moved on to other civil rights cases in South Carolina. Throughout the 1950s and 1960s, he handled cases to desegregate schools, colleges, parks, golf courses, restaurants, and beaches. He won the release of more than a dozen black men from death row. In 1979, he was appointed the first African American federal judge in South Carolina, and in 2004, the federal courthouse in the state capital of Columbia was named for him. He never retired and died in 2011 at the age of eighty-nine.[20]

Carter argued or coargued and won twenty-one cases before the Supreme Court. He was appointed to the U.S. District Court for the Southern District of New York in 1972. He still had fire in the belly in 2004, when he told the *New York Times* that much remained to be accomplished in the quest for racial equality. In his attack on segregated schools in the 1950s, he had long relied on psychologist Kenneth B. Clark's research that showed segregation harmed the learning and development of black children in public schools. The problem remained well into the twenty-first century. He said: "Black children aren't getting equal education in the cities. The schools that are 100 percent black are still as bad as they were before *Brown*. Integration seems to be out, at least for this generation."[21] He remained on the bench until his death in 2012 at the age of ninety-four.[22]

Abraham Williams was another man in another police brutality case, and the details of this kind of brutality continue to echo in those incidents reported in modern-day headlines. Because of the ruling in the *Sullivan* case, protesters today are free to express themselves: "Hands up, don't shoot;" "I can't breathe"; "Black Lives Matter"; and others became ubiquitous in the years following the spate of high-profile police shootings starting in Ferguson, Missouri, in 2014. But in 1963, Stanley and his attorneys feared there would be no relief from the libel onslaught of white supremacists. At the time, they didn't know how the *Sullivan* case would turn out. It also defied logic that a white officer would feel defamed by a flyer that was sent out to the black community—and not the white community. Would a police officer in this era be concerned about his reputation among the black citizenry? It is arguable that he would not. This was also the year that police brutality brought national attention to Gadsden and Etowah County, Alabama, during the hot and heated summer of 1963.

"The Most Lied About City in the U.S."

It seemed like the whole world watched as thousands of peaceful demonstrators descended on the Washington Mall on Wednesday, August 28, 1963. Racial tension simmered in large part due to protests in Birmingham, Alabama, that spring. Martin Luther King Jr.'s motel was bombed, and the city exploded in some of the fiercest rioting seen to date. A white man walking across the United States to draw publicity in support of civil rights was shot twice in the head on the side of the road outside Gadsden, Alabama, and that small city had seen a wave of demonstrations throughout the month of June.

At the much-anticipated March on Washington, armies of police and national guardsmen readied themselves for anything as the sign-waving demonstrators filled the half-mile mall between the towering obelisk of Washington Memorial and the marble steps of the Lincoln Memorial. Bob Dylan was there, singing with Joan Baez. Hollywood A-listers Paul Newman and his wife, Joanne Woodward, swayed alongside Marlon Brando, who appeared on the platform brandishing an electric cattle prod like the one used by police to control demonstrators in Gadsden earlier that summer. Before electric stun-gun technology developed, police used cattle prods to control crowds and disable demonstrators. These tactical weapons delivered a high-voltage shock not strong enough to kill but certainly potent enough to cause significant pain. They were designed for use at slaughterhouses to drive cattle into the killing chutes.[23]

Brando and other movie stars had been traveling all over the country to support the civil rights revolution, followed by breathless national media awed by their celebrity. Brando and Newman were in Gadsden with actors Anthony Franciosa and Virgil Fry the week before the Washington march, much to the chagrin of city leaders there. Gadsden mayor Lesley "Les" Gilliland refused to meet with the celebrity "rabble rousers," who came to town to encourage ongoing civil rights demonstrations. In a press release reprinted verbatim in the local newspaper, the *Gadsden Times*, Mayor Gilliland, Police Commissioner Joe Hubbard, and Public Works Commissioner Hoyt Warsham complained about the movie stars:

> We feel that they are serving no purpose in Gadsden except to create trouble and chaos. The only reason they are here is for the publicity they will get out of the trouble and chaos which they are creating. All of the trouble which we have had in Gadsden has

been caused by outside rabble rousers coming in here and using our Negro people for their own gain. We have nothing but contempt for people such as these movie stars who are here and the quicker they leave and go back where they came from, the better off we will all be. We believe in law and order in Gadsden. That is the approach that we have taken in all the racial difficulties. If these people violate the law, they will be put in jail. These so-called movie stars should clean up around their own doors and their own affairs before they come into our community and try to tell us what to do.[24]

The actors met with an overflow crowd of civil rights demonstrators at Union Baptist Church and learned firsthand about the responding police brutality, notably the police force's use of electric cattle prods, which seared flesh with an excruciating shock to control the marchers. One young demonstrator remembered Paul Newman weeping in the pulpit during the meeting. "He had so much compassion for the marchers, young and old men, women and children," recalled Gadsden resident Mildred Williams years later. "Paul Newman cried through the whole meeting, I believe."[25]

Wire services stories continued to track the actors as they crossed the country that summer, running pithy quotes from Brando in Gadsden: "We are here as devoted representatives of good will." And from Newman: "We are here to see if we can help the racial situation."[26] The local paper covered the actors much differently. At the bottom of a page-two story, the *Gadsden Times* informed: "The quartet plans to leave the city tonight. Each actor denied that he is in Gadsden to receive publicity."[27]

Etowah County, with its county seat of Gadsden, sits in the southernmost foothills of the Appalachian Mountains sixty miles northeast of Birmingham. Etowah is the smallest county in Alabama but densely populated nonetheless. The 1960 U.S. Census reported that almost 97,000 residents lived in its nearly 550-square-mile area. This is hilly terrain, not farming country. The people relied instead on industry. Steel plants and the Goodyear Tire and Rubber Company had been the economic drivers in the region since the late 1920s. Although the stereotypical cotton planters of the South were absent from Etowah County, that southern way of life was woven into the social fabric, like having fried chicken after church on Sunday.[28]

Gadsden's political leaders were knocked off balance as civil rights demonstrations swept through their community, especially when the glaring media spotlight hit their own city. And the local newspaper worked hard to prop up the town and its leaders with stories from the white-segregationist point of view. For example, *Gadsden Times* columnist Mary Hoffman railed about the liberal northern media in a front-page column titled "Gadsden Most Lied-About City in the U.S." The column enjoyed prime space above the masthead, a spot traditionally reserved for the biggest news of the day. She pointed to the murder of the "integrationist" William L. Moore that spring, while he was walking just thirteen miles outside of Gadsden. A thirty-five-year-old white postal worker from Binghampton, New York, Moore received international and national media coverage for his walk across several states. He was shot along the highway toward Jackson, Mississippi, where he had planned to deliver to Governor Ross Barnett a letter pleading for an end to segregation in the South. Of the murder, Hoffman wrote: "No responsible person has condoned it. But in their loathing for the South, the hate-mongers have had a Roman holiday. With a great air of virtue, they have condemned the entire South as a section of evil and lawlessness, never hesitating to employ falsehoods for their purposes."[29]

She continued to rant about the liberal media and the liberal North in general: "Wrapped in what they deem their own sanctity, they will not stop at any lie, publish any error that belittles and besmirches the South. The image of the South as a region that glories in murder and the situations that provoke it, is absurd." At the end of her column, Hoffman quoted several of the Ten Commandments, including "Thou shalt not bear false witness against thy neighbor."[30]

Two days later, the *Gadsden Times* praised Alabama governor George Wallace's appearance on NBC-TV's *Meet the Press*, where he "maintained dignity and composure," though "baited by the media." The editorial explained: "If our Northern adversaries had hoped to make a fool of the governor of Alabama, they far overshot their goal. The governor said he would make his promised stand against desegregation at the University of Alabama even if a court order were issued against his doing so. But he repeatedly pledged that violence would not be tolerated at the University of Alabama."[31] A week later, Wallace stood in a doorway at the University of Alabama to block federal marshals as black students Vivian Malone and James A. Hood showed up to start classes by federal court order. In his inaugural address earlier that year, Wallace had famously declared, "Segregation now, segregation tomorrow, segregation forever!" Yet when President Kennedy sent one hundred Alabama National Guard troops into Tuscaloosa, Wallace chose to step aside rather than incite violence.

The *Gadsden Times* editors downplayed local civil rights demonstrations throughout the summer of 1963, relegating them to the bottom of page two under small-type headlines in single columns. But the paper trumpeted racial violence happening anywhere north of Alabama. Even at the high point of demonstrations in Gadsden on June 19, those actions making national news were still relegated to page two of the paper under the small, single-column headline: "Riot Squad in Gadsden, 466 Jailed; State Troopers Disperse Crowd at Courthouse." The story informed readers that Alabama's Highway Patrol Riot Squad had "virtually" invested Gadsden and that "65 specially trained state troopers made their first move against more than 300 Negroes gathered on the lawn of the Etowah County Courthouse."[32]

Al Lingo, whose job as director of the Alabama Department of Public Safety carried the title "colonel," looked intimidating and militaristic with his stern face and riot gear. Demonstrators had fanned out to sit in at lunch counters and at the courthouse. The *Gadsden Times* provided remarkable detail on the showdown between Colonel Lingo and the protesters:

> The troopers came around the west end of the courthouse in double file and quickly made a semicircle around the lawn sitters. This circle was tightened toward the front door of the building. . . . Several of the demonstrators began to offer resistance to

the ever-tightening circle of troopers and were rapidly subdued by the night-stick-armed troopers. A few of the troopers carried electrically charged probes which are usually used to move balky cattle.... A majority of the Negroes turned and started to leave the area around the steps. Only a small handful remained. Members of the riot squad began prodding the Negroes who were leaving the courthouse steps. The demonstrators again resisted the prodding and a few intense moments of club-swinging ensued in which several Negroes, both men and women, were beaten to the ground.[33]

The civil rights protestors were dangerous enough to attack and club; their beatings and arrests were not newsworthy enough to report on the front page in Gadsden.

The next day, the *Gadsden Times* reported that Sheriff Dewey Colvard of Etowah County requested that state troopers remain in the city indefinitely. In a rare showing of both sides of the civil rights story, the newspaper also said demonstrators had complained of police brutality when officers broke up the sit-in on the courthouse lawn. It also reported that Lingo "denied his men struck anyone with billy clubs."[34] However, the story made no mention of the cattle prods. Throughout the summer, the local newspaper kept up its criticism of national media coverage, continuing to quote local and state officials under such headlines as "Angry Mayor Wants Probe of Newspaper."[35]

Mayor Gilliland had sent the Federal Communications Commission (FCC) a telegram to request an investigation of the *Brooklyn Eagle* for its "lies about Gadsden."[36] The *Eagle* had apparently mistaken Dothan, Alabama, for Gadsden in a story about civil rights demonstrations. Alabama state representative Ollie Nabors wrote a resolution that called on "[U.S.] Congress to determine whether any violations were made of Federal Communications Commission laws or other federal matters," according to the article published on the front page of the *Gadsden Times*. Apparently, the mayor did not realize that the FCC regulated electronic media such as radio or television, but exercised no authority over the print media. In a story quoting Mayor Gilliland, the newspaper reported he had consulted with lawyers about how to punish the press for its coverage of the demonstrations. The report confirmed, "He said city legal brains have been instructed to 'go to work' on legal procedures."[37] The mayor of Gadsden, Alabama, was determined to seek redress from a New York newspaper for writing what he saw as disparaging stories about him and his town.

City officials no doubt were aware of the *Sullivan* case working its way through the courts, then in its third year. The *Gadsden Times* splashed in its pages AP stories filed from Montgomery about the libel suit against the *New York Times* and the black ministers.[38] Another libel case out of Atlanta received big headlines across the South, including in Gadsden. The *Saturday Evening Post* was fighting a losing battle in a libel case arising from a gaff of an article headlined "The Story of a College Football Fix." The writer used unreliable sourcing to accuse University of Alabama football coach Bear Bryant of "fixing" a game with Wally Butts, the athletic director at the University of Georgia.[39]

The *Post*'s owner, Philadelphia-based Curtis Publishing, had long faced declining circulation figures and advertising revenues. So its editors had tried to reverse course by turning the flagship *Saturday Evening Post* into a "sophisticated muckraker."[40] Some sloppy journalism followed, including this piece. The story was big news. Newspaper editors across Alabama and Georgia knew football icons Bear Bryant and Wally Butts were heroes in their respective states. The *Gadsden Times* ran bold front-page headlines above the fold: "BUTTS WINS $3 MILLION"; and "'I Feel Like A Champ' Smiling Wally States after Jury's Verdict." Perhaps, the success of Wally Butts's libel suit inspired Gadsden officials to file their own case against Curtis Publishing, a northern media company, and led them to believe they too could win damages in court.

Mayor Gilliland filed his libel suit in August 1963. In a national television broadcast that same month, when the movie stars had zoomed into town, ABC News in New York had erroneously attributed quotes praising the civil rights demonstrators to Mayor Gilliland rather than Marlon Brando. ABC said Gilliland described the civil rights movement as a grassroots democratic movement that would sweep the nation. Local journalists at the *Gadsden*

Times crowed their glee for days in their news pages when the mayor announced his intention to sue ABC for $1 million for the error and promised to donate the jury award to the city's general treasury. "I'm fed up with this sort of thing," said Gilliland. He instructed city attorney Roy Davis McCord to prepare the suit, and he told the *Gadsden Times* that he didn't know whether the suit would be filed on his or the city's behalf.[41]

News outlets normally don't report that someone is considering a lawsuit. Typically, it isn't news; anybody can threaten to file one. The convention in journalism is to wait until the suit is filed, then write about it. The *Gadsden Times* featured a much-longer story when the suit was filed four days later. The suit charged that the 12:55 p.m. broadcast on August 23 beamed from New York and played over local AM radio station WGAD was "false, untrue and was maliciously uttered with the desire to bring ridicule and disrespect to the city and its mayor." City attorney McCord told the *Gadsden Times* that the ABC report caused "serious damage to the governmental functions of our city, the state and the nation and contributed to the race relations problems in Gadsden."[42] The suit charged that the Hollywood actors were "agitators who came to Gadsden to increase agitation, disorder and violence." The money from the suit would go to the city's general treasury, McCord said.

The *Gadsden Times* quoted the city attorney complaining generally about outside media for making things worse in Gadsden. The newspaper also pointed out how local coverage had been much different from national coverage, quoting McCord: "Our local news media have done a wonderful job in carrying the factual news and are to be commended for their genuine efforts and cooperation."[43] So really it was just a matter of time before ABC News would find itself in the crosshairs of frustrated city leaders intent on maintaining the racial status quo. The second libel suit from Gadsden came from Sheriff Dewey Colvard, and like *Sullivan*, this case arose out of criticism of police brutality against civil rights demonstrators.

March on Washington Flashback: Sheriff Dewey Colvard's Cow Prods

The famous playwright Lillian Hellman sat against a marble column on the steps of the Lincoln Memorial, watching television camera crews setting up to film the March on Washington. It was 7 a.m., and she enjoyed the cool morning air while waiting to meet up with the grandson of her beloved childhood nurse, a black woman named Sophronia Mason. On freelance assignment for *Ladies' Home Journal,* she'd planned to sprinkle her coverage of the big event in Washington, D.C., with memories of her childhood in New Orleans for the December issue of the magazine. Wanting a southern perspective, editors had commissioned Hellman, a noted figure in the American theater for forty years, writing in an introduction to her article: "For a present day assessment we decided to turn away from cold political analysts, seeing instead the artist, whose insights probe the true humanity of events." In "Sophronia's Grandson Goes to Washington," Hellman wove into her story about the march her attempt to meet up with a young Alabama protester, Sophronia's grandson, who had agreed to rendezvous on the steps below Mr. Lincoln.[44]

She didn't know it at the time, but his bus wouldn't arrive until that afternoon. The planned meeting, Hellman wrote, had brought back memories of the South's searing racism and her own memories of rebelling against it. She wrote: "I realized again how deep were my roots in the South, how I had loved it and not loved it, and how so much of me had been molded by a Negro woman, and molded to last for good." When her family moved to New York City, they couldn't afford to take Sophronia with them, but Hellman returned home to visit her most years until Sophronia died when Hellman was twenty-five years old and becoming a noted New York intellectual. She had rebelled against her mother's "rich, middle-class" Alabama family and instead took inspiration from her father's side. She considered his family "a group of rather mixed-up eccentrics" who "deeply believed in the equality of the Negro." Most certainly it was Sophronia who opened Hellman's eyes to the injustices of racism and molded her into a bit of a rebel and most certainly a liberal. As she aimed to blend the personal and political for the *Ladies' Home Journal* article, she sent Sophronia's grandson money for the bus ticket—although that detail was not in the article. They did not find each other in the sea of demonstrators, but she found a considerable amount material in her interviews with other marchers, focusing on three youths from Gadsden, Alabama.[45]

In a flashback sequence, she wrote about these youths, who made the long bus ride from Gadsden, and their descriptions of what they had endured back home as part of the civil rights revolution. She wrote about police officers using electric cattle prods on black protesters who had a lay-in at the Etowah County courthouse in Gadsden. One of the young men said of the electric shocks: "It's just awful when you're sweating, it's just awful how it comes through you. But nobody screamed except one boy when they put the cow prodders to his pants. You know, the place in his pants."[46]

The youths told her that when they were hauled to the Alabama State Penitentiary, guards crammed 175 people in one big room with no beds or cover and dirty food twice a day. Two other boys got sick, so they pled to the police for help. "We asked the sheriff for a doctor we knew, but he said no nigger doctor was coming into his jail," Hellman quoted the youngster without identifying him. Eventually, the sick boys were taken to the hospital. Hellman wrote, "Another sheriff and two cops came, saying to him, 'You, boy, are you really sick or just making up?' The boy said he wasn't going to answer. That made them mad, so they got out their electric cow prodders right in the hospital room and put them to the boy, and all he could do was lie there and holler." Hellman asked her source how the boy fared, and the youngster told her that his friend "still drags his legs, and the doctor said maybe he always would." A teen girl at the march also told Hellman that police put the prod to her breast during the protest in Gadsden.[47]

Hellman then quoted Alabama senator John Sparkman claiming that the use of cow prods on protestors was nothing new in police departments. He also complained to her that the northern press always played down the racial unrest in the North and that the only injuries from demonstrations in Alabama so far were sustained by the police. Hellman wrote: "The Southern answer is often an attack on the hypocrisy of the North, and has been since the Civil War. . . . I went out of the Senate Office Building thinking that the argument for states' rights was now reduced to the argument for the right of each police department to act as it saw fit." After she filed her story, editors at *Ladies' Home Journal* were thrilled with the imagery, introducing the article with an editor's note: "Miss Hellman brought to the march the clear eye of a trained observer, the sensitivity and skill of one of America's major dramatists, and the tempered affection for the South that characterizes her work in such plays as *The Little Foxes, Another Part of the Forest,* and *Toys in the Attic.*"[48]

Editor Caskie Stinnett sent Hellman an edited copy of the article marked with only minor changes before it was published in December 1963. He gushed: "I can't say that I'm surprised at receiving such a fine article from you because I was quite sure that we would, but I wanted you to know that I was genuinely delighted."[49] Before Hellman's story ran in the magazine, another *Journal* editor, Davis Thomas, praised her work in a personal note to her: "It's a wonderful piece—filled with meaning and beautifully writen [sic], and I'm proud to publish it in our magazine. All I can add is a question—when will you feel able to undertake another assignment for us?"[50]

The people in Gadsden—and other readers across the South—were not so happy with Hellman's article. Angry letters poured into the editorial offices on Fifth Avenue in New York City. Mrs. T. R. Gribon of Montgomery, Alabama, defended the police tactics described in Hellman's article:

> Use of electric prods and tear gas have never been classified as brutish acts and they are both harmless. Rather it is a humane method of mob control and never permanently harms anyone. The riot police are trained with the hopes that they will never be needed, but they are called only in times of trouble. They are taught their first duty is to protect life and property. They are never

used in any other place than to control mobs.... The incident of the "lay-in" on the courthouse lawn at night in Gadsden, Alabama was a disgrace to the entire Negro race. People passing in automobiles and on the streets reported the disgraceful actions of these people. The police tried in every reasonable way to get them to go home and as a last resort used the electric cow prodders. To a reasonable thinking person it would seem appropriate that if people acted like cattle then they should be treated like cattle.

Gribon also doubted the veracity of Hellman's reportage: "The 'hospital' incident simply could not have happened.... It is gross misrepresentations such as the writing of Miss Hellman and the grossly exaggerated stories about Birmingham that cause misunderstanding and bad feelings among the Negro people. Our good Negro citizens differentiate between the truth and distortions they read, and the kindest thing I can say about Miss Hellman is that she has a great imagination."[51]

Another reader, who signed her letter "A Southern Lady Ex-subscriber," noted her "increasing discontent" in the magazine over the last two years. "But an article in the December issue which arrived today is the last straw! 'Sophronia's Grandson Goes to Washington.' Really! And in the Christmas issue, too, which is ordinarilly [sic] so full of good cheer.... This is still a Ladies' Home Journal?" Yet another angry reader, Ruby Richardson of Florence, Alabama, wrote of the damage Hellman's article—and others like it—had caused southern society. She fumed, "The colored people are losing all their pride in their race and their respect for white people. A few colored and a few white are causing all the trouble. There is a dividing line now that separates friends and neighbors not races."[52] Another disgruntled reader, Mrs. A. W. Carnes of Birmingham, labeled the magazine's editors as serious troublemakers: "I have today notified Publishers Clearing House to cancel my subscription to your magazine.... I do not wish to give support to a paper of your type. We could well do without The Curtis Publishing Company and it is my wish to see you disbanded [sic]. I would very much like to see the House Unamerican [sic] Activities investigate your works."[53]

Hellman did not name names in her story, but Etowah County

sheriff Dewey Floyd Colvard was outraged by the article too. He charged Curtis Publishing with libeling him, specifically citing Hellman's descriptions of police brutality in his jurisdiction. In the March 1964 issue of *Ladies' Home Journal*, editors ran the lengthy demand for a retraction penned by Colvard's attorney, Roy D. McCord, who was also Gadsden's city attorney and the lawyer representing the mayor in his libel suit against ABC. McCord objected to Hellman's descriptions of police operation, especially the references to cattle prods and mistreatment of prisoners in the penitentiary and hospital. McCord wrote: "The article, as written and published, is slanderous, false and untrue, and as such Attorney I demand a full retraction of not only the above matters but all other printed insinuations and slurs against my clients, the Sheriff of Etowah County, Alabama, and his deputies."[54]

Editors published his letter in full along with the requested retraction. "As requested by Mr. McCord, attorney for Sheriff Colvard and his deputies, the Ladies' Home Journal and its publisher retract all statements complained of in 'Sophronia's Grandson Goes to Washington.'" Once a prosperous trailblazer in the magazine industry, the struggling Curtis Publishing was eager to stay out of court. Curtis was drowning in litigation, and by the end of 1963, the company was facing almost $30 million in libel suits.[55] So when the Gadsden sheriff threatened to sue, the gun-shy Curtis was quick to issue that retraction.

Colvard filed suit in March 1964, the same month Curtis issued the retraction. McCord took the papers to the courthouse about two weeks after the U.S. Supreme Court overturned the *Sullivan* decision, making it much more difficult for public official plaintiffs to win such a case. The Colvard suit is strikingly similar to the *Sullivan* case. Police commissioner L. B. Sullivan hadn't been named in the *New York Times* advertisement that detailed the police treatment of protesters in Alabama. Likewise, Hellman named no public authorities in her article. Both lawmen, Colvard and Sullivan, however, insisted the pieces describing police violence against protesters referred to and disparaged their conduct as officers of the law. Both demanded a retraction and both sued.

In court documents, Colvard said the "sensational" story was "wholly untrue and not founded in fact," and demanded $1 million in compensatory and $2 million in punitive damages.[56]

Like Sullivan, Sheriff Colvard had been long accustomed to getting favorable media attention, especially from the *Gadsden Times*. Thin and dapper in a dark suit and tie, his rugged, crinkly face was not an uncommon sight in the local news. Typically, he'd have his picture taken with a new technological gadget, such as the department's first polygraph machine or a new radio system, with the newspaper boasting about his being on top of the latest techniques and technologies in law enforcement. Colvard was a hometown hero, born and raised in Gadsden, serving in World War II in the Pacific, then working at the local Goodyear Tire and Rubber Company before going into law enforcement. Beginning in January 1952, Colvard served as constable, a typical title for a small-town police officer, for six years before being elected sheriff in 1959. He and his wife, Virginia, raised two boys, Wayne and Jimmy, in Gadsden.[57]

Colvard and McCord probably had good reason to think they would win the case. Sprinkled throughout the news in the previous year, including page one of the *Gadsden Times*, were stories of Curtis Publishing defending itself against the $10 million libel suit filed by Bear Bryant for the story in the *Saturday Evening Post*. Birmingham lawyer Eric Embry, also on the *New York Times*' defense team in the *Sullivan* suit, represented Curtis in the Bryant libel suit. He would defend Curtis in the suit arising from Hellman's article in *Ladies' Home Journal.* In the fall of 1963, Embry argued that Curtis Publishing couldn't get a fair trial in the state of Alabama, and a play-by-play of the Butts and Bryant cases was covered extensively in wire stories that ran in the *Gadsden Times* and other newspapers across the state. He argued it would be impossible to find an unbiased jury with Bear Bryant as plaintiff. He introduced in the Bryant trial evidence, five thick volumes, that contained seventy-seven newspaper stories attacking the *Saturday Evening Post*'s article about the alleged 1962 football fix. A federal jury in Atlanta had already awarded the former Georgia athletic director, Wally Butts, $3 million in damages. Embry argued before federal judge Hobard H. Grooms that the *Saturday Evening Post* and Curtis Publishing had been vilified by the Alabama media for the magazine's coverage of the civil rights movement since 1954. Surely McCord and Colvard saw this coverage and viewed Hellman's article as a chance to cash in on a lucrative legal trend and punish the liberal media.

The bellicose Hellman was furious that *Ladies' Home Journal* refused to stand by her. Editors gave her space to make a statement below McCord's letter demanding a retraction and below their own retraction. Hellman's note read:

> I was evidently misinformed about minor matters of fact. For example, I quoted the young Negroes from Gadsden as saying that a boy who was lying in a hospital bed had cow prodders put to him by a sheriff and two cops. Curtis Publishing Company has been informed by the Sheriff of Etowah County that neither he nor his deputies used cow prodders on the boy. I therefore wish to apologize to Mr. Colvard because, as a white woman born in the South and whose roots are most affectionately there, I do not blame any white Southerner for not wishing to be unjustly involved. But the fact remains that the cow prodders were used on the boy I wrote about by men I cannot identify at this minute of going to press. My article, in all important matters, tells the truth and I wish to disassociate myself from the above retraction. What is true should not be obscured by fear of lawsuits.[58]

Hellman's personal diary included even more violent details related to her by the protestors.[59] She had noted the increasing use of libel to assail coverage of the civil rights movement, complaining in a letter to a friend, "These law suits [*sic*] are getting to be regulation stuff in an attempt to shut up the press." She then joked, "I am off to do some more harm by covering the Pope's visit to Israel and Jordan and when I come back I hope we can all meet."[60] That visit to the Holy Land was an assignment for *Ladies' Home Journal,* which heralded the piece the next month in the April issue.[61]

Linked with many left-wing causes, Hellman was known for her strong personality and for standing by her convictions. For that, she had been blacklisted in Hollywood during the 1950s when she refused to denounce friends who had been labeled communists. Widely considered America's leading female playwright, Hellman had a thirty-year career on Broadway, writing about characters set in Alabama, along the Gulf Coast, and in New Orleans. She also wrote movie scripts for a time in Hollywood.[62]

After seeing the retraction and Hellman's note in the magazine, an angry writer from Mobile, Alabama, raged at *Ladies' Home Journal* editors, piling on more criticism: "Lillian Hellman's birth was a geographical accident; she is not a Southerner. She obviously is not a good Christian either or she could not so easily excuse her slanderous defamation of Mr. Dewey Colvard's character with the airy statement. 'I was evidently misinformed about minor matters of fact.' Minor indeed! With comrades like her working to drive the wedge between races and sections of this wonderful country, America doesn't need outside enemies."[63]

The *Gadsden Times* closely followed Sheriff Colvard's libel suit, eagerly defending him in its news columns. In a front-page story, editors ran an article headlined "Magazine Admits Article on City, Area Was Untrue," printing verbatim a telegram dispatched from *Ladies' Home Journal* editor Davis Thomas to Colvard's lawyers.[64] Although the *Gadsden Times* article, written by staff writer Mary Hoffman, appeared to be a news story, it was steeped in opinion, again railing against the northern media. In the second sentence, Hoffman complained the *Journal*'s "lies pertain to the South in general and to the Gadsden-Attalla area in particular." The lengthy story, which jumped to the second page, read: "Indignant citizens of the community, many of whom have already cancelled their subscriptions to the magazine, will regard the retraction as acknowledgment that alleged incidents described by Lillian Hellman as having actually occurred, did not happen and could not have happened as Miss Hellman pictured them." The article complained that Hellman "has long enjoyed picturing the South as a region of . . . immorality and dry rot." The *Times* heaped more praise on the sheriff and continued to scold *Ladies' Home Journal* in several more paragraphs: "Sheriff Colvard is to be commended for placing this matter in the hands of an attorney and demanding a hearing in the name of truth and decency. Once again, The Times feel [sic] that the time for a newspaper or magazine to check on facts is before malice and lies have done their work, but it is delighted that the retraction is to be 'unqualified.'"[65]

In order to win this case, Curtis among other things had to prove in its defense that what Hellman wrote was true. Did, for example, Colvard and his deputies use cattle prods to control demonstrators? It was well documented that the police across the South employed them against demonstrators, and Hellman would have had no reason to doubt the youths who told her about the police prodding and shocking them. Colonel Lingo of the Alabama State Patrol brought cattle prods to Gadsden during that summer in 1963 in an effort to quell hundreds of demonstrators marching through the city day after day, the same protests that Hellman wrote about in the magazine. A *Gadsden Times* reporter's account most certainly would not have vilified the police the way Sheriff Colvard felt demonized by *Ladies' Home Journal*. In coverage of those protests held the summer before, June 1963, reporter M. L. Ray wrote in the *Gadsden Times* that law enforcement did indeed use those prods, according to the play-by-play account via the local story, but it was likely the state police rather than the sheriff's deputies who used the weapons. Perhaps a protester would not recognize the difference between a local sheriff's deputy and a state trooper, particularly if they wore riot gear.

Colonel Lingo became legendary for his brutality. He strutted about during demonstrations in Alabama's hot spots, decked out in helmet and uniform and carrying a nightstick on his belt. Later in the *Gadsden Times* story about the local protests, the reporter brought up the use of cattle prods again during the summer demonstrations. He wrote: "A majority of the Negroes turned and started to leave the area around the steps. Only a small handful remained. Members of the riot squad began prodding the Negroes who were leaving the courthouse steps. The demonstrators again resisted the prodding and a few intense moments of club-swinging ensued in which several Negroes, both men and women, were beaten to the ground. One girl, apparently trying to return to the steps[,] was driven back by three patrolmen into a cluster of bushes along the front sidewalk." It's possible that Sheriff Colvard—rather than the state troopers—had control over the prisoners once they were hauled off to jail. Hellman quotes the demonstrators' reference to the "sheriff" and they refer to more than one sheriff, so it is likely that these were probably sheriff's deputies working for Colvard, but it is impossible to be sure.

The U.S. Supreme Court had by then established the actual malice rule in *Sullivan*. In order for a public-official plaintiff such as Sheriff Colvard to win, he would need to prove that Hellman had written that story with the knowledge that it was false, or that she should have known its falsity. Demonstrating actual malice would have been very difficult for Colvard to do. And the debate over whether the story was true or false continued to rage among *Ladies' Home Journal* readers in letters to the editor. One New York City reader, Lorraine Hansberry, complained about the retraction and insisted that the gist of the story was true: "We are all being mocked when the words 'sheriff' or 'deputies' are allowed to confuse events." She quoted a *New York Times* article, published on June 19, 1963, and datelined Gadsden, Alabama, about police brutality during the demonstrations: "State troopers swinging nightsticks and wielding electrically charged prod poles, drove more than 300 demonstrators from the Etowah County courthouse lawn early today. The state police summoned by the local authorities clubbed and jabbed Negroes who did not move away from the courthouse fast enough."[66]

Hansberry pointed out that Hellman was quoting in good faith what the civil rights protesters told her. "Are we now to suppose that victims of this brutishness, young boys and girls, must be as precise as seasoned journalists of what may be the world's most meticulous newsgathering agency? That those on whom a club or cattle prod is being used are not being objective enough to note whether that particular grisly caricature of 'law enforcement' is a 'state trooper' or 'local police'? It is as if we were now to disregard the Diary of Anne Frank because she misspelled the names of her oppressors or said they arrived to arrest her and her family on the wrong day!" Hansberry's defense of Hellman, argued for two typewritten pages, insisted she had been treated unjustly for reporting about widely known police brutality in the South: "Sly attacks on infinitesimal particulars in her report are not only an affront to her personally but to the highest levels of American culture. . . . The truth is that bestial and inhuman acts are committed daily by law enforcement officials in the South and there are, these days, few of us left who do not know it. It is also the truth that American Negroes are in such an aggrieved and desperate mood, watching the cream of our youth get their heads split open in trying to achieve rights which are already on the books of this nation. . . ."[67]

Another reader, Louise Davis, from Indian Rocks Beach, Florida, typed a postcard to Hellman after she read the *Ladies' Home Journal* retraction. "Good for you for not subscribing to the retraction—I do so admire people who have the courage of their convictions!" she wrote. "There are so few of them, nowadays. Working, as I do, among the Negro people here, I haven't the slightest doubt that what you wrote about is true. What does surprise me, is that the caliber of the Ladies' Home Journal staff would not rather make a thorough investigation, rather than make a retraction. I wish I knew if they did investigate or just 'chickened out.' Of course, law suits [*sic*] are horribly expensive, but then, integrity should never be for sale. I think you were brave to write the article, and God bless you in any future work taking much courage."[68] Another reader, Mrs. Floyd D. Lofland Jr. of Colorado Springs, Colorado, asked editors for more coverage of race issues: "I fear for the South if the white cannot learn to accept the Negro as an equal—but what of the Negro who cannot control his feeling of resentment for not having had complete freedom all his life? Where is the answer to our problem? Could you publish more articles of this kind to help your readers to understand both sides of the situation?"[69]

Like other members of the northern media who had been sued for libel in Alabama, Curtis Publishing had tried to get the case thrown out for lack of jurisdiction.[70] Alabama courts, however, had consistently rejected that idea. By the end of 1964, as Curtis was scrambling to settle out of court, the company reported a net loss of $4.2 million for the third quarter of that year and an operating deficit of $8 million for the first half of the year.[71] Colvard had originally filed suit in the Circuit Court of Etowah County, but Curtis was successful in securing transfer of the case to U.S. District Court for the Northern District of Alabama, citing conflict-of-interest concerns given that Colvard would be party to a libel case in his home county.[72]

Many Gadsden residents had a negative view of the March on Washington. The *Gadsden Times* had griped about it in an editorial on the eve of the event. The march would likely be violent, the editorial warned. And it was unthinkable that President Kennedy could actually sanction the demonstration.[73] The newspaper also ran several wire stories about trains and buses heading toward nation's capital, with crowds estimated in the hundreds of thousands. Another AP story focused on how the trip to Washington would be expensive for many of the marchers.[74] The bottom line was that the March on Washington was a big national story on the civil rights front, and Gadsden officials were livid that Hellman found a local angle for the *Ladies' Home Journal* story. With the timing of the *Sullivan* decision, however, the law was now on Curtis Publishing's side. Just like Commissioner Sullivan, Sheriff Colvard was an elected police official, and like Sullivan, he sued despite not being named in an article about police brutality. A federal judge in Birmingham dismissed the suit six months after the actual malice doctrine was articulated by the U.S. Supreme Court.[75] This ruling was one of the fastest responses to *Sullivan* by a southern court, and Colvard, unlike Bull Connor, did not appeal.

The sheriff went on to an unprecedented five terms in office. After being hospitalized for an unexplained seizure while on vacation in Panama City, Florida, he died in July 1974 at age fifty-eight before beginning that fifth term. His wife, Virginia Colvard, was appointed by Governor George Wallace to be the county's first female sheriff to finish out the calendar year and until a new election could be held. Dewey Colvard was the only sheriff in county history to be elected without opposition and the only elected to a fourth term much less a fifth.[76] It is unlikely that he felt defamed by Hellman's article.

Freedom Summer, 1964: *Mississippi Burning*

Of all the southern lawmen of the civil rights era, Sheriff Lawrence Rainey of Neshoba County, Mississippi, certainly was among the most litigious. Over a twenty-year period, Rainey filed six libel suits against the media, all stemming from coverage about his possible involvement in the notorious murders of three civil rights workers during Freedom Summer 1964. Rainey was suspected but never convicted of the crime, which garnered national attention, became a defining moment in the civil rights movement, and later was the subject of the 1988 movie *Mississippi Burning*. Rainey was dismayed to find himself portrayed as the villain of the story rather than the hero.

The three civil rights workers, Michael Schwerner and Andrew Goodman, white men from New York City, and James Chaney of Meridian, Mississippi, who was black, were in Neshoba County to investigate the burning of a black church that was also a base for voter-registration drives. It was June 1964, Freedom Summer, and hundreds of civil rights volunteers headed South to set up schools and work voter-registration drives in the state. Volumes have been written about what happened the night of June 21, 1964. Cecil R. Price, Rainey's only deputy, stopped the civil rights workers' car and hauled the men to jail in Philadelphia, booking them on speeding charges and for allegedly burning the church themselves. After several hours in jail, they were released and then disappeared into the night. Six weeks later, federal authorities discovered their bodies buried in an earthen dam in Neshoba County, after receiving a tip from a paid informant.[77]

It was widely speculated that Deputy Price and members of the Ku Klux Klan killed the three men, but no state charges were ever filed. Federal authorities instead brought suit in 1965 against Rainey, Price, and sixteen others for violating the civil rights of the three workers.[78] The Federal Bureau of Investigation said Sam Bowers, the Klan's imperial wizard, gave the order to eliminate Schwerner, whom the KKK had nicknamed "Goatee." The FBI said the murders were planned and organized with Edgar Ray Killen, Bowers's right-hand man in the eastern Mississippi KKK, along with other Klansmen. Rainey and seven other defendants were acquitted of the charges. Price, Bowers, and five others were convicted. The jury could not agree on the remaining men, all suspected Klansmen.[79]

The murders and trial captured the nation's attention and spawned scores of articles and books. But the era of D. W. Griffith's wildly successful film, *Birth of a Nation,* had long since passed. In 1915, the film's heroic cavalry, dressed in white sheets, saved white purity from black contamination in the post–Civil War South. But some fifty years later, the Klan faced criticism even in some southern newspapers. Still other regional publications maintained a stony silence. This time, it was not the Negro that was evil, according to many mainstream reports. It was the white sheriff, his deputy and the white sheet-bedecked local rabble. Sheriff Rainey hired James McIntyre, his lawyer in the federal case, and started filing libel suits. In 1966, Rainey, Price, and Neshoba justice of the peace Leonard Warren sued the New York Herald Tribune Company, WCC Books, and William Bradford Huie for the latter's news articles and his book, *Three Lives for Mississippi.*[80] Rainey sought $3 million in damages, claiming that thirty-three separate passages in the book libeled him. For example, Huie wrote that most of the violence against civil rights workers and blacks occured in small towns like Philadelphia and McComb, with the larger cities being "relatively safe for 'agitators.'" The big-city politicians know "the smart way to resist 'agitators' in Mississippi is not to break their heads but to protect them and let time and circumstance break their hearts. The men with power in Mississippi know this. Only the peckerwood politicians and the jerks in the backwoods don't know it."[81]

Rainey also objected to the characterization of Neshoba as a "maximum-danger county." Huie wrote that the three civil rights workers "knew it was one of the counties where the sheriff had been elected on the promise that he'd 'handle the niggers and the outsiders.' They knew the sheriff and his only deputy had friends who were Ku Klux types."[82] Huie also quoted an anonymous elderly black resident of Neshoba discussing the presence of the media and the outside civil rights workers for the summer. He told Huie: "When you leave, then it gets might [sic] lonesome out here. There ain't nobody under these pine trees except us and the big man with guns buckled on and the red light flashing on top of his big car."[83]

Deputy Price filed identical libel suits against the New York Herald Tribune Company, WCC Books, and Huie, also seeking $3 million.[84] He objected to thirty-one separate passages in Huie's book. Among them: "Sheriff's deputy Cecil Price believed he was protecting the State of Mississippi, and acting in its best interest, when he arrested Michael Schwerner and when he delivered him to his murderers."[85] Justice of the Peace Leonard Warren also sought $3 million, objecting to fifteen specific passages in Huie's book and the general implication that he was involved in the murders. Huie had described Warren this way: "A third, but not usually uniformed, law-enforcement figure at the courthouse is Justice of the Peace Leonard Warren. His office is in the courthouse, and most miscreants are brought before him. He attracts attention by being the physical opposite of Rainey and Price: skinny, no more than 140 pounds, chicken-necked, with a prominent Adam's apple. He, too, likes to don the cattleman's hat, the gun, and the nightstick and work as a part-time cop."[86]

Like Price and Rainey, Warren objected to being called a "white supremacy terrorist" and to Huie's description of "a Master Plan for Protection" that the killers were to have carried out.[87] Huie described the four-part plan for maintaining the racial status quo, each "successively more violent, with all plans 'activated as necessary.'" Plan one involved cross-burnings and leaflets; plan two progressed to arson and dynamite; plan three called for whippings;

plan four advocated extermination. Huie wrote: "During the second week in May 1964 a decision to activate Plan Four was reached by a group of terrorists in Mississippi." The target was "the Jew-Boy with the beard," Mickey Schwerner.[88] Clearly, the traditional lynching, a public spectacle of racial honor and terror, was no longer hailed as heroic and acceptable in polite southern society. While the northern press condemned the murder of the three civil rights workers, most of the southern press remained silent.

Suing for libel had become a fashionable thing by this time, and other Neshoba County Klan members (as identified by the FBI) filed more SLAPP suits against the press. Of the nineteen men indicted on federal conspiracy charges, five sued Time, Inc., publisher of *Life* magazine for a December 1964 article identifying them as members of the Klan. Bernard Lee Akin, his son Earl, along with Tommy Horne, James Thomas Harris, and Oliver Warner Jr., said that their business pursuits had been damaged by the *Life* story about the slaying of the three civil rights workers. Represented by former Birmingham mayor Arthur Hanes, each sought $1 million in damages. Federal judge Seybourn H. Lynne of Birmingham dismissed the cases in February 1966 because they missed the one-year statute of limitations by one day.[89]

The questions of whether Sheriff Rainey was a public official, public figure, or private citizen for libel purposes would plague him for a quarter century after the murders. If the court found him to be a public figure, he would have to prove actual malice, meaning that the defendants published with knowledge of falsity or reckless disregard for the truth. If Rainey was classified as a private citizen, the standard of fault—negligence—would be much lower and much easier for the plaintiff to prove. The law was against him, but he also was his own worst enemy. Emerging as a southern folk hero to the locals, Rainey basked in his legend immediately following his arrest on December 4, 1964. He told reporters at the time, "It took me an hour to get to work today, I had to shake so many hands."[90] In essence, Rainey had said the publicity surrounding the murder of civil rights activists improved a white man's status in the South in the 1960s. So how could he have been defamed by the coverage that followed?

The sheriff certainly enjoyed support from local media. Situated about forty miles south of Philadelphia, Mississippi, the *Meridian Star* editorialized after the murders: "The student volunteers, the beatniks, the wild-eyed left wing nuts, the unshaven and unwashed . . . go on meddling and muddling. The poison pen sweepings of the gutters of journalism go on printing their lying trash. . . ."[91] The *Neshoba Democrat* editor Jack Tannehill complimented the sheriff this way: "When he sees a drunk nigger on the street, instead of just grabbing him, Lawrence will say, 'Now, boy, you get on home now 'fore I have to run you in.' That's the kind of man Lawrence Rainey is."[92]

But broad national and even international coverage of the murders had seared Rainey's image into the American consciousness. Especially memorable and unflattering was the famous photograph of a smirking Rainey stuffing a huge wad of Red Man tobacco in his mouth during his arraignment in the federal case in which he was accused of violating the three workers' civil rights. After that image appeared in magazines and newspapers across the country, Pinkerton Tobacco Company, based in Toledo, Ohio, mailed Rainey a complimentary case of Red Man. The famous Rainey also appeared in advertisements for a Mississippi chiropractor. But when his term as sheriff ended in 1967, the term-limited lawman said he couldn't find a job.[93]

He sued *Time* magazine for libel the next year, claiming that he had a "priceless, untarnished, and unblemished and unassailable reputation" when yet another article was published.[94] Rainey sought $50,000, claiming his reputation had been ruined by a story that suggested he was a "Klan sympathizer or member" and that the story erroneously said he was convicted with Bowers and five other codefendants of violating the three workers' civil rights.[95] The following passage published in the February 1968 *Time* article was the crux of the complaint and seemed to be more about a Klan lawyer who did not even represent Rainey: "Whenever Ku Klux Klansmen needed legal aid in Mississippi, they invariably turned to Lawyer Travis Buckley. A cocky, stocky, pugnacious little man with jug ears, Buckley, 35, was chief defense attorney in last October's trial of Imperial Wizard Sam Bowers, Neshoba County Sheriff

Lawrence Rainey, and 17 others accused of conspiring to kill three civil rights workers in 1964. Bowers and six co-defendants were convicted, but Buckley filed an appeal that has kept them all out of jail. Next on his agenda was the defense of Bowers—and another gang of Klansmen—in the fire-bomb murder of Vernon Dahmer, a Hattiesburg, Miss., N.A.A.C.P. official. As always, Buckley was outwardly confident." Once again, Rainey turned to James McIntyre, his lawyer in the civil rights cases, to represent him. In 1969, five years after *Sullivan,* a U.S. District judge in Meridian dismissed Rainey's case against *Time*. The magazine argued successfully that Rainey was a public official when the events took place and that he remained a public figure after vacating the Neshoba County Sheriff's Office. As such, he had to prove that *Time* acted with actual malice by knowingly publishing false information or acting with reckless disregard for the truth. Rainey was unable to meet that legal standard.[96]

Undeterred by his loss to *Time*, Rainey filed other libel suits, moving from the written word to made-for-TV movies. Along with Price, Rainey sued CBS and the producers of the television movie *Attack on Terror: The FBI versus the Ku Klux Klan in Mississippi.* Price and Rainey sued when it first aired in 1975 and again when it was broadcast late-night in 1977. Each plaintiff sought $1.5 million in compensatory and punitive damages for each broadcast. In its defense, CBS said producers consulted with FBI officials involved in the case, relied on government documents and uncontested court testimony in telling the story, which was based on Don Whitehead's book of the same name. The film was made in good faith, without actual malice, attorneys for CBS asserted. It did not use Rainey's or Price's names or the names of the town or county where the murders occurred. In this post-*Sullivan* world of libel, CBS also argued that the story involved the actions of public officials in the recent past and was a matter of public interest.[97] Rainey and Price again had the burden of proving that CBS acted with knowledge of falsity or reckless disregard for the truth.

This was not the only difficulty for them in the CBS case. The pair had signed releases in 1968, giving actor Jack Lemmon and his Jalem Productions the right to use "the character, personality, physical attributes and/or biographical information concerning me and to portray in any way it deems appropriate."[98] In exchange for $6,000 apiece, both Rainey and Price agreed they would not sue for libel, slander, or invasion or right of privacy. The agreement even allowed Jalem to use the real names of the civil rights workers. Inexplicably, the agreement Rainey and Price had signed off on involved the making of the movie called "Three Lives for Mississippi," based on the book by Huie. Two years before, they had unsuccessfully sued the writer, claiming that the book had libeled them. The movie was never made, however, and CBS bought the rights originally purchased by Jalem. There was no stipulation in the agreement regarding the selling of those rights.

In his claim, Rainey said he was fired from his job as a security guard at a supermarket after the CBS's airing of *Attack on Terror* in 1975. He said when his term as sheriff ended in 1967, he "was refused employment in Mississippi and surrounding states because of the adverse publicity surrounding the trial."[99] Since then, Rainey said, he had worked at "numerous meager jobs," and after the publicity subsided he was able to find a job as a security guard at a grocery store owned by an African American man. His situation had been improving, Rainey said, until CBS brought up the murders again. Rainey complained that the film depicted him as "a person bent on violence, that he had conspired with others to kill and murder three human beings, and that he was and is guilty of un-American racial prejudice against persons of other than the White Race and guilty of conduct unbecoming to public officers." Further, he said CBS and the movie's director, Quinn Martin, portrayed him as "a white supremacy terrorist" and "a Ku Klux Klan sympathizer and/or member."[100]

Judge Harold Cox of the U.S. District Court, the judge who heard the Justice Department's conspiracy case against the murderers of Chaney, Goodman, and Schwerner, granted CBS's motion for a summary judgment in 1976, citing the *Sullivan* decision. He said the plaintiffs were public officials at the time, and the events depicted in the movie were of national interest. In dismissing the case, Cox pointed out that Rainey and Price did not claim the movie was false; "instead these plaintiffs complain only that eight years have passed and these defendants should have let sleeping dogs lie."[101]

Another made-for-TV-movie awakened still another sleeping dog in the 1970s, bringing yet another courtroom battle, this time initiated by the commander of the Alabama National Guard unit in Tuscaloosa charged with protecting the Scottsboro Boys. In 1931, nine black teens were accused of raping two white women aboard a freight train near Scottsboro, Alabama. The incident spawned a set of legal cases that highlighted issues of institutionalized racism and the right to a fair trial and that are commonly cited as one of the most egregious examples of the miscarriage of justice in American courts. In NBC's fictionalized adaptation of the case, *Judge Horton and the Scottsboro Boys*, which aired in April 1976, the judge in the case, unlike the rest of the town, comes to believe that the boys are innocent, setting them free against the advice of his friends and family. As a result, the community turns against him. In real life, all nine were sentenced to death but were eventually pardoned or paroled.

Colonel Joe W. Burleson of Tuscaloosa sued NBC and two affiliate stations in Alabama for $1.2 million after the broadcast, charging that the network portrayed him as "cowardly, unwilling to do his military duty, unable to maintain security and unwilling to protect the black defendants."[102] Bull Connor's attorney, Jim Simpson, served as Burleson's attorney. Unwilling to undertake a protracted legal battle, NBC settled the suit for $30,000 in March 1977.[103]

Buford Boone and the Imperial Wizard

Born in 1908, James Buford Boone grew up on his family's hundred-acre farm in Newnan, Georgia, picking cotton in the fields alongside a family of black tenant farmers. The denim overalls and straw hats of his youth were replaced with tweed jackets and bow ties as the clean-cut Boone headed to journalism school at Mercer College in Macon, Georgia, the geographic center of the state. The

Figure 6. A young Buford Boone grew up picking cotton on his family's farm outside Macon, Georgia. The unassuming editor of the *Tuscaloosa News* would become a powerful voice against the KKK in Alabama.
—The University of Alabama Libraries Special Collections.

bookish and spectacled Boone edited the student newspaper, the *Cluster,* and after graduation, he took his first job as a reporter for the *Macon Telegraph.*

With his unassuming demeanor, he wielded a powerful pen. Boone would become an unlikely foe for one of the most infamous white supremacists of the civil rights era.[104] Like most southern editors, Boone was never a liberal. Nor was he an integrationist. However, he would be considered a liberal extremist by his community for his editorial position that the U.S. Supreme Court's school desegregation orders must be obeyed by southern communities. Boone's ancestors were Confederates on both sides of the family, and a great-grandfather had been killed at Bull Run. But his grandfather, who also had been injured in the war and lived well into his nineties, slowly evolved to believe black people should be treated as human beings. The farmer and state legislator even said so publicly later in life and planted the seeds of justice that his grandson would grow years later.[105]

When the United States entered World War II, Boone left the *Macon Telegraph* to serve as a wartime special agent for the Federal Bureau of Investigation, writing speeches for J. Edgar Hoover. After the war, he returned to the *Telegraph* as managing editor before being wooed to the *Tuscaloosa News* as editor and publisher in 1947. As a young journalist, Boone had benefitted from strong mentors, notably Mark Ethridge, one of the South's most noted progressive editors, who had moved on to edit the *Louisville Courier-Journal* during the civil rights era.[106]

Two years after his arrival in Tuscaloosa, Boone startled many readers with his aggressive condemnation of the Ku Klux Klan in 1949. He wrote a four-part series exposing the local Klan's secret start-up meetings, asking how a group labeled "subversive" by the United States attorney general was able to meet in the Tuscaloosa County Courthouse on Friday nights.[107] He used an unnamed source attending the meetings to report the goings-on verbatim. At a meeting May 6, 1949, for example, Klansmen discussed a membership application from a "possible candidate for sheriff." Boone wrote that at another meeting, there was discussion about a local police officer who had to work the night shift and could not attend the gathering. During the meeting, Klansmen also complained about several undesirable situations in town, such as whites and blacks crowding into the same elevator at the First National Bank Building and how some black dishwashers in local restaurants laughed and talked with white waitresses.[108]

Boone also discussed the ceremonial elements of the meetings, referencing his interview with an anonymous member. He wrote somewhat mockingly that an entire meeting was used to demonstrate and practice the Klan's secret handshake.[109] After the series ran, Boone editorialized that the local Klansmen were "more than a little gullible. They are forking over $10 [dues] for the privilege of affiliating with an organization which in present times is becoming more and more a discredit to itself. . . . We wouldn't classify the members of the local Klan as hoodlums, although they could become hoodlums under the protection of their masks and robes."[110] Boone also wrote that he had a list of the members of the local Klan, about forty men, but had decided not to publish them "at present. We have placed the list in safekeeping. Whether it is brought out and published, or is given to law enforcement officers called upon to investigate illegal activities by hooded men in this area, will depend entirely upon the local Klan."[111]

The KKK responded with a demonstration of its own. With the help of the Birmingham Klavern, a group of 126 men donned their white robes and hoods and paraded around the *Tuscaloosa News* building on a steamy June night in 1949. But the Klan remained quiet in the months following the march, and other journalists praised Boone for putting the fledgling local group on the defensive before it got too bold.[112] In town, there was a flurry of discussion about the series, and some businesses selling the newspaper refused to display a *Tuscaloosa News* placard advertising the series. Some parents insisted their sons no longer work as newsboys, fearing they might be attacked.[113] Due mostly to Boone's editorials, the Klan disappeared into the night in central Alabama, for the time being.

By 1955, a year after the *Brown* decision, Tuscaloosa was a growing town of more than fifty thousand residents, a third of them black. A paper mill and rubber-manufacturing plant made the small city an industrial center that contrasted sharply with the nearby lush and lovely University of Alabama, which had more than eight thousand students, faculty and administrators.

Many southern editors had ignored the implication of *Brown* and would do so for years, but Boone faced it head on when the U.S. Supreme Court ordered the university to accept Autherine Lucy in 1956. The Klan had made symbolic threats, but on Lucy's first day of class, a Friday, all was quiet. The next two nights, however, crowds of students and townspeople marched and chanted "Keep Bama White!"[114]

On Saturday night, things turned ugly. The crowd of demonstrators swelled with people who worked in the nearby factories, and a prelaw student in a bowtie and jacket urged crowds to gather Monday morning when Lucy returned for classes. Spotted in the crowd was "Dynamite" Bob Chambliss, who would set the bomb seven years later that killed four little girls at the Sixteenth Street Baptist Church in Birmingham. The enraged crowd rocked a bus from side to side, almost overturning it, after it noticed black people inside. The weekend mobs attracted national media coverage, and the university president met with his staff on Sunday morning, agreeing to send in thirty state troopers to help the thirty Tuscaloosa policemen keep the peace on campus.[115]

When twenty-six-year-old Lucy, a library-science graduate student, returned to classes Monday morning, only fourteen officers were present to protect her, and the enraged crowd pelted her with gravel and eggs, chasing her from one building to another. Chants of "Hey, hey ho! Where did Autherine go?" and "Hey, hey, ho, where in the hell did the nigger go?" echoed throughout the campus. Lucy was trapped for three hours before finally being rushed out of the back of the library, planted face down in the backseat of a police car that sped off campus. That night rowdy protestors waving Confederate flags worked themselves into a frenzy before police fired teargas to them breakup. University leaders used that mob violence as an excuse to expel Lucy after three days, ostensibly for her own protection.[116]

Down the street at the offices of the *Tuscaloosa News*, a troubled Boone sat down at his typewriter and hammered out his editorial. Published the next morning, the piece condemned the protestors and shamed university leaders, insisting federal law must be obeyed: "The community of Tuscaloosa should be deeply ashamed—and more than a little afraid. . . . No intelligent expression ever has come from a crazed mob, and it never will."[117] Boone urged calm and reasonable discussion in his editorial headlined "What a Price for Peace." He pondered with his pen: "What does it mean today at the University of Alabama, and here in Tuscaloosa, to have the law on your side? The answer has to be nothing—that is, if a mob disagrees with you and the courts." Back in the press room, *Tuscaloosa News* distributor J. T. Sullivan picked up the first copy of the paper that rolled off the presses. "I handed it to Mr. Boone," he recounted, "and I asked him was he trying to put me out of business, and he said, 'If necessary, yes,' and by that he meant, we must obey the law or we have to suffer the consequences."[118]

Boone's stance was widely discussed and resulted in canceled newspaper subscriptions. Bricks crashed through his living room window, but no one was hurt. Late-night calls were filled with taunts and threats, and he had his shotgun at the ready in his modest Tuscaloosa home. Merchants pulled their ads, shocked at Boone's stinging criticism of university trustees—prominent businessmen from around the state—for caving into the racist mob. The editorial was reprinted in newspapers as far away as London, and out-of-town subscriptions swelled as Boone found himself on a national stage. Editors at the *New York Herald Tribune* asked him to write another front-page editorial.[119]

By the end of the month, the university trustees expelled Lucy after her attorneys said the university had conspired with the mob to prevent her admission. By then, the White Citizens' Council had enrolled forty thousand new members in Alabama, and the Tuscaloosa chapter was led by a former student who had been expelled for inciting the mob.[120]

Boone, meanwhile, tried to maintain a good relationship with the White Citizens' Council.[121] He also kept detailed files on the group's leader, Leonard R. Wilson. When Boone was asked to speak about desegregation issues at the organization's regular meeting, he accepted the invitation, and local radio station

WTBC broadcast what promised to be a dramatic moment. Although there were a few hecklers who vowed to kill the next black person who stepped on the Alabama campus, Boone was treated cordially at the packed meeting on the second floor of the Tuscaloosa County Courthouse. In his Georgia drawl, he told the packed room of white men: "It's easy to blame our trouble on things that are far away. We can criticize the Supreme Court and mentally horse whip [sic] the NAACP, but our problem is with ourselves. . . . I believe the Supreme Court decision was morally right, even though my background of southern living and southern tradition tells me it will be strange to see colored faces at the University of Alabama. . . . But we have been telling the rest of the country to go to hell and we can't do that and get away with it."[122] After the raucous meeting Boone wrote a note to himself and put it in his files: "[Reporter] Bob Kyle told me that I looked like I was scared to death when I started speaking and that if I had been any worse I would have had to sit down. I told him that this was one time that he was wrong, that I was terribly nervous but I wasn't scared."[123]

He won the sole Pulitzer Prize for editorial writing in 1957 for his stance on the desegregation attempt, but he played down the award locally. He refused to be interviewed by *Time* magazine, telling the reporter, "Please be kind to me and forget it."[124] Like Hodding Carter in Mississippi and Ralph McGill in Georgia, Boone became well known outside his state.[125] He even turned down an offer from New York publisher Alfred A. Knopf to write a book on the southern moderate's position. Boone told Knopf he was busy running a daily newspaper and did not want to become too detached from the community.[126] Besides, he barely had time to do a little fishing and some volunteer work in town.

Seven years after Lucy's expulsion, the university was finally desegregated when Vivian Malone and James Hood enrolled in 1963. The most vivid and enduring image of that peaceful day was Governor George Wallace standing at the schoolhouse door and defiantly blocking the entrance of the administration building in a widely televised showdown with federal marshals. Boone often sharply criticized the governor in his editorials, arguing that Wallace encouraged the violence and lawlessness and that he was the chief architect of the atmosphere spawning the bombings and murders of black Alabama citizens by white extremists. By the 1960s, Boone's efforts to prevent the expansion of the local KKK seemed futile, and one of the country's largest Klan organizations in the country was now based in Tuscaloosa and led by a local tire salesman named Robert Shelton.[127]

Shelton, who would become infamous as the imperial wizard of the United Klans of America, Knights of the Ku Klux Klan, sent Boone hate mail in response to his editorials. He blasted the editor during his nighttime speeches on the back of flatbed trucks at his Klan meetings out in the country. Despite the desegregation of the University of Alabama, Jim Crow laws were ever present in Alabama. In July 1964 with the passage of the Civil Rights Act, the previously all-white restaurants and movie theaters were integrated by test groups of local blacks. The KKK under Shelton threatened and boycotted local businesses that served or employed black citizens.[128]

In an editorial headlined "Ready for Mob Control?" Boone described the Klan as a lawless gang that police had to rein in. He opined: "Supreme commander of these reckless and irresponsible white elements is a sickly-looking, pitiable little man named Robert Shelton. He has no life savings at stake in any private business enterprise. He has been reduced to living as a human jackal on a racket known as the Ku Klux Klan."[129] Boone was dismayed to see whites had kicked several black men out of Tom's Snack Bar. Whites also marched in front of the movie theater bearing signs that read, "Will you pay a buck to sit next to a coon?"[130] Boone called those signs "asinine" in his editorial. He said later: "It reached a point where the business community was about to submit to the rule of the Ku Klux Klan. They were afraid, and I said I'm not going to let this group of cutthroats take over our community."[131]

Members of the Klan raided as many as three thousand papers from the *Tuscaloosa News* coin machines around town in an attempt to squelch the coverage.[132] As Boone challenged the supremacy of whiteness in Tuscaloosa, the Klan resorted to thieving like a pack of juvenile delinquents. But Shelton took the fight into the Alabama court system in July 1964, filing a libel suit against Boone and the *News* less than four months after the U.S. Supreme Court overturned *New York Times v. Sullivan*.[133] Shelton's $500,000 suit included a litany of complaints that had become commonplace in such suits. He claimed that he suffered extreme embarrassment by Boone's editorial and damage to his character and reputation, that he was subject to "public contempt, ridicule and shame," and that his "profession, business or trade" had been damaged as a result.[134] Boone viewed this legal development as an opportunity to do more reporting, using the suit to delve deeper into Klan activities. During the discovery phase of the case, Boone's attorney, Bruce McEachin, sought membership rosters of the state and county Klan, any photos of Klan meetings, rallies, or cross burnings, copies of the Klan's newspaper, the *Fiery Cross*, and copies of the group's bylaws and other written Klan material. He also sought Shelton's income tax returns to determine whether the imperial wizard had truly been damaged in his business as a result of the editorials. Boone argued the editorial was a matter of public interest and that his free speech and press rights were clearly protected by the First Amendment.[135]

In his original complaint, Shelton did not use the words *actual malice*. At this point, the law held that public-official plaintiffs had to prove the defendant's words met that standard, but not public figures, as Shelton surely was. Boone's attorney, however, was sure to address the issue, arguing that Shelton did not "sufficiently allege" that Boone published the editorial with reckless disregard for the truth.[136] Meanwhile, Shelton filed a second $500,000 libel suit against Boone in 1965 in circuit court in Tuscaloosa, for another editorial that ran in July 1964.[137] He complained that the second editorial was false and defamatory, noting that Boone called him "a threat to the general public" and "a leader of 'gorillas' uncaged but waiting to bite, as one who 'crawls' out at night to use the cover of darkness to defy and disobey the law and to lead others to do so."[138]

During his deposition, Shelton refused to answer 139 of the 210 questions posed by McEachin, mostly queries related to Klan activities and his work as the Klan leader. It seemed that Boone was putting Shelton on trial. For example, McEachin asked Shelton details of his whereabouts and activities relating to the beatings of the Freedom Riders in Birmingham on Mother's Day in 1961. Shelton argued he was protected by his First Amendment right of association. Circuit Court judge Walter B. Henley ordered Shelton to answer 64 of the 139 questions the Imperial Wizard originally refused to answer.[139] But he did not require Shelton to hand over membership lists or photographs taken during Klan rallies, meetings, or cross burnings. Judge Henley said Boone would first have to prove that the group was engaged in or sanctioning illegal activities before it could be compelled to reveal members' names. He did require Shelton to provide copies of all editions of the group's newspaper, the *Fiery Cross*. Boone appealed the judge's ruling to the Supreme Court of Alabama.[140] He argued that he sought to prove Shelton's bad reputation existed before Boone's editorials ran.[141]

Ironically, in appeal documents, Shelton's attorney relied on *NAACP v. Alabama*, in which the U.S. Supreme Court ruled that Alabama officials could not require the NAACP to hand over its membership lists.[142] In that case, Shelton argued, the court recognized "the vital relationship between freedom to associate and privacy in one's association." Turning over the Klan roster would "affect adversely" the group's efforts "to foster beliefs which they have a right to advocate."[143] Also, Shelton argued, the Klan was not party to the suit—he was suing as an individual. In Shelton's second case, Alabama's high court refused to hear Boone's appeal to require the Klan leader to answer the questions posed to him in his deposition. Once again, as the court battle continued into 1967, Boone wanted membership lists and answers to specific questions about Klan activities.[144]

Since Shelton alleged that he had been harmed financially

by Boone's editorials, the judge agreed that the plaintiff should hand over his tax returns from 1963 through 1966, along with all accounting records showing his income. Those records reflect a steady increase in his paycheck as Shelton became more involved in the Klan. In 1963, Shelton reported to the Internal Revenue Service (IRS) that he earned $1,875 as a salesman, and listed his wife, Betty, as a housewife on their joint return.[145] In 1964, the year Shelton filed suit, he reported to the IRS that he earned $3,576, a third of that income from his public relations work for the United Klans of America. In 1965, his income continued to increase steadily. Shelton listed his only occupation as president of the United Klans of America, with all of his wages—$4,663.23—coming from that group. He reported a remarkable income jump to $18,061.21 in 1966 in the same occupation as Klan leader. Clearly, Boone's attorney argued, Shelton had not suffered in his business as a result of the editorials.[146] Quite the opposite—organized bigotry, racism, and violence paid Shelton huge dividends.

At his lawyer's suggestion, Boone even thought about throwing a libel suit back at Shelton and the Klan after the imperial wizard called the publisher either a "rattlesnake" or a "rat-snake" during an April 1966 Klan meeting. However, he later discarded the idea.[147] Throughout the lengthy court battle, Boone kept tabs on Shelton's activities, receiving memos from his reporters that read like FBI reports. According to reporter Jimmy Mizell's internal memo to Boone, Shelton told members at a rally on April 17, 1965, that he would fight to protect Klan membership rosters just as the courts protected those of black organizations. Shelton also told the crowd that members of the media were welcome at the rally and that he had just talked to a reporter and photographer from the *Tuscaloosa News* before coming on stage. He got plenty of laughs and applause when he said into his microphone, "The only thing I ask is if you bring Buford with you, leave him in the middle of the highway."[148]

Boone also worked with the House Un-American Activities Committee (HUAC) in its investigation of Shelton.[149] Boone agreed to mail committee members a photo of Shelton at an August 1965 rally with the three men accused of the murder of civil rights demonstrator Viola Liuzzo.[150] Boone wrote Donald Appell, HUAC's chief investigator: "I have been astonished at the Klan's parading of the three accused of the [Liuzzo] murder at weekend meetings. And they may be planning to keep on presenting them as the Klan's current heroes. I think it is good that they are doing this, for it is proof through Klan action of how extreme, how unreasonable they are and of how much they approve of violence for their cause."[151] Further, Boone staked out his reporters at a KKK meeting at Tuscaloosa's Stafford Hotel in August 1967 on the advice of his lawyer, who believed that it would help to know who was coming and going when it came time to select a jury in the libel trial.[152]

At trial in 1968, McEachin argued that Shelton was a public figure and must prove actual malice, citing *Associated Press v. Walker*, which had been decided in July 1967.[153] He argued that Klan activity was a matter of public interest, and Boone's editorials had focused on concerns about mob violence in the streets of Tuscaloosa. McEachin also argued that Shelton had received so much publicity that it was impossible to tell which (if any) news stories actually damaged his reputation. The Tuscaloosa jury awarded Shelton a measly $500 in punitive damages, refusing to award compensatory damages.[154] Boone paid the next day. After the verdict was released, the segregationist *Clarion-Ledger* in Jackson, Mississippi, speculated that white southerners were turning on the Klan and that moderates, angry with the Klan for civil rights murders, church bombings, and other violence, used the suit to expose some of the inner workings of the secret organization.[155] Members of the jury privately told *Tuscaloosa News* employee Bob Kyle that Boone had "overstepped his bounds" in the editorial about Shelton and should "be paddled a little."[156] "The fact that none appeared to want to burn Boone up with a big verdict against him," Kyle stated, "was . . . the most significant development, particularly as regards [to] future litigation."[157] Shelton later dropped the second case.

Throughout the legal battle and his coverage of civil rights issues, Boone managed to keep his sense of humor in the face of a steady stream of hate mail. One of the more civil letter writers from out of town, C. A. Hull, asked Boone: "Are you white or black? You may plead the Fifth Amendment if you wish."[158] The editor answered Hull: "In answer to your question, the *Tuscaloosa News* is black and white and read all over."[159]

Boone, an unassuming, lifelong southerner, had stared down one of the most notorious Klansmen in the country. To the white supremacists in his community, Boone aided and abetted those who would threaten their core beliefs and their way of life. He had called a racist icon "a pitiable little man" and a "jackal" and lived to talk and write about it. Although middle-class support of the Klan was beginning to wane, Boone was clearly ahead of his time. Most southern moderates were afraid to say what they were thinking: separate may not really be equal. But Boone had his newspaper and his conscience and enough courage to exercise both. He could have censored himself or decided not to fight Shelton's libel suits so ardently. As Justice William Brennan Jr. wrote in his opinion in *Sullivan,* First Amendment freedoms must take into account self-censorship. Journalists such as Boone must feel free to speak their minds on controversial public issues without the fear of bankruptcy from libel suits.

A few months after the libel cases were decided and dropped, Boone handed over the editor's job at the newspaper to his son, who had been running a paper in Virginia. Autherine Lucy earned her masters degree at the University of Alabama in 1992, graduating with her daughter. Boone was given an honorary doctorate from the university and established a scholarship for journalism students. He died February 7, 1983, twenty-seven years to the day of his publication of his Pulitzer Prize–winning editorial, "What a Price for Peace."

This chapter detailed libel suits filed by five police officers arising from police brutality of African Americans and civil rights demonstrators. The two officers in Darlington, South Carolina, waged war on NAACP leaders who criticized them for beating up a black man for no apparent cause other than driving a nice car with out-of-state license plates. That case dragged on from the 1961 incident until 1968, when the plaintiffs or their legal counsel finally realized, post-*Sullivan,* that they couldn't win the case. It was quietly removed from the docket, although NAACP attorneys long remained wary it would be reinstated. Similarly, the mayor of Gadsden, who sued ABC in 1963, saw that the case dragged on for years before it was removed from the docket and quietly disappeared. Also in Gadsden, the local sheriff sued *Ladies' Home Journal* although, like Lester B. Sullivan, he was not named in an article about police brutality, specifically about the use of electric cattle prods on civil rights protesters. A federal judge in Birmingham dismissed the suit six months after the *Sullivan* doctrine was created, one of the fastest responses to that landmark case.

The pattern continued with multiple suits filed by three officers of the law in Philadelphia, Mississippi, including the infamous former sheriff Lawrence Rainey. By the late 1960s and into the early 1970s, *Sullivan* had been widely studied and understood by the southern legal community. The U.S. Supreme Court had extended the actual malice standard to public figures in *Associated Press v. Walker.* Such administrative delay as seen in some of the cases presented here is integral to our system of civil rights law, critical race theorists have argued correctly. CRT scholars such as Richard Delgado, distressed over the slow pace of racial progress in the United States, have pointed out that periodic legal victories such as *Brown* or the 1964 Civil Rights Act, are held up as proof that the legal system is fair and just. But Delgado argues that such victories "are then quickly stolen away by narrow judicial construction, foot-dragging and delay."[160] Indeed it is arguable that the impact of *Sullivan*—most certainly a legal victory for free speech advocates, the press, and African Americans—was dulled initially by that very foot-dragging and delay. This point is further illustrated in the next chapter, which tells the story of three New York City area police officers who shot and killed black men and sued over criticism of their official actions.

CHAPTER 5

"Wanted for Murder"

In the summer of 1964, New York City Police lieutenant Thomas Gilligan shot and killed a fifteen-year-old black youth. A year later in June, patrolman Henry Martinez shot and killed a twenty-two-year-old black man in Newark, New Jersey, after a routine traffic stop. The next month, Brooklyn-based patrolman Sheldon Liebowitz shot and killed a mentally disabled black man on the street.

After all three shootings, local civil rights leaders and their enraged followers protested in the sweltering streets, and in all three instances, they held "Wanted for Murder" signs, which displayed mimeographed photos of the officers and included their names and badge numbers. All three police officers sued those same civil rights leaders for libel, with at least one case winding its way through the court system for more than three years. This trio of libel cases further shows that police officers and their lawyers, eager to suffocate any criticism, were slow to absorb and react to the landmark *Sullivan* decision. This chapter also presents similar cases with police-officer plaintiffs in Savannah, Georgia, and in Akron, Ohio. These cases illustrate that northern police officers could be as litigious as their southern counterparts when criticized about their actions on the job. This chapter includes a case involving yet another KKK plaintiff, this time from Maryland, taking on the NAACP for criticizing his actions as a white supremacist and getting him fired from his day job.

"This Is Worse Than Mississippi!"

On July 16, 1964, a Thursday, Patrick Lynch was washing down the sidewalk with a garden hose outside a white, six-story brick apartment house at 215 East Seventy-Sixth Street in Manhattan, where he worked as the building superintendent. At 9 a.m., the day was already boiling hot, and in this working-class, white neighborhood, it was becoming more common to see black youths on the sidewalks. They were waiting for the summer-school bell to ring across the street at Wagner Junior High School, which kids from both Manhattan and the Bronx attended during the break from the regular school year. Shirley Robinson, a black fourteen-year-old, later said Lynch, a white man, looked annoyed that some black teens were on his side of the street, and he sprayed them with his garden hose to encourage them to scoot along.

"There were about seven kids near the stoop of the building and when he started spraying water, somebody yelled, 'Say mister, look out!' The superintendent then said—and I heard him—'I'm going to wash all the black off you.'" She said some of the boys threw bottles and trashcan covers at Lynch, who finally ran into the apartment building. One of the youths, fifteen-year-old James Powell, chased Lynch inside. A minute later, Powell bounded back out on the street. "When he came out, he was even laughing and kind of like running," Shirley said.[1]

Police lieutenant Thomas Gilligan, dressed in civilian clothes and off-duty at the time, had taken a small radio to a TV repair shop next door to the apartment building when he heard the ruckus. He hurried onto the street and later said he identified himself as a police lieutenant, flashing his badge and revolver, but Powell came toward him with a three-and-a-half-inch pocketknife. Gilligan said he advised Powell to stop, and he fired a warning shot, but the boy kept coming at him. Gilligan then fired at Powell in self-defense, he later said, and the second of three bullets tore through the boy's right forearm and hit his chest. Another went through his abdomen and out his back, killing him instantly in front of his friends. Shirley later told a reporter from the *New York Times* that she didn't hear the police lieutenant warn Powell before he fired the shots. She also said the youth was not armed. "I saw the boy go into the building and he didn't have any knife then." However, white adult witnesses said he did.[2]

Within minutes an angry crowd, mostly black teenagers arriving for classes, filled the street and shouted at the stunned police officer. Gilligan was still standing there when some girls on the street became hysterical. One young teen, tears streaming down her cheeks, screamed at him, "Come on, shoot another nigger!" Others yelled, "This is worse than Mississippi!" A crowd began throwing rocks and bottles at an estimated seventy-five police officers, who had descended into the Upper East Side neighborhood within two hours of the shooting, and a full-scale riot ensued. Civil rights leaders from Harlem hastened to the East Sixty-Seventh Street police station to learn more about the shooting. Members of the local chapter of the Congress of Racial Equality (CORE), along with the local NAACP branch and other civil rights groups in Harlem demanded an investigation and announced later that there would be a demonstration outside the precinct the following day.[3]

Gilligan acted in self-defense, Deputy Chief Inspector Joseph Coyle told reporters later that day: "The youths and the superintendent had some heated words and the superintendent ran into the building with the boys in pursuit. He saw the boys banging on an apartment door with a garbage can lid and ordered them to stop." Gilligan, a highly decorated military veteran of World War II with sixteen years on the job, weighed two hundred pounds and stood six feet tall. Surely such a large, experienced officer could disarm a teenager who was much smaller physically, argued civil rights leaders, including CORE director James Farmer. Powell, five feet six and 122 pounds, had lived with his widowed mother in the Soundview, a housing project at 1686 Randall Avenue in the Bronx, and he was an only child. He had finished the ninth grade at Samuel Gompers Vocational High School and enrolled in a remedial-reading course at summer school.[4]

Everyone seemed to be asking the same question: Why couldn't

Gilligan resolve the conflict without killing the teenager? Even if he did have a three-and-a-half-inch blade, did Gilligan have to kill him? Two days of mourning followed as tension filled the streets. Emotions were already running high that summer with all eyes on Mississippi and the hunt for the three civil rights workers in Neshoba County. At the public viewing of James's body on Saturday night, more than three hundred people filed past his body in the open casket, and his weeping mother, Annie Powell, became overwrought as she neared the coffin. Many heard her cries as she was helped to a car: "They murdered my baby. That's all it was. Murder." That night, more than a thousand mourners stood outside the Levy and Delany Funeral Home on Seventh Avenue, near 132nd Street, to pay their respects.

Two weeks before the shooting, President Lyndon Johnson had signed the landmark Civil Rights Act of 1964 into law, banning discrimination on the basis of race, color, religion, sex, or national origin. Powell was killed the same night Senator Barry M. Goldwater of Arizona received the Republican presidential nomination in San Francisco. In his acceptance speech, Goldwater spoke of the need for more law and order to a national audience. A radical conservative, the senator declared, "The growing menace in our country tonight, to personal safety, to life, to limb and property, in homes, in churches, on playgrounds and places of business, particularly in our great cities is the mounting concern—or should be—of every thoughtful citizen in the United States." On the campaign trail, Goldwater was a vocal opponent of the Civil Rights Act and blamed black leaders such as CORE's James Farmer and March on Washington organizer Bayard Rustin for promoting civil disobedience, weakening respect for authority, and encouraging lawlessness in American cities.[5]

After the shooting, seething protesters rioted across Harlem for six nights, leaving 1 rioter dead, 118 injured, and 465 arrested. More than two hundred stores were damaged. Riots struck other cities that summer, including Philadelphia, Chicago, and Jersey City, as rage bubbled up after people had endured decades of police brutality, desperate poverty, and systemic racism.[6] Calling for Gilligan's arrest, Farmer and others held a CORE rally at the corner of 125th Street and Seventh Avenue in Harlem. Speakers stood on kitchen chairs on the sidewalk, and other groups, including members of the Harlem Progressive Labor Movement, were on hand. Reverend Nelson Dukes of the Fountain Spring Baptist Church called for an impromptu march to the nearby Harlem police stationhouse to demand justice. The crowd followed him and tried to push its way through the front door, but they were blocked by five policemen in locked arms. Rioters near the precinct threw bottles and bricks at the police, and glass bottles and garbage can lids rained down from rooftops as the Tactical Patrol Force was ordered to disperse them, lunging toward the crowd with their batons and firing shots into the air to quell the crowd. This enraged the mob further, and someone heaved a Molotov cocktail at the police, who pushed the hundreds of demonstrators back a few blocks to the corner of 125th Street and Lenox Avenue. Protesters were arrested and charged with disorderly conduct after they sat down in the middle of the street and refused to move. They shouted: "Killer cops must go! Police brutality must go!" The *New York Times* later described the tactical patrol force as "a group of about 200 handpicked men, all over six feet tall, all trained in judo and all under 30 years of age. The force was organized in 1958 as a roving unit that could be dispatched to danger areas."[7]

On Sunday afternoon, Farmer appeared on WABC-TV's *Page One* in New York City, when the topic of the previously scheduled appearance was changed to discussion of the riots. He charged that brutal police actions were fueling the already outraged rioters. "I was up there this morning for five hours, and what I saw was a blood bath," he said. "I saw also police shooting into windows, into tenement houses and into the Theresa Hotel. . . . Now I'm not saying that the community, the people in the community of Harlem, were blameless. There was bottle-throwing, but when people throw bottles, when they throw bricks, it's the responsibility of the police to arrest, or at least restrain the culprits, the guilty parties, not indiscriminately to shoot into hotel windows and tenement houses, not to beat people who are merely walking down the street as I saw happen."[8]

Born in Marshall, Texas, in 1920, Farmer was the grandson of a slave and the son of the first black man to earn a doctorate in the state. Like his father, a Methodist minister, he focused on education throughout his life and, as a child prodigy, knew how to read, write, and count in the first grade. In 1938, he enrolled at Howard University's School of Religion. Heavily influenced by one of his favorite professors, Farmer became a devotee of Gandhi's ideas on nonviolent resistance. Farmer was a big man with a booming voice and careful diction, seemingly perfect for preaching the gospel. But he stung from the denial of service in whites-only restaurants and having to sit in the "nosebleed" section at the movie theater. He and two others formed a fledgling civil rights group that would become CORE and initiated the 1961 Freedom Rides to desegregate interstate transportation. As the CORE director, he helped organize the March on Washington in 1963 and had become a major target of arrest and violence as one of the most recognized civil rights leaders of the day, having spent many weeks in jail on disturbing the peace charges.

He was fearless in his criticism of the police during his forty-five minutes on WABC-TV that afternoon. Farmer continued: "I saw some young men walking down the street and heard police scream, 'Let's get those niggers,' and they dashed in. . . . The police were hysterical." He then called for Gilligan's suspension and immediate arrest and renewed the standing CORE demand for a civil review board to study all police use-of-force cases.

Rent-strike leader Jesse Gray spoke at Mount Morris Presbyterian Church in Harlem on that Sunday afternoon, encouraging citizens to take to the streets. "Before today is over, we'll be able to separate the men from the boys," he preached into the hot, airless sanctuary. "Only one thing can solve the problem in Mississippi," Gray harangued, "and that's guerrilla warfare. I'm beginning to wonder what's going to solve the problem here in New York." The crowd shouted back, "Guerilla warfare!"[9] The riled-up crowd erupted later that day in front of the West 123rd Street Police

Station, with the *Times* reporting: "Just before the funeral began, bottles began crashing to the street. Suddenly there were shrieks from the corner of Seventh Avenue and 132d Street, and patrolmen, waving nightsticks, charged into crowds that were pouring out from behind barricades. The crowd broke up when shots were fired into the air. Three busloads of specially trained antiriot policemen drew up and helped put down the outburst, but not before one man was knocked to the ground. . . . The pattern was the case that prevailed much of the night: missiles and gasoline-filled bottles thrown at police, with shots returned."[10]

New York's twenty-five-thousand-man police force worked twelve-hour shifts and the Transit Authority temporarily discontinued service at the Harlem station at 125th Street, calling for extra transit police to beef up patrols on trains passing through Harlem. Police closed fifty-seven blocks to traffic in the area, where the "frenzied, embittered crowds had swarmed." And taunting police, protestors yelled, "Killers! Killers!" The Transit Authority diverted buses from other regular routes as riots spread. "By 3 a.m., three and a half hours after the riot started, the situation was not under control," the *Times* reported. "Police roamed the streets with revolvers drawn." The despised white police with their white steel helmets had run out of ammunition in those early morning hours and called for more boxes of .38-caliber rounds. Under orders, they were emptying their revolvers into the air to control and disperse crowds peacefully but using force when necessary.

The next day, civil rights leaders, including Farmer, held another rally at Mount Morris Presbyterian, calling the riots "New York's night of Birmingham horror" in reference to the police dogs and water jets used against black children the year before in Alabama. Early in the week, groups of CORE members picketed Police Headquarters. "Gilligan!" leaders yelled. "Must go!" answered the picketers. In counterprotest, an estimated 250 white teenagers hurled eggs at them. "Go back to Harlem!" some shouted.[11] Dusk brought the third straight night of rioting as demonstrations swept across the East River to the

Bedford-Stuyvesant section of Brooklyn. Gathering at Fulton Street and Nostrand Avenue, the main business streets, demonstrators shouted, "Killer Cops Must Go!" CORE's office was situated at 307 West 125th Street on the main business street of Harlem. From there Farmer emerged as about 150 mostly black teenagers gathered in front of the headquarters. He told the group that he had talked to the mayor and that Gilligan would appear before a grand jury investigating the shooting. The crowd roared, with someone shouting, "They should kill him!" Farmer appealed to them to go home, but protesters yelled out, "We are not going home, we are home."

The Harlem Defense Council had published a poster reading, "Wanted for Murder." It included a photo of Gilligan in his police uniform and identified him as "Gilligan, the cop." Newspaper, television, and radio reporters focused on that poster as they covered the marches, and protesters attached the placards to buildings and utility poles across the city. Young girls and boys handed out stacks of the flyers to protesters. On day three of the riots, more mimeographed leaflets from the Harlem Defense Council appeared on the streets, urging residents to defend themselves against the police and calling for the continuation of demonstrations to protest police brutality.[12]

Within a week of the shooting, a New York County grand jury began its inquiry. The Patrolman's Benevolent Association provided legal counsel for the thirty-six-year-old Gilligan, who took sick leave for the rest of the summer. He was said to have on his right hand knife wounds inflicted by Powell. Police officials refused to disclose his whereabouts to reporters, and journalists staked out his home in a middle-income apartment building on the Lower East Side, where he lived with his wife and ten-year-old daughter on the fifth floor. Neighbors told journalists that the family had left with their daughter to stay with Mrs. Gilligan's parents to avoid hostile demonstrations around their home.[13]

Gilligan, who served in the Marine Corps in World War II and in Korea, was receiving seventy-seven dollars a month for a "military service disability," reported the *Times*, eager to scrape up any morsel of information it could find. Journalists also checked out reports that Gilligan was a patient in the Veterans Administration hospital, but they were unable to verify this rumor. The *Times* detailed his impressive police record, pointing out that he had been considered a hero since an episode when he shot, then arrested a car thief in Stuyvesant Town three years earlier. He received a citation for meritorious police duty for that incident, one of nineteen honors for outstanding police work since he joined the force in 1947. Four of those citations came after Gilligan disarmed men with guns, according to newspaper reports.

At the invitation of Mayor Robert Wagner, Dr. Martin Luther King Jr. flew to New York City four days after the riots ended for a series of private meetings. Holding an impromptu news conference at the airport, King said: "It would have been wise to suspend the police lieutenant who murdered the Negro boy, and we feel the Negro boy was murdered."[14] King and Farmer appeared on a series of television programs, notably an NBC News panel entitled *Who Speaks for Harlem?* on July 26. They also continued to do impromptu interviews with the media and were among the thirty-five civil rights leaders who held a conference with Mayor Wagner and Police Commissioner Michael Murphy to try working out solutions to the unrest and volatile relationship between the police and black citizenry. Again, African American leaders proposed that the mayor create an independent civilian review board to hear charges of police brutality, appoint one of the three black captains already on the force to command the police in Harlem, and discontinue the assignment of rookie officers to Harlem. They also asked Commissioner Murphy to suspend Gilligan until the investigation was concluded and to order his officers to stop using live ammunition against the riots.

In September 1964, Gilligan was exonerated by a grand jury, which concluded there was insufficient evidence to indict him. Internal police department investigations determined that he had killed in self-defense when Powell attacked him with a knife. District Attorney Frank S. Hogan issued a fourteen-page report on the city's investigation, making clear that various witnesses' versions of the facts did not agree. In response to what was widely called the Hogan Report, NAACP leader Roy Wilkins said: "They can explain and explain until they're blue in the face, but they'll never explain why it's necessary for a police officer to shoot a 15-year-old kid. It just doesn't go down."[15]

The following May, Gilligan filed in New York County two libel suits totaling $5.25 million and focusing on the poster that read, "Gilligan, Wanted for Murder." The first suit sought $3.75 million from a long list of defendants: Martin Luther King Jr.; James Farmer and CORE; the Progressive Labor Movement and William Epton, its chairman; the Tri-Line Offset Company, which printed the flyer, and Michael Crenovick, its president; and Jesse Gray, leader of the Harlem rent strikes; and the Harlem Defense Council.[16]

William Epton, a thirty-two-year-old self-described pro-Chinese communist, worked out of the same headquarters on Lenox Avenue as did the Harlem Defense Council and the Harlem Action Group. In particular, he appealed to the top police brass that off-duty police officers should not be allowed to carry their guns. Jesse Gray, a Louisiana native, came to New York City to work as a tailor, also serving as a longtime community activist in Harlem. He organized demonstrations against abominable conditions in Harlem's slum areas and gained media attention in 1963 when he led scores of tenants, holding rats both dead and alive, to a hearing in civil court to illustrate the infestations in the apartment buildings. He launched rent strikes when no measures were taken to improve conditions.[17]

Gilligan also sued Reverend King in federal court in Atlanta for $1.5 million. According to the police officer, the civil rights leader had made, during several television interviews in July 1964, false allegations that he was guilty of murder. King's attorneys worried their client could not get a fair trial in Atlanta, a city in the Deep South, and asked the U.S. District judge Frank A. Hooper to transfer the case to New York. Initially, Hooper refused after the February 1966 hearing but agreed when King promised to waive the one-year statute of limitations and to accept service of the suit in New York. He required that King submit an affidavit to the court to this effect, and King did so.[18] Two years had passed since *Sullivan* had been overturned, and here was yet another libel suit filed by a police-officer plaintiff about speech relating to his actions on the job. Perhaps King was confident that he would win this one too.

In the three suits, Gilligan accused the civil rights activists of collusion, specifically printing and distributing leaflets that pictured him in uniform and called him a murderer. He said King, Farmer, and others had conspired to damage his name and reputation, attempting to cut off his income by having him removed as a New York City police officer. He said that before this episode, he had an outstanding reputation for honesty, intelligence, integrity, and valor. He also used the language of the *Sullivan* decision, complaining that the defendants acted with actual malice. In short, Gilligan complained that he had been falsely accused of murder. The second suit, filed in Manhattan Supreme Court, seeking $1.5 million from Farmer and CORE, stemmed from Farmer's suggesting that Gilligan had been treated in a mental institution. Farmer was accused of saying on television that Gilligan "presently is in a mental institution receiving treatment." In the suit, Gilligan also charged that Farmer urged his arrest on a murder charge. He complained that posters were circulated during the official investigation of the Police Review Board in an attempt to get him fired.[19]

Gilligan's attorneys also took the position that he was not an elected official under the meaning of the *Sullivan* decision, whereas Sullivan was an elected police commissioner, more of a politician than policeman. Gilligan argued that he was one of thousands of low-ranking government employees who are not public officials. Therefore, he should not have to prove "actual malice," the standard of fault in which the plaintiff must prove that the defendant communicated the allegedly libelous information "with knowledge of falsity or reckless disregard for the truth." If he was considered a public official under the *Sullivan* rule, Gilligan reasoned, so would all local employees of the government, including "firemen, postal men, secretaries, waitresses, garbage collectors ad finitum."[20] Gilligan said he was merely a "municipal servant."

The defendants filed a motion to dismiss the suit later that summer. Citing Sullivan extensively, they argued that that they had a First and Fourteenth Amendment right to criticize a police officer in his official duties. "Plaintiff sounds a completely false alarm when he warns that all local employees" would automatically be considered public officials for the purposes of a libel suit. "If the official actions of a maid or a secretary or others employed by New York City are ever of 'great public concern' the constitutional privilege will apply."[21] Epton's attorney, Shirley Fingerhood, argued that the Gilligan poster, like the *New York Times ad,* "Heed Their Rising Voices," that prompted the *Sullivan* case, represented the "expression of grievance and protest on one of the major public issues of our time" and thus warranted constitutional protection.[22] Epton said that as "a negro," he had long been vocal about the issue of police brutality and that it was his right to continue that public conversation. "I am entitled to publish criticism," he argued, "which I believe to be true, whether or not it can be proved true." Epton pointed to the conflicting witness testimony. Some witnesses said that Gilligan acted in self-defense and that Powell had a knife; others contradicted those observations. So the truth might not be knowable. He also pointed out that Gilligan was not removed from his job, was not demoted in the police force, and suffered no financial loss.[23]

The defendants argued that police should indeed have to prove "actual malice" rather than meeting the much easier "negligence" standard of fault. As if savoring *Sullivan,* and confident of a win in court, they continued to quote extensively from the Supreme Court's opinion, including the history of the case and its relationship to the civil rights fight. They argued that the *Sullivan* opinion was designed to help foster robust debate on public issues and to bring about "political and social changes desired by the people." Farmer's and King's attorneys argued that in a literal sense, anyone who occupied a position in government, even a minor position, is a public official. "It is not the title of his office but the duties . . . which the particular officer" executes that matters. And indeed, police officers—more than so many other government officials—exercise significant power over the citizenry.[24]

Farmer's attorneys filed an additional motion to dismiss the libel suit in November of 1965, arguing that he and CORE were not affiliated with either the Harlem Defense Council or the Progressive Labor Movement. Farmer said he had nothing to do with the creation of the poster or its distribution. In his affidavit taken on September 19, 1965, Farmer said he didn't know who had printed the poster or circulated it. Relating to the separate case against Farmer for his television interviews, he said he had no recollection of making such statements. In his motion to dismiss, Farmer said he tried to check the accuracy of all of his statements, but Gilligan refused to be interviewed by Farmer's lawyers and the New York Police Department refused to hand over any documentation. Farmer argued he could not mount a defense because Gilligan would not tell the truth.[25] In his original suit, Gilligan filed an affidavit that his lawyers believed should suffice. It read in part: "I went out onto the street from where the store was. I saw one James Powell with an open blade knife running into a building after the superintendent. I identified myself as a police lieutenant, flashing my badge and revolver. James Powell came after me with a knife in his hand. I ordered him to stop and I fired a warning shot, but Powell kept coming. Then, in self-defense, I fired my revolver and killed James Powell." In October of 1964, Justice Joseph Brust of the Supreme Court of New York denied motions to dismiss the case, ruling that the defendants must proceed to trial. The civil rights leaders appealed in early January of 1965.[26]

More than three years of legal wrangling ensued, and the Supreme Court of New York ultimately agreed with the civil rights leaders in this case. Gilligan, like Sullivan, was a public official for the purposes of the libel suit.[27] This case, then, became notable in legal jurisprudence as definitively extending the actual malice standard to police officers, not just law enforcement officials who are elected to lead a police department. But they still had to go to trial. On April 25, 1968, three weeks after the assassination of Martin Luther King Jr. in Memphis, the New York appellate court informed Gilligan that he must prove the civil rights leaders acted with actual malice. King was still listed as a defendant on the appellate court's documents that returned the case for trial.[28]

Issuing a scathing dissent, however, Justice J. Stevens pointed to Farmer's affidavit asserting that he had nothing to do with the creation, printing, or distribution of the Gilligan poster. Stevens heaped scorn on Gilligan's choice of defendants, asserting that there was no evidence that Farmer or CORE were involved in distributing the poster or leaflets. "The conclusion is irresistible that plaintiff merely cast his lawsuit net into the sea of civil rights workers and organizations, hoping, willy-nilly, to snare them in its mesh." Stevens also underscored the importance of public scrutiny of police actions: "If the official conduct of a police official is immune to critical appraisal or public disapproval he becomes a preferred member of society." He explained, "Public opinion, which is the most effective check on official abuse, can never be aroused and any and all acts of such an official are protected either by a veil of secrecy or the critic is subjected to costly litigation."[29]

In the separate suit against Farmer, the one targeting his remarks about Gilligan undergoing treatment at the VA Hospital, the state Supreme Court refused to dismiss the complaint, affirming the lower court's ruling that a trial must proceed. Again, Stevens dissented, noting that Gilligan had refused to allow the defense attorneys to interview him. How would Farmer's attorneys establish truth or falsity of the claim?[30] All they had to go on was Gilligan's original affidavit, in which he stated: "I have never been examined by a psychiatrist nor have I ever been confined to a mental institution or psychiatric ward of any hospital or otherwise, including a veteran's hospital. I have never been treated for any mental or emotional shock."[31]

Wire services reports focused on the appellate court ruling that Gilligan had a legal right to press the libel claims, and the story reported that this position boosted "police morale" in New York City and around the country.[32] In the meantime, court officials found still other ways to punish the civil rights leaders. William Epton, a self-acknowledged Marxist, was convicted for inciting the Harlem riots, even though, in the words of the New York court, there was "no evidence that the defendant . . . had any hand in causing the riots that began on the evening of July 18, 1964." But the appellate court held that he violated the law—that his words and actions created a "clear and present danger" the state was justified in stopping. The court noted that Epton told the crowd the day the riots started, "They [the police] declared war on us and we should declare war on them and every time they kill one of us, damn it, we'll kill one of them and we should start thinking that way right now."[33] Sentenced to one year in prison, Epton was the first person convicted of criminal anarchy since the Red Scare of 1919.[34]

Later newspaper reports pointed to the inconsistencies in the police department's descriptions of Gilligan's injuries after the shooting. He had four months of sick leave and took a desk job in November 1964. On his return to duty, Police officials said that Gilligan had broken a bone in his hand during the scuffle that immediately preceded the shooting. However, they initially said the officer had suffered a knife wound on his right hand, not a broken bone.[35] Gilligan retired from the police force in April 1968, the same month that the New York Appeals Court kicked the libel cases down for trial. He had been on sick leave for a year after suffering a back injury on the job.[36]

Here is where the case goes cold. The New York County clerk and the clerk of the New York State Supreme Court converted the Gilligan libel-case files to microfilm in 1981. There is no record of the adjudication of these libel suits, so it is likely that the cases were dismissed. Historian Gil Troy has pondered the disappearance of these cases from public record. He asks: "Did the defendants settle confidentially? Did the plaintiffs drop the suit?"[37]

Regardless of the mystery, the defendants undoubtedly spent untold sums defending themselves in court for years. Gilligan's lawyer was Roy Cohn, nationally famous as chief counsel for Senator Joseph McCarthy's anti-communist witch hunt. He would later represent Donald Trump. Cohn died in 1986, disbarred and owing $3 million in back taxes, having been tried and acquitted three times in federal court on charges ranging from conspiracy to bribery to fraud.[38]

Gilligan died in 2014, at the age of eighty-eight, some fifty years after shooting Powell. As historian Michael Flamm describes, the ex-police officer had disappeared into the shadows after his retirement, living in a small house in East Hampton on Long Island. Some ten years before Gilligan's death, Flamm tried to interview him for his book on the riots, but the retired officer refused. "It was a long time ago and I don't ever want to get into it again," Gilligan explained. "That chapter of my life is closed."[39]

"The Gun Suddenly Went Off"

In the second New York City–area case, the police seemed concerned more about how they released information to the media than about the shooting of an unarmed black man during a routine traffic stop. Henry Martinez, a patrolman in Newark, New Jersey, shot Lester Long in the back of the head after stopping him because of a noisy muffler and a defective headlight in the early morning hours of June 12, 1965. Police said they saw Long driving fast in his black 1955 Chevrolet and weaving in and out of traffic. Officer Martinez said he figured he and his partner would merely ticket Long for careless driving, but the twenty-two-year-old Newark man handed over a driver's license and registration that registered two different names. Martinez and his partner, William Provost, ran a check on Long from a nearby telephone booth. While holding him in their squad car, the patrolmen asked Long for his social security number. From the record check, the officers learned that Long was wanted for four traffic violations and contempt of court, so they advised him that they were going to search, then arrest him. The police later reported that when they asked Long for other identification, several social-security and draft cards, all with different names, spilled out of his wallet.

The officers said Long became increasingly angry and began cursing them. The twenty-nine-year-old Martinez, a five-year veteran of the Newark Police Department, explained the shooting when he wrote up the incident report later that night: "The prisoner stated 'You Motherfuckers ain't searching me and you ain't going to get me to that fucking precinct.'" Martinez said that as he prepared to handcuff him, Long yelled, "I'll kill both you motherfuckers before you take me to the precinct."[40]

"I then heard my partner yell 'Look out Hank he has a knife [sic] turning to see my partner reach out to prevent me from being stabbed causing a laceration on his right forearm in doing so. We scuffled in the car attempting to disarm him and place him under arrest. He then opened the rear door and ran across Broadway towards the corner of Broadway & Oriental St., where the undersigned got out of the car hollering several times. He did not heed my warning and I fired 1 shot from my Service Revolver NPD#2831, at the fleeing prisoner."[41]

One shot was all it took to kill the fleeing man. Martinez said he and his partner ran to Long's body and saw his open knife on the sidewalk. A crowd formed in front of the dead man with the bloody head wound as an ambulance and backup squad car arrived. Martinez and Provost were ordered back to the precinct in hopes that the police could avoid another riot. The department issued conflicting statements in the following days, first saying Martinez's gun went off accidentally when he tripped on a curb in pursuit of his fleeing prisoner. *Newark Evening News* reporter Hy Kuperstein interviewed Martinez at the precinct to make his Saturday afternoon deadline. He reported that Martinez said he was not trying to hit Long but slipped as he drew his gun. The officer stated: "The gun suddenly went off. The man was about 30 feet from me. I wasn't trying to shoot him but he was hit."[42] Newark Police director Dominick A. Spina lamented the fact that Kuperstein was able to interview Martinez back at the station and that Martinez gave "misinformation" to the reporter and caused "so many problems."[43] Spina wrote to Newark mayor Hugh J. Addonizio: "You will note that this investigation indicates that there is a difference of opinion between Patrolman Martinez and Mr. Kuperstein as to the exact language used at the time Martinez was interviewed by Mr. Kuperstein" In fact, Kuperstein states that Martinez was "highly emotional and appeared to be confused and distraught." Martinez later told his superiors that he didn't remember telling Kuperstein that he slipped.[44]

The next day, June 13, the police reported that Martinez fired when he saw that Long had a knife and had slashed at the officer's partner, Provost.[45] After investigating the shooting, Spina told an exasperated Mayor Addonizio: "There is no indication whatsoever in his original report that he stumbled and fell. Captain [Anthony] Kessup reported that Martinez appeared to be nervous and in a state of shock. I have further ascertained that Patrolman Martinez did go to a psychiatrist several times after the shooting."[46]

Leaders of the Newark CORE chapter demanded that Martinez be suspended while the investigation continued. They created, mimeographed, and distributed handwritten signs that read: "Stop Police Brutality. Our neighbor, Lester Long Jr., was murdered by a policeman last Friday night on the corner of Oriental and Broadway, shot in the back of the head." The flyers urged people to join CORE at a protest on June 16 at 7 p.m. at the street corner where Long was killed. In response, city leaders suspended Martinez while the investigation was pending.[47] The mayor said he ordered Martinez's suspension to prevent racial disorder, noting that nearly half of Newark's four hundred thousand residents were African American. CORE leaders, however, complained that Martinez was still being paid and that he was actually working a desk job at the police director's office.[48] Then more than 150 Newark police picketed in front of city hall around the clock for five days to protest the suspension; many were joined by their wives and children along with police officers and civic groups from nearby towns. The Junior Chamber of Commerce placed a coffin on the steps of City Hall with a sign reading: "Here lies the Newark Police department [sic], slain by . . ." The rest of the sign was ripped off.[49]

Mayor Addonizio accused demonstrators on both sides of "helping to split our community in two" and of "providing a rallying point for every malcontent, hothead and bigot in the area." The mayor and police department also opposed the idea of creating a civil review board to investigate the police. They pointed out that over the preceding five years, police had arrested more than one hundred thousand people with only twenty-eight complaints of brutality. And of those, the police found every one unsubstantiated.[50] CORE's local director, Fred Means, called these figures "very definitely misleading," arguing that black citizens didn't file complaints because they feared and distrusted law enforcement. A *Newark Evening News* article quoted a representative of the ACLU likewise calling the city's statistics "meaningless" and arguing that "for every complaint that's made, there are 50 to 100 that aren't made."[51]

CORE continued to complain that the police department's account of the shooting "was confused and unclear." "There is a strong possibility," CORE suspected, "that the patrolman abused his powers and misused his revolver." Indeed, the officers hadn't had time to get their stories straight before they filed their report on the shooting. Hundreds of CORE members and others responded to Director Means's call "to turn this town peacefully and non-violently upside down" by marching to city hall to protest police brutality.[52]

Martinez wasn't off the street for long. He was reinstated after eleven days, when the Newark Human Rights Commission concluded from its investigation that there was no evidence of racial prejudice in Martinez's shooting of Long.[53] An Essex County grand jury also determined Martinez was legally justified in the force used against the victim. The mayor ordered an investigation into how the conflicting reports about the shooting were released to the public, believing their muddled information brought about the unrest and demonstrations.[54] Newark Police director Spina delivered the results of that second investigation on August 5, 1965.

"In all good conscience, it is my personal opinion and I coincide with the recommendation made by Deputy Chief [Floyd] Harle that no charges can be upheld and substantiated against Patrolman Martinez." He attached to his report a new policy, General Order Number 65–14, which put tighter controls on the release of information to the news media. After the Long shooting, only police supervisors and command officers were allowed to release "pertinent news."[55]

Martinez sued local chapters of CORE and the NAACP for libel in late July of 1965. He complained that "he was deprived of his position as a patrolman, his reputation has been and will be injured due to the great deal of publicity attached to his illegal suspension, he has suffered and will suffer mental anguish requiring medical attention, and he and his family have suffered special damages and his position in the community has been seriously damaged." Farmer, CORE's national director, was handed court documents accusing him of libel "conspiracy" shortly before he spoke at a civil rights rally organized in Military Park. Under heavy police guard because of death threats, Farmer addressed a crowd of about seven hundred people, demanding the creation of a civilian police-review board. He had distributed a flyer that read in part, "Henry Martinez is a murderer," and for that and the other flyer, he and eleven others faced defamation suits.[56]

Two years after the shooting in August of 1967, weary of the legal battle, CORE settled out of court for an undisclosed sum.[57] The same NAACP and CORE lawyers were fighting legal battles on a variety of fronts to secure basic civil rights for African Americans. The libel suits pulled them away from such cases and into civil court, case after case, year after year. The Baltimore *Afro American* offered context to the CORE libel case in 1965, pointing out that similar suits had been filed by police officers accused of brutality in six states.[58] News articles rarely provided such context for the libel onslaught by this time, for many observers had not yet connected the dots, which showed the growing trend of SLAPP suits in the United States.

The Possibility of "Police Culpability"

Almost a year to the day after the Gilligan incident, another police shooting brought attention to police brutality and resulted in yet another libel suit in the New York City area. An African American man known by his neighbors to be mentally ill shadowboxed on the sidewalk in his Brooklyn neighborhood of Bedford-Stuyvesant on a hot and steamy day in July 1965. He often prayed and talked to himself but otherwise seemed harmless. New to the beat on this particular day was Sheldon Liebowitz, a white twenty-eight-year-old rookie patrolman, who spotted the man, Nelson Erby, behaving strangely. Witnesses differed on what happened next. Some said Erby had dropped to his knees to pray for rain, for relief from the heat, as he had done many times before.

Patrolman Liebowitz ordered him to stop, but Erby did not "move along" as the officer instructed. The official police report said Erby hit out at the police officer, the two struggled, and Erby pulled out a knife with a five-inch blade. The police said Leibowitz was handcuffing Erby to arrest him for disturbing the peace when Erby lunged at him, and then in the ensuing struggle, the officer was hit in the left forearm by a bullet from his own pistol. A passing truck driver, twenty-year-old Stewart Maxwell, told police that Erby had the gun and that Maxwell hopped out of his vehicle and hit Erby with a nightstick he kept in his truck. Leibowitz was able to get his gun back and shoot Erby after the man ignored his warning to stand back.[59]

Two-time Pulitzer Prize winner Homer Bigart wrote about the dramatic scene in the *New York Times*, reporting that some one hundred witnesses saw the street struggle and Erby's demise: "With bullets in his abdomen and arm, Erby staggered westward on Nostrand Avenue, passing a shoe store, a bar and a doughnut stand. He lurched out into the street between two parked cars, then staggered slowly into the open doorway of Little King & Queen, an infants-wear store. He collapsed inside and died before an ambulance could take him to Cumberland Hospital."[60] Police said Erby had been arrested twelve times and was twice convicted of felonious assault, including an attack on a police officer in 1958.[61]

Brooklyn district attorney Aaron E. Koota worried about another shooting setting off another series of riots. He issued a statement to the press promising a thorough investigation and urging people to stay home rather than protest in the streets. He advised: "To the people of the Bedford-Stuyvesant community, I say remain calm. Do not lose your heads."[62]

The local chapter of CORE reacted swiftly. Members of CORE claimed that Erby "was mentally defective" and "like a child" and that the police should have treated him as such.[63] Instead, they said Erby was shot in cold blood by an inexperienced officer who didn't know the neighborhood or Erby. At a rally at Jefferson and Nostrand avenues the night after the shooting, former Brooklyn CORE chairman Oliver Leeds addressed a seething crowd of about 125 people from a wooden platform. Leeds called the shooting "a typical day in the life of a black man in Bedford-Stuyvesant—a shooting of a Negro by a white policeman."[64]

CORE brought forth witnesses who said that Erby never had possession of the patrolman's gun and that there had been no knife. The organization held a protest at the intersection where the shooting occurred and organized a march over the bridge from Brooklyn, a total of eight miles, to police headquarters in Manhattan. Some 150 demonstrators carried signs protesting police brutality with such messages as "Down with the Killers in Blue" and sang "We Shall Overcome." Marchers passed out leaflets demanding a civilian review board to independently consider evidence in such cases, along with fielding community complaints about police.[65]

During the grand jury investigation in the following days of late July 1965, CORE members were routinely quoted in several newspapers throughout the city, arguing that Erby's arrest record was irrelevant to the shooting. They also released his autopsy report showing he had been shot five times.[66] Meanwhile, Liebowitz faced several threats by telephone while recovering from the gunshot wound in his arm, so authorities moved him to a different hospital where he was placed under twenty-four-hour guard.[67]

CORE's James Farmer sent Police Commissioner Vincent Broderick a telegram saying the shooting indicated the possibility of "police culpability." His telegram was widely covered and quoted by the media. Hearing from thirty-six witness, an all-white grand jury determined Erby had been shot in the chest rather than the back, evidence that Erby was moving toward the police officer rather than away.[68] It declined to indict Liebowitz on criminal charges, and CORE leaders said they were "seriously disturbed" by the patrolman's exoneration. A statement, also widely quoted in local newspapers, read: "We again emphasize that this case, as countless cases in the past, dramatizes the vastly inadequate system of police review adjudication in New York City."[69]

CORE attorney George Schiffer filed a complaint in State Supreme Court in Brooklyn, accusing prosecutors of illegally using grand juries as trial juries. He argued that Brooklyn district attorney Koota "whitewashed" Patrolman Liebowitz and the case and that Erby's family deserved a more thorough investigation into the incident. On September 5, 1965, he told the *New York Times*: "Since Erby's death, seven people have been killed by the police that we know of—some accidental, some justifiable, and some highly questionable. . . . The attitude in this case seemed to be that Erby was a worthless guy."[70]

Liebowitz filed a libel against CORE in October 1965, naming several members personally, along with other civil rights groups that had engaged in public dialogue about this shooting specifically and police brutality generally. Liebowitz said the civil rights leaders "conspired and maliciously and willfully participated in a plan and course of action designed to defame and injure the plaintiff in his good name and reputation in his profession as a policeman, to destroy his income and livelihood, and to remove [the] plaintiff as a police officer" in New York City. At the crux of his complaint was a poster or handbill that stated, "Wanted for Murder," and included a picture of him in his police uniform, his name, and his precinct. The item was signed by the Harlem Defense Council.[71]

Seeking $2.5 million in damages, Liebowitz's attorney used the language of the *Sullivan* decision delivered months earlier, asserting that the poster was published with actual malice, with reason to believe it false and with the intent of exposing him to "hatred, contempt, ridicule and aversion and injure and dishonor him" as a police officer. Like Gilligan, he even sued the printer who stamped the poster. The NAACP mounted a vigorous defense, filing motion after motion and pointing to the March 1964 *Sullivan* case and Justice Brennan's clearly stated opinion about a citizen's right and duty to criticize police actions. More than a year later, at the end of 1966, New York County judge Abraham Geller dismissed the suit.

By the early 1960s, the NAACP had become rather well equipped to contend with the libel onslaught in addition managing its civil rights caseload. Its Legal Defense and Educational Fund, created in 1940, employed a staff of nine lawyers by 1963, while still calling on local lawyers throughout the states to help with various local cases. The NAACP legal budget was $625,000 in 1962, increasing dramatically to more than $1 million in 1963. It was learning how to fight this expensive legal battle deployed by plaintiffs to shut down civil rights reporting in the United States.[72]

"Either He Is for the Union or the Klan"

The glow of a fifty-foot burning cross flickered across Vernon John Naimaster's face as the acting grand dragon stood before some two thousand fellow KKK members in a Maryland cow pasture on a crisp November night in 1965. The thirty-six-year-old bus driver had seen his media blitz pay off in the sheer numbers of Klansmen swarming at the rally, the first one seen in the state in forty years. He'd publicized the big event on the radio and been interviewed by television and newspaper reporters, and here he was in a dark business suit and straw hat flanked by two Klansmen in white robes and miters.

"I'm the bus driver that they was talking about," Naimaster said from the back of a flatbed farm truck draped in black paper wreaths and in American and Confederate flags. He promised the new Maryland Klan would not bring violence to the state. "We will not entice violence, but we won't walk away from it either," he drawled.[73]

Naimaster had been a driver for the Baltimore Transit Company for twelve years. He told reporters that he had helped set up other rallies throughout the country and that Alabama-based Robert Shelton, imperial wizard of the United Klans of America, had offered him the title of grand dragon of the Maryland Klavern. Shelton was slated to headline the rally but canceled at the last minute for unspecified Klan business elsewhere. Naimaster said, "Tears are probably rolling from his eyes because he couldn't get here."[74]

Shelton had sued *Tuscaloosa News*' editor Buford Boone for his anti-Klan editorials the year before and the suit was ongoing. Across the road from the cow pasture, a huge sign leaned against a tree, its message criticizing the chief justice of the U.S. Supreme Court: "Save America: Impeach Earl Warren." Justice Warren led a liberal majority that had expanded civil rights and civil liberties during the 1950s and early 1960s, and the farmer who rented his field to the Klan in Rising Sun, Maryland, about fifty miles northeast of Baltimore, undoubtedly knew the sign would please the rally-goers.[75]

Naimaster had estimated that a crowd of eight to nine thousand supporters might be on hand, but media reports variously estimated between two and three thousand, trampling the corn husks and cow manure, attended the three-hour event. Rebel yells burst from the crowd around the fifty-foot, burlap-wrapped burning cross, and a red-robed man chanted: "Forward the white race. Segregation forever." The speakers alternately spewed racist jokes and raged against President Johnson, the newly enacted civil rights laws, and the evils of race mixing. Naimaster chimed in, "Christianity is my guide. The way it is being destroyed today is outrageous to me. It's got to stop."[76]

The new grand dragon said he had gathered a group of Klansmen to train as "security guards," getting the idea from the helmeted Delaware Klansmen who prowled through the crowd at the Rising Sun rally to provided "security" for the Klan leaders and the fiery cross. The Delaware grand dragon, "an ex-vice cop" named Ralph Pryor, informed the press that his guards were highly qualified because they were former military paratroopers, army rangers, and police officers.⁷⁷

The Baltimore *Evening Sun* reported: "As the Klan rally drew to a close with the cross burning beneath a moonlit sky, Mr. Naimaster said he was pleased at the turnout. 'Terrific,' he said. 'I think this will certainly help strengthen the Klan in Maryland. I got so many applications it will take me two years to answer them.'"⁷⁸

Not everyone was pleased with the resurgence of the Klan in Maryland. Two nearby churches, one Presbyterian and another Catholic, scheduled prayer vigils the same night to protest the Klan rally, along with participants from nearby Lincoln University in Oxford, Pennsylvania, just across the state line. Prayer-vigil attendees signed petitions protesting the presence of the Klan and delivered them to the governors of Maryland and Pennsylvania. A total of ten churches, local Democratic and Republican committees, and the AFL-CIO chapter worked together on the effort, and the vigils were publicized from local pulpits, through handbills, and newspapers.⁷⁹

The Saturday-night KKK rally got wide coverage in the Baltimore press, and the Baltimore Transit Company was flooded with complaints about Namaister and demands to fire him. Long-time Baltimore NAACP branch president Lillie Jackson sent a telegram to transit company leaders, asking for an investigation into the matter, and that telegram was published in local newspapers. Jackson pointed out that the Maryland grand dragon was employed by a public utility providing mass transportation for the city of Baltimore. The bus company was part of the Metropolitan Transit Authority, created by Maryland General Assembly, and that most of the passengers riding the buses were black.⁸⁰

She said her office had been bombarded with calls from concerned African Americans who depended on the bus system for their transportation. She received several tips that Naimaster was recruiting Klan members and spreading antiblack and anti-Jewish propaganda on company property during working hours. Callers also told her that Naimaster had been suspended from the job in the recent past for assaulting an elderly black passenger on a bus he was driving. Riders on Baltimore's city buses told her they feared for their safety.[81]

Within days, the bus company fired Naimaster, citing "actions which have resulted in turmoil, discussion and apprehension among our employees" and violation of a company rule that employees "shall foster friendly relations between the company and the general public."[82] The Transit Workers Union, bargaining for about 1,850 bus drivers—500 were African Americans—called a meeting to look into the controversy. Just days after the rally, the union board ordered Naimaster to appear before it and answer questions about his Klan activities and statements in the press. As a result, he began backing away from his leadership role in the KKK, announcing that he had just turned over his duties to another Klansman and that he would merely be an active member.[83]

At a standing-room-only meeting of about 250 drivers, about half of whom were black, the union board president, Frank P. Baummer, said there was no evidence Naimaster had violated any union law. One driver, unable to contain himself, yelled: "You mean, Mr. President, that a man who belongs to an organization which throws bombs into a church and kills our children, can work beside me?"

Another driver yelled, "You know that the Klan is a terrorist and corrupt organization, Frank!"

Still another driver asserted, "What bothers me is the feeling I have when I pull up to a curb, or have to speak to someone on the bus who has had one beer too many. How do they know I'm not the Klansman?"

A black driver joined in: "How do you think we, as colored people, feel working with this man?"

From the back of the room, another voice broke through the rumbling and threats to boycott. "Either he is for the union or the Klan. He can't be for both."

Still another called out, "We have to do this. We must denounce him and now."

The union members then unanimously adopted a resolution denouncing Naimaster.[84]

Amid threats of a strike if Naimaster got his job back, Baltimore

NAACP president Jackson and her daughter, Juanita Jackson Mitchell, the president state NAACP, testified at an arbitration hearing held in March 11, 1966, expressing their concerns over a KKK leader working as a public employee. Bus company officials worried about violence on Naimaster's bus, the possibility of a strike, and a boycott by black riders. Upholding the termination of Naimaster, the arbitrator, Clair V. Duff, wrote, "The company was not required to wait until it became a battleground in the civil rights movement before taking action." As for Naimaster's "freedom of belief," Duff noted that his conduct went beyond mere belief when he became a "zealous advocate of intolerance and racial hatred."[85]

Seeking $200,000 in damages, Naimaster sued Jackson, the local branch of the NAACP, and Juanita Jackson Mitchell. He said their telegrams, complaints, and testimony at the arbitration hearing degraded him and "exposed him to public hatred, contempt and ridicule, aversion and disgrace, and were calculated to produce an evil opinion of him in the minds of right-thinking persons and deprive him of his employment."[86]

Before this case, Mitchell had faced down a $1 million libel suit filed by a police officer and saw this latest complaint as yet another SLAPP suit, an effort to silence her criticism of Naimaster and the KKK.[87] Mitchell, the first African American woman to practice law in Maryland, wrote that the suit's sole purpose was to harass and punish the NAACP and stop members from exercising their First Amendment right to "criticize and protest on matters of public importance and national concern."[88]

Mitchell and her husband, Clarence, who ran their own Baltimore law firm, Mitchell and Mitchell, turned to Robert Carter of the NAACP Legal Defense Fund to represent her and her mother. They worked with Carter to move the case from Baltimore County to federal court on First and Fourteenth Amendment grounds. The Mitchells considered the Baltimore County Circuit Court an unfriendly venue, pointing to its decisions restricting black access to juries and discriminatory rulings relating to housing covenants. They also pointed out that candidates seeking office on a platform of racial segregation received overwhelming support in the local elections in fall 1966. Baltimore was a southern town, they said, and the possibility of impaneling a jury sympathetic to the Klan was highly probable. At this point, they knew the law was on their side, thanks to *Sullivan*, but they worried that the local court would deviate from the law. A federal judge in Baltimore denied the Mitchell's motion to move the case from state court, and the Fourth Circuit Court of Appeals affirmed that decision in 1970.[89]

NAACP leaders were encouraged by the U.S. Supreme Court in *Associated Press v. Walker* in 1967. The court had extended *Sullivan*'s actual malice standard to public figures, and they reasoned that Naimaster would surely fall under this plaintiff category. He had publicly pronounced that he was revitalizing the Maryland KKK, granted interviews with journalists, and led a rally attended by hundreds. In court filings, NAACP lawyers argued that, like General Edwin Walker at Ole Miss, Naimaster had "thrust himself into the vortex of an important controversy" and that, in doing so, he had "made himself a public figure."[90] They also pondered the idea that the *Sullivan* rule was not limited to protecting newspaper or media defendants—that any "speaker deserves as much protection from the first amendment as the newspaper publisher."[91]

In 1973, after four days of testimony, an all-white jury rejected Naimaster's libel claims. Noted Maryland civil rights lawyer Gerald A. Smith had signed on to the defense team at that point, and the case had been moved to Annapolis in Anne Arundel County. The *Sullivan* and *Walker* decisions would have been well understood there and explicated to juries. And times were changing, perhaps. "By that time," Smith said, "people wanted to distance themselves from the activities of the Klan."[92]

"They Beat Me All the Way to the Paddy Wagon"

Local NAACP Chapter president Edwin Parms of Akron, Ohio, fired off a telegram to Mayor John Ballard and gave copy to the newspaper in September of 1966, calling for the immediate suspension of four police officers involved in the arrest and beating of a black man named Kenneth Rowe until an investigation was completed and a report made public. He said the NAACP would call for a protest march on Akron City Hall if the officers were not suspended pending a hearing. Parms, a prominent black attorney who grew up in the city, followed through on his promise. Ten days after the arrest, nearly three hundred demonstrators marched in silent protest, delivering to the mayor a list of demands for dealing with all police brutality charges. Gary Sampson, a reporter for the *Akron Beacon Journal,* got a copy of Parms's telegram and wrote about the incident that prompted the NAACP protest:

> Kenneth J. Rowe, a 24-year-old black man, said that officers Warren L. Hayes and William O. Rice beat him after they stopped him for running a red light on September 10. Patrolmen Jerry Green and Jay C Carano arrived at the scene as backup and said Rowe got hostile after he learned he was being arrested rather than receiving a traffic ticket. Police said they had to chase Rowe for more than a mile at speeds over seventy miles per hour and that Rowe refused to submit to a search once he finally pulled over. For his part, Rowe said he only fought back when the officers began beating him while he was being lead from the cruiser to a police wagon. Rowe, a Goodyear Aerospace employee and part-time mechanical engineering student at the American Technical Institute in Akron, was charged with resisting arrest, reckless driving and running a red light.

Parms told the *Akron Beacon Journal* that the NAACP march was in protest of the "many incidents" of police brutality over the last ten years. "There will be no singing or talking during the march," Parms said. He advised those who would attempt to make the march anything but peaceful to stay home. He also urged students to stay at school. The mood of townsfolk grew tense as Howard Lewis, the head of the local Ku Klux Klan, threatened to hold a countermarch. The newspaper reported that Rowe challenged the officers to take a lie-detector test to determine who was telling the truth. Rowe, married and the father of a six-month-old son, Kenneth Jr., had served as an Army paratrooper and was a squad leader in Vietnam as well as an instructor for Vietnamese soldiers. But he had experienced some minor trouble with the law when he got home and had been convicted of intoxication in 1965 and fined $5 plus court costs. He also had "a number of traffic violations," according to the local newspaper.[93] After the beating and arrest, Rowe remained in the hospital for twelve days.

When Rowe was released, Akron mayor John S. Ballard held a two-and-a-half-hour hearing in his office, listening to testimony from nine people, starting with Rowe. He had agreed to hold the inquiry at the request of John A. Bailey, an attorney for the four officers. Bailey said that the mayor, who was also head of the city's Safety Division, had the right to hold the administrative hearing under the Akron city charter. If the officers used more force than necessary, Ballard stated, they could be suspended "or worse."[94]

Represented at the hearing by Parms, Rowe said he was driving west on Wooster Avenue at about 4 a.m. on September 10, heading for a bar on Copley Road. He saw the traffic light turn red. "I ran it anyway," he explained, "because it was early in the morning and I didn't see any other cars." Then he saw the flashing red lights of the police cruiser in his rearview mirror. He pulled over and got out of his vehicle, walking back to the patrol car that pulled in behind him, its lights flashing. Rowe said two officers sat in the front seat of the car, so he got in the back seat and produced his driver's license. The officers then began debating whether they should cite him or arrest him. He said Officer Hayes wanted to just give him a ticket, but Officer Rice wanted to arrest him for either speeding or running the red light. "Then Rice turned to me and said, 'Mr. Rowe, you're under arrest,'" Rowe recalled. "I asked him, 'Don't you usually just give citations in these cases?' But he said, 'You've got to see a judge,' or something like that."[95]

"Well, that's how you usually treat my people anyway," Rowe told Officer Rice. "Then he got out and got in the back seat and hit me three or four times on the left side of the head." Rowe testified that he and Rice struggled in the back of the cruiser while Hayes got out of the front seat and opened the rear door. Hayes "kept hitting me on the leg, either with his club or fist, and pulling me out the door." Rowe then said Rice pulled him from the car. "I saw him reach for his gun . . . and I thought, Oh, God, I'm going to be shot." He said Rice clubbed him from behind with his nightstick, handcuffed him, and clubbed him again before heaving him into the back of the cruiser. As Rice radioed the station, Rowe yelled, "Help! They're out here beating me!"

Rowe testified to the mayor: "I don't know if the radio man heard me or not." Then a second cruiser arrived, and Patrolmen Green and Carano began talking outside Rice and Hayes' car. "I was pleading for mercy. I told them I was hurt. One of them told me to shut up."

"Then the paddy wagon arrived and they told me to get out and when I did Rice hit me again and knocked me down. He reached down and pulled me up by my sweater. When he pulled me up I kneed him in the groin," Rowe admitted. "Then they were all on me, jockeying for position, yelling, 'Let me hit him!' They beat me all the way to the paddy wagon."

Rice and Hayes testified next, agreeing with the story up until they decided to make the arrest. Rice said that Rowe had "turned hostile and abusive and began swearing at us and cursing and saying he could whip me any time." Rice said: "I told him he was under arrest and ordered him out of the cruiser so that we could search him. I told him this was necessary. I asked him to get out three times, and he refused. Then I reached in to pull him out and he struck me on the right shoulder." Rice said he went into the cruiser after Rowe, and they wrestled and punched each other until Rowe threw him forward against the back of the front seat and pinned him. Hayes said that after he saw Rowe punch his partner, he began beating him "on the legs, ribs and arms" with his night stick "in an effort to subdue him." Both officers testified that they finally got Rowe out of the car and were trying handcuff him when he took another swing at Rice. Hayes said he hit Rowe on top of the head with his nightstick and Rice handcuffed him. When they got Rowe into the back seat again they radioed for the paddy wagon, advising the dispatcher that Rowe would need medical attention.

Officer Hayes said: "If we had wanted to use excessive force, one man could have done it. We wanted to avoid that. That's why it took two of us to bring him under control." The officers said they did not draw their guns. Rice said he took his pistol out of its holster and "threw it over the front seat when I thought I felt him reaching for it while we were wrestling in the back seat." Officer Carano and Green testified that they arrived in the second cruiser at the same time as the paddy wagon. Carano said he saw Rice deliver one blow after Rowe kneed him in the groin. The two officers in the paddy wagon said when they arrived, Rowe was standing by the police cruiser. Officer William H. Howland, driver of the paddy wagon, testified: "He (Rowe) was yelling and screaming. I didn't pay much attention to what he was saying. No one struck him. The only time we touched him was to search him." Robert Deen, owner of Deen's garage, testified that when he arrived with a tow truck to impound Rowe's car, both police cars were there, but the paddy wagon hadn't arrived yet. He said the prisoner was in the front seat of one of the cruisers. He said Officer Rice asked the prisoner to get out of the car and placed his hand on the man's shoulder. The prisoner got out and then kneed Rice, Deen said. According to Deen, Rowe was "fighting all the way. He called them a lot of names. He threatened them."

After the booking at Police Headquarters, Rowe was admitted to City Hospital with a damaged left eye, scalp cuts, a concussion, and broken facial bones. Rice, the only officer who said he had been injured, testified that he suffered neck and back sprains along with bruises on his hands. Rice's physician, Dr. Charles E. DuVall, testified that he had diagnosed Rice's conditions on September 14 and that he had treated Rice for similar complaints on multiple occasions. This medical information suggested that Rice had gotten into brawls before.

After the hearing, Mayor Ballard, a former FBI agent, said he wanted to study a report from Rowe's doctor before deciding whether to suspend the officers pending further investigation. Ballard said: "I know I face the extremely difficult question: Whether excessive force was used. I will search my conscience and try to arrive at what I feel is just and right."

Rowe filed charges of assault and battery against Rice and Hayes in early October. The city of Akron took his affidavit seriously, arresting the two officers and charging them for the crime. They were released on bond. Later that month, two of the officers, Green and Carano, sued Parms and Rowe for $10,000 each, plus court costs and attorneys' fees, for defamation. The officers said that because of Parms's telegram and resulting newspaper coverage, they had suffered "great mental anguish, humiliation and embarrassment" and that their professional standing and reputations were damaged. In identical suits, they complained that members of the public had been calling and threatening them and their families on the telephone. They complained that they had been subject to "investigations and interrogations" by their Akron Police Department superiors, the mayor of Akron, and the FBI. The officers' complaint charged that Rowe falsely said, "He beat me while I was handcuffed and under arrest." They also complained that the statement was widely published in the press, starting with Gary Sampson's story in the *Akron Beacon Journal*.[96]

In court filings, Parms countered that his statements were true and therefore could not be libelous. Meanwhile, the criminal case against the officers proceeded quickly. In November, the officers' trial for assault and battery kicked off in Municipal Court with much fanfare and media scrutiny. The Akron City prosecutor Ed Pierce made the case for Rowe, arguing that the young engineer was not resisting arrest but resisting assault. Pierce told the court that such a beating could happen to anyone, anytime, and that the city must take police brutality seriously. "Someday we are going to be driving alone late at night. Someday we are going to be in that car," the prosecutor explained. "It's time we tell the police how we want them to use force. When you become a police officer, you get the badge, the club, the gun, but you have to have humanity too."[97] Rowe testified that he did not hit the officers with his fist, and only kneed Rice in self defense.

Defense attorney John A. Bailey, hired by the Fraternal Order of Police, said the issue at hand wasn't the magnitude of Rowe's crime, but whether the arrest was lawful and whether the police were using "such force as is reasonably necessary."[98] Judge Joseph I. Wetli, brought in from the Municipal Court of Oregon,

Ohio, a Toledo suburb, found the officers innocent of assault and battery on November 22, 1966. "I won't split hairs about how much force should have been used in subduing the prisoner once he was under arrest," Wetli ruled. "The weight of the evidence seems to indicate to me, however, that it was Rowe who provoked the officers to violence, and not the other way around." "Rowe, because of his race, may feel he has been abused," the judge admonished, "but he should have consideration for other people."[99]

City prosecutor Pierce echoed the NAACP request that the Akron needed a citizen board to review all cases in which police brutality is charged. "Akron police ought to have a community relations division," Pierce told reporters after the verdict in the assault and battery case, "and teach their boys how to bring a person out of a car without beating the tar out of him." Pierce was most certainly aware of the pending libel suit. "Rowe stands to lose his shirt," he told reporters. On top of that, he had to file a complaint and go to court rather than go before a civil review board. Mayor Ballard, however, said he was against such a board. He waited to issue a ruling in his own inquiry after the court had done so.[100]

After the officers' criminal trial, Rice and Hayes filed suit against Rowe, each seeking $10,000 in actual and punitive damages plus court costs and attorneys' fees. Rowe now faced a total of $40,000 in libel suits from the four officers who arrived on the scene that night. In their complaint, Rice and Hayes said they were forced to appear in court three different times and pointed out that they were found not guilty. They characterized the entire event as a "malicious prosecution" that caused them to suffer "mental anguish, humiliation, worry and nervousness."[101]

NAACP lawyers Robert Carter and Lewis M. Steel signed on to help Akron lawyer Norman Purnell with Rowe's defense. Both New York lawyers were well-seasoned in the area of libel law by this time. In the process, they also agreed to represent Rowe. The exchange of calls and letters between the lawyers in Akron and New York City followed all that fall and winter. In November of 1966, Steel advised Parms, who was still battling Green and Carano in court, that the *Sullivan* ruling should grant him "ample protection." Steel said, "As I read *Sullivan,* the plaintiff would have to prove that you were aware that your statements were erroneous in order to recover." He said the Rowe case was more complex and that a jury might decide that Rowe lied in making his accusations, and thus the officers would be able to prove actual malice. Steel also worried about the big picture, when anyone makes police brutality charges: "A person under arrest would always find himself faced with large libel verdicts if he ever complained of police misconduct. . . ."[102]

With their First Amendment defense, the attorneys discussed filing a motion for summary judgment, hoping for a quick win under the *Sullivan* decision. Steel also pondered the issue of "truth" in the defense. In a letter to Purnell, he wrote: "I would hope that we could develop facts indicating that Rowe was in the custody of police during the time he claims to have been beaten and that only he and the police were witnesses."[103] Purnell and Steel also agreed that the defense of privilege would be appropriate in the Parms and Rowe cases, because the issue was of public concern. Purnell wrote Steel: "This defense is based upon the theory that the defendant, in the interest of society tells third persons certain matters which he, in good faith, believes to be true. It is my further assertion that the duty need not be a legal one, but merely a moral or social duty."[104] Steel agreed that the telegram to Mayor Ballard should be considered privileged, but he pondered whether Parms's release of that telegram to a journalist at the local newspaper would be considered such. Steel surmised: "Parms as an NAACP branch president would have such a duty to comment on police brutality to the Mayor. . . . I am not sure that such privilege would cover release of statements to a newspaper involving the conduct of a third party." He continued to worry that Rowe's defense would be more complicated and thus difficult, and he hoped that the free-speech argument would hold up in court.[105] In a return letter, Purnell said the Rowe case was certainly winnable but depended on whether or not the jury felt that Parms "went too far" in contacting a reporter at the *Akron Beacon Journal* with the contents of the telegram.[106]

For several weeks in early 1967, Purnell toiled on with the "qualified privilege" defense. But by April, Steel told him he was off base. From New York, he kept coming back to the *Sullivan* case, which would make Parms's case a slam-dunk win. "Because I do not believe that plaintiff can possibly prove malice on the part of Parms," Lewis argued, "this case does not appear overly worrisome." He was more worried about the cases against Rowe and advised that winning would require intensive research.[107] Lawyers also agreed that Parms had merely called for the officers' suspension until a fair and impartial investigation was completed. Bob Adler, a civil rights attorney in New York, concluded, "This seems to me to be fair comment in its most classic sense." In their defense strategy, they pondered whether they should argue for the extension of privilege to Rowe. Adler reasoned, "The only alternative would be to put a muzzle on the victim of a beating lest he find himself sued for defamation." Rowe was out of the public eye when the beatings occurred, so it was his word against the officers'. As they filed various motions and pleas in the libel cases, the lawyers also discussed Akron's ongoing school desegregation cases and a formal protest against the city school board's redrawing of the boundary lines for each school in an apparent effort to keep schools all-white and all-black. As usual, civil rights attorneys had much more on their plates than the SLAPP suits.[108]

By late 1967, the case was taken off the court docket. Lawyers for the police surely understood the implications of *Sullivan* by this time and gave up the fight. In later years, Parms would be most noted for his successful 1972 federal lawsuit requiring the fire department and police force to hire blacks in the city of Akron. Around town, his nickname became "Do-you-want-a-job-Parms" because he always asked African Americans if they needed a job and worked to connect them with potential employers.[109]

Another "Slaughtered Youth"

NAACP lawyers in New York wished that Westley Wallace "West" Law would just slow down. The head of the NAACP branch in Savannah, Georgia, had passion and vigor, but he also ushered in a host of headaches for the national organization. These days it seemed like the civil rights fight came with too many civil suits, and in April of 1966, the national NAACP organization was reeling from a case stemming from the Savannah branch's actions. A grocery store owner sued the NAACP to recover economic losses after Law organized pickets in front of the market. It all started in May of 1962 when Robert Bolton, a fourteen-year-old black youth, was accused by his employer of stealing merchandise. The youngster told his mother that the owner slapped and kicked him after the accusations were made. She then complained to the police, who did nothing. So she appealed to West Law and the local chapter of the NAACP for help. Law organized picketing and a full economic boycott of the grocery store until owner Haldred Overstreet won a temporary restraining order against the NAACP to stop the picketing. The Georgia Supreme Court later agreed that the national chapter of the NAACP was liable for intimidating grocery store customers, blocking sidewalks, and causing scattered incidents of violence, along with lost business. The U.S. Supreme Court initially agreed to consider one of the questions in the case but dismissed the writ of certiorari in April 1966, causing the Georgia ruling to stand. This case provided another financial burden on the cash-strapped NAACP, and it would create tension between the New York office and local NAACP leaders in Savannah.

Two years later, on April 26, 1968, a Savannah police officer shot and killed a black teenager, and Law again took the lead in protesting the action. He issued a statement about the killing of sixteen-year-old Lewis Mack: "It appears to us that the policemen involved are not telling the whole truth, but apparently have killed an unarmed Negro youth in cold blood and are now busily constructing a justifiable alibi for their crime." Law said the "slaughtered youth" was slightly built and his body was "riddled with bullets."[110]

The incident was widely reported in the media, including the *Savannah News-Press*. The paper quoted police detective H. E. Fields saying he shot Mack after the teen and two other "colored" men attacked, beat, mugged, and robbed him.[111] The use of force was self-defense, insisted Fields, a police officer for ten years, the last six as detective. Fields sued the newspaper and Law as president of the local NAACP chapter and the national NAACP in New York in May 1968, complaining in his libel suit that the newspaper didn't check the reliability of Law's statements. He declared that Law, the NAACP, and the newspaper had injured him in his profession as a police officer and characterized him as a criminal to the public. Fields sought $50,000 in general damages and $100,000 in punitive damages.[112]

Law held several mass meetings to discuss the case, much to the concern of NAACP general counsel Robert Carter in New York, along with Savannah attorney Gene Gadsden, who served as chair of the NAACP's local legal-redress committee. The newspaper hired Savannah attorney Thomas Gignilliat to mount its defense, and he was eager to collaborate with Carter and Gadsden. Carter characterized the suit "as a reasonably serious issue" and was clearly growing weary of such libel assaults in civil court. Carter and Gadsden agreed that Law must keep his public statements about the case to a minimum. In a letter to Law, Carter referred to the costly Overstreet case and urged, "Please be careful in issuing any statements, since we don't want to be in a position of having our defenses eliminated by anything you might say without the advice of counsel. . . . We cannot afford to pay another $60,000 fine."[113]

Law responded to Carter: "I was somewhat disturbed by the tone of the letter in as much as one would assume . . . I had no right to criticize a policeman. . . . I do hope I will be allowed to honestly condemn bad public conduct or police brutality when Negroes are victimized in this town." Law said he consulted with his public relations chairman and couldn't understand why

Carter was siding with the Savannah NAACP executive committee against him. Law also vented a bit about the condition of race relations in Savannah and about the attitudes of the police. "There are many racists among the white policemen in this town," Law complained. "It is obvious that Detective Fields and his lawyer are 'NAACP haters' and 'negro haters.' It appears to me that public officials can be criticized and that [the lawsuit] is simply an attempt to intimidate me and the NAACP."[114]

Carter responded to Law's letter, again referring to financial losses the NAACP had faced, although the figure differed slightly. The attorney explained the NAACP's legal and fiscal position in no uncertain terms:

> Because of ill-advised action some time ago, this office was forced to pay approximately $65,000 for acts about which we knew nothing. The Association cannot be placed in that kind of posture a second time. It would seem to me that having been warned once that you would be aware that when lawyers say go slow, that you would understand and appreciate that advice to act with restraint is intended only as a precautionary measure and has nothing whatever to do with taking sides. If we lose this, are you prepared to pay damages? I am not certain that the NAACP can't win this lawsuit, but since we have been sued, I want you to give out no public statements about this matter except on specific advice of Gadsden or myself.[115]

West Law had to conduct himself with discretion and prudence; the resources of the NAACP were nearly exhausted by the many legal challenges the organization was battling around the country.

Attorneys for the NAACP and the newspaper moved for dismissal of the libel case, asserting that the statements were truthful and protected by the First and Fourteenth Amendments under *Sullivan*. They said the *Savannah News-Press* article said nothing defamatory about the detective in the statements and series of articles published between April 27 and May 8, 1968. The newspaper reported the mugging of Fields, the slaying of the alleged mugger, Lewis Mack, the call for an investigation by the NAACP, the arrest of other suspects, information about ballistic reports, the coroner's report, and the filing of a wrongful-death suit against the mayor and other city officials by Mack's mother in U.S. district court. Motions in the libel case were initially set for a hearing on October 29, 1968, then pushed back to December. But the case quietly disappeared from the docket. At this point, more than four years after *Sullivan*, it was likely attorneys for the police detective knew they couldn't win.

This chapter focuses on a trio of police brutality cases in the New York City area in addition to cases in Akron, Ohio, and Savannah, Georgia. In all instances, civil rights leaders were sued for speaking out in defense of their communities and the victims of police violence. These intimidation lawsuits certainly SLAPPed the local chapters and national office of the NAACP. The Martinez case was settled out of court for an undisclosed sum. The Gilligan case disappeared from the docket but only after years of legal wrangling. The Liebowitz case was also retired. The resolutions of the Georgia and Ohio cases were also unclear. Likely, the police officers' lawyers told them they couldn't prevail in court. By the mid to late 1960s in a post-*Sullivan* environment, SLAPP targets had the upper hand and rarely lost, but it is impossible know how much money the defendants paid in attorneys' fees and how many nights of sleep they lost. It is also impossible to know how many people were discouraged from speaking out from fear of costly libel suits.

Legal scholars Pring and Canan have identified scores of police SLAPPs not related to civil rights issues during the 1970s and 1980s, noting that these suits are particularly unjust due to the "formidable power" police exercise in their communities. They argue, "Police SLAPPs will continue as long as they receive a neutral response (let alone encouragement and financial support) from police higher-ups, government officials, and police associations, lawyers, and unions. Until these authorities and our laws and judges make it clear that such suits are unacceptable, they may well continue to censor the message by censuring the messengers."[116]

CHAPTER 6

Sullivan Sinks In

On a Monday night, April 17, 1967, a desperate Rosemary Vital Harris called the New Iberia, Louisiana, police when her husband came home drunk and started hitting her yet again. She later learned that phone call was a big mistake, that she would not be rescued that night by the men in blue. She would instead suffer more violence, this time at the hands of the police, and given the reputation of local law enforcement among African Americans in New Iberia, NAACP leaders did not doubt her story as relayed to them the next day. "Two policemen came and one of them told me I had to go too. They took both of us," said the twenty-eight-year-old Rosemary. They put her husband, Lester, in one interrogation room and Rosemary in another, explaining that she must file the complaint at the police station rather than from home. She heard Lester screaming as police beat him in the room down the hall. Then they turned on her. She recounted, "After a while a big fat policeman came in and started asking how many children I had so I told him six."

One of Rosemary Harris's children was a teenager at the time, living with an aunt, and the other five lived with her. The officer had seen her small baby in bed when he responded to the domestic-disturbance call. Harris kept asking to go home because her sick mother-in-law and her baby needed her, but the police officer, Lieutenant Henry Dorsey Jr., instead quizzed her about her work. She told him she cleaned a white lady's house four days a week and worked another job washing dishes at a café on Center Street. He finally stood up and told her he was taking her home, ignoring her protests. "In the first place I didn't have any business to go to the Court House because I had called for help," she later said.

Dorsey violated police regulations when he took Harris home alone that night. Policy dictated that two officers must accompany a woman when they transport her in a squad car. Driving toward home in the cruiser, Harris said, the police officer propositioned her for sex. In her written statement filed with the local NAACP chapter the next day, she said: "He asked me if I could fix him up. I told him no. He said now come on and let's not lose time so he carried me on a road cross Hopkin I believe it was dark I couldn't see. . . . He told me to set [sic] close to him. I was scared of him and I asked if he was going to kill me out there." He took her to a deserted spot—she was not sure about the location—and told her to get in the back seat and take her clothes off. The next day Harris described the assault to NAACP leaders: "I didn't take everything off. I just took my pants off. I was crying and scared and he told me to raise my leg up. I told him that was the first time that happened to me. I never been in jail or been involved in trouble and when I called for help I think I should get it but not that way. I was so scared my heart was beating fast. I am still nervous of that."[1]

By 1967, attorneys around the United States, even those in the South, were coming to terms with the legal ramifications of the *Sullivan* case. And undoubtedly, when Harris went public with her charges of rape against Dorsey, his lawyer told him libel law was not the best option to silence the public criticism that would surely ensue from Harris's allegation. This chapter focuses on the route a police officer might take to silence criticism instead of libel law. It also analyzes libel cases filed by James Earl Ray, the confessed assassin of Martin Luther King Jr., whose suits prompted courts to expand on the libel-proof doctrine, perhaps illustrating courts' growing impatience with the ongoing SLAPP suits. The chapter also looks at the actions of and libel suit filed by the "toughest cop in America," Frank Pape in Chicago. Lastly, this chapter presents Neshoba County sheriff Lawrence Rainey's last-ditch effort to cash in on the negative publicity generated by the film *Mississippi Burning* released in 1989 and the murder of three civil rights workers during Freedom Summer of 1964.

Down in the bayou regions of southern Louisiana, a distraught Rosemary Harris sought help from the local chapter of the NAACP after Dorsey's attack. When she came to him, NAACP branch president Dr. James Henderson urged her to file a complaint with the police department. NAACP officers said it had been rumored for years that Dorsey, a twelve-year veteran on the force, had sexually abused black women. So when Harris told them she had been raped in the back of a police car, they believed that they finally had firsthand evidence. The NAACP met with the police chief, demanded Dorsey's suspension pending a rape prosecution, and held lengthy, tense meetings with city officials.[2]

The New Iberia district attorney told Harris that he could not file rape charges against Dorsey because she did not fight the officer physically to prevent the rape.[3] NAACP leaders found this contention absurd. Harris did what she could to survive the attack, they asserted. Officer Dorsey was short but stocky, most certainly stronger than Harris, but fighting him might have resulted in her death, they believed. The NAACP branch led a march to city hall two days after the attack, demanding justice and protesting police brutality in general and this rape specifically. That civil action got the attention of local white leaders. Dorsey was suspended from the police force for conduct unbecoming an officer, and the district attorney convinced a New Iberia grand jury to indict him for simple battery and kidnapping. Mayor J. Allen Daigre also wrote the city's Fire and Police Civil Service Board a letter expanding on the reasons for Dorsey's dismissal, informing it that he "seized and carried Rosemary Vital Harris from her residence to the City Police Headquarters without her consent and without valid reason . . . and returned [her] to her residence in a police vehicle unaccompanied by any other officer."[4]

The service board met two months later on June 15, to hear Dorsey's suspension appeal. His attorney, J. Minos Simon, a widely noted Lafayette, Louisiana, lawyer with a talent for courtroom theatrics, argued that there was no written code of conduct regarding the transportation of a female in a patrol car without another officer. Simon called three other police officers to testify at the hearing, and all admitted that, at one time or another, they too had transported women in patrol cars unaccompanied. All three officers said they had never been criticized for violating this unwritten rule. There was no mention of the rape or Harris's race in the local newspaper's story on the hearing, although her race was likely assumed given that the article mentioned she had contacted the NAACP. The story focused only on Dorsey's violation of the policy on transporting women and the fact that police officers violated this rule regularly.[5]

The civil service board ruled that the city reinstate Dorsey but with a loss of pay for thirty days. The decision triggered public outcry, an uproar led by the local NAACP membership. The town newspaper, the *New Iberian,* ran a letter from Mayor Daigre asking the board to reconsider its ruling. He argued that Dorsey had been indicted by a grand jury and that the police chief's original dismissal was based on Harris's entire written statement, which included "violations of the law and immoral conduct." The mayor complained that the board refused to hear Harris's full statement or consider Dorsey's indictment. "I cannot believe that you intended to compel the City to reinstate and re-employ in the same position, a police officer who stands charged with Simple Kidnapping and Simple Battery," Mayor Daigre responded. "The continued employment of any police officer with such charges is prejudicial to departmental service and to the public interest." The NAACP also protested the civil service board's decision, sending a telegram to the *New Iberian*.[6]

The NAACP, mayor, and police chief met with the local Catholic leader, Bishop Warren L. Boudreaux, at his home and sent a telegram to the newspaper about the meeting. Louisiana NAACP field director Harvey Britton, who was based in New Orleans, also met with the New Iberia police, mayor, and city attorney to complain about the board's decision to reinstate Dorsey. Bowing under pressure, the civil service board reversed itself four days later on June 19, agreeing that Dorsey should remain suspended until the conclusion of his trial. If he was exonerated by the court, board members agreed, he would be reinstated, retroactive to his suspension date with full pay. In a letter addressed to the mayor and published in the *New Iberian*, the board informed him that its members did not realize they could consider the April indictment as evidence.[7] This decision was also met with anger, but this time it came from members of the white community. A letter to the editor from "A concerned citizen, Charles A. Dorsey," most certainly a relative of Henry Dorsey, took the board to task for the reversal of its original decision. He said it was "inconceivable" that a police officer would be charged with simple kidnapping: "Certain elements in the community have repeatedly requested that colored officers be employed in patrol cars to answer complaints of their own race. These elements have been denied their request and there has been a continuous agitation to dramatize the need." Charles Dorsey complained that the mayor and police chief overreacted and brought about all this damaging publicity. He blamed the NAACP and city leaders for pressuring the civil service board into changing its original decision.[8] The NAACP filed a police brutality complaint with the FBI on behalf of Lester Harris, who had been beaten in jail. As evidence they had photographs of Harris that showed several bruises on various parts of his body. The Justice Department did not respond to those complaints, according to NAACP documents.[9]

After a local jury acquitted him on the assault and battery charges,[10] Dorsey sued the NAACP and Mayor Daigre for $1.5 million in damages. Instead of utilizing state statute, he filed against the defendants under a federal law, ironically the Civil Rights Act of 1871 (also known as the Anti-Ku Klux Klan Act), a Reconstruction-era statute aimed at battling violations of former slaves' constitutional rights, which were systematically abused in the postbellum South. The law reads: "Every person who, under color of any statute, ordinance, regulation, custom, or usage, of any State or Territory, subjects, or causes to be subjected, any citizen of the United States or other person within the jurisdiction thereof to the deprivation of any rights, privileges, or immunities secured by the Constitution and laws, shall be liable to the party injured in an action at law, suit in equity, or other proper proceeding for redress." More to the point, the court had to determine: Has Dorsey been deprived of a "right" secured by the "Constitution and laws"?[11] He claimed that he was deprived of due process and equal protection under federal law, not state law.

Dorsey did not sue for libel. By 1967, the actual malice rule established in *Sullivan* would have been more fully understood, especially by Dorsey's attorney, Minos Simon. In both cases, civil rights groups and other individuals had publicly criticized the actions of a police officer. Instead of libel, Dorsey's attorney wanted to establish a different liability: the NAACP and mayor had conspired to get him fired. Their complaints and demands to the civil service board had caused his firing, he asserted in the suit filed in U.S. District Court in Lafayette on November 9, 1967. He wanted the court to enjoin the defendants from depriving him of due process and equal protection, which was denied him in the civil service board's June 19 decision. He named Dr. J. B. Henderson, president of the local chapter of the NAACP; Harvey Britten, the NAACP's acting field director; Mayor Daigre, Chief of Police Lee Fournet, and the four members of the Fire and Police Civil Service Board. All told, Dorsey sought $392 in back pay, $1 million in punitive damages (punishment of the defendants for their speech), and $500,000 for "embarrassment, humiliation and mental anguish."[12]

Dorsey also complained in the lawsuit that the NAACP's meeting with Bishop Boudreaux—and a telegram to the newspaper about it—was meant to intimidate members of the civil service board in this predominantly Catholic community. On top of that, Dorsey charged, the mayor's letter published in the *Daily Iberian* was intended to "expose said members to public censure" for their original decision to reinstate him. He complained that when the civil service board wrote the mayor back, informing him that the board reversed itself, that letter was published in the local newspaper. In sum, Dorsey complained that the named defendants wrote and publicized letters about the incident, conducted public demonstrations, and met with the local Catholic bishop to lobby him into speaking out about the issue.[13]

Louis Berry, a black attorney from Alexandria, Louisiana, served as local counsel for the NAACP, with the help of Michigan attorney Joan Franklin from the national NAACP office. They filed a motion to dismiss the case in January 1968, arguing that Dorsey failed to state a claim upon which relief could be granted. Franklin argued that there is no federal constitutional right of employment at a specific job and that Dorsey failed to show that there was purposeful discrimination as required by law, citing multiple wrongful termination cases after 1950. She also made this case about free speech: "The only discernable basis for plaintiff's legal pursuit of defendants is their publicized objection to his continued active presence on the police force, based on his treatment of Mrs. Rosemary Harris."

Franklin wrote, almost mockingly: "Casual familiarity with the American form of government, as relayed in elementary and secondary history and civics textbooks, would expose the wrongheaded basis of [the] plaintiff's attack. Suffice it to say that recent Supreme Court decisions continue to confirm the First Amendment rights of citizens to peacefully associate, assemble, demonstrate and petition for redress of grievances." Next, she cited *Sullivan,* by then four years old, arguing that her clients had the right to protest the conduct of a public official, in this case, a police officer. Franklin declared, "The First Amendment alone warrants the dismissal of the complaint."[14] Despite these compelling arguments for dismissal, the case was placed on the U.S. District Court, Western District of Louisiana calendar for Wednesday, March 6, 1968, before Judge Richard J. Putnam.

Dorsey's attorney, Minos Simon, may have seen this case as a losing proposition. He submitted a written memorandum to Judge Putnam and waived his oral argument, saying he would be in another Lafayette court for an unrelated jury trial. Tellingly, he did not attempt to reschedule the court appearance when he learned of the conflict. In his memorandum to the judge opposing the NAACP's motion to dismiss, Simon called the mayor's letter addressed to the civil service board and published in the *New Iberian* a "conspiratorial vessel of destruction" against Dorsey. Simon never spoke about the truth or falsity of the complaints alleged by the NAACP, the mayor, or other defendants. He ignored the charges of simple battery and simple kidnapping. There is certainly no mention of rape. "To grant [defendants] the immunity they claim under the auspices of free speech," Simon argued, "would require the court to hold that the First Amendment masks a license authorizing them to destroy the rights of others who have fallen from grace." Simon urged broad interpretation of federal law in this context.[15]

Judge Putnam dismissed the case on March 12, 1968. Franklin later commented to Britton: "Occasionally, the Southern 'gentlemen' who people the courts in the South do the correct thing. I don't care what motivated the judge who judged correctly. The important thing is that he did do so in this case. Let us hope that we continue to be [so] lucky."[16] The judge even agreed that Dorsey should pay for the defendants' court costs. Franklin's bill alone was more than $900. She argued that the suit itself was "an injustice perpetrated on the defendants," particularly the New York–based NAACP, "by hauling them into court on a complaint as patently frivolous as that in this case, causing them to incur substantial travelling and preparatory expenses and attorney[s'] fees." She pointed out that the court requires a local counsel to be present—in this case Louis Berry—to assist the out-of-state legal team.[17] Dorsey immediately appealed to the Fifth Circuit in New Orleans in April of 1968, with oral arguments made that December. Charges for simple battery and simple kidnapping were still outstanding in New Iberia.

In its ruling, the Fifth Circuit relied in part on a Pennsylvania case in which the Third Circuit ruled in 1950 that a township policeman must be reinstated using the law from that state rather than federal law and that a right of employment is not secured by federal law or the Constitution. The court said Dorsey could have tried the state courts of Louisiana and perhaps argued that the civil service board acted unlawfully and that the NAACP conspired and prompted this unlawful action. But he chose the federal courts. The Fifth Circuit affirmed the trial judge's decision, ruling that whatever rights Dorsey may have to be reinstated derive solely from Louisiana law: "The Louisiana Constitution specifically authorizes modification of an order when the prior Board decision was undesirable, unnecessary, or contrary to the public interest."[18] In short, the Fifth Circuit said Dorsey's claim was "without merit" in March 1969. Dorsey asked the court to reconsider and the appellate court denied a rehearing a month later. The U.S. Supreme Court also declined to hear the case. By then, former NAACP attorney Thurgood Marshall had been named to the high court, but he recused himself when the court reviewed the case.[19] Dorsey continued to serve on the New Iberia police force until his retirement years later. His assignments after this case included security in the local courtroom and serving papers for the court.[20]

The Dorsey case is labeled a libel case in the voluminous legal files of the NAACP. By 1969, libel law after *Sullivan* was widely understood on the bench and among many civil rights attorneys: criticism of a police officer in his official capacity was now protected speech. But the reality on the ground remained uninformed, and in *Dorsey*, the local chapter and national office of the NAACP had faced yet another expensive, time-consuming battle in court. It was also unusual for a police-officer plaintiff to sue the mayor and even his own police chief.

The mayor's daughter, Hilda Daigre Curry, continued the family tradition of New Iberia leadership. Curry's grandfather, Joe Daigre, had served as mayor from 1929 to 1940, and her father from 1963 to 1988. She filled the office from 2005 through 2016. Sitting in her brown-paneled executive suite in city hall overlooking Bayou Teche and amid miles of sugar cane, she remembers being a sophomore in high school when much of the turmoil of the era transpired. Although she doesn't remember the specifics of the Dorsey case, she remembers fearing for her father's safety for some of his progressive stances. "My daddy had such integrity. He wanted to do the right thing. He was really a wise man," she said in the summer of 2016. But that came at a price. At home, there were guns at the ready under the bed. She remembers the marches and the countermarches, but New Iberia, like Dorsey's case, never rose to national prominence. She recalls: "Dad said, 'Don't worry, it's going to be peaceful.' And it was."[21]

James Earl Ray and the Libel-Proof Doctrine

Cultural historian Grace Elizabeth Hale writes, "No one is ever more white than the members of a lynch mob."[22] Spotlighting spectacle lynching within the popular-culture frame of "making whiteness," she illustrates that newspaper coverage of a lynching is "central to the power" of the event. Within this context, the confessed assassin of Martin Luther King Jr. believed he had achieved the pinnacle of whiteness in his efforts to perpetuate the supremacy of his race. James Earl Ray reveled in the media coverage of his murder of the nation's leading civil rights leader in April 1968. He enjoyed his eminence in the newspapers he read every day in his jail cell, but he came to despise the way journalists were covering this most spectacular lynching of all.[23] Where were his accolades? Even the southern press distanced itself from this particular race-making effort. But to Ray, the national news magazines and northern reporters were the worst offenders, and he railed against them with his lawyers from his jail cell in Nashville, Tennessee. He first began plotting his libel suits within weeks of his June 1968 arrest, targeting several publications for coverage of King's murder, the two-month international manhunt, his capture at London's Heathrow Airport, and his initial incarceration in Tennessee.[24]

Atlanta attorney J. B. Stoner agreed to represent Ray in a series of libel suits just months after the assassin's capture. Puffing on a cigar and smiling broadly, Stoner held a press conference outside the Tennessee State Prison in Nashville after visiting Ray, promising to punish the media for what he considered unfair coverage.[25] Stoner, an avowed white supremacist, would be convicted in 1980 for the 1958 bombing of a Birmingham church.[26] He called his indictment a set up in the late 1970s: "This is all part of the plot to destroy me and the white race and to promote race mixing with the niggers," he told reporters with United Press International. When Ray hired him, Stoner was head of the National States Rights Party and often carried a briefcase bearing a sticker that read "Rights for Whites."[27] Reporters quoted his colorful one-liners, such as: "We didn't shed no tears when Saint Martin Lucifer Coon was shot." He also mounted unsuccessful campaigns for the U.S. Senate and Georgia governor on white-supremacist platforms, including a proposal to allocate funds for one-way tickets to send blacks back to Africa.[28]

Ray's criminal lawyer at the time, former Birmingham mayor Arthur Hanes, refused to have anything to do with Stoner, threatening to abandon Ray if he allowed Stoner to represent him in the libel cases, or in any legal matter. Meanwhile, freelance writer William Bradford Huie convinced Ray to give him exclusive rights to his story for $40,000.[29] Published in 1970, the resulting book, *He Slew the Dreamer,* offers a first-person account of Huie's investigation of Ray, including the journalist's written correspondence with the killer and his conversations with Hanes. Huie, an eighth-generation Alabama native, had achieved considerable fame as a writer, selling forty million copies of his several books with most titles adapted into Hollywood films. Among them were the *Revolt of Mamie Stover* in 1951 and the film adaption starring Jane Russell in 1956, along with *The Americanization of Emily* in 1964, with the movie version starring A-listers James Garner and Julie Andrews.[30]

Huie served in the U.S. Navy during World War II and drew from his overseas experiences in much of his writing. When he worked out the book deal with Ray, Huie had become well known for elbowing in on the hottest civil rights story of the day. Other reporters scornfully dubbed his work "checkbook journalism," after he caused a firestorm with his paid-for exclusive interview of the two white men who were found not guilty of Emmett Till's murder in Money, Mississippi.[31] The 1955 killing of the black Chicago youth visiting Mississippi and the resulting trial, along with the Montgomery Bus Boycott, had catapulted the civil rights fight onto the front pages of newspapers and TV broadcasts around the country and world. The school desegregation case, *Brown v. Board of Education,* had been widely condemned in the South the year before. The day the Warren Court released the opinion had been referred to as Black Monday across the South, and southerners labeled Chief Justice Earl Warren the anti-Christ. But Rosa Parks's refusal to give up her bus seat in Montgomery and Emmett Till's murder in 1955 provided the emotional spark that helped jumpstart the civil rights movement in the United States. After the Till murder trial, J. W. Milam and Roy Bryant confessed to Huie their killing of the black youth. In an article for *Look* magazine headlined "The Shocking Story of Approved Killing in Mississippi," Huie narrated a step-by-step the killers' retelling of how they tortured and executed Till for reportedly whistling at a white woman, Carolyn Bryant, Roy's wife.[32]

Born in Hartselle, Alabama, in 1910, Huie finished his bachelor's degree at the University of Alabama in two-and-a-half years, married his grammar-school sweetheart, and took a job at the *Birmingham Post* for four years before trying to make his living as a freelancer. He'd made it to the big leagues by the early 1940s when he replaced H. L. Mencken as one of the top editors of the *American Mercury,* a national magazine. But still he knew how to talk to native white southerners in Alabama and convinced Bryant's and Milam's lawyers that the tell-all story was a good idea. Huie secured signed releases and paid Bryant and Milam $3,150 for the story about how they killed fourteen-year-old Till, wrapping the cord of a cotton gin fan around his body and chunking his mutilated corpse in the Tallahatchie River. Protected by double jeopardy—the men could not be tried twice for the same crime—they caused a sensation nationwide with the graphic, tell-all horror story.

Indeed, Huie's checkbook gave him the access to King's accused assassin that no other reporter could get. The privilege included virtually unlimited letters to and from James Earl Ray in 1968 and chats with Ray's attorneys, Arthur Hanes and later the famous Texas lawyer Percy Foreman. "He's burned up at some of his publicity and wants me to sue some magazines for libel," Hanes told Huie in July 1968.[33] Hanes and Ray complained that the press was calling Ray *the* killer, rather than the *alleged* killer. Ray told his lawyer: "Every newspaper and magazine is trying to make it look like nobody in the world likes me. Tell Mr. Huie that I'll give him the names and he can go find people who like me."[34] The more reporters waded into Ray's seedy past as a life-long con, a bumbling burglar, and a prison escapee, the angrier he got. "He's mad about all the lies that have been printed about him," Hanes told Huie of the very thorough reporting. "One magazine says his father died as an alcoholic. Ray says the man is not only alive but he's too stingy to buy whiskey. He says all the stories about him chasing whores and wasting money in nightclubs are lies. He says, 'Every newspaper and magazine is trying to make me look like nobody in the world likes me.'"[35] Court officials in Memphis had refused to allow Huie to visit Ray, forcing the pair to continue writing letters while Ray awaited trial. For more than a year, Hanes served as a go-between for Ray and Huie, ferrying messages back and forth. Ray told Hanes: "Tell Mr. Huie that I'll give him the names and he can go find people who like me." Hanes passed along the message to Huie: "So he wants you to find people who like him and present him as a man who is liked."[36]

Hanes also complained that Ray focused more on filing libel suits than on his criminal defense, and Huie thought Ray's obsession with libel was "silly." By 1968, libel law under the *Sullivan* and *Walker* cases had become well established and understood. Both public officials and public figures had to prove actual malice to prevail as plaintiffs, and southern juries were no longer so sympathetic to the white supremacy cause that included violence. Huie wrote about Ray's libel fixation in his book, *He Slew the Dreamer:* "Mr. Hanes would listen to Ray no more than a moment before he cut him off; and when Ray wrote to me about libel suits, I ignored him."[37]

Hanes's refusal to file the suits in a timely manner irritated Ray and drew him closer to Stoner, who also visited him regularly in jail. Ray loved to listen to Stoner expound on all the money they would make when they won a few big libel judgments. Ray pondered the timing of the suits, though. Should he wait until his criminal trial was over? Should he file immediately? In one of his many letters to Huie, written in longhand on yellow legal pads, Ray pondered the question and made a plan. He informed Huie: "Stoner wants to file the libel suits right now, while Mr. Hanes wants to put the libel suits off till after the trial. I want the libel suits filed now. In fact I want the libel suits filed at the same time that you publish how much people who have known me like me. . . . I'm going to retain Stoner to file the libel suits." Stoner also promised to mobilize the National States Rights Party to raise money for his defense and to help Ray's family financially, his two brothers John and Jerry Ray in particular. The brothers and Stoner speculated that they could raise "hundreds of thousands" of dollars for the slayer of Martin Luther King.[38] They held a press conference in Memphis announcing the creation of a nationwide defense fund and called for contributions. None came. The only money received by Ray came from Huie for the exclusive book deal and that went primarily to his attorneys' fees.

As Huie's book research proceeded into 1969, he came to believe Ray acted alone rather than as part of a larger conspiracy. He spent months studying Ray, tracing the man's life from his birth in Alton, Illinois, in 1928, through his dirt-poor childhood in Missouri, to the death of his mother, and during his time living with his grandmother. Young Jimmy Ray dropped out of the eighth grade when he was fifteen years old and began bouncing from one minimum-wage job to another while drifting to California and Chicago. Huie followed Ray's route for a year and a half, fleshing out his own first-person narrative and publishing Ray's many letters throughout his book. Huie traced Ray's two-year stint in the Army where he drank and fought too much, his discharge from the military, and his arrests for vagrancy and burglary. Huie interviewed anyone he could find where Ray worked as a house painter, gathering government documents as Ray went in and out of prison in Illinois, Kansas, and Missouri.

By 1962, Ray was serving his third year of a twenty-year sentence in the Missouri State Penitentiary for armed robbery of a Kroger supermarket in St. Louis. When President Kennedy was shot, a prisoner at the Jefferson City prison speculated that somebody was paid to assassinate the president and that he probably made a million dollars for it. A second prisoner speculated, "The man who murders King will make another million." Ray was later quoted by yet another prisoner as saying, "That's the million I'm gonna collect."[39] Three years later, he escaped from prison with his brother's help, took an assumed name, and hid out in Chicago working as a dishwasher. Huie retraced Ray's trail to Chicago and his later trip to Canada, where Ray attempted to get a Canadian passport under an assumed name. Huie wrote: "Behind the wheel of his beat-up red Plymouth, driving from Detroit to Montreal in July 1967, James Earl Ray apparently attracted no attention. . . . He was bareheaded, with his thick black hair cut a bit longer than a crew cut. He wore no glasses. He was thirty-nine, but could be taken for thirty-five. He was five feet eleven inches and weighed only 165, so except for a paunch which he has a habit of rubbing, he looked thin."[40] Huie pondered Ray's intentions in his book, taking the reader with him as he retraced the criminal's steps, which were detailed by him in one of his many letters scribbled on those yellow legal pads.

Wrote Huie: "So on September 14, 1968, carrying with me Ray's diagrams and explanations, I flew to Montreal to try to confirm his story of what caused him to risk a return and what caused him to travel directly from Montreal to Birmingham, a city which Ray had never visited before but which was often visited by Dr. King."[41] Ray failed to get new identification documents in Canada, and he said he robbed a "whorehouse" of $1,700 before heading South to Birmingham, Alabama, in 1967. Here Ray lived under an assumed name and bought a white Ford Mustang with cash and a .22 rifle. Huie writes pages and pages about a mysterious man named "Raoul," who Ray suggested was a co-conspirator to the murder. But ultimately, Huie concluded that Ray acted alone. He tried for months to convince Ray to tell the truth, deciding that the con artist thrived on the mystery and the contest of wits with his attorney and his famous biographer. Huie concluded toward the end of his book: "He killed Dr. King to get attention, and he's afraid of losing it."[42]

Ray pled guilty to King's murder in March of 1969 and was sentenced to ninety-nine years at the state penitentiary in Nashville. Realizing that he had been portrayed as a villain rather than a hero in Huie's book and in other retellings of the story, Ray spent the rest of his life insisting that his confession had been coerced and demanding a trial. He fired his expensive and flamboyant second attorney, Percy Foreman, and became his own jailhouse lawyer, with occasional advice coming from Stoner. He declared himself a pauper and succeeded in getting his court costs waived. He had plenty of time to file libel suits, along with appeals, for a new criminal trial. Ray, who lived in solitary confinement for the first five years, started his libel onslaught against Huie in 1970, complaining that he initially cooperated with the writer on a book entitled *They Slew the Dreamer,* not *He Slew the Dreamer.*

For Ray, this book was his chance to talk about conspiracy theories, but mainly he wanted it to be a celebration of the King assassination. Instead, *He Slew the Dreamer* turned out to be a condemnation. Ray did not know of Huie's change of heart about how the murder was carried out until the book was released. Huie had also written several stories for *Look* magazine as teasers for his new book, which came out in 1970. U.S. District judge Robert M. McRae Jr., who had dismissed Ray's habeas corpus claim and thus denied him of a trial in the criminal case, also dismissed the libel suit as frivolous.[43]

Ray's next libel suit targeted journalist Gerold Frank Jr., author of *An American Death: The Hunt for Martin Luther King's Killer,* a 1972 book detailing King's assassination and the hunt for and subsequent court machinations involving Ray.[44] Frank, a Cleveland native who worked for hometown newspapers in Ohio and then New York City, found success writing book-length nonfiction bestsellers. He had authored *The Boston Strangler,* which was adapted into the 1968 movie starring Henry Fonda and Tony Curtis. He pioneered the "as told to" form of celebrity biography, most famously with the book *I'll Cry Tomorrow,* a 1954 tell-all by singer and actress Lillian Roth, which was adapted into a 1955 film of the same name. One of the earliest books by a celebrity (with a ghostwriter) on addiction, the book and film drew widespread attention to alcoholism as a disease. Actress Susan Hayward was nominated for an Academy Award for her performance as Lillian Roth. Frank also worked with Zsa Zsa Gabor on her autobiography released in 1960, and he published the definitive celebrity biography of Judy Garland in 1975. Between his stints ghostwriting for actresses, from 1968 to 1971, Frank delved into Ray's story and the King assassination, conducting scores of interviews and relying on court records, police reports, and private diaries and letters.[45]

Like Huie, Frank found no conspiracy. He believed that Ray acted alone and that he was a savage racist who thought no jury would convict a white man for murdering a black man. Frank concluded that Ray wanted to continue to baffle the world by escaping jail and then to remain an enigma after his capture. He also might have wanted to be perceived as just the hired gunman, since inmates in this role are at the top of the prison pecking order. By pleading guilty, Frank reasoned, Ray could avoid a trial that might prove he was a lone wolf, not a hired assassin.[46] Ray first sued Frank in 1973, filing at U.S. District Court in Memphis, but that case, like the one against Huie, would be dismissed as frivolous. In the Frank case, the court ruled that there was a lack of jurisdiction because the writer lived and worked in New York City.[47]

Ray's most notable libel suit came next and was actually combined with a suit for civil rights violations and stemmed from a *Time* magazine article about another new book on the King assassination. Reporter George McMillan spent about seven years researching his book, *The Making of an Assassin: The Life of James Earl Ray,* published in 1976. The Knoxville, Tennessee, native wrote regularly about civil rights in the South, freelancing for magazines such as *Look, Life,* and *the Saturday Evening Post,* and newspapers such as the *New York Times* and *Washington Post.* In the late 1960s, McMillan and his wife, journalist Priscilla McMillan, were living in Atlanta while he freelanced and taught journalism at the historically black Clark College. McMillan told his students: "I'm not one of those damned white liberals. I'm not making any sacrifice. I am paid well to stand here and lecture to you." White civil rights activist and liberal philanthropist Leslie Dunbar hired McMillan to train black journalists. The West Virginia native, an Emory University political science professor, believed that with civil rights demonstrations breaking out across the country, the events and issues needed to be covered by more black reporters working for mainstream publications.[48]

After King's assassination, McMillan spent hundreds of hours with Ray's father, George "Speedy" Ray along with his brothers and sister, paying them a total of $3,850 for their interviews and research help. As the book was hitting stores in January 1976, *Time* magazine revisited King's assassination, focusing on the emerging controversy surrounding the FBI's harassment of the civil rights leader.[49] The *Time* article was based on McMillan's book and said that Ray was a drug dealer while in prison in Missouri. Known as the "merchant," he dealt in speed, prison food supplies, and other contraband. The story also quoted former inmates as saying Ray fantasized about killing King while he was incarcerated in Jefferson City. According to fellow prisoner Raymond Curtis, Ray figured there must be a bounty on King's head and jokingly called King his "retirement plan."[50] Like Huie's and Frank's books, the *Making of an Assassin* concluded that Ray likely acted alone.

Ray sued *Time* and McMillan in federal court in Memphis, seeking $500,000 in punitive damages from multiple defendants.[51] The original complaint was rife with spelling errors and even misspelled McMillan's name, using instead "McMillian." Ray also named Willaim Huie and Gerold Frank again. Ray accused Huie and Frank of furnishing false information about him to McMillan through their separate books on the assassination. Still other defendants were Tennessee assistant attorney general W. Henry Haile, U.S. District judge Robert M. McRae Jr., and McRae's clerk, Brenda Pellicciotti. Haile was the state lawyer who opposed Ray's efforts to withdraw his guilty plea. Ray complained that Haile acted in collusion with *Time* and McMillan, helping supply information to the magazine and timing the article to influence the Sixth Circuit Court of Appeals' ruling in his criminal case. In so doing, Ray said Haile and the others conspired to violate his civil rights. McRae was the federal judge who denied Ray's motion to withdraw his guilty plea for King's assassination, and the Sixth Circuit would affirm that decision.[52] Ray accused McRae and his clerk of playing politics by refusing to forward parts of the hearing transcript to the appeals court. Ray also lumped in an additional "defamation of character" complaint against Huie stemming from an interview the journalist underwent with Dan Rather on CBS in 1976.

For their part, Frank and Huie said they never talked to McMillan about helping him with his book and did not know that a story about Ray was to be published by *Time* until after the fact. Frank and Huie pointed out that the only possible reference to them in the article was a mention of "experienced writers who spent years researching books on the assassination."[53] On top of that, Frank and Huie argued, any background McMillan would have used from their books was not actionable because Tennessee's one-year statute of limitations for libel suits had long passed. Frank complained to the court: "For a second time, at great expense and inconvenience, I am forced to defend myself some 1,000 miles from my residence against the meritoriously bankrupt suits of a convicted slayer who obviously has nothing better to do with his time but institute these frivolous suits."[54]

After Judge McRae requested dismissal by claiming judicial immunity, Ray dropped the judge and his clerk as parties to the suit. Another flaw in Ray's case was that the civil rights law he relied on protected against violations in state law, and McRae was on the federal bench. Former Assistant Attorney General Haile also argued that when the original petition for habeas corpus was put on the docket in July 1975, he was no longer working for the government and had set up his own private practice. He had left his state position in June of that year, and another assistant attorney general handled Ray's Sixth Circuit appeal for a new criminal trial.[55]

Time's lawyers all but scoffed at Ray's claims: "It is inconceivable that a single article published nearly eight years after the assassination, the last of his many criminal adventures, could further affect or damage his reputation."[56] In his motion to dismiss, *Time* magazine's attorney Leo Bearman Jr. argued that the story had nothing to do with the appeal before the Sixth Circuit but rather was prompted by revelations of the FBI's "vicious vendetta" against King. They also pointed out that Ray did not even allege injury to his reputation in his libel claim. Further, they argued the story might have even helped Ray's case, quoting sections of the article that questioned whether the crime had been solved and thus perhaps casting some doubt on Ray's guilt. For example, McMillan wrote: "Nearly eight years later, the widespread feeling still persists that King's murder has not been solved." And "Certainly there are a number of unanswered questions." And "Did Ray . . . really kill King? The evidence against him is persuasive, but it is also largely circumstantial. The case might be tough to prove in court."[57] *Time* also argued that Ray was a public figure.[58] He had "injected himself into the controversy about the assassination of Dr. King by pleading guilty to the assassination and by providing information about it to writers with the understanding that his revelations would be published." And most notably, in a motion to dismiss the libel suit, *Time* attorneys argued that Ray was libel proof: "Plaintiff, by virtue of his present conviction culminating his life as a habitual criminal, is incapable of sustaining injury to his reputation. Ray was convicted for burglary and sentenced in Los Angeles in 1949. In 1952, he was convicted for robbery in Chicago, served 22 months in prison, and was released in March 1954. In 1955 he robbed an Illinois post office and forged postal money orders. He served time at the federal penitentiary at Leavenworth, Kansas, for this offense and was released in April 1958. He was convicted for an October 1959 robbery in St. Louis and sentenced to 20 years at the Missouri State penitentiary at Jefferson City. He escaped in April 1967." *Time*'s attorneys detailed these crimes example by example.[59] In 1976, the "libel-proof" defense was a young concept but not without precedent. Appellate courts had accepted this doctrine the year before in *Cardillo v. Doubleday*, when the Second Circuit affirmed the dismissal of a libel action brought by an incarcerated criminal who was named in the book, *My Life in the Mafia*.[60]

Judge Harry Wellford dismissed all of Ray's libel suits in September 1976, ruling that he was indeed "libel proof."[61] He had pled guilty to murdering King. Wellford also noted that Ray had pled guilty to two prior felonies and was a prison escapee. Since Ray was a habitual criminal subject to widespread publicity, it would be impossible to injure his reputation further, Wellford said. The courts had previously noted that Ray was "internationally famous," and Wellford held there was no question he was a public figure for First Amendment purposes under the *Walker* case. Any coverage about Ray was of public interest, and he would have ample opportunity to refute the articles he deemed false or unfair. Wellford also agreed that this suit was clearly an attempt on Ray's part to secure a review and retrial of his criminal case. The judge denied yet another motion by Ray to reinstate the libel suits, and the Sixth Circuit affirmed the decision in 1978.[62]

Huie said later that he wished he'd never gotten involved in Ray's story. "Ray represents the biggest mistake I have ever made in my life. . . . The Ray case cost me twenty-five thousand dollars to defend. I have never 'lost' a suit, what I 'lose' is what I must pay the lawyers who defended me successfully. . . . I write for money. I have earned a great deal of money in writing, but I never kept any of it."[63]

By 1980, Ray still had some fight left in him. Again representing himself, Ray sued the U.S. Department of Justice and Conrad Baetz, formerly an investigator for the House Select Committee on Assassinations. As in other filings, the original complaint contained spelling errors and confused phrasing. The court commented that Ray's claim was "less than clear" when he charged that the Justice Department "improperly, and with reckless disregard of the truth amounting to malice, continually attributed various crimes to Ray that allegedly enabled Ray to financially survive during his period as a fugitive." Ray said any speculation on the part of Justice Department investigators would hurt his chance for parole in Tennessee. He also charged that Baetz instructed one of his investigators to steal letters from his brother Jerry Ray in his hotel room in Washington, D.C. These were letters from Ray to Jerry. This act, Ray argued, was a violation of his Fourth Amendment rights and amounted to an unlawful search. He also said Baetz had libeled him in a July 22, 1979, interview published in the *St. Louis Post-Dispatch*. He sought $25,000 in actual damages and $50,000 in punitive damages for the Fourth Amendment and libel claims.[64]

The U.S. District Court dismissed the suit, and the Eighth Circuit affirmed, agreeing that Ray did not have a case. He had failed to state a claim upon which relief could be granted because such investigations were under the purview of the Justice Department. Investigators were just doing their job in investigating Ray's actions while he was on the run, the court held. Investigators had come to the conclusion that Ray acquired funds by nefarious means. The local court and the Eighth Circuit also affirmed the dismissal of Ray's two claims against Baetz. In the Fourth Amendment privacy case, Baetz and his investigators filed affidavits denying that they took property from Jerry Ray's hotel room. Even if they had, the court reasoned, the letters were owned by Jerry and not James, so the latter had no expectation of privacy for what was in those letters once he sent them to his brother.[65]

Regarding the libel claim, the *Post-Dispatch* article discussed the possibility that in 1966 or 1967, a St. Louis attorney offered a man named Russell G. Byers $50,000 to kill King. The story reported that Byers refused the offer from the attorney, who had since died. Baetz was interviewed for the article because he had investigated Byers's story. Baetz said in the article that he believed one of Ray's brothers served as an intermediary between Ray and the St. Louis attorney who allegedly offered to pay for King's murder. The article said that Baetz's investigation failed to prove any such link. The Eighth Circuit promptly dismissed the libel suit, noting that Ray was indeed libel proof.[66]

Sixteen years had passed since *Sullivan* and twelve years since the court had extended the actual malice standard to public figures in *Walker*. Ray's chances of winning a libel case, even in southern courts, had long passed. Southern judges and juries had begun seeing the writing on the courtroom wall by the mid-1970s, and public sentiment had turned against violent extremists of Ray's ilk. Through a series of libel cases, many not relating to the civil rights movement, courts had applied the *Sullivan* edict and worked through some of the finer points of the actual malice standard. But still, for extremists such as Ray, it took a bit longer to receive and digest the message. He died in prison in 1998, having never won a libel case.

Frank Pape: "The Toughest Cop in America"

The story of Chicago police detective Frank Pape could come out of an old black-and-white movie, a film noir, a story of tough cops taking on the city's unsavory underbelly. In photographs splashed across the front pages of Chicago newspapers in the 1940s and 1950s, Pape sported a fedora and a double-breasted suit; he was a hero hauling wise guys off to jail. The flinty detective was dubbed "The Toughest Cop In America" by Chicago crime reporters, and the establishment crowd didn't seem to care much about how Pape and his boys kept the city safe. Plus, stories of cops with Tommy guns bringing down robbers in a hail of bullets made for exciting reading.[67] Pape and his detectives secured some eight hundred criminal convictions, sent five convicted killers to the electric chair, and waged twenty-three gun battles over almost three decades. Pape was said to be the inspiration for a 1950s TV show, *M Squad*, which focused on a Chicago police lieutenant and his elite detective squad with actor Lee Marvin playing the lead role.[68]

But Pape's old-school tactics came under intense scrutiny with increased awareness of police brutality—especially against minorities—by the 1950s. As hundreds of thousands of southern blacks migrated to northern cities, Chicago police did their part to maintain the color line, keeping the immigrants out of "white" parks and public spaces and ignoring vigilante acts of violence aimed at keeping segregated neighborhoods intact.[69] Many white Chicagoans worried about the growing black population, and there were more than a dozen brutal attacks and murders of black citizens during the Red Summer riots of 1919 as tensions escalated along with competition for jobs and housing in crowded urban areas across the country. Another population boom from 1940 to 1960 brought half a million African Americans into the city in search of job opportunities, and police brutality symbolized powerfully the unresolved racial tensions of the day.[70]

So when a black man became a suspect in the robbery and murder of a white Chicago insurance salesman in 1958, Pape used tactics on a raid of the man's house that would help lead to his professional downfall. Without a search or arrest warrant, Pape led twelve officers in a predawn raid on James Monroe's apartment on October 29, 1958. Monroe lived just two-and-a-half miles from the murder scene and had a criminal record for burglary and auto theft. What happened in that apartment would be disputed for years. Pape said he and his officers treated Monroe, his wife, and six children with respect, that Monroe quietly agreed to be escorted into a waiting squad car and taken down to the station for questioning. But Monroe charged that he and his family were brutalized and humiliated in the raid.[71]

The Illinois branch of the ACLU hired a prominent civil rights attorney to represent Monroe, arguing that the police violated his rights under the Fourteenth Amendment, Reconstruction-era legislation enacted by Congress to protect black citizens from incidents of racial violence where local law enforcement had failed to protect them (or had even perpetrated the violence). In his civil rights complaint filed six months after the incident, Monroe said Pape and his officers broke through the front and back doors of the apartment, came into his bedroom pointing their pistols and shining flashlights in their faces. "Chief Pape cursed Mr. Monroe and threatened to shoot him if he didn't move fast. Mr. Monroe was naked. He left the bedroom at gunpoint. He was forced to stand in the center of his living room naked. . . . Chief Pape was questioning Mr. Monroe. He kept calling him 'nigger' and 'black boy' and hit him in the belly with his flashlight several times." Monroe also charged that a detective kicked and pushed his children to the floor. "The police searched every room," he recounted. "They ransacked the closets, throwing all the family's clothing on the floor. They opened and dumped all the drawers in the various pieces of furniture. They ripped open all the mattresses. Mr. Monroe was then allowed to dress. His hands were chained together and he was escorted outside."[72]

In March 1950, Monroe filed his complaint in the Northern District of Illinois, seeking $200,000 in damages against Pape, the twelve officers who participated in the raid, and the city of Chicago. The ACLU relied on part of the Civil Rights Act of 1871, also known as the Ku Klux Klan Act. But the court dismissed the complaint, finding that the federal code did not provide a cause of action against state officers who conducted a search that violated state law. The Seventh Circuit affirmed, suggesting that Monroe seek relief in Illinois state courts.[73] But the U.S. Supreme Court reversed the lower courts in February 1961, finding that the federal civil rights statutes could indeed provide remedy to Monroe. In an opinion by Justice William O. Douglas, the court famously wrote that the "legislation was passed to afford a federal right in federal courts because, by reason of prejudice, passion, neglect, intolerance or otherwise, state laws might not be enforced and the claims of citizens to the enjoyment of rights, privileges and immunities guaranteed by the Fourteenth amendment might be denied by the state agencies."[74]

The next year, in November 1962, Monroe's lawyers made a convincing case that Detective Pape and the other officers broke into the Monroe apartment, assaulted them and took James Monroe to the police station where he was held for ten hours without being charged or advised of his rights. He wasn't even allowed to call an attorney or his family. An all-white jury found Pape and four of his detectives liable for violating the civil rights of Monroe and his family, awarding $13,000 in damages.[75] The judge denied the defendants' motion to vacate the jury award but did reduce the damages to $8,000.[76] The police officers paid the judgment. Pape, long accustomed to favorable press, refused to comment to the swarms of reporters waiting outside the courthouse. His codefendants, though, harshly criticized the jury verdict, calling it "a travesty on justice, a severe blow to law enforcement."[77]

While the civil rights complaint worked its way through the court system, the U.S. Commission on Civil Rights, which was created by Congress in 1957, had filed a report entitled *Justice*, a three-hundred-page paperback, the last of five volumes. It devoted a section to police brutality, citing the facts in *Monroe v. Pape*.[78] A week after the report was released, *Time* magazine carried a story on its findings in its November 24, 1961, issue: "Justice carries a chilling text about police brutality in both the South and the North—and it stands as a grave indictment, since its facts were carefully investigated by field agents and it was signed by all six of the noted educators who comprise the commission."[79] The article discussed the Monroe case and quoted the complaint in detail, ending with the note that although "the officers were not punished" for their early-morning actions, "Monroe has carried a suit to the Supreme Court [and] is still seeking a civil judgment." The description of the Monroe incident in *Justice* contained the subhead, "Search, seizure, and violence: Chicago, 1958," and detailed ten other examples of police brutality across the country.[80]

Pape sued *Time* for libel. The article did not explain, he contended, that the charges as described by *Time* were made by Monroe rather than independent findings of the commission.[81] At trial, eight of the police officers who went on that early morning raid testified on Pape's behalf, swearing that the events in the *Time* article were inaccurate. The magazine's lawyers argued for dismissal on the grounds that the article constituted fair comment on a government report and therefore was privileged under Illinois law. The researcher who helped put the *Time* article together testified that she read several articles in various newspapers as well as dispatches from *Time's* Chicago correspondent. All corroborated the civil rights report. She said she considered the full context of the report and believed *Time*'s article on it "was true as written."[82]

The district and appeals courts agreed that Pape, as deputy chief of detectives of the Chicago Police Department, was a public official and that *Time's* story concerned his official conduct. The district court dismissed the case in May 1962, finding the story was not clearly false. However, the appeals court said *Time*'s omission of the word "alleged" constituted the publication of a false report, remanding the case for a jury trial in December 1965. A jury, then, would decide whether the *Time* article was published with actual malice under the *Sullivan* precedent. The U.S. Supreme Court had ruled on *Sullivan* the year before, and thus the landmark case became the basis for the district court to grant summary judgment for *Time*. After another try at the district court level, the Court of Appeals reversed again in April 1966 and ruled that the issue of actual malice was one for the jury to determine.

The U.S. Supreme Court heard the case in 1971, holding that the U.S. Court of Appeals for the Seventh Circuit did not correctly apply the *Sullivan* precedent. The high court noted that Pape did not object to *Time* magazine's characterization of what he did in Monroe's house but rather condemned the magazine's description of what the Civil Rights Commission said he did there. Pape said he was damaged because *Time* attributed Monroe's accusations "to an authoritative official source."[83] *Time* magazine paraphrased the commission report, and the high court said Pape had to show that the magazine printed its story about the commission report knowing it was false or exercising reckless disregard of its falsity. Justice Stewart wrote in the majority opinion that *Time* made an inexact interpretation of an ambiguous document. In other words, the *Justice* report was already "bristling with ambiguities" before it was interpreted by *Time* editors.[84] But the fact that *Time* left off "alleged" did not constitute actual malice. This case was one of three decided by the U.S. Supreme Court on the same day, February 24, 1971, in an effort to clarify the *Sullivan* decision.[85]

While Pape's case wound its way through the court system, he took a four-year leave of absence from the police department to oversee security at the Arlington Park Racetrack in suburban Chicago. When he returned to the department in 1965, much to the chagrin of civil rights groups, the department had adopted an official motto, "To Protect and Serve," but the police culture felt much the same.[86] In 1966, King had famously said, "I think the people of Mississippi ought to come to Chicago to learn how to hate." Civil rights demonstrators and later anti–Vietnam War protestors were routinely abused by police, notably at the Democratic National Convention in the tumultuous summer of 1968. *Time* magazine reported at the time: "With billy clubs, tear gas and Mace, the blue-shirted, blue-helmeted cops violated the civil rights of countless innocent citizens and contravened every accepted code of professional police."[87]

But this was the way officers like Pape knew how to do business. He made commander of Chicago's Englewood District, which was plagued with gangs and racial polarization.[88] He later described his reaction on hearing rumors of a gang war, saying that he "went around to the places all these punks hang out and I said, 'I hear you are going to have a gang war. Fine. I'll be there with five of my guys with baseball bats, and you all better bring a lot of cars, because when we get done with you there won't be enough ambulances to take you to the hospital.'"[89] Pape was proud to note that no gang war erupted after that.

He retired at the rank of captain in 1972, having worked for the Chicago Police Department for thirty-nine years. Some fifteen hundred people, including Mayor Richard Daley, attended his retirement dinner. But Pape was bitter in his later years. Disappointed at how policing had changed, he declared in 1994 that he would not join the police department "nowadays." Foreshadowing the militarization of police forces in the twenty-first century, Pape said: "Criminals respect one thing—that you have more muscle than they have. When you've got that, they listen. The police force is our peacetime army, but they are getting no support anymore from John Q. Public. Today, every move a policeman makes is scrutinized by the public, more so than the criminal. . . . Damn shame really."[90] Frank Pape died of a heart attack in March 2000 at the age of ninety-one.

Seventeen years later, the U.S. Justice Department found that things hadn't changed enough since Frank Pape's glory days, issuing a damning report on Chicago police brutality in January of 2017. The report concluded that the police were poorly trained and quick to turn to excessive or deadly force, most often against minority residents and without facing consequences. The 164-page report, issued in the final days of President Barack Obama's administration, called for sweeping reforms and condemned the department's pervasive "code of silence," which enables police officers to lie to protect themselves and each other.[91] The investigation came after the court-ordered release of a video showing a white police officer shooting black teenager Laquan McDonald sixteen times and after revelations that city officials worked to keep the video from the public for almost a year. The review of the twelve-thousand-officer department, issued by then U.S. Attorney General Loretta Lynch, echoed accusations—that police target minorities—from black and Hispanic Chicagoans over the decades. She cited Department of Justice statistics showing that the police use force almost ten times more often against black suspects than whites.[92]

Codename MIBURN

With much fanfare, the movie *Mississippi Burning* appeared in theaters across the nation in December 1988. In the film starring Gene Hackman and Willem Defoe, FBI agents poured into fictional

Jessup County to investigate the murder of three civil rights workers, mirroring the true story that captured the nation's attention during Freedom Summer of 1964. The hulking, tobacco-chewing sheriff in the film was Ray Stuckey, a thinly veiled stand-in for the Sheriff Lawrence Rainey, who had long been suspected of having something to do with the murders of James Earl Chaney, Andrew Goodman, and Michael Schwerner. Rainey had unsuccessfully sued media companies in five different cases before 1988; he had been unable to prove actual malice as required in *Sullivan* and then *Walker*. Still, he tried again, seeking $8 million from Orion Pictures, claiming that he was identifiable as the sheriff in the movie and that the depiction was false and defamatory.[93]

In his 1989 claim, Rainey said: "The film depicts [me] as a terrorist. . . . They didn't use my name . . . [but] they intended that sheriff to be me. . . . The character in the movie was a big man like me, and he chewed tobacco like I chew tobacco all the time. . . . The actor had twice as big a chew of tobacco as I ever had, but they might as well have called him Lawrence Rainey." The former sheriff also said he had not been a public official since 1967 and therefore should be considered a private citizen for the purposes of the libel suit, particularly given that he "had not had access to the media."[94]

He said was leading a "quiet and peaceable life with his family" in rural Lauderdale County, outside Meridian, Mississippi, with "a priceless, untarnished, unblemished, and unassailable reputation" until the movie was released.[95] With renewed fame, or infamy, after the release of *Mississippi Burning*, Rainey appeared on the morning news shows, as well as ABC's *Nightline* and the news magazine *A Current Affair*, to tell his side of the story: he had nothing to do with the murders; he was at his wife's hospital bedside in Meridian that night.[96] Having occupied the spotlight's white-hot center in 1964, Rainey still had access to national media in 1988. All he had to do was pick up the telephone and offer to tell his side of the story to any news outlet in the country—the very activity that the nation's high court referred to when explaining public officials' higher standard in proving fault in *Sullivan*. According to established law by 1988, public officials (and public figures, as established in *Walker*) by their very definition are newsworthy characters and are often discussed in the context of significant public events. Therefore, they have easy access to the media in order to refute what they see as false or misleading statements about them.

In his libel complaint, Rainey said that after *Mississippi Burning* was released, he was afraid he would lose his job as a security guard for a black-owned firm in Mississippi. "I've got a good relationship with blacks," he told the *Clarion-Ledger* in Jackson. "I'm working for a black man and a black company, but he is getting a lot of feedback for working me."[97] His employer, E. E. McDonald, an African American minister, said he had received a great deal of pressure to fire Rainey. He said he would not do so. "He's a good employee, and he's just like my brother," McDonald said. "I teach love, not hatred. I teach forgiveness. This was in '64. We are in '89. We shouldn't look back. We should look forward, and this man has a right to work and support his family just like any other man."[98]

Raised on a small farm near Philadelphia, Mississippi, Rainey attended school to the ninth grade, then took a job as a laborer and later as a car mechanic before landing his first job as a police officer with the Canton, Mississippi, Police Department in 1956. He went to work as a Philadelphia police officer in 1958 and, after three months, became the assistant chief of police. He moved up to deputy sheriff of Neshoba County in 1961 under Sheriff E. G. "Hop" Barnett, later a codefendant in the civil rights trial. By 1963, Barnett was term limited, so Rainey ran for sheriff.

He ran a campaign that assured local whites he would be able to deal with the highly publicized invasion of civil rights workers threatened during Freedom Summer. An advertisement run in the local newspaper assured readers that he was "the man who can cope with the situations that may arise."[99] In court documents, Orion's attorney, Jack Ables III based in Jackson, Mississippi, asserted that Rainey played the "strong man" to maintain the racial status quo in Neshoba County, pointing out that no black citizen had been allowed to register to vote in Neshoba County from 1955 to 1964. Ables also introduced into evidence official reports showing that at least thirty churches were burned or bombed in the Mississippi in 1964 and that prior to 1967, no white person in Mississippi had ever been convicted of illegally killing a black person.[100]

After he won the election in November 1963, Rainey appointed Cecil Price, a former dairy worker, appliance repairman, fireman, and police auxiliary member as his uniformed deputy. At six feet two inches tall and 240 pounds, Rainey had a confident swagger in his trademark western tan clothes and cowboy hat, his patrol car filled with guns, ammunition, and Red Man tobacco.[101] He and Price patrolled the rural Neshoba County, which is roughly 25 square miles, with hill country made up of piney woods and cow pastures. The county seat of Philadelphia stands at its center.

Attorney Ables pointed out that, in the film *Mississippi Burning,* Sheriff Stuckey is not present at the shooting. In the Hollywood version of the story, the sheriff's alibi is solid—he was playing poker with his wife's brother and his two cousins, losing $11.38 during the night.[102] Most notably in Orion's defense, however, Ables sought to prove truth, which is an absolute defense in defamation suits. The defense would prove, Ables warned from the outset, that Rainey was involved in the murders despite the fact that a court had acquitted him of violating the young workers' civil rights in the 1967 federal case that had become one of the FBI's biggest investigations, codenamed MIBURN.[103] "Because Rainey seeks relief for defamation based on the 'implication' of involvement in the events," Ables argued, "Orion is entitled to prove the truth of Rainey's involvement in the events he alludes to in his complaint."[104] Ables then set out to prove that Rainey was a member of the Klan, to establish his presence at Klan meetings, and to show his close connections to local Klan members including Imperial Wizard Sam Bowers, who ordered the elimination of the despised civil rights worker, "Goatee," or Michael Schwerner, and who later served a life sentence for the 1966 bombing death of the civil rights leader Vernon Dahmer.

Ables said he would introduce at the libel trial evidence that had not been available in the 1967 trial and that would incontestably demonstrate Rainey's involvement in the conspiracy to kill Schwerner, Goodman, and Chaney. In court documents, Ables said Rainey and the other defendants in the civil rights case "took the defensive tack that membership in and activity by the 'White Knights of the KKK' in 1964 was noble, selfless, and patriotic. The 3,000-page transcript is replete with this drivel. Rainey then presented himself as a 'Christian' sentinel guarding white Neshoba Countians against hordes of black communists who were there, among other things, marshaling local blacks to sign pledge cards to rape a white woman at least once a week all summer during 1964."[105] Ables introduced into evidence hundreds of pages from the 1967 trial transcript and testimony from Klan members connecting Rainey to the Klan and connecting the Klan to the murders.

He pointed out that the Klan had raised money for Rainey's defense in the criminal trial, and he tracked Rainey from Klan rally to Klan rally throughout the state and region as he spoke to thousands of KKK members in Bogalusa, Louisiana, and in Meridian, Waynesboro, Mathiston, Yazoo City, and Greenville, Mississippi. Rainey appeared on the official program of most of these rallies, and his comments were quoted in local press accounts. In Greenville, for example, Rainey appeared with Cecil Price and Byron de la Beckwith, who was civil rights leader Medgar Evers's assassin, before cheering crowds. He appeared at rallies as late as 1975, Ables said, introducing multiple newspaper articles tracking his KKK rally appearances.[106] Ables wrote: "These matters establish, among other things, Rainey's Klan membership, his presence at and participation in Klan meetings and actions in Neshoba County, Mississippi, his knowledge of and authority over Klan activities in the vicinity and his communication on these matters with the man who first ordered the murder of Michael Schwerner by the White Knights of the Ku Klux Klan. All of these matters are relevant to a defense predicated on 'truth.'"[107]

Ables also connected Rainey to noted Klan leader Robert Shelton of Tuscaloosa, Alabama, who spent time in Philadelphia within a few days of the Neshoba County murders and publicly labeled the disappearance of the workers a hoax. Rainey had picked Shelton up from the airport and escorted him to Klan rallies in his patrol car.[108] Shelton, whose own libel suit against Buford Boone of the *Tuscaloosa News* was working through the courts, had posted the bonds for KKK members accused of killing Viola Liuzzo a month earlier. Liuzzo, a white housewife and mother of five from Detroit, had traveled to Selma in the wake of the Bloody Sunday attempt to cross the Edmund Pettus Bridge. Shuttling demonstrators back from Montgomery after the march, she was shot on Highway 80 after a car tried to force her off the road.[109]

As part of the libel suit, Ables filed five sets of admissions for Rainey to answer. They included 509 requests for the plaintiff to admit to a wide range of historical facts. Rainey's lawyer, James McIntyre, complained at the volume of work Ables was creating with the admissions: "They keep coming in daily . . . and are unduly burdensome and expensive on the plaintiff. . . . The plaintiff is a poor man, without the financial resources [available to Orion]."[110]

Rainey had complained that *Mississippi Burning* made him look like "a person bent on violence." So Ables detailed his history of police brutality, focusing on Rainey's involvement in at least four shootings when he was a police officer. In October 1959, Officer Rainey shot and killed an unarmed black man named Luther Jackson, who had wrecked his car in Philadelphia. Rainey had told journalist William Bradford Huie that Jackson was "a Chicago nigger. He had me down choking me." In another incident, Deputy Rainey shot and killed a handcuffed, twenty-seven-year-old black man he was transporting with Sheriff Barnett to the State Mental Hospital at Whitfield. Rainey told Huie: "This crazy nigger. He grabbed a gun out of the glove compartment, and I killed him in an exchange of gunfire." In two other instances, Rainey exchanged fire with a white man but allowed that man to surrender unharmed. He also shot a Choctaw Indian in the mouth.[111]

Ables said in court filings, "Of the four people who Rainey admits shooting and or killing, only the white man survived uninjured. The Indian was wounded. The two black victims were either sick, drunk, shaken up from a car wreck, handcuffed, unarmed and/or in the custody of two armed peace officers. They nevertheless failed either to surrender successfully or overcome Rainey and his armed associates."[112]

Ables also detailed how Rainey had courted media attention and allowed his face, half-naked torso, and reputation to be used to advertise for a Meridian chiropractor not long after the murders, with Rainey describing how his civil rights fight had taken its toll on his back. The ad for Dr. Jim Barfoot read, "World Famous Neshoba County Sheriff Says 'Civil Rights Got Him Down in the Back,'" and explained that Rainey's "long hours and hard work keeping 'law and order' in his county'" had caused his back pain.[113]

With preparations for the libel trial underway in 1990, Ables deposed Rainey in his law office in Jackson, Mississippi. The deposition was part of the discovery process during which the litigants gathered information to prepare for trial. In his testimony, Rainey again denied his involvment in the murders: "I wasn't even in the county that week."[114] Pressing him, Ables questioned the veracity of his alibi, essentially putting the former sheriff on trial for murder, albeit in his law office.

RAINEY: "You see, that's been 25 years ago."

ABLES: "I understand that. But this is the biggest thing that ever happened in your life, I imagine."

RAINEY: "Yeah, and the aggravatingest thing."

ABLES: "I'm sure it is. Nobody much let this get out of your memory all these years, have they?"

RAINEY: "And these dad-blamed moviemakers and news reporters and all, they just keep it going."[115]

Rainey said he had never been a member, much less a leader, of the KKK. When Ables contradicted him with evidence, though, he admitted to attending the Klan rallies and getting applause when he was introduced.[116] As the deposition continued, Ables focused on Rainey's actions as sheriff and interrogated him on his whereabouts during the night of the murders. After his wife got out of the hospital, the family went down to the coast on holiday, and Rainey said he was playing miniature golf in Biloxi when he heard about the discovery of the bodies of the civil rights workers buried in the earthen dam. When Ables asked him about the guns that he owned, the sixty-six-year-old Rainey turned to his lawyer and asked, "James, what does this here have to do with about what we've got against the movie?"

MCINTYRE: "Nothing, but he's got the right to ask questions."

ABLES: "I'm going to try not to keep you a bit longer than we have to, believe me."

RAINEY: "In other words, he's making money off of Orion that we ought to be getting. I can't blame him for spending all this time, though, because he's getting rich off them."[117]

Ables also questioned Rainey about the other libel suits he'd filed over the years, and the witness launched into a diatribe about the press. "All them ruint me. That's the reason I don't like to have nothing to do with the news media."[118]

Ables's questions next explored Rainey's memberships beyond the KKK. He asked about a hunting club and for details about his other associations in Philadelphia, again working to weave connections to the Klan. Rainey again turned to his lawyer and said, "Jim, I thought this would be on the movie. I didn't know it was going to start a new investigation and go through the court all over again."[119]

The former sheriff complained that he had received calls from reporters all around the world after *Mississippi Burning* was released. "I got phone calls," he admitted, "all during the night from reporters in other countries. I didn't know to this day you show anything in foreign languages."

Ables asked him about his employment history after 1964. Since the murders and his acquittal, Rainey had bounced around, working various security jobs, one at a Meridian grocery store and another at McRae's Department store at a nearby suburban mall. He confessed he had difficulty holding a job since the 1967 trial on the conspiracy charge. He tried to secure employment elsewhere as a police officer but was unsuccessful, and he was passed over for a position as a guard at the Mississippi State Penitentiary at Parchman Farm.

After *Mississippi Burning* was released, Rainey said he was heckled at the mall: "As soon as that movie runned all them riff-raffs and troublemakers like hanging around the mall know who I was and they'd come by: Well, you white son of a bitch, said, 'you ain't going to kill no more blacks like in Mississippi Burning and all' and cussing and cussing."[120] Rainey said his boss moved him to the Mississippi Welcome Center since the security firm, McDonald Security Company, had recently gotten that contract.

Ables pressed Rainey on any possible financial damages he might have suffered as a result of the film: "So, you haven't lost any money or anything or lost a position or anything on account of the movie? You've still got your job and making the same money essentially?"

RAINEY: "Well, I've lost a lot of time."

ABLES: "What kind of time did you lose?"

RAINEY: "About these reporters and interviewers calling me, coming on the job."

ABLES: "Do they dock your pay for talking to them?"

RAINEY: "Well, he never—but it's still your attention is broke on the job."[121]

Married three times with two grown children, Rainey also complained about people calling him and threatening him and his wife on the telephone. Ables requested a list of the threats after Rainey said his wife kept a notebook with the times of the calls and what each person said. McIntyre agreed to provide the list to Ables, over Rainey's objections.

RAINEY: "Now wait a minute. We can't keep put all—we got to keep an ace in the hole."

MCINTYRE: "No, you hadn't. They are entitled to see it."

ABLES: "I'm entitled to see all your aces and your jokers too."[122]

Perhaps most damning was that Ables introduced as evidence a 1970 oral history with Paul B. Johnson Jr., the governor of Mississippi from 1964 to 1968.[123] Johnson implicated Rainey and Price in the murders in his interview: "Actually, one thing that is not known to the people anywhere in this country is that these Klansmen—of course I knew them very well—did not actually intend to kill these people. What happened was that they had been taken from the jail and brought to this particular spot. There were a good many people in the group besides the sheriff and deputy sheriff and that group. What they were going to do, they were going to hang these three persons up in a big cotton sack and leave them hanging in the tree for about a day or a day and a half, then come out there at night and turn them loose. They thought that they'd more or less scare them off." But, according to Johnson, they accidentally killed Chaney, the black civil rights worker, who "was acting kind of smart aleck and talking pretty big, and one of the Klansmen walked up behind him and hit him over the head with a trace chain that you use, you know, plowing and that sort of thing. . . . The chain came across his head and hit him just above the bridge of the nose and killed him as dead as a nit. After this boy had been killed, then is when they determined, 'Well, we've got to dispose of the other two.' Very, very few people know."[124]

Ables also waded through several defense tactics executed by Rainey's attorney during the federal trial for civil rights violations. At the trial McIntyre claimed that the three bodies were illegally exhumed because the FBI had no permit for their exhumation from the Mississippi State Board of Health. Ables asked during the deposition, "What difference would it make to you whether they dug them up or not with the right paper work? I'm just wondering, why would you need a motion to be made like that?" In other words, to an innocent man, it shouldn't matter. Rainey replied, "I don't remember why now."[125]

Ables also subpoenaed the state fire marshal's records from the devastating blaze at Mt. Zion Church, the fire that the three civil rights workers were investigating in Neshoba County and that led to their deaths. He also subpoenaed the fire marshal's records on the burned Ford station wagon the workers had been driving when they were killed. And he subpoenaed the files from the Mississippi Highway Patrol investigation of the murders.[126]

Ables secured an affidavit from the pioneering African American comedian and civil rights activist Dick Gregory, who had been traveling in Europe when a reporter told him the three civil rights workers had disappeared after their arrest in Neshoba on June 21, 1964. Gregory said he flew home immediately and met with CORE leader James Farmer in Meridian to see how he could help. Farmer and Gregory knew it was dangerous to go to Philadelphia, so they gathered up a group of sixteen cars full of civil rights workers to drive with them from Meridian. They were stopped and detained by a blockade of about 150 members of the highway patrol. Gregory told them he was there to investigate the disappearance of the civil rights workers and asked to speak to Sheriff Rainey and Deputy Sheriff Price.

The civil rights caravan reached the courthouse, and Rainey agreed to meet with him. Gregory's affidavit reads: "Upon being asked why the boys had been arrested, Sheriff Rainey personally responded that he (Rainey) had arrested the three, Schwerner, Chaney and Goodman, because they were driving 75 miles per hour inside the City of Philadelphia. Cecil Price then inserted that he (Price) had arrested them. Sheriff Rainey and Deputy Sheriff Price then stopped talking and looked at one another for several moments. Then they both looked together at the county prosecutor. Nothing more was said by either about this subject." Apparently, the two law officers had not yet gotten their stories straight. Gregory said that as he and Farmer walked out of the office, "the only way to get to the truth of the matter was to offer a substantial sum of money as a reward. I said to Mr. Farmer, 'Jim, if CORE will put up $100,000, we'll have this case solved in a week.' Rainey and Price acted very bothered. . . ."[127]

Gregory offered a reward of $25,000 for information leading to the discovery of the bodies. He said that in July 1964, "I received a letter informing me, almost with pinpoint accuracy, where the three bodies were buried." Gregory was not called to testify at

Rainey's 1967 trial, and in his 1990 affidavit, he said Rainey had "never testified to his admission that he arrested them as he stated to me. . . . I am informed that Sheriff Rainey later claimed not to have been in Philadelphia the afternoon of June 21, 1964."[128]

Ables also filed his own affidavit with the court in June 1990, asserting that McIntyre told him he had evidence indicating how Chaney, Goodman, and Schwerner actually died, suggesting that evidence on the matter heard in the 1967 conspiracy trial was not factual. McIntyre, according to Ables, had substantial volumes of documents and statements relating to the murders. Ables reported, "He stated he might write a book about this someday but, referring to his client, stated that he would have to, and I quote, 'wait until after Lawrence is dead' before doing so."[129]

Ables then flooded the court with exhibits of Klan literature, including KKK recruiting materials, text from the initiation ceremony of the KKK in Mississippi, an application for citizenship in "the invisible empire," the White Knights of the KKK of Mississippi, and flyers from the Legal Defense Fund seeking money "to assist white Christian victims of political arrest and persecution in Mississippi." All told, Ables filed thirty-seven exhibits, which consisted of more than fifteen hundred pages, along with six affidavits. He also said he was preparing to call witnesses who could testify about the sheriff's involvement in the murders.[130] Rainey dropped the case against Orion Pictures in August 1990. His attorney filed a motion to dismiss the suit, and the judge's order of dismissal came down the next day.[131] Rainey, the stalwart of southern libel plaintiffs, had reached the end of the line. Twenty-six years had passed since *Sullivan* had been overturned. Members of the media, exercising their First Amendment right and responsibility to report on events about public officials and on events of public interest, had spent untold millions trying to defend that right.

Rainey died of throat and tongue cancer in 2002 at the age of seventy-nine. McIntyre represented Edgar Ray Killen in 2005, the man who was convicted of manslaughter for planning and directing the murders of Chaney, Goodman, and Schwerner. McIntyre was disbarred in 2008 after being found guilty of comingling his personal and business funds with those of his clients.[132]

This chapter focuses on how a police officer might silence criticism of his actions in the post-*Sullivan* era without resorting to libel law. By the late 1960s, the meaning and ramifications of the *Sullivan* case were taking hold in southern jurisprudence. The chapter also analyzes the losing battles initiated by James Earl Ray, Frank Pape, and Lawrence Rainey. Police officers had finally and consistently begun losing the SLAPP battle in court. Under the new actual malice standard of Sullivan, libel law no longer provided legal protection for criminal violence practiced by the police. But the public discussion of police brutality continues, as discussed in the U.S. Justice Department's damning report of Chicago law and order in 2017. Less publicized has been the ongoing battle in New Iberia, Louisiana, where the NAACP has continued to lead protests of yet another black man killed by police, this time while in the custody of an Iberia Parish sheriff's deputy. Victor White III died from a gunshot wound in 2014 while sitting handcuffed in the back of a police car.

CONCLUSION

The Writing on the Courtroom Wall

What an uncanny déjà vu. Place the photographs side by side, images of protestors in Ferguson, Missouri, from 2014, and those of the civil rights demonstrations in the American South some fifty years earlier. "Black Lives Matter" placards might be a modern equivalent of the iconic "I Am A Man" signs from the 1968 Memphis sanitation workers' strike.[1] Michael Brown, an eighteen-year-old African American, was shot and killed by a white police officer in Ferguson on August 9, 2014, sparking widespread demonstrations and a national conversation about the militarization, tactics, and institutional racism of the police in the United States.

But what about all that time in between? Released in 1991, the grainy footage of the beating of taxi driver Rodney King by Los Angeles police officers catapulted the issue of police brutality into mainstream America's consciousness at that time. Within hours of the four officers' acquittal for the assault, riots spread across Los Angeles, lasting six days, killing sixty-three people and injuring two thousand more before the California governor deployed the National Guard to regain control of the city. King had led police on a high-speed chase, refusing to pull over because a DUI charge would be a violation of his parole for a previous robbery conviction.

More recently, iconic images from the 1960s found their way back to mainstream media in the wake of the Ferguson controversy and in the aftermath of still more high-profile cases of police officers shooting black males in cities across the United States. All these years later, as coverage of white police officers shooting black citizens dominated the headlines month after month, the national conversation has swarmed around the issue of police brutality and has brought questions about how far we have come—or have not come—since the days of Bull Connor and Lester B. Sullivan. It is difficult to know what the twenty-first-century protests will mean for America's not so postracial society.

Fast-forward to Ferguson, Missouri, to police officer Darren Wilson's shooting of Mike Brown, and placards reading "Wanted for Murder" became ubiquitous calls for justice but brought no libel suits such as those filed by Officer Gilligan in New York City in 1965 as well as Officers Sheldon Liebowitz and Henry Martinez. Today, lawyers would advise police officers (along with any public official or public figure) that it would likely be a waste of time and money to file a suit under such circumstances. It seems that today Americans take for granted their right to criticize police officers' actions in their official capacity. The handwritten signs of protesters around the country have denounced the police abuse and violence again and again since Ferguson:

"Hands up, don't shoot."[2]

"I can't breathe."[3]

"I am Mike Brown."[4]

Though not as famous, other modern-day placards held by demonstrators have been equally bold in their criticism of police behavior in Ferguson and elsewhere:

"KKK in Uniform, License to Kill, Please Stop!"

"Police everywhere, justice nowhere."

"The Whole Damn System is Racist as Hell."

"Wanted For Murder."[5]

That last sign could be a flashback to 1964, when New York City erupted in riots after police shot yet another black man and when it became apparent that it was not just southern lawmen seeking to silence criticism of their official actions through libel. The evolution of libel law during the civil rights movement involved so much more than Commissioner Sullivan failing to prove that the *New York Times* acted with actual malice, the new standard of fault that constitutionalized libel law. This battle involved so much more than the nation's high court extending that requirement to public figures in General Edwin Walker's case, which was spawned from the Ole Miss riot in 1962. It was also waged in the series of more obscure yet hard-fought libel cases supported by an army of civil rights lawyers, sometimes paid by the NAACP and most times not, representing local journalists and activists in communities and court rooms receiving little or no national media attention.

Undoubtedly, southern lawmen such as Sheriff Lawrence Rainey of Neshoba County and Colonel T. B. Birdsong of the Mississippi Highway Patrol had long felt under siege. In July 1964, for example, the Council of Federated Organizations (COFO), a coalition of civil rights groups in Mississippi that sponsored Freedom Summer, brought suit against Rainey, Birdsong, and other state officials under a federal Reconstruction-era statute, charging that they had failed to protect the three young civil rights workers—Chaney, Goodman, and Schwerner—and calling for an emergency appointment of federal commissioners throughout the state empowered to arrest anyone violating civil rights laws.[6] The suit charged that the disappearance of the three civil rights workers was part of a statewide conspiracy between law enforcement agencies and the KKK to deny black citizens their constitutional rights. COFO workers took 257 testimonies from black Mississippians who had suffered harassment and police brutality, choosing 57 of the most powerful stories by people who were not afraid to give their names for a publication titled *Mississippi Black Paper*.[7]

In his foreword to the book, noted theologian and ethicist Reinhold Niebuhr wrote: "The documents disclose a society in which the instruments of justice are tools of *in*justice. On the evidence of these affidavits, it seems that there are no limits to inhumanity, cruelty and sheer caprice in a closed society. . . . The crimes described in the following pages, committed either by local officials or with their connivance, include the bombings of homes and churches, the arrests of Negroes on false charges for every type of fanciful law infraction, and—most frightening of all—a brutality by the police that frequently approaches sadistic cruelty and on occasion has resulted in actual murder."[8] What Niebuhr calls legalized injustice mirrors most certainly what the critical race theorists of the 1970s were describing, as more racial minorities entered the legal profession and the academy.

Critical race theory has challenged the ways we think about race and how racial power is constructed, with CRT scholars illustrating that racial discrimination has been systemic and institutional since our nation's founding. This study offers further evidence of that institutional racism through the prism of libel law. It delves into how white supremacy contributed to the shaping of legal doctrine up to 1964 and beyond and hopefully encourages us to continue following the threads of the messy and massive literature on the relationship between race and the law. Racism has historically been a part of the structure of legal institutions, and CRT provides a valuable and productive framework to help make sense of those relationships and formations. CRT began as a movement in the law, specifically studying how race and racism have structured the law and thus society, and expanded to other areas of inquiry, including cultural and social history.

In his classic article in the *Harvard Law Review*, Derrick Bell argues that civil rights progress for African Americans always coincided with the self-interest of elite whites.[9] He points out that the country faced massive unrest after World War II as black servicemen came home looking for freedom and equality after fighting for it overseas. The country was locked in the Cold War with the Soviet Union, and American leaders hated seeing stories of racist sheriffs, the lynchings, and the beaten, bloody civil rights demonstrators jailed for exercising their First Amendment rights to petition their government for redress of grievances. Bell pointed out that the country was losing the public relations war on the international stage, and government officials needed to do something about it, so the U.S. Justice Department sided with the NAACP Legal Defense Fund in its fight to desegregate schools. "The interests of whites and blacks, for a brief moment, converged," wrote CRT scholars Richard Delgado and Jean Stefancic, in agreement with Bell's initially controversial findings.[10]

In keeping with this theory, in the realm of libel law, the *New York Times* was facing extinction as libel cases continued to pile up. The *Times* employed some of the best legal minds in the country to blunt the massive effort of mostly southern politicians and police to bury the newspaper and its reporters under libel suits in court and thus stop them from covering the civil rights movement. Other mainstream media companies also faced financially crippling SLAPP suits, and they all needed to win. Of course, covering the civil rights demonstrations and other issues relating to the emerging race beat down South was the right action to take. The civil rights movement was news—often big news. But ultimately, the white-owned media had to beat Sullivan and Connor and their ilk in court. Scholars found Bell's argument audacious at the time, but ten years later, legal historian Mary Dudziak's research came to the same conclusion in her *Stanford Law Review* article, "Desegregation as a Cold War Imperative." Her study of U.S. Department of Justice and U.S. Department of State files reveal that government officials had generated a stream of memos and cables outlining the importance of improving the United States' image to the rest of the world in its fight against communism. Again, she has discovered that this problem of optics was part of the rationale for federal assistance with the school desegregation cases in the 1950s.[11]

A consistent theme throughout U.S. history is the government's effort to suffocate dissent. So many of these libel suits were SLAPPs intended to resurrect sedition law, and they are a reminder that the government's attempt to silence its critics is nothing new. The SLAPP was just a newly conceived and effective way to do it. SLAPP plaintiffs rarely win nowadays, and thirty-one states have enacted anti-SLAPP legislation, with state courts upholding the constitutionality of such laws. Anti-SLAPP legislation is meant to provide a remedy for defendants to make a motion to dismiss the case because it involves speech on a matter of public concern. The plaintiff then must show probability that he will win the suit and that under libel law, he is likely to win. If he is unable to demonstrate that likely outcome, the plaintiff must pay attorneys' fees for the defendant, a legal rule surely serving as a deterrent to filing such intimidation lawsuits to silence the speaker. In federal court, results have been mixed, with some circuits applying anti-SLAPP remedies and others not. As such, twenty-first-century legal threats of a vengeful government official against the press continue to be worrisome absent a federal SLAPP statute.

During his campaign and while in office, President Donald Trump called the media "dishonest scum" and "the enemy of the people" for writing articles about him and his platform that he did not like, and journalists and media scholars worried about an all-out assault on the First Amendment as part of the Trump battle cry. Back in 2016 in Fort Worth, Texas, presidential candidate Trump proceeded with what had become his customary rant against the media, especially the *New York Times* and the *Washington Post,* and later CNN, promising to retool libel law to punish them for what he saw as critical coverage of him and his campaign. He railed: "One of the things I'm going to do if I win, and I hope we do and we're certainly leading. I'm going to open up our libel laws so when they write purposely negative and horrible and false articles, we can sue them and win lots of money. We're going to open up those libel laws. So when the *New York Times* writes a hit piece which is a total disgrace or when the *Washington Post,* which is there for other reasons, writes a hit piece, we can sue them and win money instead of having no chance of winning because they're totally protected."

To clarify, journalists are not "totally protected" from libel suits when they cover issues of public concern. Truth is the ultimate defense in a libel suit, and if reporters get it wrong, there are certainly ramifications. If they get the story wrong and the plaintiff is a public official or public figure, reporters may still lose a libel case if actual malice—that they published content they knew was incorrect or should have known it was incorrect—is proven in court. *Goldwater v. Ginzburg,* a libel suit filed by then Republican presidential candidate Barry Goldwater in 1964, offers such an example. Goldwater successfully sued *Fact* magazine and its publisher, Ralph Ginzburg, for a story entitled, "The Unconscious of a Conservative: A Special Issue on the Mind of Barry Goldwater." The partisan magazine mailed a survey to 12,356 psychiatrists asking whether the senator from Arizona was psychologically fit to serve as president. The poll was to serve as a warning to the American people as Goldwater kicked off the final leg of his campaign. Some 2,417 psychiatrists responded and the magazine published a sampling of the comments. Some said the request was unethical, but many described Goldwater as having a personality disorder or psychosis. Some said he was trying to prove his "manliness."[12]

Ginzburg offered a triumphant conclusion in the article that said Goldwater was paranoid, unfit for office, and troubled by "intense anxiety about his manhood." After a fifteen-day trial, a New York jury found evidence of actual malice, awarding Goldwater $75,000 in punitive damages, and the U.S. Court of Appeals affirmed.[13] Ginzburg argued unsuccessfully that he had exercised his First Amendment right to free speech and press, citing *New York Times v. Sullivan.* The U.S. Supreme Court declined to review the case, thus letting the appellate affirmation stand. The magazine had been warned by some psychiatrists that such an evaluation must take place in a clinical setting, and after the verdict, the American Psychiatric Association issued "the Goldwater rule" forbidding practitioners from commenting on such matters. They must first conduct an interview with the subject and obtain consent to discuss that professional opinion with a third party. This rule or position has not been without controversy, with some professionals and pundits arguing that at times a "duty to warn" overrides other considerations.[14]

Justice Black wanted to hear the Goldwater case, insisting that *Sullivan* did not go far enough to protect the press from the "grave dangers" created by libel actions. He called the Court of Appeals' affirmation in favor of Goldwater "repressive and ominous." Justice Douglas joined Black in his dissenting opinion, which asserted: "This suit was brought by a man who was then the nominee of his party for the Presidency of the United States. In our times, the person who holds that high office has almost unbounded power for good or evil. The public has an unqualified right to have the character and fitness of anyone who aspires to the Presidency held up for the closest scrutiny."[15]

In keeping with Black's dissent, I argue that journalists, and by default, society, are owed the right to report and discuss the actions of those running for and sitting in elected office, as well as police officers, who are in a position to exert enormous power over the citizenry. Our government most certainly has a role in protecting journalists and journalism from frivolous and costly libel suits. But the issue reaches beyond the fear of SLAPP suits against the press. If civil rights leaders or anyone criticizing the actions of police or public officials fear such costly suits, they might also be afraid to speak on such vital issues as police brutality or even the behavior of the president of the United States. Black was considered an absolutist, along with Douglas, who believed that "the First Amendment bars in absolute, unequivocal terms any abridgment by the Government of freedom of speech and press." His was an unusual stance, but one worth noting.

And certainly, journalists would disagree with the characterization that the nation's most heralded newspapers, the *New York Times* and *Washington Post*, are "enemies of the people." They continue to lead reportage on issues of police violence against the citizenry, with the *Post* winning the Pulitzer Prize in 2016 for coverage of police killings of civilians. The police have long provided information about officers killed in the line of duty, but there was no central, publicly available repository for journalists–and thus the public–to better understand how and how many citizens had been killed by officers. The *Post* created a database containing the details of 990 fatal police shootings in the United States in 2015 and has continued the tally in subsequent years.

Key findings included the fact that unarmed African Americans were at a much higher risk of being shot after routine traffic stops than any other group, and that fifty-five officers involved in fatal shootings in 2015 had been involved in a previous deadly incident while on duty. Police agencies are not required to report the shooting of civilians to a central repository that is available to the public, so these basic facts were missing in our increased national conversation about police brutality.[16] *Sullivan* freed the press to ramp up its watchdog reporting on a wide range of issues, and that yielded the Watergate stories and increased scrutiny on America's role in the Vietnam War along with the historic Pentagon Papers coverage. That scrutiny continues today as part of our democratic tradition.

The uneasy relationship between public officials and the government is as old as the nation itself. President George Washington railed about editor Philip Freneau of the *National Gazette*, who supported Thomas Jefferson's ideology and criticized the president's financial policies. The president despised the *Gazette* and famously called the editor "that rascal Freneau."[17] Perhaps the modern-day equivalent is "dishonest scum" and "enemy of the people"?

The layers at the intersection of race, law and journalism are much deeper and more complex than historians and legal scholars have generally assumed. In a broader sense, this line of libel cases woven throughout the civil rights movement might remind us that major social (and legal) change rarely takes place as a result of once incident in history, but rather is the result of many actors and actions whose significance accumulates over time. This point is true of many social and political movements, and it further challenges our academic tendency to write about law and history as a parade of Great Men and Great Moments, or in this instance, Great Court cases, as *Sullivan* surely was.

NOTES

PREFACE: AN AWAKENING

1. John H. Scott and Cleo Scott Brown, *Witness to the Truth: My Struggle for Human Rights in Louisiana* (Columbia: University of South Carolina Press, 2003).
2. U.S. v. Manning, 205 F. Supp. 172 (W.D. La. 1962).
3. Larry Still, "La. Farmer Still Faces Reprisals," *Jet,* April 15, 1965, 14.
4. New York Times v. Sullivan, 376 U.S. 254 (1964); Anthony Lewis, *Make No Law: The Sullivan Case and the First Amendment* (1991; reprint, New York: Vintage, 1992).
5. Carol Anderson, *White Rage: The Unspoken Truth of Our Racial Divide* (New York: Bloomsbury Publishing, 2016), and "Ferguson Isn't about Black Rage against Cops. It's about White Rage against Progress," *Washington Post,* August 29, 2014.
6. Popham quoted in Gene Roberts and Hank Klibanoff, *The Race Beat: The Press, the Civil Rights Struggle, and the Awakening of a Nation* (New York: Alfred A. Knopf, 2006), 185.

INTRODUCTION

1. Catledge to *Miami Herald* editor Lee Hills, December 30, 1960, folder Litigation: Libel-Alabama Case, 1960–1964, box 16, Turner Catledge Papers, MSS 116, Manuscript Division, Special Collections Department, Mitchell Memorial Library, University Libraries, Mississippi State University, Mississippi (hereafter Catledge Papers).
2. Catledge to Mr. W. F. Aycock Jr., Memphis Publishing Company, March 23, 1962, ibid.
3. Catledge to Wes Gallagher, October 11, 1962, ibid.
4. New York Times Co. v. Sullivan, 376 U.S. 254, 270 (1964), *rev'd,* 273 Ala. 656 (1962).
5. *Sullivan,* 376 U.S. at 294–95 (Black, J., concurring). Appointed to the U.S. Supreme Court by President Franklin D. Roosevelt in 1937, Black was the senior senator from Alabama and an active supporter of the New Deal. After the Senate confirmed his appointment, the press reported that Black had been a member of the Ku Klux Klan in Alabama for two years in the 1920s. From humble and rural beginnings, Black believed membership would gain him political advancement. To control the damage after the story broke, Black delivered an eleven-minute

radio address in October 1937 in which he decried racial and religious intolerance and praised the liberal policies of Roosevelt's New Deal.

6. Lawrence M. Friedman, *American Law in the Twentieth Century* (New Haven: Yale University Press, 2002).

7. Anthony Lewis, *Make No Law: The Sullivan Case and the First Amendment* (New York: Vintage, 1992), 157; Kermit L. Hall and Melvin I. Urofsky, *New York Times v. Sullivan, Civil Rights, Libel Law, and the Free Press* (Lawrence: University Press of Kansas, 2011).

8. Hall and Urofsky, *New York Times v. Sullivan*, 86–87, 182, 202.

9. Rodney A. Smolla, *Suing the Press* (New York: Oxford University Press, 1986), 43.

10. George W. Pring and Penelope Canan, *SLAPPs: Getting Sued for Speaking Out* (Philadelphia: Temple University Press, 1996).

11. Brown v. Board of Education of Topeka, 347 U.S. 483 (1954). See also Derrick A. Bell Jr., *Race, Racism, and American Law*, 2nd ed. (Boston: Little, Brown, 1980), and Ian Haney Lopez, ed., *Race, Law and Society* (Burlington, Vt.: Ashgate Publishing, 2007). The first edition of Bell's book was published by Little, Brown in 1972.

12. Smith v. Allright, 321 U.S. 649 (1944), outlawing the all-white Democratic primary.

13. See, for example, Alston v. School Board of City of Norfolk, 112 F.2d 992 (4th Cir. 1940).

14. Loving v. Virginia, 388 U.S. 1 (1967).

15. Shelley v. Kraemer, 334 U.S. 1 (1948). The use of racial covenants in real estate emerged in 1917 when the U.S. Supreme Court ruled that city segregation ordinances violated the Fourteenth Amendment in Buchanan v. Warley, 245 U.S. 60 (1917), a case detailed in this book.

16. Boynton v. Virginia, 364 U.S. 454 (1960).

17. Plessy v. Ferguson, 163 U.S. 537 (1896).

18. Howard K. Smith, *Events Leading Up to My Death: The Life of a Twentieth-Century Reporter* (New York: St. Martin's Press, 1996), 274.

19. Associated Press v. Walker, 388 U.S. 130 (1967); Curtis v. Birdsong, 360 F.2d 344 (5th Cir. 1966).

20. "Curtis Publishing Is Named in a $3 Million Libel Suit," *New York Times*, February 27, 1964.

21. See for example, Rainey v. CBS, Case No. E78–0121 (Cir. Ct. Miss. filed October 3, 1978).

22. Ray v. Time, 582 F2d. 1280 (6th Cir. 1978).

23. Lewis, *Make No Law*; Hall and Urofsky, *New York Times v. Sullivan*, 202.

24. See, for example, Roberts and Klibanoff, *The Race Beat*, and David R. Davies, ed., *The Press and Race: Mississippi Journalists Confront the Movement* (Jackson: University Press of Mississippi, 2001).

25. Henry Mayer, *All on Fire: William Lloyd Garrison and the Abolition of Slavery* (New York: St. Martin's Press, 1998), 76. See also Amy Reynolds, "William Lloyd Garrison, Benjamin Lundy and Criminal Libel: The Abolitionists' Plea for Press Freedom," *Communication Law & Policy* 6 (Autumn 2001): 577–607.

26. Mayer, *All on Fire*, 84.

27. Ibid., 90.

28. Ibid., 93.

29. Ibid., 114. See also Reynolds, "William Lloyd Garrison, Benjamin Lundy and Criminal Libel," 594.

30. Cornish is perhaps best known, though, for editing *Freedom's Journal*, the first African American owned and operated newspaper in the United States, with John B. Russwurm in 1827. The newspaper only existed for two years, yet what they famously wrote in the first issue has been widely quoted: "Too long have others spoken for us," and "We wish to plead our own cause." See Armistead S. Pride and Clint C. Wilson II, *A History of the Black Press* (Washington, D.C.: Howard University Press, 1997), 32.

31. Arthur J. Kaul, "Hazel Brannon Smith and the *Lexington Advertiser*," in *The Press and Race: Mississippi Journalists Confront the Movement*, ed. David R. Davies (Jackson: University Press of Mississippi, 2001), 233–64.

32. Harrison Salisbury, "Fear and Hatred Grip Birmingham," *New York Times*, April 8, 1960.

33. This point has been widely established in the literature. See Howard K. Smith, *Events Leading Up to My Death*; J. Mills Thornton III, *Dividing Lines: Municipal Politics and the Struggle for Civil Rights in Montgomery, Birmingham, and Selma* (Tuscaloosa: University of Alabama Press, 1991).

34. Smith, *Events Leading Up to My Death*, 268.

35. Friedman, *American Law in the Twentieth Century*, 584.

36. Associated Press v. Walker, 388 U.S. 130 (1967).

37. Walker v. Carter, Cause No. 6182 (Cir. Ct. Miss. filed September 7, 1963).

38. Rainey v. Orion Pictures, No. E89-0014 (Cir. Ct. Miss. filed February 21, 1989).

39. Allison Graham, *Framing the South: Hollywood, Television, and Race during the Civil Rights Struggle* (Baltimore, Md.: Johns Hopkins University Press, 2001), 147.

40. Liebowitz v. Farmer et al., No. 17506-65 (NY Sup. Ct. filed October 19, 1965), at 5.

41. "Request for a Reprise," *Time*, March 28, 1969.

42. Ray v. Time, 452 F. Supp. 618, 622 (W.D. Tenn. 1976), *aff'd*, 582 F.2d 1280 (6th Cir. 1978).

43. Enakshi Roy, "Social Media, Censorship and Securitization in the United States and India" (Ph.D. diss., Ohio University, 2017).

CHAPTER 1: BEFORE *NEW YORK TIMES V. SULLIVAN*

1. Biographical sources on Bass include Charlotta A. Bass, *Forty Years: Memoirs from the Pages of a Newspaper* (Los Angeles: self published, 1960), Southern California Library for Social Studies and Research in Los Angeles; Rodger Streitmatter, *Raising Her Voice: African-American Women Journalists Who Changed History* (Lexington: University Press of Kentucky, 1994); Stanley Nelson, Soldiers Without Swords documentary; James Phillip Jeter, "Rough Flying: The California Eagle (1879–1965)" (paper presented at the Twelfth Annual Conference of the American Journalism Historians Association, Salt Lake City, Utah, October 7, 1993).

2. George W. Pring and Penelope Canan, *SLAPPs: Getting Sued for Speaking Out* (Philadelphia: Temple University Press, 1996).

3. "Ku Klux Monopolizes Watts," *California Eagle*, April 10, 1925, 1.

4. "Editor Visits Klan Chie[f]tan in His Lair," *California Eagle*, April 17, 1925.

5. Ibid. See also Bass, *Forty Years*, 57.

6. "Ku Klux Klan Cohorts Seek Eagle Editor's Arrest," *California Eagle*, May 8, 1925, 1.

7. Ibid.

8. "Chief Mogul of Ku Klux Klan Procures Warrant for Editor and Managing Editor of 'The Soaring Eagle,'" *California Eagle*, May 19, 1925, 1.

9. Garrison v. Louisiana, 379 U.S. 64 (1964).

10. "Chief Mogul of Ku Klux Klan Procures Warrant for Editor and Managing Editor of 'The Soaring Eagle,'" *California Eagle*, May 19, 1925, 1.

11. Bass, *Forty Years*, 27.

12. Ibid., 28.

13. Patrick S. Washburn, *The African American Newspaper: Voice of Freedom* (Chicago: Northwestern University Press, 2006).

14. Bass, *Forty Years*, 33.

15. Helen Taylor, "It's the California Eagle's 70th Birthday," *Daily People's World*, September 29, 1949, 5, cited in Streitmatter, *Raising Her Voice*, 97. See also Washburn, *The African American Newspaper*, 134.

16. "To the Readers of the Eagle," *California Eagle*, May 22, 1925, 1.

17. "Negroes' Rights Involved, Ku Klux Case Is Set for 18th of June," ibid., May 22, 1925, 1.

18. "Ku Klux Klan Case against Eagle Editors up on Next Thursday," ibid., June 12, 1925, 1.

19. "Imperial Representative G. W. Price Star Witness for Prosecution," ibid., June 19, 1925, 1.

20. Ibid.

21. "Judge J. S. Chamber Sin [sic] Notable Decision Find Defendants in Ku Klux Klan Case Not Guilty," *California Eagle*, June 26, 1925, 1.

22. "More Expressions Anent the Eagle vs. The Ku Klux Klan," ibid., July 3, 1925, 6.

23. "Judge J. S. Chamber Sin [sic] notable Decision Find Defendants in Ku Klux Klan Case Not Guilty," 1.

24. Bass, *Forty Years*, 58.

25. For a detailed analysis of this topic, see Patrick S. Washburn, *A Question of Sedition: The Federal Government's Investigation of the Black Press during World War II* (New York: Oxford University Press, 1986).

26. At the top of the ticket was Vincent Hallinan of San Francisco, a prominent attorney of Irish descent who specialized in civil liberties cases. The Progressives received 14,000 votes out of 61 million cast, which was 0.2 percent of the vote. For an analysis of Charlotta Bass's role in that campaign, see Gerald R. Gill, "'Win or Lose—We Win': The 1952 Vice Presidential Campaign of Charlotta A. Bass," in *The Afro-American Woman: Struggles and Images*, ed. Sharon Harley and Rosalyn Terborg-Penn (Port Washington, N.Y.: Kennikat Press, 1978), 109–34.

27. Ibid. See also Kathleen A. Cairns, *Front-Page Women Journalists, 1920–1950* (Lincoln: University of Nebraska Press, 2003).

28. Streitmatter, *Raising Her Voice*, 104.

29. FBI report quoted in ibid, 104.

30. "Whipped the Klan," editorial, *California Eagle*, June 26, 1925, 6.

31. Jeffrey J. Pyle, "Race, Equality and the Rule of Law: Critical Race Theory's Attack on the Promises of Liberalism," *Boston College Law Review* 40, no. 3 (May 1999): 787–827.

32. George C. Wright, *Racial Violence in Kentucky, 1865–1940: Lynchings, Mob Rule, and "Legal Lynchings"* (Baton Rouge: Louisiana State University Press, 1990), 262.

33. The employment of African Americans at the U.S. Post Office was not without controversy. By the early 1900s, some forty blacks worked as clerks and letter

carriers. Whites complained about the hiring practices, and local black groups pushed back over discrimination, appealing to Louisville's postmaster. For more details, see George C. Wright, *Life behind a Veil: Blacks in Louisville, Kentucky, 1885-1930* (Baton Rouge: Louisiana State University Press, 1985), 93.

34. Kathryn St. Clair, "Slipping Backwards: The Supreme Court, Segregation Legislation, and the African American Press, 1877-1920" (Ph.D. diss, University of Tennessee, 2007).

35. Buchanan v. Warley, 245 U.S. 60 (1917). The Civil Rights Act of 1866 states, "All citizens of the United States shall have the same right, in every state and territory, as is enjoyed by white citizens thereof to inherit, purchase, lease, sell, hold and convey real and personal property." See *U.S. Statutes at Large* 14 (1866): 27-30. Segregated housing continued after *Buchanan* through restrictive covenants, private agreements prohibiting the sale of homes to blacks and other minorities, which were used to block them from moving into white neighborhoods.

36. George C. Wright, "Black Political Insurgency in Louisville, Kentucky: The Lincoln Independent Party of 1921," *Journal of Negro History* 58, no. 1 (1983): 8-23.

37. Wright, *Racial Violence in Kentucky*, 263. Wright's research delved into at least 353 lynchings that took place in Kentucky up to 1940.

38. Ibid., 263.

39. "Editors Fined $250 Each Note Appeal, Kentucky Newspapermen Found Guilty of Libeling Judge," *Baltimore (Md.) Afro-American*, December 4, 1926, folder 001423-011-0964, box G-75, Series A: The South, Part 12: Selected Branch Files, 1913-1939, Papers of the National Association for the Advancement of Colored People, Manuscript Division, Library of Congress, Washington, D.C. (hereafter Fleming v. Fleming v. Commonwealth, NAACP Papers).

40. "Justice Mocked Again . . . ," *Louisville (Ky.) Leader*, April 10, 1926.

41. "Madisonville Sets Stage . . . ," ibid., April 17, 1926.

42. As cited in "Editors Fined $250 Each Note Appeal."

43. Fleming v. Commonwealth, 235 Ky. 454 (1926); and Bard v. Commonwealth, 217 Ky. 479 (1926).

44. Martha Summers to Weldon Johnson, December 8, 1926, Fleming v. Commonwealth, NAACP Papers.

45. Bunyan Fleming to G. P. Hughes, December 6, 1926, Fleming v. Commonwealth, NAACP Papers.

46. Mark Robert Schneider, *African Americans in the Jazz Age: A Decade of Struggle and Promise* (New York: Rowman & Littlefield Publishers, 2006), 68.

47. Cole v. Commonwealth, 22 Ky. 350, 356 (1927).

48. "Editors Fined $250 Each Note Appeal," *Baltimore Afro-American*.

49. "N.A.A.C.P. Sends $500 Legal Fee for Colored Editors on Trial," November 5, 1926, Fleming v. Commonwealth, NAACP Papers.

50. Laffoon was a life-long fixture in Kentucky politics, serving as governor of the Commonwealth from 1931 to 1935. He is noted for appointing a record number of honorary Kentucky colonels, including Harland Sanders, who used the title when he opened his chain of Kentucky Fried Chicken restaurants. See Vernon Gipson, *Ruby Laffoon: Governor of Kentucky, 1931-1935* (Hartford, Ky.: McDowell Publishing, 1978).

51. "Kentucky Justice," *Oakland (Calif.) Western American*, December 10, 1926.

52. Warley to Johnson, December 13, 1926, Fleming v. Commonwealth, NAACP Papers.

53. Wright, *Racial Violence in Kentucky*, 201.

54. For a detailed account of the lynching, see Jack E. Davis, "'Whitewash' in Florida: The Lynching of Jesse James Payne and Its Aftermath," *Florida Historical Quarterly* 68, no. 3 (January 1990): 277–98.

55. Ibid., 287.

56. *St. Petersburg (Fla.) Evening Independent*, February 14, 1946, cited in Davis, "'Whitewash' in Florida," 289.

57. "Two Governors on Race Relations," *Collier's*, February 23, 1946, 94.

58. Caldwell v. Crowell-Collier Publishing Company, Civil Action No. 152 (D. Fla. filed March 20, 1946); *Jacksonville Florida Times-Union*, March 21, 1946, as cited in Davis, "'Whitewash' in Florida," 293.

59. Trial transcript in *Crowell-Collier Publishing Company*, quoted in Davis, "'Whitewash' in Florida," 293. See also the *Tallahassee (Fla.) Daily Democrat*, "Cites Handicap in His Handling of Racial Issue," March 9, 1948, 1.

60. As quoted in Davis, "'Whitewash' in Florida," 294.

61. Caldwell v. Crowell-Collier Pub. Co., 161 F.2d 333 (5th Cir. 1947).

62. Davis, "'Whitewash' in Florida," 297.

63. *Tallahassee (Fla.) Daily Democrat*, August 8, 1949, as cited in Davis, "'Whitewash' in Florida," 298.

64. Cecil J. Williams, *Freedom and Justice: Four Decades of Civil Rights Struggle as Seen by a Black Photographer of the Deep South* (Macon, Ga.: Mercer University Press, 1995), 27.

65. Wim Roefs, "Leading the Civil Rights Vanguard in South Carolina, John McCray and the *Lighthouse and Informer*, 1939–1954," in *Time Longer Than Rope: A Century of African American Activism, 1850–1950*, ed. Charles M. Payne and Adam Green (New York: New York University Press, 2003), 462–91. For a more detailed study of John Henry McCray, see Sid Bedingfield, *Newspaper Wars: Civil Rights and White Resistance in South Carolina, 1935–1965* (Urbana: University of Illinois Press, 2017); and John W. White, "Managed Compliance: White Resistance and Desegregation in South Carolina, 1950–1960" (Ph.D. diss, University of Florida, 2006).

66. Theodore Hemmingway, "South Carolina," *The Black Press in the South, 1865–1974*, ed. Henry L. Suggs (Westport, Conn.: Greenwood Press, 1983).

67. John H. McCray, "Is Willie Tolbert, Jr. Guilty? Condemned Man Tells His Story," *Lighthouse and Informer*, October 1, 1949.

68. State of South Carolina v. John H. McCray (June 20, 1950), General Sessions Court, Greenwood County, South Carolina.

69. Grace Elizabeth Hale, *Making Whiteness: The Culture of Segregation in the South, 1890–1940* (New York: Vintage Books, 1998).

70. State of South Carolina v. Tolbert, Greenwood County Court, 1949. For more discussion of the case, see Charles Franklin Beall Jr., "With Malicious Intent: John McCray, Willie Tolbert and the Struggle for Equal Justice in South Carolina." This document was Beall's undergraduate thesis at the University of Virginia. The author located a copy in the box 4, John Henry McCray Papers, 1910–1987, South Caroliniana, Carolina Library, University of South Carolina, Columbia (hereafter McCray Papers). Beall and his academic adviser, Patricia Sullivan, conducted oral history interviews with McCray on several occasions. *Greenwood (S.C.) Index-Journal*, August 9, 1949.

71. Beall, "With Malicious Intent," 23, citing *Greenwood (S.C.) Index-Journal*, August 10, 1949.

72. *Greenville (S.C.) News*, August 11, 1949; *Anderson (S.C.) Independent*, August 10, 1949.

73. Beall, "With Malicious Intent," 24. He cites court documents found in State v. Tolbert.

74. John H. McCray, "Is Willlie Tolbert Jr. Guilty?" *Lighthouse and Informer,* October 1, 1949. The article was reprinted in its entirety in court records for State v. McCray.

75. McCray, "Is Willie Tolbert Jr. Guilty?"

76. Ibid.

77. *Anderson (S.C.) Independent,* October 28, 1949, cited in Beall, "With Malicious Intent." See also State v. Booth, discussed in ibid.

78. Beall, "With Malicious Intent," 39.

79. State v. McCray and State v. Booth (S.C. Cir. Ct. January 1950).

80. Mrs. Deling Booth, interview by Charles Franklin Beall Jr., February 21, 1987, Columbia, South Carolina, in Beall, "With Malicious Intent," 41.

81. *Baltimore (Md.) Afro-American,* January 14, 1950, cited in Beall, "With Malicious Intent."

82. Letter from McCray to "Fellow Citizen," May 16, 1950, folder: Greenwood County, S.C. (libel case), 1950–1959, box 4, McCray Papers.

83. Ibid.

84. "NNPA Fights Attack on Freedom of Press: Newspaper Talk," *Chicago Defender,* January 28, 1950, 1.

85. "Our Opinions: Freedom of The Press," *Chicago Defender,* January 21, 1950, 6.

86. These letters to McCray are found in folder: Greenwood County, S.C. (libel case), 1950–1959, box 4, McCray Papers. W. T. Murray to McCray, June 19, 1950, ibid. Julian Morgan and James A. Hodge to Mrs. Liverman, May 17, 1950, ibid.

87. John W. White, "Managed Compliance," 37.

88. Ibid.

89. Bedingfield, *Newspaper Wars,* 124.

90. *Lighthouse and Informer,* July 9, 1949, cited in Roefs, "Leading the Civil Rights Vanguard," 471.

91. Sengstacke to McCray, June 27, 1950, folder: Greenwood County, S.C. (libel case), 1950–1959, box 4, McCray Papers; Undated press release, ibid.

92. Johnie M. Robinson to John McCray, July 10, 1950, folder: Greenwood County, S.C. (libel case), 1950–1959, box 4, McCray papers.

93. "Funds Collected At Special Rally for John H. McCray at Progressive Democrat Institute," May 12, 1950; Principal James A. Miller, Holmes School, to McCray, May 12, 1950, folder: Greenwood County, S.C. (libel case), 1950–1959, box 4, McCray papers.

94. White, "Managed Compliance," 37.

95. McCray to Roy D. Stutts, October 3, 1952, folder: Greenwood County, S.C. (libel case), 1950–1959, box 4, McCray Papers.

96. Beall, "With Malicious Intent," 54.

97. State v. McCray, 222 S.C. 391 (1952), *aff'd,* 73 S.E.2d 1 (S.C. Cir. Ct. 1951).

98. "The Case of McCray," *Baltimore (Md.) Afro-American,* August, 21, 1951.

99. "Prison Sentence Won't Silence Crusading Editor," *Pittsburgh (Penn.) Courier,* December 13, 1952.

100. Beall, "With Malicious Intent," 59.

101. White, "Managed Compliance," 38.

102. "Get Up or Shut Up," *Lighthouse and Informer,* May 6, 1950, 1. He failed to reach that voter-registration target. However, an estimated seventy thousand

blacks qualified to vote in 1950, an increase from an estimated fifty thousand in 1948. See Bedingfield, *Newspaper Wars*, 128.

103. "How to Make a Martyr," *Chicago Defender,* December 6, 1952, 10.

104. Beall, "With Malicious Intent," 68; Bedingfield, *Newspaper Wars*, 215.

105. Beall, "With Malicious Intent," 63.

106. Kari Frederickson, *The Dixiecrat Revolt and the End of the Solid South, 1932–1968* (Chapel Hill: University of North Carolina Press, 2001), 211.

107. McCray to Mr. S. L. Latimer Jr., editor, *The (Columbia, S.C.) State*, April 17, 1959.

108. Richard Kluger, *Simple Justice: The History of Brown v. Board of Education and Black America's Struggle for Equality* (New York: Alfred A. Knopf, 1976), 14, 302.

109. White, "Managing Compliance," 24.

110. Peter F. Lau, *Democracy Rising: South Carolina and the Fight for Black Equality since 1865* (Lexington: University Press of Kentucky, 2006), 192.

111. Kluger, *Simple Justice*, 15–18.

112. Ibid., 18.

113. DeLaine to McCray, February 21, 1955, folder: Politics, box 3, McCray Papers.

114. J. A. DeLaine, "August 1962—Some Reminiscence of My Life, Vacation Reflections," ibid. DeLaine traveled to Ghana in 1962 to visit his daughter, one of the first blacks to serve in the Peace Corps. He also traveled to Liberia and Israel, writing long letters to McCray.

115. Kluger, *Simple Justice*, 19.

116. Ibid.

117. Lau, *Democracy Rising*, 202.

118. Kluger. *Simple Justice*, 21.

119. Ibid., 25.

120. Ibid.

121. Ibid., 1.

122. Ibid., 525.

123. DeLaine sued his insurance company, Hanover Fire Insurance Company of New York, for $3,500 in 1955, seeking to recover the insurance money. The company settled out of court for an undisclosed sum a year later. See DeLaine v. Hanover Fire Insurance, No. 4823 (D. E. Div. S.C. filed March 28, 1955).

124. DeLaine, "August 1962—Some Reminiscence of My Life," folder: Politics, box 3, McCray Papers.

125. Williams, *Freedom and Justice,* 41.

126. "Bishop George W. Baber Dedicates 'DeLaine-Waring A.M.E. Church,'" DeLaine's remarks, n.d., folder: Politics, DeLaine, box 3, McCray Papers.

127. "DeLaine Is in NY; Gives Side in Case," *New York Post,* October 19, 1955.

128. DeLaine to McCray, August 22, 1961, folder: Politics, box 3, McCray Papers.

129. "Dear Editor," *Sumter (S.C.) Daily Item,* September 13, 1955, in Nash v. Sharper, folder 001477-039-0674, Jan. 1, 1955–Dec. 31, 1956, Series A: The South, Part 23: Legal Department Case Files, 1956–1965, Papers of the National Association for the Advancement of Colored People, Manuscript Division, Library of Congress, Washington, D.C. (hereafter Nash v. Sharper, NAACP Papers).

130. "Dear Editor," *Sumter Daily Item,* September 13, 1955, 1, and Complaint, October 24, 1955, both in Nash v. Sharper, NAACP Papers.

131. Complaint, October 24, 1955, both in Nash v. Sharper, NAACP Papers.

132. Nash v. Sharper, Case No. 4101, Opinion No. 17175 (S.C. filed June 18, 1956).

133. Jack Greenberg to Lincoln C. Jenkins, October 1, 1956, Nash v. Sharper, NAACP Papers.

134. Demurrer to Complaint, November 16, 1955, Nash v. Sharper, NAACP Papers.

135. Greenberg to Reverend J. M. Hinton, October. 26, 1956, ibid.

136. Jenkins to Greenberg, October 30, 1956, ibid.

137. Greenberg to Reverend J. M. Hinton, October 26, 1956, ibid.

138. "Conscience-Stricken Plaintiff Vows Not to Spend Damage Fine," *Durham Carolina Times*, November 24, 1956, 1.

139. "He Wanted the Money, We Paid Him, Still Wanted Integration," *Baltimore (Md.) Afro-American*, November 27, 1956, 23.

140. Ibid.

141. Greenberg to Hinton, October 26, 1956, Nash v. Sharper, NAACP Papers.

142. "Presbyterians Aided NAACP in Settling Suit," *Indianapolis (Ind.) Recorder*, May 18, 1957, 16.

143. Ibid.

144. Randall v. Sumter School District Number 2, Sumter, S.C., 232 F. Supp. 786, 789 (E.D.S.C. 1964).

145. Ian F. Haney Lopez, *White by Law: The Legal Construction of Race* (New York: New York University Press, 1996), 17.

146. "Memory Hold the Door," Shepard Kollock Nash (1893–1980), accessed July 24, 2018, http://guides.law.sc.edu/MemoryHoldTheDoor-VolumeIII/NashShepardKollock.

147. John A. Whalen, *Maverick among the Magnolias: The Hazel Brannon Smith Story* (N.p.: Xlibris, 2000), 28.

148. Ibid., 31.

149. Hazel Brannon, "Through Hazel Eyes," *Lexington (Miss.) Advertiser*. She complained about the whisky and gambling in her columns dated January 31, 1946, and February 7, 1946, and challenged the sheriff directly in her column dated February 28, 1946. She continued to complain about these issues in columns dated March 7, 1946; March 14, 1948; March 21, 1946; and March 28, 1946.

150. Hazel Brannon, "Through Hazel Eyes," *Lexington (Miss.) Advertiser*, April 11, 1946.

151. Ibid., April 25, 1946.

152. T. George Harris, "The 11-year Siege of Mississippi's Lady Editor," *Look*, November 16, 1965, 121–25.

153. Hazel Brannon, "Through Hazel Eyes," *Lexington (Miss.) Advertiser*, ibid., May 20, 1954.

154. Ibid., September 23, 1954.

155. See Whalen, *Maverick among the Magnolias*, for Hazel Brannon Smith's frequent battles with segregationists in Mississippi.

156. Hazel Brannon Smith, "Through Hazel Eyes," *Lexington (Miss.) Advertiser*, July 8, 1954.

157. Ibid.

158. Hazel Brannon Smith, "Through Hazel Eyes," *Lexington (Miss.) Advertiser*, July 15, 1954.

159. Ibid.

160. Ibid.

161. Hazel Brannon Smith, "Through Hazel Eyes," *Lexington (Miss.) Advertiser*, July 22, 1954.

162. Smith v. Byrd, No. 39755, 225 Miss. 331 (1955); 83 So. 2d Lexis 588, at *173 (Miss. 1955).

163. "The Last Word," *Time*, November 21, 1955.

164. Smith v. Byrd, 225 Miss. 331 (1955).

165. Ibid. at 345.

166. Ibid.

167. Hazel Brannon Smith, "Through Hazel Eyes," *Lexington (Miss.) Advertiser*, November 10, 1955. At the end of 1955, the state Supreme Court overruled a suggestion of error filed by Sheriff Byrd's attorneys.

168. Untitled memo, n.d., folder 9, Correspondence, 1955–1956, Hazel Brannon Smith Papers, Mitchell Memorial Library, University Libraries, Mississippi State University, Mississippi (hereafter Smith Papers).

169. Smith to Hodding Carter Jr., September 15, 1956, folder 9, Correspondence, 1955–1956, Smith Papers.

170. Included in the group were Ralph McGill of the *Atlanta Constitution*, J. N. Heiskell of the *Little Rock (Ark.) Gazette*, Mark Ethridge of the *Louisville (Ky.) Courier-Journal*, and Francis Harmon, former owner of the *Hattiesburg (Miss.) American*.

171. Hodding Carter Jr. to Norman Isaacs, October 12, 1961, folder: Hodding Carter Correspondence (Tri-Anniversary Committee, 1961–1962), Smith Papers.

172. Ibid. Carter also wrote a story in support of Smith, "Woman Editor's War on Bigots," which first appeared in the *St. Louis Post Dispatch*, November 26, 1961. It was later included in an anthology of Carter's work, *First Person Rural* (New York: Double Day, 1963).

173. Confidential Memorandum to Tri-Anniversary Committee, October 26, 1961, folder: Hodding Carter Correspondence (Tri-Anniversary Committee, 1961–1962), Smith Papers.

174. Hazel Brannon Smith, "Through Hazel Eyes," *Lexington (Miss.) Advertiser*, December 4, 1958.

175. Ibid., July 20, 1961.

176. Whalen, *Maverick among the Magnolias*, 157.

177. Smith quoted in ibid., 158.

178. *Lexington (Miss.) Advertiser*, October 24, 1963.

179. Ibid.

180. Ibid.

181. Whalen, *Maverick among the Magnolias*, 159.

182. Duard Le Grand, "Hazel Smith Is All-Southern Editor," *Lexington (Miss.) Advertiser*, June 6, 1968. Smith faced another libel suit in May 1966, this one filed by the prominent Lexington businessman Homer Daniel after she was quoted as saying at a public meeting: "You do not want Homer Daniel. He has been positively identified as a member of the Ku Klux Klan, and has been positively identified as leading a caravan of Klansmen through the colored section of Lexington." Daniel sued Smith for $100,000, but the suit was dismissed after a year and a half of legal wrangling.

183. Hazel Brannon Smith, "Through Hazel Eyes," ibid., June 6, 1968.

184. Whalen, *Maverick among the Magnolias*, 318.

185. Copy of Mizell telegram, in Pruitt v. Mizell, Legal Department Case Files, 1956–1965, Series A: The South, Part 23: Legal Department Case Files, 1956–1965, Papers of the National Association for the Advancement of Colored People,

Manuscript Division, Library of Congress, Washington, D.C. (hereafter Pruitt v. Mizell, NAACP Papers).

186. Pruitt v. Mizell (Fla. 2d Cir. Ct. filed October 11, 1955).

187. Ibid., 4.

188. Don Mizell quoted in "Pioneering Mizell Family's History Spans 100 Years," *Fort Lauderdale South Florida Times,* February 25, 2011, accessed July 24, 2018, http://www.sfltimes.com/uncategorized/pioneering-mizell-familys-history-spans-100-years.

189. Ibid.

190. Von Mizell to Roy Wilkins, January 10, 1956, Pruitt v. Mizell, NAACP Papers.

191. Bill Taylor to Francisco Rodriguez, June 11, 1956, in Pruitt v. Mizell, NAACP Papers.

192. Robert M. Ratcliffe, "Behind the Headlines: Ducking Preachers, Not Cops!" *Pittsburgh (Penn.) Courier,* June 23, 1956, A8. Ratcliffe reported, "Fort Lauderdale's Dr. Von D. Mizell will pay the $15,000 awarded to white supremacy leader Prentice Pruitt in a libel suit (he says it would be useless to continue to fight the case in Florida courts)."

193. Savannah News-Press, Inc. v. Harley No. 37840, 100 Ga.App. 387 (1959), *rev'd,* 111 S.E.2d 259 (Ga. Ct. App. 1959).

194. *Harley,* 100 Ga.App. at 391.

195. L. Scott Stell Jr., J. H. Bennett, and E. Cooper, "Church Labels Shooting as Murderous," *Savannah News-Press,* June 1, 1959, reprinted in ibid.

196. Ibid.

197. *Harley,* 100 Ga.App. at 388.

CHAPTER 2: "HEED THEIR RISING VOICES," THE *SULLIVAN* CASE, AND TURMOIL FOR THE *TIMES*

1. New York Times v. Sullivan, 376 U.S. 254 (1964).

2. Association of Citizens' Councils of Mississippi press release, November 17, 1961, folder 28, box 1, Citizens' Council Collection, Department of Archives and Special Collections, University of Mississippi, Oxford.

3. "Join Citizens' Council," *Meridian (Miss.) Star,* September 10, 1961; "Citizens' Councils Must Be Strong to Protect S.C. If Crisis Comes," *Charleston (S.C.) News and Courier,* July 14, 1958; and "Citizens' Council Gets Credit," *Jackson (Miss.) Daily News,* April 11, 1963, folder 18, box 1, Citizens' Council Collection, Department of Archives and Special Collections, University of Mississippi, Oxford.

4. The standard history of the Alien and Sedition Acts of 1798 is James Morton Smith, *Freedom's Fetters: The Alien and Sedition Laws and American Civil Liberties* (Ithaca, N.Y.: Cornell University Press, 1956).

5. Invaluable discussion of events leading up to the passage of the Alien and Sedition Acts of 1798 can be found in Norman L. Rosenberg, *Protecting the Best Men: An Interpretive History of the Law of Libel* (Chapel Hill: University of North Carolina Press, 1986). John C. Miller, *The Federalist Era,* 1789–1800 (New York: Harper, 1960) is also an excellent introduction to the earliest party system.

6. Rosenberg cautions against characterizations that only Federalists sought to silence critics and that Jeffersonians were libertarians by modern standards. Although Jefferson and his Democratic-Republicans considered the congressional acts unconstitutional, they did not believe in the absolute freedom of political expression. They did not focus on protection of government as an entity but rather protection for the reputations of public leaders, or the "the best men." See Rosenberg, *Protecting the Best Men,* 89–100.

7. Proponents of the acts were quick to point out that the law differed from traditional seditious libel tenets in that it included the principle of truth as a defense. *U.S. Statutes at Large* (1798): 596, as discussed in Rosenberg, *Protecting the Best Men.*

8. See generally Smith, *Freedom's Fetters,* and John C. Miller, *Crisis in Freedom* (Boston: Little, Brown and Company, 1951).

9. For details on the Zenger trial and free speech in general, see Lucas A. Powe Jr., *The Fourth Estate and the Constitution* (Berkeley: University of California Press, 1991); Leonard W. Levy, *Emergence of a Free Press* (New York: Oxford University Press, 1985); Leonard W. Levy, *Legacy of Suppression: Freedom of Speech and Press in Early American History* (Cambridge, Mass.: The Belknap Press of Harvard University Press, 1960); and William Lowell Putnam, *John Peter Zenger and the Fundamental Freedom* (Jefferson, N.C.: McFarland & Company, 1997).

10. J. Herbert Altschull, *From Milton to McLuhan: The Ideas behind American Journalism* (White Plains, N.Y.: Longman, 1990), 122.

11. Ibid., 119–126.

12. Anthony Lewis, *Make No Law: The Sullivan Case and the First Amendment* (New York: Random House), 65.

13. The three-fifths compromise is located in US Const, Art I, Sec 2, Par 3: "Representatives and direct Taxes shall be apportioned among the several States which may be included within this Union, according to their respective Numbers, which shall be determined by adding the whole Number of free Persons, including those bound to Service for a Term of Years, and excluding Indians not taxed, three fifths of all other Persons."

14. "Heed Their Rising Voices," *New York Times*, March 29, 1960, 25.

15. For details on this case, see Taylor Branch, *Parting the Waters: America in the King Years, 1954–1963* (New York: Simon and Schuster, 1988), 277.

16. Ibid.

17. "Amendment XV," *New York Times*, March 19, 1960, 20.

18. "Heed Their Rising Voices," *New York Times*, March 29, 1960, 25.

19. Lewis, *Make No Law,* 9.

20. *Montgomery (Ala.) Advertiser,* April 7, 1960.

21. Petitioners' brief, New York Times v. Sullivan, 376 U.S. 254 (1964) (Case No. 40).

22. Kermit L. Hall, "'Lies, Lies, Lies': The Origins of New York Times Co. v. Sullivan," *Communication Law & Policy* 9 (Summer 2004): 391–421, quoting Merton Roland Nachman, Sullivan's attorney, who argued his case before the U.S. Supreme Court.

23. Kermit L. Hall, "Justice Brennan and Cultural History: New York Times v. Sullivan and Its Times," *California Western Law Review* 27, no. 2 (1991): 339–59.

24. Kermit L. Hall and Melvin I. Urofsky, *New York Times v. Sullivan, Civil Rights, Libel Law, and the Free Press* (Lawrence: University Press of Kansas, 2011), 11–12.

25. Sullivan quoted in Diane McWhorter, *Carry Me Home: Birmingham, Alabama, the Climactic Battle of the Civil Rights Revolution* (New York: Simon & Schuster, 2001), 164. See also Branch, *Parting the Waters,* 283.

26. Branch, *Parting the Waters,* 280.

27. *Montgomery (Ala.) Advertiser,* February 26, 1961, as cited in "Affidavit in Support of Motion for Temporary Relief and Order to Show Cause," filed by Bernard Lee, in the case of Abernathy v. Patterson, supporting court documents found in folder 3, box 4, Papers of Vernon Z. Crawford, McCall Library, University of South Alabama, Mobile (hereafter Crawford Papers).

28. Branch, *Parting the Waters*, 289.
29. Roberts and Klibanoff, *The Race Beat*, 231.
30. "*Times* Retracts Statement in Ad," *New York Times,* May 16, 1960, 22.
31. Patterson v. New York Times, Civ. A. No. 1707-N (Ala. filed May 30, 1960). The Patterson and Parks cases were later moved to federal court. See Parks v. New York Times Company, 195 F. Supp. 919 (M.D.Ala. 1961).
32. NAACP v. Alabama ex rel. Patterson, 357 U.S. 449 (1958), 360 U.S. 240 (1959), 368 U.S. 16 (1961).
33. Hall and Urofsky, *New York Times v. Sullivan*, 91; Branch, *Parting the Waters*, 186–87.
34. Howell Raines, *My Soul Is Rested: The Story of the Civil Rights Movement in the Deep South* (1977; reprint, with a new subtitle, New York: Penguin Books, 1987), 304.
35. Represented by Roland Nachman, Sellers and Parks had found some success with libel suits three years before against the New York pulp magazine, *Ken*, which said Montgomery suffered from widespread illegal gambling and prostitution. Parks, Sellers, and then Mayor W. A. Gayle claimed the article, "Kimono Girls Check in Again," was false and defamatory and reflected badly on them as guardians of the city's welfare and reputation They demanded $750,000. *Ken* settled the suit for $15,000 and issued an apology. See Hall, "'Lies, Lies, Lies,'" 391, 414.
36. Judge Walter B. Jones, "Off the Bench," *Montgomery (Ala.) Advertiser,* March 12, 1962.
37. Ibid., March 26, 1962.
38. Ibid., "Off the Bench," undated clipping, *Montgomery (Ala.) Advertiser,* Judge Walter B. Jones Biographical File, Alabama Department of History and Archives, Montgomery.
39. Judge Walter B. Jones, "Off the Bench," *Montgomery (Ala.) Advertiser,* December 7, 1959.
40. "Judge Jones Given Press Honor," ibid., February 22, 1958.
41. Harrison E. Salisbury, *Without Fear or Favor* (New York: Times Books, 1982), 385.
42. Roberts quoted in ibid., 382.
43. Ibid.
44. Hall and Urofsky, *New York Times v. Sullivan*, 46, 199.
45. Brief and Arguments of Appellants, Abernathy, Shuttlesworth, Seay, and Lowery, filed October 5, 1961, in New York Times v. Sullivan, 273 Ala. 656 (1962), 144 So. 2d 25 (Ala. 1962), folder 2, box 4, Civil Rights Series, Crawford Papers. See also Branch, *Parting the Waters*, 370–71.
46. Affidavit in Support of Motion For Temporary Relief and Order to Show cause, by Bernard Lee, in the case of *Abernathy v. Patterson*, supporting court documents found in folder 3, box 4, Crawford Papers.
47. Hall, "Justice Brennan and Cultural History," 348.
48. *Montgomery (Ala.) Advertiser*, April 7, 1960. Hall and Urofsky deconstruct the editorial and Grover Hall's reaction to the ad in detail in their book *New York Times v. Sullivan*, 29.
49. Testimony of Harry W. Kaminsky, William Parker, L. B. Sullivan, and others, court documents in folder 2, box 4, Civil Rights Series, Crawford Papers.
50. New York Times v. Sullivan, 273 Ala. 656 (1962), 144 So. 2d 25 (Ala. 1962).
51. Hall, "Justice Brennan and Cultural History," 17.
52. "Four Negro Clerics, New York Times," *Jet*, February 16, 1961, 4.
53. Branch, *Parting the Waters*, 442.

54. Lawrence M. Friedman, *American Law in the Twentieth Century* (New Haven, Conn.: Yale University Press, 2002).

55. Lois G. Forer, *A Chilling Effect: The Mounting Threat of Libel and Invasion of Privacy Actions to the First Amendment* (New York: W. W. Norton and Company, 1987), 61. See also Clifton O. Lawhorne, *Defamation and Public Officials: The Evolving Law of Libel* (Carbondale: Southern Illinois University Press, 1971), 230-31.

56. Rosenberg, *Protecting the Best Men*, 243-44. See also Bernard Schwartz, *Super Chief: Earl Warren and His Supreme Court; a Judicial Biography* (New York: New York University Press, 1983), 538.

57. Lewis, *Make No Law*, 103.

58. *Sullivan*, 376 U.S. at 271-73.

59. John Stuart Mill, *On Liberty* (1859; reprint, Oxford, U.K.: Blackwell, 1947), 15; John Milton, *Areopagitica*, in *Complete Prose Works of John Milton*, vol. 2, 1643-1648, ed. Don M. Wolfe (New Haven, Conn.: Yale, 1959).

60. *Sullivan*, 376 U.S. at 273.

61. W. Wat Hopkins, *Mr. Justice Brennan and Freedom of Expression* (New York: Praeger, 1991), 163.

62. Hopkins, *Mr. Justice Brennan*, 84; Holmes's dissent, in Abrams v. United States, 250 U.S. 616 (1919).

63. Salisbury, *Without Fear or Favor*, 380.

64. Ibid.

65. Harrison Salisbury, "Fear and Hatred Grip Birmingham," *New York Times*, April 12, 1960, 1.

66. Ibid.

67. Connors quoted in Salisbury, *Without Fear or Favor*, 379.

68. "*New York Times* Slanders Our City—Can This Be Birmingham?" *Birmingham (Ala.) News*, April 15, 1960.

69. As quoted in New York Times v. Connor, 365 F.2d 567 (5th Cir. 1966), 575. See also "Alabama Groups Protest to Times," *New York Times*, May 4, 1960, 1; "3 in Birmingham Ask a Retraction," *New York Times*, April 27, 1960, 28.

70. The Birmingham Chamber of Commerce passed a resolution condemning Salisbury and the *Times* for damaging the city's reputation and requested space in the newspaper for a rebuttal. The chamber also offered to pay for a *Times* reporter to visit the city again in order to double-check the accuracy of its rebuttal. Resolution dated April 21, 1960, folder 9, box 7, James T. "Jabbo" Waggoner Papers, 1954-1963, Department of Archives and Manuscripts, Birmingham Public Library, Alabama (hereafter Waggoner Papers).

71. Connor v. New York Times, Civil Action No. 9634 (N.D.Ala. filed May 6, 1960).

72. Lindsey v. New York Times, Civil Action No. 9711 (N.D.Ala. filed July 20, 1960). This suit was filed in the same court and later consolidated with the other Birmingham suits. Lindsey dropped the suit July 13, 1964, saying he could not win in light of the *Sullivan* decision. See "Suit against Times Ended in Alabama," *New York Times*, July 14, 1964, 17.

73. Simpson to Waggoner, April 19, 1960, folder 10, box 7, Waggoner Papers.

74. Simpson quoted in McWhorter, *Carry Me Home*, 21.

75. Lanier v. New York Times, Thompson v. New York Times, Parsons v. New York Times, Case Nos. 9659, 9660, 9221 (N.D.Ala. all filed in 1960).

76. Salisbury, "Fear and Hatred Grip Birmingham," 1.

77. Ibid.

78. Salisbury, *Without Fear or Favor,* 383.
79. According to an interview conducted by Lucas Powe and printed in his *The Fourth Estate and the Constitution* (Berkeley: University of California Press, 1991), the Bessemer indictments worried Salisbury "for several years since no DA was willing to take the political risk of dismissing them. Finally one quiet day three or four years later they were dismissed." See author's notes, 312n14.
80. Salisbury, *Without Fear or Favor,* 383.
81. Ibid., 384.
82. Grover Hall, "Checkmate," *Montgomery (Ala.) Advertiser,* May 22, 1960, 15.
83. Salisbury, *Without Fear or Favor,* 382.
84. Sitton quoted in ibid., 384.
85. Memo for the file, November 27, 1962, folder: Sitton, Claude, 1961–1968, box 6, Catledge Papers.
86. Memo for Mr. Catledge from the National News Desk, November 25, 1962, ibid.
87. Roberts and Klibanoff, *The Race Beat,* 240.
88. Morgan v. Commonwealth of Virginia, 184 Va. 24 (1946). For a detailed narrative on the Freedom Riders, see Raymond Arsenault, *Freedom Riders, 1961 and the Struggle for Racial Justice* (New York: Oxford University Press, 2006).
89. David Halberstam, *The Children* (New York: Ballantine Publishing Group, 1998), 293.
90. McWhorter, *Carry Me Home,* 21, 37, 55, 258.
91. Undated internal memo, folder 10, box 7, Waggoner Papers. Before closing the Birmingham parks, city officials studied how Lester B. Sullivan shut down the public parks in Montgomery rather than implementing desegregation as ordered by a federal district court. Birmingham officials noted in this memo that all black employees of Montgomery parks were dismissed, and the white employees were redistributed to other public jobs.
92. Arsenault, *Freedom Riders,* 136. He and other historians have relied on volumes of FBI correspondence to piece together events that led to the Klan's unfettered access to the bus terminals in Birmingham and Montgomery. This includes documentation on Klansman-turned-FBI-informant Gary Thomas Rowe, who told the FBI that Connor secretly met with Bobby Shelton, a Tuscaloosa tire salesman and the imperial wizard of the Alabama Knights of the Ku Klux Klan. Arsenault writes that Connor's "behind-the-scenes role was a crucial element of the evolving plan to teach the Freedom Riders a lesson they would never forget." Connor reportedly promised Shelton fifteen or twenty minutes to beat the Freedom Riders before the police would arrive at the bus terminal.
93. Branch, *Parting the Waters,* 431.
94. Halberstam, *The Children,* 293.
95. McWhorter, *Carry Me Home,* 338.
96. Salisbury, *Without Fear or Favor,* 388.
97. Connor v. New York Times, 144 So. 2d (Ala. 1962).
98. Constance Baker Motley, *Equal Justice under Law: An Autobiography* (New York: Farrar, Straus and Giroux, 1998). Motley was the first African American woman to argue a case before the U.S. Supreme Court, winning in *Meredith v. Fair,* James Meredith's legal push to be the first black student to attend the University of Mississippi in 1962.
99. Ibid., 121.
100. Proctor quoted in Dennis Washburn, "Judge Grooms Receives Honorary Doctorate," *Birmingham (Ala.) News,* April 3, 1977.

101. Grooms quoted in McWhorter, *Carry Me Home,* 247.

102. Salisbury, *Without Fear or Favor,* 388.

103. Trial transcript, copy, folder 9, box 1, Connor v. New York Times Collection, Department of Archives and Manuscripts, Birmingham Public Library, Alabama (hereafter Connor v. New York Times Collection).

104. Ibid., 16.

105. Ibid., 27.

106. Trial transcript, copy, p. 40, folder 9, box 1, Connor v. New York Times Collection.

107. Ibid., 74.

108. Ibid., 82–103.

109. Trial transcript, copy, p. 104, folder 9, box 1, Connor v. New York Times Collection.

110. Ibid., 116.

111. Ibid., 117–20.

112. Trial transcript, copy, p. 123, folder 9, box 1, Connor v. New York Times Collection.

113. Ibid., 121.

114. Exhibits 26–51, ibid., 146–55. These twenty-five exhibits were newspaper articles introduced by Embry and illustrating the violence perpetrated against black citizens in the region.

115. Trial Transcript, copy, p. 155, folder 9, box 1, Connor v. New York Times Collection.

116. Ibid., 162.

117. See Andrew M. Manis, *A Fire You Can't Put Out: The Civil Rights Life of Birmingham's Reverend Fred Shuttlesworth* (Tuscaloosa: University of Alabama Press, 1999), 235.

118. Grooms in 144 So. 2d at 574.

119. Arrest record of Fred Lee Shuttlesworth, October 16, 1963, roll 9.11, microfilm, Birmingham, Alabama, Police Department Surveillance Files, AR1125, Department of Archives and Manuscripts, Birmingham Public Library, Alabama.

120. Trial transcript, copy, pp. 162–63, folder 9, box 1, Connor v. New York Times Collection.

121. Ibid., 207.

122. Letter from Morgan to Mrs. Hall Livingston, October 8, 1957, James W. Morgan Papers, File #266.24.29, Department of Archives and Manuscripts, Birmingham Public Library, Alabama (hereafter Morgan Papers).

123. Trial transcript, copy, pp. 260–61, folder 9, box 1, Connor v. New York Times Collection.

124. Ibid., 263–64.

125. Ibid., 265–67. "Birmingham's Million Dollar Building, Plush New Edifice Houses Multi-million Dollar Enterprises of A. G. Gaston," *Ebony,* June 1960, 25–26. In the photograph illustrating the article, Birmingham mayor J. W. Morgan is shaking hands with Mr. and Mrs. A. G. Gaston, thanking them for the "fine building added to our city" at the building's dedication.

126. Trial transcript, copy, p. 274, folder 9, box 1, Connor v. New York Times Collection.

127. Ibid., 277–78.

128. Ibid., 278–79.

129. Trial transcript, copy, pp. 325–27, folder 9, box 1, Connor v. New York Times Collection.

130. Ibid., 328.
131. Ibid., 341, 347–48. Embry read a story from the *Birmingham News*, March 12, 1963, edition quoting Connor and entered it into evidence.
132. Trial transcript, copy, pp. 362, 366–67, folder 9, box 1, Connor v. New York Times Collection.
133. Ibid., 386–87.
134. Ibid., 388–89.
135. Trial transcript, copy, pp. 395–96, folder 9, box 1, Connor v. New York Times Collection.
136. Ibid., 401–2.
137. Ibid., 404–5.
138. Trial transcript, copy, pp. 408–9.
139. Ibid., 410–11.
140. Judge's instructions to the jury, in Trial transcript, copy, pp. 1–22, folder 9, box 1, Connor v. New York Times Collection.
141. Ibid., 4.
142. Ibid., 6.
143. Judge's instructions to the jury, in Trial transcript, copy, pp. 7–22, folder 9, box 1, Connor v. New York Times Collection.
144. "Connor Awarded $40,000 in NY Times Libel Suit," United Press International story, undated, folder 9, box 1, Connor v. New York Times Collection.
145. "Times Is Cleared in 2 Libel Suits," *New York Times*, September 18, 1964, 22.
146. New York Times v. Connor, 365 F. 2d. 567 (5th Cir. 1966).
147. Judgment, August 4, 1966, ibid.
148. *Connor*, 365 F. 2d. at 577.
149. Salisbury to Catledge, January 30, 1961, folder: Litigation (Libel-Alabama Case, 1960–1964), box 16, Catledge Papers.
150. Howard K. Smith, *Events Leading Up to My Death: The Life of a Twentieth-Century Reporter* (New York: St. Martin's Press, 1996), 268.
151. Ibid., 271.
152. Ibid.
153. "Bi-Racial Buses Attacked, Riders Beaten in Alabama," *New York Times*, May 15, 1961, 10. See also Smith, *Events Leading Up to My Death*, 272.
154. Smith, *Events Leading Up to My Death*, 272.
155. Ibid., 269. Pretrial documents in *Connor v. CBS* show that CBS conducted seventy-seven interviews in Birmingham during preparation of the documentary, "Who Speaks for Birmingham?" See pretrial documents in folder 14, box 7, Waggoner Papers.
156. "People Are Asking: 'Where Were the Police,'" *Birmingham (Ala.) News*, May 16, 1961, 1.
157. Ibid.
158. Howard K. Smith, "Who Speaks for Birmingham?" *CBS Reports*, New York, May 18, 1961.
159. Shuttlesworth, one of the four ministers sued by Sullivan in 1960, was a big target, having successfully challenged, among many other things, a Birmingham city ordinance that forbade whites and blacks from playing together. Shuttlesworth v. Gaylord, 202 f. Supp. 59 (N.D. Ala. 1961). Struck down by Judge H. H. Grooms, the ordinance had listed forbidden interracial activities, including cards, dice, dominoes, checkers, softball, basketball, baseball, football, golf, track, and others.

160. Shuttlesworth's battles with Birmingham officials have been well documented in Manis, *A Fire You Can't Put Out*. See Smith, "Who Speaks for Birmingham?"

161. "People Are Asking: 'Where Were the Police?'" *Birmingham News*, May 16, 1961.

162. Simpson to CBS, November 6, 1961, folder 10, box 7, Waggoner Papers.

163. Simpson to Connor, Morgan, and Waggoner, November 24, 1961, folder 10, box 7, Waggoner Papers.

164. Ibid.

165. Simpson to Waggoner, Connor, and Morgan, December 4, 1961, folder 11, box 7, Waggoner Papers. Simpson told his clients that the retractions "in no wise [sic] remedied the situation" and proceeded to file suit.

166. Smith, *Events Leading Up to My Death*, 276.

167. Connor v. CBS, No. 10068-S; Morgan v. CBS, No. 10067-S; Waggoner v. CBS, No. 10069-S, (N.D.Ala. all filed in 1961). As was the case with many of the nearly identical suits, these three were consolidated not long after they were filed in 1961.

168. U.S.A. v. Penton, Montgomery Alabama, Case No. 1741-N (M.D.Ala filed August 3, 1961).

169. Arthur Osgoode, "Decision on CBS Libel Film Suits Delayed by Johnson," *Montgomery (Ala.) Advertiser*, March 12, 1962.

170. Arsenault, *Freedom Riders*, 215.

171. See Branch, *Parting the Waters*, 420. See also J. Mills Thornton III, *Dividing Lines: Municipal Politics and the Struggle for Civil Rights in Montgomery, Birmingham, and Selma* (Tuscaloosa: University of Alabama Press, 2002).

172. Halberstam, *The Children*, 309.

173. Ibid.

174. Sullivan quoted in Arsenault, *Freedom Riders*, 217.

175. Klansman quoted in ibid, 220.

176. Pierce v. Moon, Pierce v. Dunjee, combined, No. 150825, District Court, Oklahoma City; "NAACP Calls Killing of Negro a Lynching in Letter to Chief," *Black Dispatch*, February 26, 1960, 1.

177. "NAACP Calls Killing of Negro a Lynching," 1.

178. Bob Burke and Angela Monson, *Roscoe Dunjee, Champion of Civil Rights* (Edmond, Okla.: UCO Press, 1998), 15–19.

179. Moon to Carter, January 10, 1961, and Pierce v. Moon, folder: 001477-039–0156, Series A: The South, Part 23: Legal Department Files, 1956–1965, Group V, Box 132, Papers of the National Association for the Advancement of Colored People, Manuscript Division, Library of Congress, Washington, D.C. (hereafter Pierce v. Moon, NAACP Papers).

180. Porter to Carter, January 9, 1961, Pierce v. Moon, NAACP Papers.

181. Stewart to Carter, March 3, 1961, ibid.

182. Carter to Stewart, March 23, 1961, ibid.

183. Carter to Roy Wilkins, October 7, 1960, ibid.

CHAPTER 3: WHILE *SULLIVAN* IS ON APPEAL...

1. David L. Hudson Jr., "Ben Elton Cox: Civil Rights Leader to High Court Litigant," Newseum Institute, January 2007, accessed July 24, 2018, http://www.newseuminstitute.org/2007/01/16/ben-elton-cox-civil-rights-leader-to-high-court-litigant/.

2. "Freedom Rider Endured Jail, Shootings, Attacks to Get Out Black Vote," *Jackson (Tenn.) Sun,* undated item, http://orig.jacksonsun.com/civilrights/sec5_freedomrider_cox.shtml.

3. Adam Fairclough, *Race and Democracy: The Civil Rights Struggle in Louisiana, 1915–1972* (Athens: University of Georgia Press, 1995), 290.

4. State v. Cox, No. 46,395 (Sup. Ct. La. petition for rehearing filed July 12, 1963).

5. State v. Cox, 245 La. 303 (1963).

6. Fairclough, *Race and Democracy,* 293.

7. Ibid., 292.

8. *The Crisis,* January 1963, 43.

9. State v. Cox, No. 44,287 (Cir.Ct.La. 1964).

10. State v. Cox, 167 So. 2d 352, 354 (Sup. Ct. La. 1964).

11. Ibid. at 355.

12. Ibid. at 355–56.

13. Ibid. at 357.

14. CORE v. Clemmons, 323 F.2d. 54 (5th Cir. 1963).

15. Cox v. Louisiana, 379 U.S. 536 (1965).

16. Cox v. Louisiana, 348 F2d 750, 752 (5th Cir. 1965).

17. Aaron Henry with Constance Curry, *Aaron Henry: The Fire Ever Burning* (Jackson: University Press of Mississippi, 2000). See also Minion K. C. Morrison, *Aaron Henry of Mississippi: Inside Agitator* (Fayetteville: University of Arkansas Press, 2015).

18. According to Constance Curry: "While it appears that the 1962 charge was trumped up and a case of harassment, Aaron Henry's bisexuality was later assumed by his friends and associates. The essence of their interview comments was: 'We all knew it, it made no difference to us, and it had no impact on his political life nor on his contributions to the freedom movement.'" Curry, *Aaron Henry,* 128n. Henry's memoir was completed by Curry after Henry's death. She added this note.

19. "New Trial Opens for Aaron Henry, Youth Accuses Official of NAACP with Making Immoral Advances," UPI wire story, *Memphis (Tenn.) Commercial Appeal,* May 22, 1962.

20. *Aaron Henry,* 124.

21. Ibid., 123.

22. Ibid., 125.

23. Exhibit B, United Press International, Henry v. Pearson, No. 5724, Coahoma County Circuit Court, 158 So. 2d 695 (Miss. 1963).

24. Brief for Appellant, 2, Henry v. Pearson, No. 42758, 253 Miss. 62 (1963) (filed September 9, 1963).

25. *Aaron Henry,* 125.

26. Henry v. Pearson, 158 So. 2d 695 (Miss. 1963).

27. Henry v. Collins, 158 So.2d 28 (1963).

28. Yasuhiro Katagiri, *The Mississippi State Sovereignty Commission: Civil Rights and States' Rights* (Oxford: University Press of Mississippi, 2001), 11–12.

29. DeCell to Governor Coleman, December 17, 1957, SCR ID# 1-16-1-19-1-1-1, Mississippi State Sovereignty Commission Records, 1956–2002, Mississippi Department of Archives and History, Jackson (hereafter Sovereignty Commission), accessed July 21, 2018, http://www.mdah.ms.gov/arrec/digital_archives/sovcom/result.php?image=images/png/cd01/000720.png&otherstuff=1|16|1|19|1|1|1|709|#.

30. Ibid.

31. DeCell to Governor Coleman, January 6, 1958, SCR ID# 1-16-1-2-1-1-1, Sovereignty Commission, accessed July 21, 2018, http://www.mdah.ms.gov/arrec/digital_archives/sovcom/result.php?image=images/png/cdo1/000630.png&otherstuff=1|16|1|2|1|1|1|621|.

32. Landingham to Director, State Sovereignty Commission, January 26, 1959, SCR ID# 1-16-1-21-2-1-1, Sovereignty Commission, accessed July 21, 2018, http://www.mdah.ms.gov/arrec/digital_archives/sovcom/result.php?image=images/png/cdo1/000723.png&otherstuff=1|16|1|21|2|1|1|712|.

33. Ibid.

34. Ibid.

35. Landingham to Director, State Sovereignty Commission, October 13, 1959, SCR ID# 1-16-1-27-1-1-1, Sovereignty Commission, accessed July 21, 2018, http://www.mdah.ms.gov/arrec/digital_archives/sovcom/result.php?image=images/png/cdo1/000824.png&otherstuff=1|16|1|27|1|1|1|727|.

36. Memo to file, Zack J. Van Landingham, February 23, 1960, SCR ID# 1-16-1-35-1-1-1, Sovereignty Commission, accessed July 21, 2018, http://www.mdah.ms.gov/arrec/digital_archives/sovcom/result.php?image=images/png/cdo1/000828.png&otherstuff=1|16|1|35|1|1|1|814|.

37. Ibid.

38. Ibid.

39. Memo to file, Zack J. Van Landingham, May 6, 1960, SCR ID# 1-16-1-42-1-1-1, Sovereignty Commission, accessed July 21, 2018, http://www.mdah.ms.gov/arrec/digital_archives/sovcom/result.php?image=images/png/cdo1/000898.png&otherstuff=1|16|1|42|1|1|1|881|.

40. Ibid.

41. Memo, Coahoma County—Boycotters, investigated by Tom Scarbrough, January 9, 1962, SCR ID# 1-16-1-57-1-1-1, Sovereignty Commission, accessed July 21, 2018, http://www.mdah.ms.gov/arrec/digital_archives/sovcom/result.php?image=images/png/cdo1/001044.png&otherstuff=1|16|1|57|1|1|1|1025|.

42. Ibid.

43. Noelle M. Henry v. Coahoma County Board of Education, 353 F.2d 648 (5th Cir. 1965).

44. Ibid.

45. "Jury Votes 'Guilty' For NAACP Leader, Aaron Henry Is Convicted on Morals Charge," UPI wire story, *Memphis (Tenn.) Commercial Appeal*, May 23, 1962.

46. "Aaron Henry Gets Reversal, NAACP Leader Scheduled for New Trial Due to Illegal Search," ibid., June 4, 1963.

47. "Court Reverses Henry Decision, Conviction of NAACP Chief on Morals Charge Is Upheld," UPI wire story, ibid., July 12, 1962.

48. Ibid.

49. Henry v. Pearson, No. 5724, Coahoma County Circuit Court, 158 So. 2d 695 (Miss. 1963).

50. Court transcript, 35, ibid.

51. Court transcript, 22, ibid.

52. Henry to Mr. Norwood, Boliver County deputy sheriff, March 6, 1962, Exhibit P.1., ibid. Henry had originally been arrested in Boliver, the county south of Coahoma, and jailed there. He wrote Norwood looking for his address book, which had not been returned to him when he was released from jail.

53. Court transcript, 102, Henry v. Pearson, No. 5724, Coahoma County Circuit Court, 158 So. 2d 695 (Miss. 1963). Savell was also the AP reporter sued by General Edwin Walker for his dispatches from Oxford during the Ole Miss riot.

54. At the objection of Henry's attorney, the judge instructed the jury to disregard the inflammatory statement. See *Pearson*, 158 So. 2d.

55. *Pearson*, 253 Miss. 62 (1963), *aff'd*, 158 So.2d 695 LEXIS 551 (Miss. 1963); Collins v. Henry, 253 Miss. 34 (1963), *aff'd*, 158 So. 2d 28 (Miss. 1963).

56. "Over 70,000 Cast Freedom Ballots, Henry-King Ticket Tops Mock Election," *The Student Voice*, undated copy SCRID# 1-16-1-81-1-1-1, Sovereignty Commission, accessed June 19, 2001, http://www.mdah.ms.gov/arrec/digital_archives/sovcom/result.php?image=images/png/cdo1/001149.png&otherstuff=1|16|1|81|1|1|1|1125|.

57. *Aaron Henry*, 143.

58. Henry v. Collins, 380 U.S. 356 (1965). The Collins and Pearson suits were combined.

59. *Aaron Henry*, 127.

60. For Moore's body of work on the civil rights movement, see *Powerful Days: The Civil Rights Photography of Charles Moore* (New York: Steward, Tabori and Chang, 1991).

61. Grace Elizabeth Hale, *Making Whiteness: The Culture of Segregation in the South, 1890–1940* (New York: Vintage Books, 1999).

62. Robert Massie, "What Next in Mississippi?" *Saturday Evening Post*, November 10, 1962, 18–23.

63. John Dittmer, *Local People: The Struggle for Civil Rights in Mississippi* (Urbana: University of Illinois Press, 1991), 274, quoting a transcript of Barnett's speech housed at Mississippi State University.

64. Curtis Publishing v. Birdsong, No. 22,277, 360 F.2d 344 LEXIS 7392 (5th Cir. 1966).

65. Justice Department official quoted in Massie, "What Next in Mississippi?" 19.

66. Amendment to Complaint, Curtis Publishing v. Birdsong, No. 22,277 360 F.2d 344 (5th Cir. July 14, 1966). Lower courts had addressed the question regarding whether words of general abuse and vituperation are libelous, ruling that they are not in and of themselves actionable. See Crozman v. Callahan, 136 F. Supp. 466 (W.D. Okla. 1955); Bolton v. Strawbridge, 156 N.Y.S. 2d 722 (1956); Notarmuzzi v. Schevack, 108 N.Y.S. 2d. 172 (1951).

67. Karl Fleming, *Son of the Rough South: An Uncivil Memoir* (New York: Public Affairs, 2005), 279.

68. Ibid., 278.

69. Ibid., 279.

70. "The U.S. Marshals and the Integration of the University of Mississippi," U.S. Marshals Service site, History, accessed February 10, 2019, https://www.usmarshals.gov/history/miss/02.htm and https://www.usmarshals.gov/history/miss/05.htm. See also Taylor Branch, *Parting the Waters: America in the King Years, 1954–1963* (New York: Simon & Schuster, 1988), 668.

71. Office Memorandum from Chief U.S. Marshal James McShane to All U.S. Deputy Marshals, Border Patrolmen, and Bureau of Prisons personnel who participated in the control of the riot at Ole Miss on the night of September 30, October 19, 1962, box 1, Investigation into the University of Mississippi Desegregation Riots, 1962–1963, Oxford Division, Northern District of Mississippi, Records of the United States Marshals Service, Record Group 527, National Archives and Records Administration, Southeast Region, Atlanta, Georgia (hereafter Investigation, Oxford Div., NDist. Miss., U.S. Marshals Service, RG 527, NARA).

72. Bryan to McShane, October 25, 1962; Hearell to McShane, October 22, 1962; Coen to McShane, October 25, 1962; and Alexander to McShane, October 23, 1962, all in ibid.

73. Coen to McShane, October 25, 1962; Anglin to McShane, October 25, 1962; and Official Report: Riot Control "Old Miss" [sic] Campus, submitted by Bartholomew, n.d., all in ibid.

74. Mike to McShane, October 23, 1962; Brake to McShane, October 19, 1962; Alexander to McShane, October 23, 1962, all in ibid.

75. Official report by T. B. Birdsong, pp. 8–9, folder 7, box 8, Leesha Faulkner Collection, McCain Library and Archives, University of Southern Mississippi, Hattiesburg (hereafter Faulkner Collection).

76. Ibid., 8–9.

77. Ibid., 15.

78. Branch, *Parting the Waters*, 664–65.

79. Ibid, 664.

80. Massie, "What Next in Mississippi?" 19.

81. Although he refused to dismiss the case, Judge Grooms agreed with Curtis Publishing on the class-action question. He ruled: "This is not a proper class action in that the particular part of the publication complained of refers only to those members of the Mississippi Highway Patrol who were involved at Oxford and who wore gray uniforms. Certainly not all of the [members of the department] were on duty at Oxford...."

82. Curtis Publishing cited some convincing case law on this legal point, including a case in which Curtis had been the defendant: Fowler v. Curtis Publishing Co., 182 F.2d 377 (D.C. Cir. 1950). In this case, the court held that one cab driver was not libeled by a statement calling a group of sixty-one drivers "dishonest." See also Service Parking Corp. v. Washington Times Co., 92 F2d 502 (D.C. Cir. 1937), in which one of ten parking-lot owners was denied recovery for a charge that the downtown lot owners were "chiselers."

83. Motion of Defendant to Dismiss Action for Failure to State a Claim upon Which Relief Can Be Granted, Curtis Publishing Co. v. Birdsong, No. 22,277, 360 F.2d 344 (5th Cir. 1966).

84. Application for Permission to Appeal from Orders of the United States District Court for the Northern District of Alabama, ibid.

85. *Curtis*, 360 F.2d. 344.

86. Ibid. at 348.

87. The court cited other cases that agreed such words are not of themselves actionable. Among them are Robbins v. Treadway, 1829, 25 Ky. (2 J. J. Marsh.) 540, 541, and Rice v. Simmons (1838), 2 Del. (2 Harr.) 417, 31 Am. Dec. 766.

88. Associated Press v. Walker, 388 U.S. 130 (1967).

89. Eric Pace, "Gen. Edwin Walker, 83, Is Dead; Promoted Rightist Causes in the 60s," *New York Times*, November 2, 1993; Jonathan M. Shoenwald, *A Time For Choosing: The Rise of American Conservatism* (New York: Oxford University Press, 2001), 100–124.

90. *Walker*, 388 U.S. at 159 n. 22.

91. Brief for the Petitioner, *Walker*, January 4, 1967, 13.

92. Fleming, *Son of the Rough South*, 278.

93. Associated Press wire story, October 3, 1962, in Associated Press v. Walker, 393 S.W.2d 671, 672 (Tex. App. 1965).

94. Fleming, *Son of the Rough South*, 282.

95. "The General v. the Cub," *Time*, June 26, 1964. See also Pace, "Gen. Edwin Walker, 83, Is Dead."

96. Indictment, Circuit Court of Lafayette County, Special November term, 1962, box 1, Investigation, Oxford Div., NDist. Miss., U.S. Marshals Service, RG

527, NARA. See also Claude Sitton, "Mississippi Jury says U.S. Marshal Touched off Riot," *New York Times*, November 17, 1962, 1.

97. "U.S. Court Voids Mississippi Action against Marshal," *New York Times*, September 25, 1964, 26.

98. *Walker*, 388 U.S. at 141.

99. Walker blanketed the courts in the Midwest and South with libel suits. He sued the AP for $2 million in Walker v. Associated Press, No. 16624, District Court, Tarrant County Texas; for $2 million in Civil Action No. 64–246-L, Circuit Court of Duval County, Florida; for $1 million in No. 58859, Circuit Court of Pulaski County, Arkansas; and for $2.25 million in No. 160,536, in Caddo Parish District Court, Louisiana. In the latter case, the *Times-Picayune* of New Orleans was also named. Walker filed suit against the AP and the *Denver Post* for $1 million in Civ. No. B66072, District Court in the City and County of Denver, Colorado; *Kansas City Star* for $1 million in No. 133,768, Circuit Court, Jackson County, Missouri; Van Savell and the AP, for $2 million in No. 7137, Circuit Court, Lafayette County, Mississippi. Walker's suits in which the AP was not named included libel actions for $2 million in Walker v. *Courier-Journal and Louisville Times,* Civil Action 4639, U.S. District Court, Western District of Kentucky; $2 million in Walker v. Times Publishing Company, No. 17,694-L, Circuit Court, Pinellas County, Florida; $2 million in Walker v. Pulitzer Publishing Company, No. 63C, U.S. District Court, Eastern District of Missouri, Eastern Division; $10 million in Walker v. Atlanta Newspapers, Inc. and Ralph McGill, Civ. No. 8590, U.S. District Court, Northern District of Georgia; $4 million in Walker v. The Journal Company, Civ. No. 64-C-270 and 64-C-276, U.S. District Court, Eastern District of Wisconsin; $1 million in Walker v. The Gazette Publishing Company, Civ. No. 58857, Circuit Court, Pulaski County, Arkansas; and $1 million in Walker v. Arkansas Democrat Company, Civil No. 58858, Circuit Court, Pulaski County, Arkansas.

100. Associated Press report, October 3, 1962, 393 S.W.2d 671, 672 (Tex. App. 1965).

101. "Walker Is Awarded $3 Million in a Libel Suit against the A.P.," *New York Times,* October 30, 1965. However, District Judge William Woods reduced the award against AP and the New Orleans Times Picayune Publishing Corporation, holding that a jury cannot award a plaintiff more than he asked for.

102. The trial court judge threw out the punitive damages, ruling that the AP showed no ill will, and the Texas Court of Civil Appeals affirmed in Associated Press v. Walker, 393 S.W.2d 671 (1965).

103. The case was issued as a joint opinion reported as Curtis Publishing Co. v. Butts, Associated Press v. Walker, 388 U.S. 130 (1967).

104. Brief for the Petitioner, *Walker,* January 4, 1967, 42.

105. Ibid, 30.

106. *Walker,* 388 U.S. at 159.

107. Ann Waldron, *Hodding Carter: The Reconstruction of a Racist* (Chapel Hill: Algonquin Books, 1993), 79.

108. Ibid., 2, 13, 115, 128, 158.

109. Ibid., 65–67, 70.

110. Hodding Carter, *Where Mainstreet Meets the River* (New York: Rhinehart & Company, 1953).

111. Waldron, *Hodding Carter,* 219.

112. Ibid., 249–50.

113. Hodding Carter, "The Why of Mississippi," folder 11, box 69, Hodding Carter Papers, MSS 127, Special Collections Department, Mitchell Memorial Library,

University Libraries, Mississippi State University, Mississippi (hereafter Carter Papers).

114. Ibid.

115. Paul Dietterle, "Hodding Carter Blames Many for Miss. Woes," *Manchester (N.H.) Union Leader,* October 12, 1962.

116. "Carter Calls Barnett 'Demagogue,' Editor Says Mississippi Politicians Low Caliber," *New Hampshire,* October 11, 1962.

117. Walker v. Carter, Case No. 6182, Washington County Circuit Court, Mississippi.

118. University of New Hampshire interviews, undated memo, folder 31, box 69, Carter Papers.

119. Carter to John Hohenberg, October 8, 1965, folder 22, box 23, Carter Papers.

120. Associated Press v. Walker, 388 U.S. 130 (1967).

121. Final Judgment, December 4, 1967, Walker v. Carter, Case No. 6182, Washington County Circuit Court, Mississippi.

122. McGill quoted in Leonard Ray Teel, *Ralph Emerson McGill: Voice of Southern Conscience* (Knoxville: University of Tennessee Press, 2001), 225.

123. Kytle quoted in ibid., 225–26.

124. Teel, *Ralph Emerson McGill,* 5–8.

125. Affidavit of Ralph McGill, Edwin A. Walker v. Atlanta Newspapers, Inc. and Ralph McGill, Civil Action No. 8590 (N.D.Ga. filed March 12, 1968).

126. Ralph McGill, *Atlanta Constitution,* October 2, 1962, 1.

127. Ibid.

128. Amended Complaint, 3, Walker v. Atlanta Newspapers, Inc. and Ralph McGill, Civil Action No. 8590 (N.D.Ga. filed Aug. 3, 1964).

129. Complaint, Walker v. Atlanta Newspapers, Inc. and Ralph McGill, Civil Action 8590 (N.D.Ga. complaint filed September 30, 1963).

CHAPTER 4: ... THE SLAPPs KEEP COMING

1. Affidavit of Abraham Williams, December 26, 1961, State of South Carolina, County of Darlington, and Affidavit of Aleen Fleming, December 27, 1961, Huntley v. Stanley, Section 2: South Carolina, Supplement to Part 23 (1960–1972), Series A (1965–1965): The South, Part 23: Legal Department Case Files, Papers of the National Association for the Advancement of Colored People, Manuscript Division, Library of Congress, Washington, D.C. (hereafter Huntley v. Stanley, NAACP Papers).

2. Affidavits of Abraham Williams and Aleen Fleming, ibid.

3. A. W. Stanley, appeal to African American community in Darlington, South Carolina, December 28, 1961, in C. W. Haynes v. A. W. Stanley (Ct.C.P. Darlington, S.C., filed December 12, 1963).

4. Huntley v. A.W. Stanley; Huntley v. Darlington Branch, NAACP et al.; Haynes v. A.W. Stanley et al.; Haynes v. Darlington Branch, NAACP et al. All four cases were filed in the Court of Common Pleas, Darlington, S.C. December 12, 1963.

5. I. DeQuincy Newman, undated appeal to African American community in Darlington, South Carolina, in Huntley v. Stanley (Ct.C.P., Darlington, S.C., filed December 31, 1965).

6. Matthew J. Perry to Robert Carter, March 28, 1966, Huntley v. Stanley, NAACP Papers.

7. Mike Hembree, "NASCAR Restores Beloved Tradition with Darlington's Move Back to Labor Day," *USA Today,* September 2, 2015.

8. Matthew Perry to Robert L. Carter, December 19, 1963, Huntley v. Stanley, NAACP Papers.

9. Perry to Carter, July 28, 1965, ibid.

10. Ibid.

11. Carter to Perry, August 4, 1965, Huntley v. Stanley, NAACP Papers.

12. Roy Reed, "Robert L. Carter, an Architect of School Desegregation, Dies," *New York Times*, January, 3, 2012.

13. Maria L. Marcus to Perry, August 5, 1965, Huntley v. Stanley, NAACP Papers.

14. Ibid. The argument that Marcus referred to in her letter is found in David Riesman, "Democracy and Defamation: Fair Game and Fair Comment I–II," *Columbia Law Review* 42, nos. 7–8 (September and November 1942): 1085–1123, 1282–1318.

15. Perry to Barbara A. Morris, Associate Counsel, NAACP, August 26, 1965. Huntley v. Stanley, NAACP Papers.

16. Demurrer, n.d., ibid.

17. Perry to Carter, March 28, 1966, ibid.

18. Carter to Perry, March 30, 1966, Huntley v. Stanley, NAACP Papers.

19. Perry to Carter, February 15, 1968, ibid.

20. Douglas Martin, "M. J. Perry Jr., Legal Pioneer, Dies at 89," *New York Times*, August 5, 2011. See also *Matthew J. Perry: The Man, His Times, and His Legacy*, ed. William Lewis Burke and Belinda Gergel (Columbia: University of South Carolina Press, 2004).

21. Lynda Richardson, "Public Lives: To an Architect of Desegregation, Divided We Stand," *New York Times*, May 5, 2004.

22. Reed, "Robert L. Carter." For more on Carter, see his memoir, *A Matter of Law: A Memoir of Struggle in the Cause of Equal Rights* (New York: The New Press, 2004).

23. Taylor Branch, *Parting the Waters: America in the King Years, 1954–63* (New York: Simon & Schuster, 1988), 877; Darius Rejali, *Torture and Democracy* (Princeton: Princeton University Press, 2007), 225–30.

24. "City Fathers Won't Confer with Actors," *Gadsden (Ala.) Times*, August 23, 1963, 2.

25. "Remembering Paul Newman," ibid., October 9, 2008, https://www.gadsdentimes.com/news/20081009/remembering-paul-newman.

26. Jeremy Gray, "Marlon Brando, Paul Newman Joined in Gadsden Protests; Mayor, Business Leaders Refused to Meet Them," *Birmingham (Ala.) News*, August 23, 2013, accessed July 24, 2018, http://blog.al.com/birmingham-news-stories/2013/08/marlon_brando_paul_newman_join.html.

27. Ibid.; "City Fathers Won't Confer with Actors," *Gadsden (Ala.) Times*; "Remembering Paul Newman," al.com.

28. See generally Mike Goodson and Bob Scarboro, *Etowah County*, vol. 2, Images of America (Charleston, S.C.: Arcadia Publishing, 1999).

29. Mary Hoffman, "Gadsden Most Lied-About City In U.S.," *Gadsden (Ala.) Times*, June 2, 1963, 1A.

30. Ibid.

31. "Wallace Does Himself Proud over National TV," ibid., June 4, 1963, 4.

32. M. L. Ray, "Riot Squad in Gadsden, 466 Jailed; State Troopers Disperse Crowd at Courthouse," ibid., June 19, 1963.

33. Ibid.

34. "Negro Juvenile Demonstrators Being Released," *Gadsden (Ala.) Times*, June 20, 1963.

35. "Angry Mayor Wants Probe of Newspaper," ibid., June 3, 1963.

36. Mary Hoffman, "Brooklyn Paper Continues Attack on Gadsden," *Gadsden (Ala.) Times,* June 16, 1963, ibid.

37. "Angry Mayor Wants Probe of Newspaper," ibid., June 3, 1963.

38. See for example, "Produce Data, Paper Is Told," ibid., July 1, 1963. This story related to the ruling by the Alabama Supreme Court.

39. Curtis Publishing v. Butts, 388 U.S. 130 (1967). This is the companion case to Associated Press v. Walker, the civil rights–related case also discussed in this study, which extended the actual malice standard to public officials.

40. Theodore Peterson, *Magazines in the Twentieth Century* (Urbana: University of Illinois Press, 1964), 198.

41. "Suit against Network Set by Gilliland," *Gadsden (Ala.) Times,* August 26, 1963, 2.

42. "Gilliland Files $1 Million Suit against WGAD, ABC," ibid., August 31, 1963, 2.

43. McCord quoted in "City Will File Suits against Wire Services," ibid., June 24, 1963, 2.

44. Lillian Hellman, "Sophronia's Grandson Goes to Washington," *Ladies Home Journal,* December 1963, 78–81.

45. Lillian Hellman, *Scoundrel Time* (Boston: Little, Brown and Company), 45.

46. Hellman, "Sophronia's Grandson Goes to Washington," 80.

47. Ibid.

48. Ibid., 78–79.

49. Caskie Stinnett to Lillian Hellman, September 20, 1963, folder 5, box 72, Lillian Hellman Papers, Harry Ransom Humanities Research Center, University of Texas, Austin (hereafter Hellman Papers).

50. Davis Thomas to Hellman, September 23, 1963, ibid.

51. Mrs. T. R. Gribon to the Editors, December 5, 1963, ibid.

52. "Southern Lady Ex-Subscriber" to the Editors, November 26, 1963, and Ruby Richardson to the Editors, n.d., ibid.

53. Mrs. A. W. Carnes to My Dear Sirs, December 3, 1963, folder 5, box 72, Hellman Papers.

54. Demand of retraction by Attorney Roy McCord, *Ladies Home Journal,* March 1964, 82.

55. Peterson, *Magazines in the Twentieth Century,* 198.

56. Colvard v. Curtis, Case No. 64-140 (N.D.Ala. filed March 23, 1964). See also "Curtis Publishing Is Named in a $3 Million Libel Suit," *New York Times,* February 27, 1964, 39.

57. Bill Tarvin, "Dewey Colvard Back at Helm of Etowah Sheriff's Office," *Gadsden (Ala.) Times,* March 7, 1965; Don Coughlin, "Sheriff's Force Faces Long Hours in Protecting Residents of Etowah," ibid., July 10, 1960; Howell Talley, "Duties of Sheriff More Complex Than Most of Citizens Realize," ibid., August, 23, 1961; "Funeral Services Tomorrow for Sheriff Dewey Colvard," ibid., July 5, 1974.

58. Hellman to Curtis Publishing, February 28, 1964, folder 5, box 72, Hellman Papers.

59. Deborah Martinson, *Lillian Hellman: A Life with Foxes and Scoundrels* (New York: Counterpoint, 2005).

60. From Hellman to Robert Nemiroff, December 26, 1963, folder 5, box 72, Hellman Papers.

61. *Ladies Home Journal,* April 1964.

62. Hellman, *Scoundrel Time,* 311. This book details her experience being called before the House Un-American Activities Committee (HUAC) in 1952.

63. Mrs. Cabell Outlaw Jr. to the Editors, February 24, 1964, folder 5, box 72, Hellman Papers.

64. Mary Hoffman, "Magazine Admits Article on City, Area Was Untrue," *Gadsden (Ala.) Times,* December 30, 1963, 1A.

65. Ibid., 2.

66. Hedrick Smith, special correspondent, *New York Times,* June 19, 1963, quoted in Lorraine Hansberry to Mr. Clay Blair Jr., editor-in-chief, Curtis Publishing, February 28, 1964, folder 5, box 72, Hellman Papers.

67. Ibid.

68. Postcard from Louise Davis to Hellman, October 10, 1964, folder 5, box 72, Hellman Papers.

69. Mrs. Floyd D. Lofland Jr. to the Editors, December 4, 1963, ibid.

70. Petition of the Curtis Publishing Company, Inc. for Removal, Civil Action No. 64-140 (N.D.Ala. filed March 18, 1964).

71. Robert E. Bedingfield, "Minow May Take Top Curtis Post," *New York Times,* November 12, 1964, 1.

72. Colvard v. Curtis Publishing, Case No. 9585 Etowah County Circuit Court (filed February 26, 1964) transferred to Civil Action No. 64-140 (N.D.Ala. March 18, 1964).

73. "March on Washington Laden with Explosives," *Gadsden (Ala.) Times,* August 27, 1963, 4.

74. "High Expense Is Problem for Marchers," ibid., Aug. 13, 1963, 1.

75. Robert E. Bedingfield, "Filing of $2 million Libel Suit Adds Item to Agenda at Curtis," *New York Times,* November 11, 1964, 61.

76. Gene Mitchell, "Curtain Falls on Colvard Term," *Gadsden (Ala.) Times,* January 19, 1975, 26.

77. For detailed accounts of the incident, see Seth Cagin and Philip Dray, *We Are Not Afraid: The Story of Goodman, Schwerner, and Chaney and the Civil Rights Campaign for Mississippi* (New York: Macmillan Publishing Company, 1988); and Florence Mars, *Witness in Philadelphia* (Baton Rouge: Louisiana State University Press, 1977).

78. U.S. v. Price et al., 383 U.S. 787 (1966).

79. For extensive analysis on these cases, see Cagin and Dray, *We Are Not Afraid,* 436-52.

80. Rainey v. New York Herald Tribune, No. 3063 (Cir. Ct. Miss., Dist. 8 filed April 25, 1966). Huie freelanced for the *Tribune* and drew much of his book material from his published articles. WCC Books is a division of New York Herald Tribune Company.

81. William Bradford Huie, *Three Lives for Mississippi* (New York: WCC Books, 1965), 88.

82. Ibid., 120.

83. Ibid., 142.

84. Price v. New York Herald Tribune, No. 1346 (S.D.Miss. filed May 13, 1966).

85. Huie, *Three Lives for Mississippi,* 170.

86. Ibid., 134.

87. Ibid., 105.

88. Huie, *Three Lives for Mississippi,* 107.

89. "5 Suits against Time, Inc., Dismissed by Federal Judge," *New York Times,* February 10, 1966, 29.

90. Cagin and Dray, *We Are Not Afraid,* 377.

91. *Meridian (Miss.) Star* quoted in ibid., 371.

92. Tannehill made this statement to *Life* magazine reporter David Nevin. Tannehill quoted in ibid., 377.
93. Cagin and Dray, *We Are Not Afraid*, 377, 456.
94. Rainey v. Time, No. 3363 (Cir.Ct.Miss., Dist. 8 filed September 2, 1968).
95. Declaration filed by Lawrence Rainey, September 21, 1968, Rainey v. Time (Cir.Ct.Miss 1968).
96. Court Order, *Rainey v. Time* (S.D.Miss., E.Div. filed March 21, 1969)
97. Rainey v. CBS and QM Productions, No. E75-23 (S.D.Miss., E.Div. filed 1975). Price's suit, No. E75-37, was consolidated with Rainey's. The second round of consolidated suits in 1978 were numbered No. E78-0121 and filed in the same court. Don Whitehead, *Attack on Terror: The FBI against the Ku Klux Klan in Mississippi* (New York: Funk and Wagnalls, 1970).
98. Exhibit 1, Agreement between Cecil R. Price and Jalem Productions, Inc., June 26, 1968, and Agreement between Lawrence Rainey and Jalem Productions, Inc., July 4, 1968, *Rainey*, No. E75-23 (S.D.Miss., E.Div. filed 1975).
99. Affidavit of Lawrence Andrew Rainey, No. E75-23 (S.D.Miss., E.Div. filed August 25, 1976).
100. Ibid.
101. Motion for Summary Judgment, No. E75-23 (S.D.Miss., E.Div. filed October 4, 1976).
102. Burleson v. National Broadcasting Co., Civil Action No. 7984 (Cir.Ct.Ala, Tuscaloosa filed October 15, 1977). See also Joe W. Burleson deposition, February 3, 1977, box 193, University Libraries Division of Special Collections, University of Alabama, Tuscaloosa.
103. "Tuscaloosan's Suit against NBC Settled for $30,000," *Birmingham (Ala.) Post Herald*, March 19, 1977.
104. For general biographical information, see Margaret Turner Stewart, "A Rhetorical Criticism of the Oratory of James Buford Boone," unpublished paper, 1966, folder 2, box 255, Buford Boone Papers, MSS 0187, Special Collections and Archives, University of Alabama Libraries, Tuscaloosa (hereafter Boone Papers). See also *A Voice of Justice and Reason: Buford Boone's Tuscaloosa News*, Tom Rieland et al. (1994; reissue, Tuscaloosa: University of Alabama Center for Public Television and Radio, 2004), DVD.
105. Maurine Beasley and Richard Harlow, *Voices of Change: Southern Pulitzer Winners* (Washington: University Press of America, 1979), 55.
106. Roberts and Klibanoff, *The Race Beat*, 132-38.
107. "Klan Has Been Using County Building," *Tuscaloosa (Ala.) News*, May 27, 1949, 1.
108. "Klan Afraid of 'Bad Man,'" ibid., May 29, 1949, 1.
109. "Klan Looks Forward To Time When It Can 'Run The Town,'" ibid., May 30, 1949, 1.
110. "Who Are Our Klansmen in Tuscaloosa," editorial, ibid., May 31, 1949, 1.
111. Ibid.
112. Spencer R. McCulloch, "Fighting Alabama Editor Stops the Klan," *St. Louis Post-Dispatch*, November 29, 1949.
113. Ibid.
114. E. Culpepper Clark, *The Schoolhouse Door: Segregation's Last Stand at the University of Alabama* (New York: Oxford University Press, 1995), 66-69. Roberts and Klibanoff, *The Race Beat*, 132-38.
115. Clark, *The Schoolhouse Door*, 66-69.
116. Ibid., 64, 72, 97.

117. Buford Boone, "What a Price for Peace," *Tuscaloosa (Ala.) News*, February 7, 1956, 1.
118. Sullivan interviewed in *A Voice of Justice and Reason*, DVD.
119. Roberts and Klibanoff, *The Race Beat*, 132–38.
120. Neil R. McMillen, *The Citizens' Council: Organized Resistance to the Second Reconstruction*, 1954–64 (1971; reprint, with new preface and updated bibliography, Champaign: University of Illinois Press, 1994), 48.
121. In a friendly exchange of letters, White Citizens' Council chairman Leonard R. Wilson assured Boone that his organization would cooperate with the *Tuscaloosa News* and help Boone provide accurate coverage of the council. Wilson to Boone, January 10, 1957, folder 7, box 255, Boone Papers.
122. Buford Boone, Speech to the West Alabama Citizens' Council, Tuscaloosa County Courthouse, January 4, 1957, folder 7, box 255, Boone Papers.
123. Buford Boone, Memorandum re: Speech to Citizens' Council of West Alabama, January 6, 1957, folder 7, box 255, Boone Papers.
124. Boone quoted in *A Voice of Justice and Reason*, DVD.
125. See for instance, "The Voice of Reason," *New Republic*, January 21, 1957, 5–8.
126. Boone to Knopf, May 7, 1959, folder 2, box 255, Boone Papers.
127. Harold H. Martin and Kenneth Fairly, "We Got Nothing to Hide," *Saturday Evening Post*, January 30, 1965, 28–33.
128. Arnold Forster and Benjamin R. Epstein, *Report on the Ku Klux Klan*, n.d., folder e, box 255, Boone Papers.
129. July 7, 1964, *Tuscaloosa (Ala.) News*, 1.
130. Memo from Boone's attorney, Bruce McEachin, August 18, 1964, folder 9, box 255, Boone Papers.
131. Boone quoted in *A Voice of Justice and Reason*, DVD.
132. Boone to McEachin, August 26, 1964, folder 9, box 255, Boone Papers.
133. Shelton v. Tuscaloosa Newspapers, No. 19462, (Cir.Ct.Ala., Tuscaloosa filed July 23, 1964).
134. Complaint, ibid.
135. Response, August 29, 1968, ibid.
136. Demurrer to the complaint, n.d., ibid.
137. "Shelton Files New Suit against News," *Tuscaloosa (Ala.) News*, July 15, 1965. The editorial was titled "Lullaby and Goodnight," ibid., July 8, 1964. The second suit was Shelton v. Tuscaloosa Newspapers, No. 20828 (Cir.Ct.Ala., Tuscaloosa filed July 7, 1965).
138. Shelton to Boone, July 9, 1964, folder 9, box 255, Boone Papers.
139. Court Order, January 16, 1965, Shelton v. Tuscaloosa Newspapers, No. 20828 (Cir.Ct.Ala., Tuscaloosa filed July 7, 1965).
140. Memoranda of Authorities in Support of Motion of Defendants Tuscaloosa Newspapers and Buford Boone to Compel the Plaintiff to Answer Certain Questions Propounded to Him on Oral Examination at 7, Shelton v. Tuscaloosa Newspapers, No. 19462 (Cir.Ct.Ala., Tuscaloosa filed December 16, 1964). McEachin argued that this information was needed in the discovery phase of the suit in order to "identify and locate persons having knowledge of the Plaintiff's reputation or character."
141. McEachin cited Bryant v. Zimmerman, 278 U.S. 68, 73 L.Ed. 184 (1928), in which the court upheld a state statute compelling the Klan to submit membership rosters, based on the "character of the Klan's activities."
142. NAACP v. Alabama, 357 U.S. 449, 2 L.Ed 1488, 78 S.Ct. 1163 (1958).

143. Brief and Argument in Support of Answer and Return at 7–8, Shelton v. Tuscaloosa Newspapers (Tuscaloosa Cnty. Cir. Ct. Ala, Aug. 5, 1965) (fling a petition for a writ of mandamus, before the Supreme Court of Alabama).

144. Petition for Writ of Mandamus at 2, Shelton v. Tuscaloosa Newspapers (April 6, 1967).

145. Certified copies of Shelton's tax returns from 1963–1966, folder 11, box 25, Boone Papers.

146. Demurrer, n.d., Shelton v. Tuscaloosa Newspapers.

147. McEachin to Boone, February 24, 1966, folder 11, box 255, Boone Papers.

148. Mizell to Boone, April 17, 1965, folder 11, box 255, Boone Papers.

149. Boone to Donald P. Appell, chief investigator, House Un-American Activities Committee, April 20, 1965, folder 11, box 255, Boone Papers.

150. The three men, Collie Wilkins, William Eaton, and Eugene Thomas, were charged with murder after Liuzzo, a white woman from Michigan, was shot twice in the head after the Selma to Montgomery marches in 1965. Eaton died after a heart attack before trial. Wilkins and Thomas were acquitted of the charges by an all-white jury but were later found guilty of conspiracy under the 1871 Ku Klux Klan Act, a Reconstruction-era criminal statute. See James P. Turner, *Selma and the Liuzzo Murder Trials* (Ann Arbor: University of Michigan Press, 2018).

151. Boone to Appell, May 21, 1965, folder 11, box 255, Boone Papers.

152. McEachin to Boone, August 26, 1967, folder 12, box 255, Boone Papers.

153. Supplement to Memorandum Trial Brief, February 1, 1968, Shelton v. Tuscaloosa Newspapers, 388 U.S. 130 (1968).

154. McEachin to Worrall, September 20, 1968, folder 1, box 256, Boone Papers. See also Simon Wendt, "God, Gandhi, and Guns: The African American Freedom Struggle in Tuscaloosa, Alabama, 1964–1965," *Journal of African American History*, 89, no. 1 (winter 2004): 36–56.

155. Rowland Evans and Robert Novak, "Million-Dollar Suit May Be KKK End," *Jackson (Miss.) Clarion-Ledger*, June 4, 1965.

156. Kyle to Boone, September 23, 1968, folder 1, box 256, Boone Papers.

157. Ibid.

158. C. A. Hull to Boone, March 1, 1965, folder 2, box 255, ibid.

159. Boone to C. A. Hull, March 23, 1965, folder 2, box 255, ibid.

160. Richard Delgado, ed., "Beyond Criticism—Synthesis? Left-Right Parallels in Recent Writing about Race," in *Critical Race Theory: The Cutting Edge* (Philadelphia: Temple University Press, 1995), 466.

CHAPTER 5: "WANTED FOR MURDER"

1. Theodore Jones, "Negro Killed; 300 Harass Police, Teen-Agers Hurl Cans and Bottles after Shooting by Off-Duty Officer," *New York Times*, July 17, 1964, 1.

2. Ibid.

3. Ibid.

4. Ibid.

5. Michael W. Flamm, "The Original Long, Hot Summer: The Legacy of the 1964 Harlem Riot," *New York Times*, July 15, 2014.

6. For detailed treatment of the riots, see Michael W. Flamm, *In the Heat of the Summer: The New York Riots of 1964 and the War on Crime* (Philadelphia: University of Pennsylvania Press, 2017).

7. Paul L. Montgomery and Francis X. Clines, "Thousands Riot in Harlem Area; Scores Are Hurt," *New York Times*, July 19, 1964, 1.

8. Farmer quoted in Fred Shapiro and James W. Sullivan, *Race Riots: New York 1964* (New York: Thomas Y. Crowell Company, 1964), 71.
9. Jimmy Breslin, "The Harlem Riot," *New York Herald-Tribune,* July 20, 1964.
10. R. W. Apple Jr., "Violence Flares Again in Harlem," *New York Times,* July 20, 1964.
11. "Teen-Agers Throw Eggs at CORE Unit Picketing the Police," *New York Times,* July 22, 1964.
12. "Violence Erupts for Third Night," *New York Times,* July 21, 1964.
13. Charles Crutzner, "Gilligan's Leave Is Still in Force: Police Keep Him out of Sight to Avoid Any Picketing," *New York Times,* September 2, 1964.
14. Edward J. Silberfarb, "King and Wagner in Conference," *New York Herald Tribune,* July 28, 1964.
15. David Halberstam, "Jury's Exoneration of Gilligan Scored by Negro Leaders," *New York Times,* September 2, 1964, 1.
16. Gilligan v. King et al., Index no. 8437/65 (Sup.Ct.N.Y., County of New York 1965).
17. "Jesse Gray, 64, Leader of Harlem Rent Strikes," *New York Times,* April 5, 1988.
18. "Gilligan Sues King, Asking $1.5 million," *New York Times,* March 4, 1966, 12.
19. Gilligan v. King et al. Index no. 8437/65 (Sup.Ct.N.Y., County of New York 1965); Robert E. Tomasson, "Gilligan Is Suing King and Farmer," *New York Times,* May 27, 1965, 48.
20. Plaintiff's memorandum in opposition to Defendant Epton's Motion to Dismiss the Complaint, Gilligan v. King et al. (Sup.Ct.N.Y., County of New York filing undated).
21. Defendant's Reply Memorandum, Gilligan v. King et al. (Sup.Ct.N.Y., County of New York filing undated).
22. *Sullivan,* 376 U.S. at 271, cited in Gilligan v. King et al. (Sup.Ct.N.Y., County of New York 1965).
23. Epton Affidavit and motion to dismiss, Gilligan v. King et al. (Sup.Ct.N.Y., County of New York filed September 10, 1965).
24. Gilligan v. Farmer, 30 A.D.2d 26, 216 (1968).
25. Farmer Affidavit and motion to dismiss, Gilligan v. King et al. (Sup.Ct.N.Y., County of New York filed September 10, 1965).
26. Notice of Appeal, Gilligan v. King et al.
27. Gilligan v. Farmer, 30 A.D.2d at 27.
28. Robert E. Tomasson, "Gilligan Upheld on Right to Sue Those Who Called Him a Killer," *New York Times,* April 26, 1968, 18.
29. Gilligan v. Farmer, 30 A.D.2d at 29.
30. Gilligan v. Farmer, 29 A.D.2d 935 (1968), 936.
31. Affidavit of Thomas Gilligan, Gilligan v. Farmer. See also Tomasson, "Gilligan Is Suing King and Farmer."
32. "Ruling Boosts Police Morale," *Jefferson City (Mo.) Post-Tribune,* April 29, 1966, 3.
33. People v. Epton, 19 N.Y.2d 496 (1967). See also Margaret Blanchard, *Revolutionary Sparks: Freedom of Expression in Modern America* (New York: Oxford University Press, 1992), 339.
34. Blanchard, *Revolutionary Sparks,* 339.
35. Douglas Robinson, "Gilligan Will End Leave Tomorrow," *New York Times,* November 11, 1964, 35.

36. Walter Carlson, "Gilligan May Get Surgery on Back: Operation Could Keep Him Out an Added 2 Months," *New York Times*, September 25, 1964.

37. Gil Troy, "When Trump Hatchet-Man Roy Cohn Sued Martin Luther King for Libel," *Daily Beast*, January 14, 2018, accessed July 24, 2018, https://www.thedailybeast.com/when-trump-hatchet-man-roy-cohn-sued-martinc-luther-king-for-libel.

38. Jonathan Mahler and Matt Flegenheimer, "What Donald Trump Learned from Joseph McCarthy's Right-Hand Man," *New York Times*, June 20, 2016.

39. Flamm, *In the Heat of the Summer*, 295.

40. Newark Police Department Incident Report, June 12, 1965, attached to Memorandum, Dominick A. Spina, Office of the Police Director, Newark, New Jersey, to Hon. Hugh J. Addonizio, Mayor, August 5, 1965. Available at http://riseupnewark.com/police-report-on-patrolman-henry-martinez-august-5-1965-ilovepdf-compressed.

41. Ibid. See also "Jersey Man Killed in Fight with Police," *New York Times*, June 13, 1965, 41.

42. Martinez quoted in Hy Kuperstein, "Police Bullet Kills Motorist, Say Suspected Traffic Violator Drew Knife and Ran," *Newark (N.J.) Evening News*, June 12, 1965.

43. Memorandum from Spina to Addonizio.

44. Ibid., 1.

45. Ibid. See also *Martinez v. CORE*, filed in Essex County Court, New Jersey, August 1965.

46. Memo dated Aug. 5, 1965, Office of the Police Director, Newark, New Jersey.

47. "Newark Policeman Suspended in Killing," *New York Times*, June 18, 1965, 20.

48. "Outside Police on Newark Line: They Join Pickets Protesting Suspension after Slaying," *New York Times*, June 20, 1965, 45.

49. "Police Retain Picket Protest at City Hall," AP wire service report published in the *Spokane Daily Chronicle*, June 21, 1965.

50. Brad R. Tuttle, *How Newark Became Newark: The Rise, Fall, and Rebirth of an American City* (New Brunswick, N.J.: Rivergate Books, an imprint of Rutgers University Press, 2009), 156.

51. *Newark (N.J.) Evening News*, August 5, 1965.

52. Ibid. See also "Washington Report, Fulton Lewis, Jr.," *Reading (Pa.) Eagle*, August 23, 1965.

53. "No Bias Is Found in Newark Case," *New York Times*, June 22, 1965, 55.

54. "Mayor of Newark Firm on Suspension," *New York Times*, June 21, 1965, 14.

55. Memorandum from Spina to Addonizio.

56. "Warrant Served on Farmer, Accused of Libel Conspiracy," *Ocala (Fla.) Star-Banner*, July 22, 1965.

57. "Core Settles Libel Suit with Newark Patrolman," *New York Times*, August 16, 1967, 29.

58. "Jim Farmer Sued," *Baltimore (Md.) Afro American*, July 31, 1965.

59. "City Cop Kills a Negro; '64 Riot Scene Stays Quiet," *Newsday*, July 16, 1965. Irving Lieberman and Nancy Seely, "Koota Starts Probe into Killing by Cop," *New York Post*, July 16, 1965.

60. Homer Bigart, "Policeman Kills Brooklyn Negro; CORE Disputes Police on Shooting of Ex-Convict," *New York Times*, July 16, 1965, 1.

61. Ibid., 15.

62. Ibid.

63. "Probe Clears Cop Who Shot Negro in City," *Newsday*, July 23, 1965.

64. Bigart, "Policeman Kills Brooklyn Negro."

65. Homer Bigart, "Protest Is Renewed; A Civilian Board Is Demanded Again,"

New York Times, July 17, 1965, 1; Murray Schumach, "CORE March Here Has Light Turnout," *New York Times*, July 18, 1965, 1.

66. Homer Bigart, "Shooting Inquiry Opened by Koota," *New York Times*, July 20, 1965, 19.

67. "Policeman Moved Because of Abuse," *New York Times*, July 23, 1965, 58.

68. Martin Tolchin, "Finding Released in Negro Killing," *New York Times*, August 13, 1965, 31.

69. David Anderson, "Policeman Cleared in Negro's Slaying," *New York Times*, July 28, 1965, 1.

70. David Anderson, "Grand Jury Role Assailed by Core," *New York Times*, September 5, 1965, 37.

71. Liebowitz v. Farmer, box 120, Group V, Section 2: New York, Supplement to Part 23 (1956–1976), Series B (1956–1965): The Northeast, Part 23: Legal Department Case Files, Papers of the National Association for the Advancement of Colored People, Manuscript Division, Library of Congress, Washington, D.C. (hereafter Liebowitz v. Farmer, NAACP Papers).

72. Foster Hailey, "Negroes are Divided in Battle for Equal Rights Across U.S.," *New York Times*, June 23, 1963, 56.

73. Carl Schoettler, "Klan Dragon Pledges No Violence," *Baltimore (Md.) Evening Sun*, November 8, 1965.

74. Ibid.

75. "BTC Driver Reveals He Heads Klan in Md.," ibid., November 5, 1965.

76. Larry Lewis, "3,000 Attend Klan Rally at Rising Sun," ibid., November 7, 1965; Schoettler, "Klan Dragon Pledges No Violence."

77. Schoettler, "Klan Dragon Pledges No Violence."

78. Ibid.

79. Harold Kelvin, Memorandum of Law, June 19, 1967, Naimaster v. NAACP, box 920, Group V, Section 2: Maryland, Supplement to Part 23 (1960–1972), Series A: The South, 1960–1972, Part 23: Legal Department Case Files, Papers of the National Association for the Advancement of Colored People, Manuscript Division, Library of Congress, Washington, D.C. (hereafter Naimaster v. NAACP, NAACP Papers). See also, "Md. Klan Leader Sees Big Turnout At Rally," *Baltimore (Md.) Evening Sun*, November 5, 1965.

80. "Petition for Removal," Naimaster v. NAACP, NAACP Papers.

81. Ibid.

82. "Problem: Discharge of KKK Acting Grand Dragon," Grievance Settlement, Naimaster v. NAACP, NAACP Papers. See also "BTC Fires Naimaster For Klan Activities," *Baltimore (Md.) News American*, November 12, 1965.

83. Sheldon Smith, "B.T.C. Bus Driver Who Reorganize Klan Is fired," *Baltimore (Md.) Evening Sun*, November 12, 1965.

84. "Resolution Raps Driver Who Heads Maryland Klan," *Baltimore (Md.) Afro-American*, November 13, 1965.

85. Grievance Settlement, Naimaster v. NAACP, NAACP Papers.

86. Complaint filed by plaintiff, November 10, 1966, ibid.

87. Mitchell to Robert Carter, November 22, 1966, ibid. The officer abandoned this case before trial. The NAACP Legal Defense Fund represented Mitchell in that libel case, but there is only one reference to it in the NAACP Papers and no court records.

88. "Petition for Removal," 10, ibid.

89. Naimaster v. NAACP et al., 423 F.2d 1227 (1970).

90. Kelvin, Memorandum of Law, Naimaster v. NAACP, NAACP Papers.

91. Ibid.

92. Larry S. Gibson, "Gerald A. Smith—Civil Rights Lawyer," *Afro: The Black Media Authority*, accessed July 2, 2018, http://www.afro.com/gerald-a-smith-civil rights-lawyer/.

93. Gary Simpson, "Beaten by 4 Police, Negro Driver Says," *Akron (Ohio) Beacon Journal*, undated clipping, in Green v. Parms, box 1993, Group V, Section 1: Ohio, Supplement to Part 23 (1960–1972), Series C (1956–1965): The Mid and Far West, Part 23: Legal Department Case Files, Papers of the National Association for the Advancement of Colored People, Manuscript Division, Library of Congress, Washington, D.C. (hereafter Green v. Parms, NAACP Papers).

94. Gary Sampson, "Plans Public Probe in 'Brutality' Case," *Akron (Ohio) Beacon Journal*, undated clipping, in Green v. Parms, NAACP Papers.

95. "Hard question in Rowe Case—Mayor," *Akron (Ohio) Beacon Journal*, September 28, 1966.

96. Green v. Parms, Case No. 260390, and Carano v. Parms, Case No. 260388 (Ct.C.P. Ohio, Summit County filed December 1966).

97. "Judge Finds Police Officers Innocent in Assault Case," undated newspaper clipping, in Green v. Parms, NAACP Papers.

98. Douglas Bloomfield, "Police Cleared in Akron Arrest," *Cleveland (Ohio) Plaindealer*, November 23, 1966.

99. "Judge Finds Police Officers Innocent in Assault Case," undated newspaper clipping, in Green v. Parms, NAACP Papers.

100. Bloomfield, "Police Cleared in Akron Arrest," ibid.

101. Petition, Hayes v. Rowe, October 13, 1966, ibid.

102. Steel to Parms, November 22, 1966, ibid.

103. Lewis M. Steel to Norman Purnell, December 2, 1966, Green v. Parms, NAACP Papers.

104. Purnell to Steel, January 17, 1967, ibid.

105. Steel to Purnell, January 31, 1967, ibid.

106. Purnell to Steel, April 13, 1967, ibid.

107. Steel to Purnell, January 31, 1967, Green v. Parms, NAACP Papers.

108. Bob Adler to Steel, August 4, 1967, ibid.

109. "Attorney Parms Honored for Lifetime of Accomplishment," *Akron (Ohio) Beacon Journal*, April 28, 2012, available at https://www.ohio.com/article/20120428/NEWS/304289624.

110. Statement of W. W. Law, June 20, 1968, Fields v. Law, box 676, Group IV, Section 2: Georgia, Supplement to Part 23, Series A (1956–1965): The South, Part 23: Legal Department Case Files, Papers of the National Association for the Advancement of Colored People (hereafter Fields v. Law, NAACP Papers).

111. "Mack Death Probe Sought by N.A.A.C.P.," *Savannah (Ga.) News-Press*, April 29, 1968.

112. Complaint of H. E. Fields, Case No. 5962 (Super.Ct.Ga., Chatham County filed May 28, 1968).

113. Carter to Law, June 11, 1968, Fields v. Law, NAACP Papers.

114. West Law to Bob Carter, ibid.

115. Carter to West, June 19, 1968, ibid.

116. George W. Pring and Penelope Canan, *SLAPPs: Getting Sued for Speaking Out* (Philadelphia: Temple University Press, 1996), 56.

CHAPTER 6: *SULLIVAN* SINKS IN

1. Signed statement of Rosemary Harris, April 18, 1967, Dorsey v. NAACP, box 881, Group IV, Section 3: Louisiana, Supplement to Part 23: 1960–1972, Series A (1956–1965): The South, Part 23: Legal Department Case Files, 1960–1972, Papers of the National Association for the Advancement of Colored People, Manuscript Division, Library of Congress, Washington, D.C. (hereafter Dorsey v. NAACP, NAACP Papers).

2. Adam Fairclough, *Race and Democracy: The Civil Rights Struggle in Louisiana, 1915–1972* (Athens: University of Georgia Press), 418.

3. "Rape Case of Mrs. Rosemary V. Harris by White Policemen in New Iberia, Louisiana & Police Brutality Charge against New Iberia Policemen by Mr. Lester Harris While in New Iberia City Jail," undated typewritten document, Dorsey v. NAACP, NAACP Papers.

4. Dorsey v. NAACP, Civil Action Number 13312 (W.D.La. filed November 9, 1967).

5. Morris Peltier, "Dorsey Civil Service Hearing Held Thurs.," *New Iberian (La.)*, June 16, 1967.

6. "City Asks Civil Service Board Reconsider Ruling," ibid., June 23, 1967.

7. "Board Says Dorsey Is Suspended until Court Charges Are Cleared," ibid., June 22, 1967.

8. "Views of Our Readers," *New Iberian (La.)*, undated newspaper clipping, Dorsey v. NAACP, NAACP Papers.

9. "Rosemary Harris, cont.," Fact Sheet, Dorsey v. NAACP, NAACP Papers.

10. State of Louisiana v. Dorsey, Case No. 18128 (La.Jud.Dist. 16 filed April 20, 1967).

11. Dorsey v. NAACP, Civil Action No. 26,368 (5th Cir., filed March 18, 1969).

12. Dorsey v. NAACP, Civil Action Number 13312 (W.D.La. filed November 9, 1967).

13. Ibid.

14. Memorandum in support of motion to dismiss, January 12, 1968, Dorsey v. NAACP, Civil No. 13362 (W.D.La, Lafayette Div.).

15. J. Minos Simon to Ronald Weathers (W.D.La., Lafayette Div. March, 4, 1968), Dorsey v. NAACP, NAACP Papers.

16. Joan Franklin to Harvey Britton, March 22, 1968, ibid.

17. Memorandum in Support of Bill of Costs, ibid. The word "rape" is finally used in a brief filed before the Fifth Circuit.

18. Dorsey v. NAACP, No. 26,368, 408 F.2d 1022 (5th Cir. 1969) at footnote 4.

19. Dorsey v. NAACP, No. 109, October Term 1969, Office of the Clerk, Supreme Court of the United States. It was noted in the court's denial of the petition for writ of certiorari that Justice Marshall took no part in the consideration of the petition.

20. Hilda Daigre Curry, interview with author, New Iberia, Louisiana, June 22, 2016.

21. Ibid.

22. Grace Elizabeth Hale, *Making Whiteness: The Culture of Segregation in the South, 1890–1940* (New York: Vintage Books, 1998), 230.

23. William Bradford Huie, *He Slew the Dreamer: My Search, with James Earl Ray, for the Truth about the Murder of Martin Luther King* (New York: Delacorte Press, 1969 [1970]), 157.

24. Untitled memo, roll 9.26, microfilm, Birmingham, Alabama, Police Department Surveillance Files, 1947–1980, AR1125 Department of Archives and

Manuscripts, Birmingham Public Library, Alabama (hereafter Birmingham Police Surveillance Files).

25. Huie, *He Slew the Dreamer*, 176–177; "Request for a Reprise," *Time*, March 28, 1969.

26. "Around the Nation: Conviction in Bombing in Alabama Is Upheld," *New York Times*, August 14, 1982.

27. "Stoner Extradition Delayed," UPI wire story, dated October 3, 1978, roll 9.26, Birmingham Police Surveillance Files.

28. Stoner quoted in Huie, *He Slew the Dreamer*, 155.

29. Ibid., 194.

30. Gene Roberts and Hank Klibanoff, *The Race Beat: The Press, the Civil Rights Struggle, and the Awakening of a Nation* (New York: Knopf, 2006), 101–6.

31. Ibid.

32. William Bradford Huie, "The Shocking Story of Approved Killing in Mississippi," *Look*, January 1956.

33. Hanes quoted in Huie, *He Slew the Dreamer*, 157.

34. Ibid., 161, 164. (Emphasis in the original.)

35. Ibid., 164.

36. Ray and Hanes quoted in ibid.

37. Huie, *He Slew the Dreamer*, 176.

38. Ray quoted in ibid., 177.

39. Ray quoted in ibid., 29.

40. Ibid., 35.

41. Huie, *He Slew the Dreamer*, 36.

42. Ibid., 173.

43. Ray v. Huie, No. C-69-199 (W.D.Tenn., Memphis filed December 3, 1969).

44. Gerold Frank Jr., *An American Death: The Hunt for Martin Luther King's Killer* (New York: Doubleday, 1972). Ray v. Frank, No. C-73-126 (W.D.Tenn., Memphis filed June 25, 1973).

45. Dinitia Smith, "Gerold Frank Is Dead at 91," *New York Times*, September 19, 1998.

46. Frank, *An American Death*. See also John Skow, "Random Act," *Time*, April 10, 1972.

47. Ray v. Frank, No. C-73-126 (W.D.Tenn., Memphis filed June 25, 1973).

48. McMillan quote in *Leslie Dunbar: Reflections by Friends*, ed. Tony Dunbar (Montgomery, Ala.: NewSouth Books, 2016), 30.

49. George McMillan, "The King Assassination Revisited," *Time*, January 26, 1976, 16–23.

50. Ibid., 18.

51. Ray v. Time, No. C-76-274 (W.D.Tenn., Memphis filed June 11, 1976).

52. Ray v. Rose, 392 S. Supp. 601 (W.D.Tenn., Memphis 1975), *aff'd* 535 F.2d. 966 (6th Cir. 1976).

53. *Time*, "The King Assassination Revisited," 18.

54. Affidavit of Gerold Frank, Ray v. Time, No. C-76-274 (W.D.Tenn. Memphis filed July 1, 1976).

55. Motion and brief on behalf of W. Henry Haile, *Ray v. Time* (W.D.Tenn, Memphis filed July 9, 1976).

56. Memorandum in Support of Time Inc.'s and George McMillan's Motion to Dismiss, 15, Ray v. Time, No. C-76-274 (W.D.Tenn., Memphis filed September 7, 1976).

57. *Time*, "The King Assassination Revisited," 16.

58. Citing Gertz v. Welch, 418 U.S. 323, 351 (1974), where the court further worked through the Sullivan doctrine's extension of the actual malice standard to public figures: "In some instances an individual may achieve such pervasive fame or notoriety that he becomes a public figure for all purposes and in all contexts. More commonly, an individual voluntarily injects himself or is drawn into a particular public controversy and thereby becomes a public figure for a limited range of issues...."

59. Memorandum in Support of Time Inc.'s and George McMillan's Motion to Dismiss, Ray v. Time, No. C-76-274 (W.D.Tenn., Memphis filed September 7, 1976).

60. Cardillo v. Doubleday, 518 F.2d. 638 (1975); Vincent Charles Teresa, *My Life in the Mafia* (New York: Doubleday, 1973).

61. Cardillo v. Doubleday, 518 F. 2d. 638 (1975).

62. As cited in Ray v. Rose, 392 F. Supp. 601, 613 (W.D.Tenn., Memphis 1975). Associated Press v. Walker, 389 U.S. 28 (1967).

63. "Kluxing with the Ku Klux, Then and Now," undated manuscript, folder 372, box 39, William Bradford Huie Papers, [ca. 1920]–1989, Rare Books and Manuscripts Library, Thompson Library, Ohio State University, Columbus (hereafter Huie Papers); Cammie East, "Huie Talks on Rascals, Revivals," undated newspaper clipping, folder 536, box 49, Huie Papers.

64. Ray v. U.S. Department of Justice and Conrad Baetz, 658 f.2d 608 (8th Cir. 1981).

65. Ibid.

66. *St. Louis Post-Dispatch*, July 22, 1979, cited in ibid.

67. Charles F. Adamson, *The Toughest Cop in America* (Bloomington, Ind.: AuthorHouse, 2001).

68. Ibid. See also James Janega, "Frank Pape: Chicago's 'toughest cop' Never Took Lip," *Toronto Globe & Mail*, March 8, 2000, R8; and Myriam Gilles, "Police, Race and Crime in 1950s Chicago: Monroe v. Pape as Legal Noir," in *Civil Rights Stories*, ed. Myriam E. Gilles and Risa L. Goluboff (New York: Foundation Press, 2008), 46–55.

69. Gilles, "Police, Race and Crime in 1950s Chicago," 43.

70. Ibid., 46.

71. Myriam Gilles, "Police, Race and Crime in 1950s Chicago," 46–55.

72. Brief for Petitioners, Monroe v. Pape, 365 U.S. 167 (1961). Monroe was detained for ten hours and interrogated about the murder. He was not permitted to call his family or an attorney and was released without being charged. Pape and his detectives had suspected the insurance salesman's wife for the murder. She and her boyfriend eventually were convicted of the killing.

73. Federal Civil Rights Act, 42 U.S.C. § 1983; Monroe et al. v. Pape et al., 272 f.2d 365 (7th Cir. 1959).

74. Monroe v. Pape, 365 U.S. at 175–76.

75. "Pape Suit Jury Is out in Civil Rights Case," *Chicago Daily Tribune*, December 4, 1962; and "Order Pape, 4 Others to Pay $13,000," *Chicago Daily Tribune*, December 5, 1962.

76. "Order Pape, 4 Others to Pay $13,000," *Chicago Daily Tribune*, Dec. 5, 1962.

77. "Refuses New Trial to Pape, 4 Other Cops," *Chicago Daily Tribune*, December 13, 1962.

78. U.S. Commission on Civil Rights Report, Book 5, *Justice* (Washington, D.C.: GPO, 1961), 20–21.

79. "Civil Rights: Dawdling on the Corner," *Time*, Nov. 24, 1961, accessed July 25, 2018, http://www.time.com/time/magazine/article/0,9171,828835,00.html.

80. Ibid.
81. Pape v. Time, 401 U.S. 279 (1971)
82. Ibid. at 283.
83. Pape v. Time, 401 U.S. at 285.
84. Ibid. at 290.
85. Douglas S. Campbell, *The Supreme Court and the Mass Media: Selected Cases, Summaries, and Analyses* (Westport, Conn.: Praeger, 1990), 139–40.
86. Gilles, "Police, Race and Crime in 1950s Chicago," 56.
87. "Chicago Examined: Anatomy of a 'Police Riot,'" *Time*, December 6, 1968, accessed July 25, 2018, http://content.time.com/time/magazine/article/0,9171,844633,00.html.
88. Gilles, "Police, Race and Crime in 1950s Chicago," 56.
89. Pape quoted in Adamson, *The Toughest Cop in America*, 165.
90. Anne Keegan, "Toughest Cop in Town: The Legendary Frank Pape Has Been Retired for 22 Years, but the Force Is Still with Him," *Chicago Tribune*, February 9, 1994, 1.
91. Jason Meisner, Annie Sweeney, Dan Hinkel, and Jeremy Gorner, "Justice Report Rips Chicago Police for Excessive Force, Lax Discipline, Bad Training," *Chicago Tribune*, January 13, 2017, accessed July 25, 2018, http://www.chicagotribune.com/news/local/breaking/ct-chicago-police-justice-department-report-20170113-story.html.
92. Investigation of the Chicago Police Department, January 13, 2017, United States Department of Justice Civil Rights Division and United States Attorney's Office, Northern District of Illinois, Chicago, available at https://www.justice.gov/opa/file/925846/download.
93. Rainey v. Orion Pictures, No. E89–0014, originally filed in Neshoba County Circuit Court (Cir.Ct.Miss. Dist. 8 filed February 21, 1989) and later moved to U.S. District Court for the Southern District of Mississippi, Eastern Division (S.D.Miss., East.Div.).
94. Rainey's claim, Rainey v. Orion Pictures (S.D.Miss., East.Div. February 21, 1989).
95. Complaint, ibid.
96. Transcript of Rainey deposition, January 16, 1990, 175, ibid.
97. "Ex-Neshoba Sheriff Seeks Retraction from 'Burning' Producers," *Jackson (Miss.) Clarion-Ledger*, January 31, 1989, 1.
98. Ibid.
99. "Vote for Lawrence Rainey," undated newspaper clipping, Exhibit 7, Rainey v. Orion Pictures (S.D.Miss., East.Div.).
100. Factual Appendix, filed June 12, 1990, ibid.
101. William Bradford Huie, *Three Lives for Mississippi* (Jackson: University Press of Mississippi), 82.
102. Orion's First Request for Admission by Lawrence A. Rainey, E89–0014, submitted by Jackson Ables, April 24, 1989, Rainey V. Orion Pictures (S.D.Miss., East.Div.).
103. Jack Ables, phone interview with the author, April 21, 2008.
104. Response by Orion, Rainey v. Orion Pictures (S.D.Miss., East.Div. filed June, 6, 1989). Emphasis added by Ables in the original document.
105. Ibid.
106. Exhibits F, G, and H, ibid.
107. Response filed by Orion, June 6, 1989, ibid.

108. Orion's Sixth Request for Admission by Lawrence A. Rainey, 3, Rainey v. Orion Pictures, ibid.

109. See James P. Turner, *Selma and the Liuzzo Murder Trials* (Ann Arbor: University of Michigan Press, 2018).

110. "Objections to Request for Admissions and Motion for Protective Order," Rainey v. Orion Pictures (S.D.Miss., East Div. filed May 18, 1989).

111. Citing William Bradford Huie, *Three Lives for Mississippi* (New York: WCC Books, 1965), 132.

112. Factual Appendix, 12–13, Rainey v. Orion Pictures (S.D.Miss., East Div.).

113. Seth Cagin and Philip Dray, *We Are Not Afraid: The Story of Goodman, Schwerner, and Chaney, and the Civil Rights Campaign for Mississippi* (New York: Nation Books, 2006), 376.

114. Deposition transcript, 21, Rainey v. Orion Pictures (S.D.Miss., East Div.).

115. Ibid., 35.

116. Deposition transcript, 183, ibid.

117. Ibid., 42.

118. Deposition transcript, 48, Rainey v. Orion Pictures (S.D.Miss., East Div.).

119. Ibid., 97.

120. Ibid., 202.

121. Deposition transcript, 204, Rainey v. Orion Pictures (S.D.Miss., East Div.).

122. Ibid., 238.

123. Paul B. Johnson, interview by T. H. Baker, September 8, 1970, Hattiesburg, Mississippi, transcript, Oral Histories, Lyndon Baines Johnson Library, Austin, Texas. Baker conducted this interview at Johnson's home.

124. Ibid, 32–33.

125. Deposition transcript, 219, Rainey v. Orion Pictures (S.D.Miss., East Div.).

126. Fire marshal and highway patrol subpoenas, ibid.

127. Affidavit of Richard Claxton Gregory, June 7, 1990, 4, ibid.

128. Ibid., 5.

129. Affidavit filed by Attorney Jack Ables III, June 8, 1990, Exhibit 29, Rainey v. Orion Pictures (S.D.Miss., East Div.).

130. Ku Klux Klan literature on recruitment, beliefs, and rites, Exhibit 40, ibid.

131. Order of dismissal, August 21, 1990, ibid.

132. David Stout, "Lawrence Rainey, 79, a Rights-Era Suspect," *New York Times*, November 13, 2002; Megan Wright, "Court Upholds McIntyre's Disbarment," March 12, 2010, *Mississippi Business Journal*, available at http://msbusiness .com/2010/03/court-upholds-mcintyres-disbarment/.

CONCLUSION: THE WRITING ON THE COURTROOM WALL

1. "I am Michael Brown" or "I am Mike Brown" has been emblazoned on protestors' signs and worn on sweatshirts during protests in Ferguson, Missouri, and other American cities. Similarities were noted in the media at the time. See, for example, Randy Kennedy and Jennifer Schuessler, "Ferguson Images Evoke Civil Rights Era and Changing Visual Perceptions," *New York Times*, August 14, 2014; and Mary Bowerman, "'I Am A Man' to 'I Am Michael Brown': A closer look at protest slogans," *USA Today*, December 9, 2014.

2. Witnesses reported that Brown was surrendering with his hands in the air when Ferguson police officer Darren Wilson shot and killed him. Other reports indicate that this was not true. See for example, Julie Bosman, Campbell

Robertson, Erik Eckholm and Richard A. Oppel Jr., "Amid Conflicting Accounts, Trusting Darren Wilson," *New York Times*, November 25, 2014.

3. This slogan comes from the death of Eric Garner, who died July 17, 2014, when a New York police officer placed him in a chokehold during an arrest that was captured on video. The scuffle occurred when police attempted to arrest him for selling cigarettes illegally. A grand jury declined to indict the policeman in the death. Garner's family settled with the city over his death, ruled a homicide due to compression of the neck, for $5.9 million. J. David Goodman, "Eric Garner Case Is Settled by New York City for $5.9 million," *New York Times*, July 13, 2015.

4. Across the country, demonstrators staged die-ins protesting Brown's and Garner's deaths. Other deaths prompting mass demonstrations include those of Tamir Rice, an unarmed twelve-year-old in Cleveland, Ohio, in November 2014, and Freddie Gray, who died after suffering a spinal-cord injury while in police custody in Baltimore, Maryland, in April 2015.

5. A basic Google images search using key words such as "Ferguson" and "protests" yielded a rich sample of messages on protesters' signs.

6. COFO v. Rainey, Civil Action No. 3599 (S.D.Miss. filed July 10, 1964); John Herbers, "U.S. Court Rejects," *New York Times*, July 31, 1964.

7. *Mississippi Black Paper*, for. Reinhold Niebuhr, intro. Hodding Carter III (New York: Random House, 1965).

8. Emphasis in original. Reinhold Niebuhr, foreword to ibid.

9. Derrick A. Bell Jr., "Brown v. Board of Education and the Interest-Convergence Dilemma," 93 *Harvard Law Review* 93, no. 3 (January 1980): 518–33.

10. Richard Delgado and Jean Stefancic, *Critical Race Theory* (New York: New York University Press, 2001), 19.

11. Mary L. Dudziak, "Desegregation as a Cold War Imperative," *Stanford Law Review* 41, no. 1 (November 1988): 61–120.

12. "The Unconscious of a Conservative: A Special Issue on the Mind of Barry Goldwater," *Fact*, September–October 1964.

13. Goldwater v. Ginzburg, 414 F2d 324, 337 (2d Cir. 1969), cert. denied, 396 U.S. 1049.

14. John Martin-Joy, "Perspectives: Goldwater v. Ginzburg," *American Journal of Psychiatry* 172, no. 8 (August 2015): 729–30.

15. Ginzburg v. Goldwater, No. 687, 397 U.S. 978 (1970) (Decided January 26, 1970) (Rehearing denied March 9, 1970).

16. Paul Farhi, "Post Series on Police Shootings Wins Pulitzer Prize for National Reporting," *Washington Post*, April 18, 2016.

17. Eric Burns, *Infamous Scribblers: The Founding Fathers and the Rowdy Beginnings of American Journalism* (New York: PublicAffairs, 2006).

INDEX

Aaron, Judge, 106
Aaron Henry (Curry), 323n18
ABC, 179–80, 213, 284
Abernathy, Ralph, 82, 84–86, 90
Ables, Jack, III, 285–94
abolitionists, 8–10
ACLU, 232, 278–79
actual malice standard: Birdsong's suit against Curtis Publishing and, 152–53; Birmingham cases against *Times* and, 103–4, 117–20; *Cox v. Louisiana* and, 133–34; Dorsey sexual assault case and, 260; establishment of, 91–93; fault and, 4, 92, 196, 225, 298; First Amendment and, 21, 91; *Garrison v. Louisiana* and, 21; *Gertz v. Welch* and, 341n58; Gilligan's libel suits and, 224–27; *Goldwater v. Ginzburg* and, 302; James Earl Ray's libel suits and, 267, 277; journalists today and, 301–2; Kenneth Rowe and Parms and, libel suits against, 249–50; Liebowitz's libel suit and, 236–37; Naimaster's libel suit and, 242; negligence vs., 118, 196, 225; Pape's libel suit against *Time* and, 281–82; police officers and, 13–15, 226–27, 260, 295, 297; public figures, extended to, 8, 12, 130, 153, 155–56, 213, 341n58; public figures/officials vs. private citizens and, 196, 198–99, 208, 211; public officials and, 8, 91–92, 120; Rainey's libel suits and, 196, 198–200, 284; Shelton's suits against Boone and, 208–9, 211; Walker's suits against Hodding Carter and McGill and, 160, 162. See also *Associated Press v. Walker*; *New York Times v. Sullivan*
Adams, John, 79–81

Addonizio, Hugh J., 230–32
Adler, Bob, 250
AFL-CIO, 239
Afro-American (Baltimore), 34, 45, 49–50, 62, 233
Akin, Bernard Lee, 196
Akin, Earl, 196
Akron, Ohio, 242–50, 254
Akron Beacon Journal, 243–44, 247, 249–50
Akron Police Department, 247
Alabama: Jim Crow laws in, 98, 207; KKK in (*see under* Ku Klux Klan); northern journalists in, 79; poll tax and, 87. *See also specific cities, towns, and counties*
Alabama Council on Human Relations, 97
Alabama Journal, 83
Alabama National Guard, 177, 200
Alabama Public Library Service, 104
Alabama Public Service Commission, 106
Alabama State College/University, 83–85, 89
Alabama State Penitentiary, 182
Alabama Supreme Court, 3, 5, 88, 90, 93, 98, 209
Alexander, James, 80
Alexander, John R., 149–50
Alien and Sedition Acts (1798), 79–81, 92, 316n7
American Death, An (Frank), 270–71
Americanization of Emily, The (film), 265
Americanization of Emily, The (Huie), 265
American Mercury, 266
American Psychiatric Association, 302

Anderson, A. Maceo, 53
Anderson Independent, 44
Andrews, Julie, 265
Anglin, Delmer E., 149
Annapolis, Maryland, 242
Anti-Ku Klux Klan Act. *See* Civil Rights Act (1871)
anti-lynching legislation, 37
anti-Semitism, 104–5, 158, 196, 239
anti-SLAPP legislation, 300–301
Appell, Donald, 211
Arkansas, 87, 153–54
Arsenault, Raymond, 319n92
Associated Press, 144, 154–56, 160, 162, 179, 192, 327nn101–2
Associated Press v. Walker, 153–57; actual malice standard extended to public figures, 12, 130, 153, 155–56, 213; attorneys and legal ramifications of, 267–68; damages awarded to Walker and, 327nn101–2; First Amendment and, 153, 275; James Earl Ray's libel suits and, 277; Naimaster's libel suit and, 242; Rainey's libel suits and, 284–85; Shelton's suit against Boone and, 211; Walker's suits against Hodding Carter and McGill and, 160, 162
Atlanta Constitution, 13, 160, 161–62
Atlanta Daily World, 46
Attack on Terror (TV movie), 198–200

Baetz, Conrad, 275–77
Baez, Joan, 174
Bailey, John A., 244, 247
Ballard, John, 242–44, 246–49
Baltimore, Maryland, 8–10, 15–16, 239–42
Baltimore County Circuit Court, 241
Baltimore Transit Company, 238–41
Bard, Nathan, 32–36
Barfoot, Jim, 289
Barnett, E. G. "Hop," 285, 288
Barnett, Ross, 147–48, 154, 176
Bartholomew, Edward T., 149–50
Bass, Charlotta Spears, 11, 17–29, 77, 308n26
Bass, Joseph B., 17, 20–21, 23–28
Baton Rouge, Louisiana, 130–36
Baummer, Frank P., 240

beaches, public, and access to, 73–74, 172
Beall, Charles Franklin, Jr., 51
Bearman, Leo, Jr., 274
Beasley, Hugh, 42, 44–45
Beasley, Martha, 45, 51
Beddow, Embry and Beddow, 88
Beddow, Roderick, 88
Belafonte, Harry, 83
Bell, Derrick, 6, 299–300
Bennett, J. H., 76
Benson, I. S., 53–55
Bergman, Roy, 125
Berry, Louis, 261–62
Bessemer, Alabama, 81, 96–97, 102–3, 319n79
Bethlehem Baptist Church, 76
Bigart, Homer, 234
Bill of Rights (1791), 80
Birdsong, T. B., 147–53, 298, 325n66
Birmingham, Alabama: bombings in, 99, 107–8, 112, 114, 122, 173, 204, 265; bus station beatings in, 7, 12, 100, 121–24, 319n92; protests in, 173–74; segregation of public parks in, 99, 319n91; *Times* sued by officials in, 11–12, 81, 93–98, 101–20, 318n72, 322n167
Birmingham Chamber of Commerce, 96, 104, 318n70
Birmingham City Commission, 99
Birmingham News, 88, 105, 107–8, 110, 113–14, 122–23
Birmingham Police Department, 95, 99–100, 122
Birmingham Post, 113, 266
Birmingham Post-Herald, 122
Birmingham Public Library, 104
Birth of a Nation (film), 18, 194
Black, Hugo, 4, 302–3, 305–6n5
Black Dispatch, 125–28
"Black List" (Garrison), 8–9
Black Monday, 78–79, 266
black press: in California, 17–29, 77; civil rights advocacy and, 18, 30, 40–41, 45–46, 49–50; Cornish and, 10–11, 207n30; Greenwood, South Carolina, rape case coverage and, 41–46; Kentucky rape case coverage and, 29–36; in Oklahoma City, 125–28; threats to freedom

of, 10–11, 18, 21, 25–27, 34–36, 45–46, 77
Blanche, Fred A., Jr., 132–33
Blanding, Roland E., 58–59
Bloody Sunday, 288
Boliver County, Mississippi, 324n52
Bolton, Robert, 251
bombings: in Birmingham, 99, 107–8, 112, 114, 122, 173, 204, 265; in Mississippi, 144–46, 286, 299
Boone, Buford, 160–61, 164–65, 200–212, 238, 288, 333n121
Booth, Deling, 42, 44–45
bootlegging, 65
Boston Herald, 69
Boston Strangler, The (film), 271
Boston Strangler, The (Frank), 271
Boudreaux, Warren L., 258, 260
Boulware, Harold, 47
Bowdoin College, 157
Bowers, Sam, 194, 197–98, 286
boycotts: of Hazel Brannon Smith's newspapers, 66; KKK and, 207; NAACP and, 73, 127, 141–42, 251; of white businesses, 18, 30, 130, 141–42. *See also* bus boycott in Montgomery, Alabama
Boynton v. Virginia, 6
Brake, Bennie E., 150
Branch, Taylor, 151
Brando, Marlon, 83, 174–75, 179
Breithaupt, Nell Catherine, 30, 32, 34
Brennan, William, Jr., 3–4, 68, 71, 92, 171, 212, 237
Briggs, Harry, 41, 55
Briggs v. Elliott, 41, 55
Britton, Harvey, 258–60, 262
Broderick, Vincent, 235–36
Brooklyn Eagle, 178–79
Brooks, Paul, 99
Broward County, Florida, 72–74
Broward County Medical Association, 73
Brown, Alfred, 70
Brown, Michael, 15, 296–97, 343nn1–2, 344n4
Brown v. Board of Education of Topeka: Black Monday and, 78–79, 266; *Briggs v. Elliott,* and, 41, 55; delays in implementation of, 6, 57, 63–64, 213; ignored in the South,

169, 204; resistance to, 72, 161; Robert Carter and, 169; school desegregation suits following, 167; school inequality and, 56–57, 173; Tuscaloosa, Alabama, and, 203–4; White Citizens' Council created in response to, 66
Brust, Joseph, 226
Bryan, Walter E., 149
Bryant, Bear, 179, 186–87
Bryant, Carolyn, 266
Bryant, Roy, 266
Bryant v. Zimmerman, 333n141
Bryson, L. L., 140–41
Buchanan v. Warley, 30–31, 127, 306n15, 309n35
Buckley, Travis, 197–98
Buffalo, New York, 56
Burleigh, A. A., 26–27
Burleson, Joe W., 200
bus boycott in Montgomery, Alabama, 84, 86, 89, 266
bus station beatings (1961), 7, 12, 100, 121–25, 319n92
Butts, Wally, 179, 186–87, 330n39
Byers, Russell G., 276–77
Byrd, Richard F., 66–68, 70, 314n167
Byrnes, James F., 50

Caldwell, Millard F., 37–39
California, 17–29, 77, 296
California Eagle, 11, 17–28
Calvary AME Church, Brooklyn, 56–57
Canan, Penelope, 5–6, 18, 254
Carano, Jay C., 243, 245–49
Cardillo v. Doubleday, 275
Carnes, Mrs. A. W., 184
Carolina Times, 61
Carter, Hodding, Jr., 13, 69, 157–60, 162, 206
Carter, Robert L., 127–28, 168–73, 241, 248, 252–53
Cassels, Sammy, 42–44
Catledge, Turner, 1–2, 11
cattle prods, 174–75, 178, 182–85, 187, 189, 213
CBS, 12, 81, 120–24, 198–200, 273, 321n155, 322n167
Central High School, Little Rock, Arkansas, 153, 154

Central Intelligence Agency (CIA), 28
Chadwick, John R., 104–5
Chambers, J. S., 26, 29
Chambliss, Bob "Dynamite," 204
Chaney, James Earl, 13, 193–99, 284, 287, 292–94, 298
checkbook journalism, 265–67
Chicago, Illinois, 277–83, 295
Chicago Defender, 24, 46, 48, 50
Chicago Police Department, 281–83
Chicago Tribune, 69
Christian, John, 134–35
CIA. *See* Central Intelligence Agency
Citizens' Councils: Boone and, 205–6, 333n121; *Brown* decision and, 59, 66, 78–79; *Holmes County Herald* backed by, 69; Mississippi Sovereignty Commission and, 139–41; Nash and, 59–61; Pitcher and, 132; southern newspapers and, 78
Civil Rights Act (1866), 30–31, 309n35
Civil Rights Act (1871), 259–60, 279, 334n150
Civil Rights Act (1964), 207, 213, 217
Civil Rights Acts (1957 and 1960), 124
civil rights movement: efforts to interfere with progress of, 95, 100, 135–36, 139; efforts to stop media coverage of, 98, 117–24, 156, 187, 300; Elton Cox and, 129–36; First Amendment theory and, 4, 91; journalism and, 79; jumpstart in U.S., 266; *Sullivan* and, 2, 4–5, 7–8, 35, 77, 91. *See also* Freedom Rides and Riders; King, Martin Luther, Jr.; libel law and civil rights struggle
Civil War, 87
Clarendon County, South Carolina, 11, 41, 49, 52–53
Clarion-Ledger, 154, 211, 285
Clark, Arthur, Jr., 70–71
Clark, Kenneth B., 173
Clark College, 272
Clarksdale, Mississippi, 130, 136–46, 171
class-action suits, 152, 326nn81–82
Clayton, Claude F., 155
Clemson University, 168

Cluster, 201
CNN, 301
Coahoma County, Mississippi, 137–38, 140, 142
Coahoma County Circuit Court, 143–44
Coen, Gordon D., 149
COFO. *See* Council of Federated Organizations
Cohn, Roy, 228–29
Cold War, 299–300
Cole, Nat King, 108
Cole, I. Willis, 29–36, 77
Coleman, James, 139
Collier's, 37–39, 77
Collins, Ben, 136–38, 143–44, 146, 325n58
Colored American, 10–11
Colored Funeral Directors & Embalmers Association of South Carolina, 48
Columbia Law Review, 170–71
Colvard, Dewey, 178, 180, 184–93, 213
Colvard, Virginia, 186, 192–93
Committee to Defend Martin Luther King and the Struggle for Freedom in the South, 82, 85
communism, accusations of, 28, 62, 72, 87, 187–88, 287. *See also* McCarthy, Joseph; Red Scare
communism, U.S. image in fight against, 299–300
Communist Party, American, 28
Confederacy, allegiance to, 87, 89–91, 157, 167
Congress of Racial Equality (CORE): Baton Rouge officials' suit against, 134–35; Elton Cox and, 129–32, 136; Farmer and, 216–27, 233, 235–36, 293; Gilligan's shooting of black teenager and suit against, 216–27; Goldwater and, 217; Liebowitz's shooting of Erby and suit against, 235–36; Martinez's shooting of Long and suit against, 231–33; murder of civil rights workers and, 293
Connor, Theophilus Eugene "Bull": CBS and, 12, 120–23, 321n155, 322n167; desegregation of public

parks and, 102; Freedom Rides and, 12, 99–106, 109, 112–14, 116–24, 319n92; libel suits filed against *Times* and, 11–12, 93, 95–96, 103–6, 109–10, 113–14, 116–20; Sitton story on, 98
Cook, Tom, 99–100
Cooper, E., 76
CORE. *See* Congress of Racial Equality
Cornish, Samuel, 10–11, 307n30
Cosby, William, 80
Council of Federated Organizations (COFO), 298
County General Hospital, Los Angeles, 24
Cox, Benjamin Elton, 129–36
Cox, Harold, 199–200
Cox chain, 162
Cox v. Louisiana, 130–36
Coyle, Joseph, 216
Crenovick, Michael, 223
criminal libel statutes and indictments, 21, 29, 34, 42, 92, 132–33
Crisis, The, 31
critical race theory (CRT), 6, 29, 51, 63–64, 81, 213, 299–300
cult of whiteness, 81, 157, 162
Current Affair, A (news magazine), 284
Curry, Constance, 323n18
Curry, Hilda Daigre, 263–64
Curtis, Raymond, 272
Curtis, Tony, 271
Curtis Publishing, 152–53, 179, 184–87, 191–92, 325n66, 326nn81–82, 330n39

Dahmer, Vernon, 198, 286
Daigre, J. Allen, 257–60, 263–64
Daigre, Joe, 263
Daily Democrat, 39
Daily Iberian, 260–61
Daily Messenger, 34
Daley, Richard, 282
Daly, Tom, 88, 98, 103
Daniel, Homer, 314n182
Darlington, South Carolina, 163–73, 212–13
Davis, Frank, 70
Davis, Jefferson, 90–91

Davis, Louise, 191
Dawson, William L., 49
death penalty, 172
DeCell, Hall C., 139–40
Deen, Robert, 246
Deer Creek Pilot, 139
defamation law, 16, 88, 133–36, 168. *See also* libel law; slander
Defoe, Willem, 283
de la Beckwith, Byron, 287
DeLaine, Joseph A., 11, 41, 51–57, 77, 312n114, 312n123
DeLaine, Mattie, 52, 54
DeLaine-Waring AME Church, Buffalo, New York, 56
Delgado, Richard, 213, 300
Delta Democrat-Times, 13, 69, 157–58
Democratic National Convention (1968), 282
Democratic Party, 31, 41, 64, 153, 239
Denver Post, 160
DePauw University, 40
desegregation: fights against, 85–86, 153–54; of golf courses, 172; of hospital waiting rooms, 168; of interstate travel/transportation, 6, 99, 219; of movie theaters, 207; of public beaches, 74, 172; of public parks, 102, 172, 319n91; of restaurants, 172, 207; South's refusal to acknowledge rulings on, 6–7; Warley and I. Willis Cole and, 31. *See also* school desegregation; segregation
"Desegregation as a Cold War Imperative" (Dudziak), 300
Dexter Avenue Baptist Church, 82
die-ins, 344n4
Diggs, Charles, 144
Doar, John, 137
Dorsey, Henry, Jr., 255–64, 339n19
Dorsey v. NAACP, 263, 339n19
Double V for Victory campaign, 27
Douglas, William O., 279, 303
Du Bois, W. E. B., 23, 31
Dudziak, Mary, 300
Duff, Clair V., 241
Dukes, Nelson, 218
Dunbar, Leslie, 272

Dungee, Erna, 124
Dunjee, Roscoe, 126–27
Durant News, 64, 70
DuVall, Charles E., 246
Dylan, Bob, 174

Eaton, William, 334n150
Ebenezer African Methodist Episcopal Church, 40
Ebony, 111, 320n125
Eilert, Sterling Lee, 136–37, 143
Eisenhower, Dwight D., 101, 153
Elliott, Roderick W., 55
Embry, T. Eric, 88–90, 103–15, 186–87
English common law, 79–80
Epton, William, 223, 225, 228
Erby, Nelson, 234–36
Espy, Barbara, 97
Ethridge, Mark, 202
Etowah County, Alabama, 173–80, 182–87
Evening Sun (Baltimore), 239
Evers, Medgar, 137, 139, 287

Faber, Harold, 93
Fact, 302
Fairclough, Adam, 132–33
Fairfield, Mrs. L. G. E., 105
Farmer, James, 14, 216–27, 233, 235–36, 293
fascism, 27–28, 37, 138
Faulkner, William, 158
fault in libel cases, 4, 92, 196, 225, 298. *See also* actual malice standard
FBI. *See* Federal Bureau of Investigation
FCC. *See* Federal Communications Commission
"Fear and Hatred Grip Birmingham" (Salisbury), 11–12, 94–95
Federal Bureau of Investigation (FBI): Birdsong and, 151; Boone as special agent for, 202; Charlotta Bass and, 27–28; Elton Cox and, 130; Espy's flogging and, 97; Freedom Riders and, 99, 319n92; KKK and, 196, 198, 319n92; Martin Luther King Jr. and, 274; MIBURN, 286; murders of civil rights workers and, 194; police brutality complaint in New Iberia, Louisiana, and, 259; police brutality in Akron, Ohio, and, 247; Rainey and, 292
Federal Communications Commission (FCC), 178
Federalist Party, 79–80, 315n6
Ferguson, Missouri, police shootings in, 15, 173, 296–97, 343nn1–2, 344n4
Fields, H. E., 252–54
Fiery Cross, 208–9
Fingerhood, Shirley, 225
Fire and Police Civil Service Board, 257, 260
First Amendment: *Associated Press v. Walker*, and, 153, 275; Black and Douglas and, 303; Boone and, 208; civil rights movement and theory of, 4, 91; criminal libel statutes and, 21, 133–34; criticism of public officials and, 110, 171; cult of whiteness and, 162; Dorsey's suit and, 261–62; Fields's libel suit and, 253; Gilligan's libel suits and, 225; *Goldwater v. Ginzburg* and, 302; Kenneth Rowe, libel suit against, and, 249; Mississippi Supreme Court and, 146; Naimaster's libel suit and, 241–42; Rainey's suit against Orion Pictures and, 294; self-censorship and, 92, 212; *Sullivan* and, 4, 7–8, 91, 110, 169, 172, 212, 242; Trump threat to, 301; U.S. image and punishment for exercising, 299–300. *See also* freedom of speech; freedom of the press
First Baptist Church of Birmingham, 102
Flamm, Michael, 229
Fleming, Aleen, 164–65, 168
Fleming, Bunyan, 32–36
Fleming, James, 165
Fleming, Karl, 148, 154
Florida, 18, 36–39, 71–75, 77
Folsom, Jim, 88
Fonda, Henry, 271
Foote, Shelby, 158
Foreman, Percy, 267, 270
Forer, Louis G., 91

Forrest, Nathan Bedford, 157
Fort Lauderdale, Florida, 71–73
Fort Worth Star-Telegram, 160
Fountain Spring Baptist Church, 218
Fournet, Lee, 260
Fourteenth Amendment: CORE, used against, 134–35; Fields's libel suit and, 253; *Monroe* case and, 278–79; *NAACP v. Alabama* and, 86; Naimaster's libel suit and, 241; racial segregation and, 4, 30–31, 306n15; right to criticize police officers and, 171, 225
Fourth Amendment, 276
Fourth Estate and the Constitution, The (Powe), 319n79
Fourth Street Pharmacy, Clarksdale, Mississippi, 139, 145–46
Fowler v. Curtis Publishing, 326n82
France and French Revolution, 79
Franciosa, Anthony, 174–75
Francis (ship), 9
Frank, Gerold, Jr., 270–73
Franklin, Joan, 261–62
Frederickson, Kari, 51
freedom of association, 209
freedom of speech: Black and Douglas and, 303; *Cox v. Louisiana* and, 136; efforts to shut down, 79; First Amendment and, 3–4, 68, 71; libel law loosening and, 15; Sedition Act and, 81; SLAPP suits and, 5–6, 18; *Sullivan* and protection of, 6–7; Supreme Court and libel cases in context of, 4, 91–93
freedom of the press: Black and Douglas and, 303; criticism of slavery and, 8–10; First Amendment and, 68; libel suits for civil rights reporting and, 7–8, 96–98, 100–101, 147–53, 162, 187, 300; Sedition Act and, 81; threats to black press and, 10–11, 18, 21, 25–27, 34–36, 45–46, 77; Walter B. Jones and attacks on, 88
Freedom Riders (Arsenault), 319n92
Freedom Rides and Riders: bus station beatings, 7, 12, 81, 100, 121–25, 209, 319n92; CBS documentary and, 120–23; Connor and, 99–100, 319n92; Elton Cox and, 129–30; Farmer and, 219; segregation in public transportation and, 6; Sullivan and, 124–25; Walter B. Jones and, 91
Freedom's Journal, 307n30
Freedom Summer murders (1964): COFO suit and, 298; libel suits filed for media coverage of, 7, 13, 164, 193–200; *Mississippi Burning* and, 13, 193, 257, 283–86, 288, 290–91
Freedom Vote in Mississippi, 144
Freneau, Philip, 304
Friedman, Lawrence M., 12
Fry, Virgil, 174–75

Gabor, Zsa Zsa, 271
Gadsden, Alabama, 173–80, 182–92, 213
Gadsden, Gene, 252–53
"Gadsden Most Lied-About City in the U.S." (Hoffman), 176
Gadsden Times, 174–80, 186, 188–89, 192
Gallion, MacDonald, 85
gambling, 65, 86, 313n149, 317n35
Gandhi, Mahatma, 219
Garland, Judy, 271
Garner, Eric, 297, 344nn3–4
Garner, James, 265
Garrison, William Lloyd, 8–10
Garrison v. Louisiana, 21
Gaston, Mr. and Mrs. A. G., 111, 320n125
Gayle, W. A., 317n35
Geller, Abraham, 237
Genius of Universal Emancipation, 8–10
Georgia, 18, 75–77, 179, 200–201, 251–54
Georgia Court of Appeals, 77
Georgia Supreme Court, 251
Gertz v. Welch, 341n58
Gignilliat, Thomas, 252
Gilligan, Thomas, 13–14, 214–29, 254, 297
Gilliland, Lesley "Les," 174–75, 178–80, 213
Ginzburg, Ralph, 302–3
Goldwater, Barry M., 217, 302–3
Goldwater rule, 302
Goldwater v. Ginzburg, 302–3

Goodman, Andrew, 13, 193–99, 284, 287, 292–94, 298
Goodyear Tire and Rubber Company, 175, 186
Google, 16
Graves, John Temple, 122
Gray, Fred, 89
Gray, Freddie, 15–16, 344n4
Gray, Jesse, 219, 223
Green, Jerry, 243, 245–49
Greenberg, Jack, 47, 59–61, 63
Greenville, Mississippi, 157–60
Greenwood County, South Carolina, 42–45, 51
Greenwood Index-Journal, 42, 45
Greer, Benny R., 169
Gregory, Dick, 293–94
Gribon, Mrs. T. R., 183–84
Griffith, D. W., 18, 194
Griffith, Steve, 47, 49, 60
Grimball, William H., 59–60
Grooms, Harlan Hobart: Bear Bryant's suit and, 187; Birdsong's suit against Curtis Publishing and, 152, 326n81; Birmingham libel cases and, 101–3, 107, 109, 111, 115, 117–19; desegregation cases and, 101–2; interracial play ordinance and, 321n159

Hackman, Gene, 283
Haile, W. Henry, 273–74
Halberstam, David, 99–100, 124
Hale, Grace Elizabeth, 147, 264
Hall, Grover, Jr., 83, 90, 98
Hall, Kermit L., 7, 90
Hallinan, Vincent, 308n26
Hamilton, Andrew, 80
Hanes, Arthur, 196, 265, 267–68
Hanover Fire Insurance Company, 312n123
Hansberry, Lorraine, 190–91
Harle, Floyd, 232–33
Harlem Action Group, 223
Harlem Defense Council, 14, 221, 223, 226, 236
Harlem Progressive Labor Movement, 218
Harlem rent strikes, 219, 223
Harley, J. R., 75–77
Harris, James Thomas, 196

Harris, Lester, 255, 259
Harris, Rosemary Vital, 255–58, 261
Harvard Law Review, 299
Hayes, Warren L., 243–48
Haynes, C. W., 163–64, 166
Hayward, Susan, 271
Hearell, James T., 149
"Heed Their Rising Voices" (*Times* ad), 2–3, 82–86, 89–90, 102
Hellman, Lillian, 164, 181–93, 330n62
Henderson, James, 257, 260
Henley, Walter B., 209
Henry, Aaron, 130, 136–46, 171, 323n18, 324–25nn52–54
Henry, Noelle, 139–42
Henry v. Collins, 146, 171, 325n58
Herbers, John, 137–38
He Slew the Dreamer (Huie), 265, 267–70
Hinton, J. M., 61
Hodges, Robert E., 62
Hoffman, Mary, 176, 188
Hogan, Frank S., 222–23
Hogan Report, 223
Hollis, Columbus, 32
Hollywood blacklisting, 187–88
Holmes, Oliver Wendell, Jr., 92
Holmes County, Mississippi, 64–71, 77
Holmes County Herald, 69, 71
Holmes School, Florence, South Carolina, 48
homosexuality, charges of, 136–37, 143, 323n18
Honolulu Advertiser, 69
Hood, James, 102, 177, 206
Hooper, Frank A., 223–24
Hoover, J. Edgar, 202
Hopkins, Wat, 92
Horne, Tommy, 196
House Un-American Activities Committee (HUAC), 210–11, 330n62
housing segregation, 6, 30–31, 127, 278, 306n15, 309n35
Howard, Roy, 69–70
Howard University School of Religion, 130, 219
Howland, William H., 246
HUAC. *See* House Un-American Activities Committee

Hubbard, Joe, 174–75
Hughes, G. P., 33
Hughes, Robert, 97–98
Huie, William Bradford, 194–96, 199, 265–70, 272–73, 275, 288, 331n80
Hull, C. A., 212
Huntley, Preston, 166–67

"I am Mike Brown," 296–97, 343n1
"I can't breathe," 297, 344n3
I'll Cry Tomorrow (film), 271
I'll Cry Tomorrow (Frank, Roth, and Connolly), 271
Indianola, Mississippi, 66
institutional racism, 143, 200, 296, 299
internet, attempts to silence dissent on, 16
Interstate Commerce Act, 6
intimidation lawsuits, 5, 301. *See also* Strategic Lawsuits Against Public Participation
Isaacs, Norman, 69

Jackson, Lillie, 239
Jackson, Luther, 288
Jackson Daily, 78
Jalem Productions, 198–99
James, Earl, 86, 90–93
Jefferson, Thomas, 79, 81, 304, 315n6
Jefferson County Coordinating Council, 113
Jelks, Arthur L., 132–33
Jenkins, Lincoln C., Jr., 59–61, 63
Jenkins, Perry & Pride (law firm), 172
Jenkins, Ray, 83
Jet, 90
Jim Crow laws: in Alabama, 98, 207; in California, 18; in Florida, 74; in Holmes County, Mississippi, 64–65; in Louisville, Kentucky, 30; in South Carolina, 39–40, 56
Johnson, James Weldon, 33, 35
Johnson, Lyndon, 238
Johnson, Paul B., Jr., 292
Jones, Thomas Goode, 86–87
Jones, Walter B., 86–91
journalism: actual malice standard today and, 301–2; checkbook, 265–67; civil rights movement and, 79; convention on reporting on lawsuits and, 180; financial hardship due to libel actions, 1–2, 50, 66, 69, 71, 300; government role in protection of, 303; sloppy, 179. *See also* freedom of the press
journalism education, 39–40, 272
Judge Horton and the Scottsboro Boys (TV movie), 200
Justice (government report), 280–82

Kankakee, Illinois, 129
Ken, 317n35
Kennedy, John F., 146, 148, 154, 177, 192, 269
Kentucky, 18, 29–36, 77
Kentucky Court of Appeals, 33, 35–36
Kessup, Anthony, 231
Killen, Edgar Ray, 194, 294
"Kimono Girls Check in Again," 317n35
King, Edwin, 144
King, Martin Luther, Jr.: assassination of, 7, 14, 227, 256, 267–77; defense fund for, 82, 85; felony charge for tax evasion and perjury, 82–83, 85; Freedom Riders warned by, 100; Gilligan accused of murder by, 14, 222–24, 227; harassment of, 83; on hate in Chicago, 282; libel suits, named in, 85, 223–24; *Times* ad and, 89
King, Rodney, 296
Kinloch, John, 27
Klibanoff, Hank, 85, 98
Kluger, Richard, 54–55
Knopf, Alfred A., 206
Koota, Aaron E., 235–36
Ku Klux Klan (KKK): in Akron, Ohio, 243–44; in Birmingham, 12, 99–100, 120–21, 319n92; Black and, 305–6n5; Boone and, 164–65, 201–3, 207–12; in California, 11, 17–21, 24–29; criticism of, 83, 158, 201–4, 207–8, 212, 239; desegregation of University of Alabama and, 204; in Florida, 73; Fourteenth Amendment and, 135; Freedom Riders and, 12, 99–100, 120–21, 124–25, 319n92; in Hopkins County, Kentucky, 29–30; in Maryland, 214, 237–42;

Ku Klux Klan (KKK) (*continued*)
  membership rosters, 209, 333n141; in Mississippi, 164, 193–99, 286–90, 292, 298, 314n182; in Montgomery, Alabama, 12, 84, 89, 124–25, 319n92; in South Carolina, 55–56, 62–63. *See also* Citizens' Councils; white supremacy and white supremacists
Ku Klux Klan Act (1871). *See* Civil Rights Act (1871)
Kuperstein, Hy, 230–31
Kyle, Bob, 206, 211
Kytle, Calvin, 161

Ladies' Home Journal, 164, 181–92, 213
Laffoon, Ruby, 34–35, 309n50
Lake City, South Carolina, 55–56
Landingham, Zack Van, 140–41
Laurens County, South Carolina, 42–44
Law, Westley Wallace "West," 251–53
lay-ins, 182–84
LeBlanc, Fred S., 132–33
Lee, Percy, 68
Leeds, Oliver, 235
Lemmon, Jack, 198–99
Lewis, Anthony, 7, 81, 91
Lewis, Howard, 243
Lewis, John, 100
Lexington, Mississippi, 64–71
Lexington Advertiser, 11, 64, 70, 160–61
libel law: abolitionist movement and, 8–10; abusive and vituperative words and, 152–53, 325n66, 326n87; criminal, 21; police officers and alternatives to, 256, 295; rewriting in U.S., 12, 29, 91–93; Trump's call to retool, 301. *See also* actual malice standard
libel law and civil rights struggle: introduction to, 1–16; *New York Times v. Sullivan* and, 78–128; SLAPP suits filed by police officers, 214–54; SLAPP suits following *Sullivan*, 163–213; after *Sullivan*, 255–95; before *Sullivan*, 17–77; while *Sullivan* was on appeal, 129–62

libel-proof doctrine, 14, 26, 256–57, 274–75
Liberator, 10
Liebowitz, Sheldon, 14, 214, 234–37, 254, 297
Life, 158–59, 196, 271–72
Lighthouse and Informer, 40–41, 45, 47, 49–50
Lincoln Independent Party, 31
Lincoln University, 239
Lincolnville, South Carolina, 40
Lindsey, Joe, 96, 318n72
Lingo, Al, 177–78, 189
Little Rock, Arkansas, 153–54
Liuzzo, Viola, 211, 288, 334n150
Loeb, Louis, 88, 98, 103
Lofland, Mrs. Floyd D., Jr., 191
Long, Lester, 229–33
Look, 158–59, 266, 270–72
Lopez, Ian F. Haney, 63–64
Los Angeles, California, 17–29, 296
Louisiana, 130–36, 255–64, 295
Louisiana Supreme Court, 132–34
Louisville, Kentucky, 29–36
Louisville Courier-Journal, 160, 202
Louisville Leader, 29–36
Louisville News, 29–36
Louisville Times, 69
Lowe, David, 121
Lowery, J. E., 82, 84–86, 90
Lucy, Autherine, 101, 204–6, 212
Lundy, Benjamin, 8–9
Lynch, Loretta, 283
Lynch, Patrick, 215
lynching and whiteness, 264
Lynne, Seybourn H., 196

Macbeth, Hugh E., 25–26
Mack, Lewis, 251–54
Macon, Georgia, 200–201
Macon Telegraph, 201–2
Madison, James, 92
Madison County, Florida, 36–39
Madisonville, Kentucky, 29, 32–35
Make No Law (Lewis), 7
Making of an Assassin, The (McMillan), 271–72
Malone, Vivian, 102, 177, 206
Manhattan Supreme Court, 224
March on Washington (1963), 7, 164, 173–74, 181–83, 192, 217, 219

Marcus, Maria L., 170–71
Marion County Progressive Democrats, 46
Marshall, Thurgood, 47, 55, 60, 139, 170, 263, 339n19
Martin, Quinn, 199
Martinez, Henry, 14, 214, 229–33, 254, 297
Marvin, Lee, 277–78
Maryland, 8–10, 14–16, 214, 237–42
Mason, Sophronia, 181–82
Massie, Robert, 147–48, 151–53
Maxwell, Stewart, 234
Mayer, Henry, 9
McCarthy, Joseph, 228
McCord, L. B., 52–55
McCord, Roy Davis, 180, 185–87
McCray, John Henry: as civil rights activist, 39–41, 48–50, 55, 311–12n102; Joseph DeLaine and, 52–53, 55–57, 312n114; sentenced to chain gang, 11, 49–50; Tolbert interview and libel suit against, 41–51
McDonald, E. E., 285
McDonald, Laquan, 283
McEachin, Bruce, 208–9, 211, 333nn140–41
McGill, Ralph, 13, 160–62, 206
McIntyre, James, 194, 198, 288, 290–92, 294–95
McMillan, George, 271–74
McMillan, Priscilla, 272
McNeer, W. M., 70
McRae, Robert M., Jr., 270, 273
McShane, James, 148–49, 154–55
Means, Fred, 232
Meet the Press (NBC-TV), 176–77
Memphis sanitation workers' strike (1968), 296
Mencken, H. L., 266
Mercer College, 200–201
Meredith, James, 7, 13, 130, 146–47, 154, 319n98
Meredith v. Fair, 319n98
Meridian Star, 78, 197
MIBURN, 286
Mike, Ernest S., 150
Milam, J. W., 266
Mill, John Stuart, 92
Miller, Loren, 28

Milton, John, 92
minstrel shows, 129
Mississippi: black Chicago youth killed in, 266; bombings in, 144–46, 286, 299; KKK in, 164, 193–99, 286–90, 292, 298, 314n182; poll tax and, 87; white supremacy and white supremacists in, 138, 147, 153, 157–58. *See also* Freedom Summer murders; University of Mississippi (Ole Miss) riots; *specific cities, towns, and counties*
Mississippi Black Paper, 298–99
Mississippi Burning (film), 13, 193, 257, 283–86, 288, 290–91
Mississippi Highway Patrol, 147–51, 293
Mississippi Press Association, 65
Mississippi Sovereignty Commission, 139–41
Mississippi State Patrol, 141
Mississippi Supreme Court, 67–68, 143–44, 146, 314n167
Missouri. *See* Ferguson, Missouri, police shootings in; St. Louis, Missouri; University of Missouri
Missouri State Penitentiary, 269, 272, 275
Mitchell, Charles, 9
Mitchell, Clarence, 241–42
Mitchell, Juanita Jackson, 240–42, 337n87
Mizell, Don, 73–74
Mizell, Isadore, 73
Mizell, Jimmy, 210
Mizell, Von, 71–75, 315n192
Monoghan, Noel, 141
Monroe, James, 278–81, 341n72
Monroe v. Pape, 279–80, 341n72
Montgomery, Alabama: black students expelled in, 83–85; bus boycott, 84, 86, 89, 266; bus station beatings in, 12, 124–25, 319n92; gambling and prostitution in, 86, 317n35; segregation of public parks in, 319n91; *Sullivan* and, 1–3, 7, 78, 86–91; voter-registration efforts in, 81, 124
Montgomery Advertiser, 83–84, 87–88, 90, 98
Montgomery County Courthouse, 89

Moon, E. C., Jr., 125–27
Moore, Charles, 146–47
Moore, William L., 176
Morgan, James: libel suit against CBS, 123, 322n167; libel suit against Times, 96; photo in Ebony, 111, 320n125; Salisbury article and, 103–4, 106, 110–12, 114, 119
Mosby, Marilyn, 15
Motley, Constance Baker, 101, 319n98
Mount Morris Presbyterian Church, 219–20
M Squad (TV show), 278
Mt. Zion Church burning, 292
Mule's Ear, 40
Murphy, Michael, 222
Murray, W. T., 46
Murrow, Edward R., 120
Murtagh, Walter L., 65
Musselman, A. J., 72, 75
My Life in the Mafia, 275

NAACP. See National Association for the Advancement of Colored People
Nabors, Ollie, 178
Nachman, Roland, 317n35
Naimaster, Vernon John, 237–42
Nash, Shepard K. "Shep," 58–64
Nashville Banner, 161
National Association for the Advancement of Colored People (NAACP); Aaron Henry and, 130, 136–42, 171; Basses and, 23–25; civil rights lawyers supported by, 298; Dorsey case and, 255–63; John Patterson's desegregation fight and, 85–86; Joseph DeLaine and, 52–55; KKK in Maryland and, 214, 239–42; Legal Defense Fund, 35, 47, 127, 237, 241, 299–300, 337n87; Liebowitz's libel suit and, 237; Louisiana criminal libel statute and, 132–33; Martinez's libel case and, 233; McCray and, 40–41, 47–48, 52–53, 55; NAACP v. Alabama, 85–86, 88, 170, 209; Pierce v. Moon and, 125–28; police brutality and, 216, 223, 242–43, 248–50, 252–54, 259, 295; Robert Carter and, 170; Savannah grocery store boycott and, 251; school desegregation and, 57–64, 101, 206; Stanley's libel cases and, 165–68, 170–72, 212–13; Von Mizell and, 71–75; Warley and I. Willis Cole and, 31–36. See also Henry, Aaron

National Association of Press Photographers, 88
National Council of Churches, 69
National Gazette, 304
National Governor's Association, 38
National Negro Press Association, 32
National States Rights Party, 265, 268
Nazism, 27–28, 37, 138
NBC, 176–77, 200, 222
Negro Newspaper Publishers Association (NNPA), 46, 48
Neimore, John, 23
Neshoba County, Mississippi, 193–98, 217, 257, 285–88, 292–93
Neshoba Democrat, 197
Newark, New Jersey, 214, 229–33
Newark Evening News, 230, 232
Newark Human Rights Commission, 232
Newark Police Department, 230–33
Newberry County, South Carolina, 47–49
New Deal, 305–6n5
New Hampshire (student newspaper), 159
New Iberia, Louisiana, 255–64, 295
New Iberian, 258–59, 262
Newman, I. DeQuincy, 166–67
Newman, Paul, 174–75
Newnan, Georgia, 200
New Orleans Times Picayune Publishing Corporation, 327n101
News and Courier, 78
Newsweek, 148, 154, 160
New York Appeals Court, 228
New York City, 10–11, 13–15, 214–29, 234–37, 254, 297–98
New York County, 221, 223, 228, 237
New York Herald Tribune, 205, 331n80
New York Herald Tribune Company, 194–95, 331n80
New York Police Department, 226
New York Post, 56

New York State Supreme Court, 226–28, 236
New York Times: Birmingham bus station beatings and, 121; Birmingham Chamber of Commerce and, 318n70; Birmingham libel cases against, 11–12, 81, 93–98, 101–20, 318n72; Catledge and libel suits against, 1–2, 11; civil rights coverage by, efforts to stop, 300; George McMillan's writing for, 271–72; "Heed Their Rising Voices," 2, 82–86, 89–90; police brutality and, 190, 215–16, 218–22, 234, 236, 303; Robert Carter, interview with, 172–73; Salisbury and libel actions against, 1–2, 11–12, 88, 96–98, 101–6, 108–16, 118–20; Trump's rants against, 301
New York Times v. Sullivan: ABC, suit against, and, 213; Associated Press v. Walker, and, 12, 130, 155–56; Birmingham suits against Times and, 100–101, 103, 117, 119–20; civil rights movement and, 2, 4–5, 7–8, 35, 77, 91; Cox v. Louisiana and, 133–34; criticism of government and public officials and, 3–4; Curtis Publishing, suits against, and, 152–53, 185–86, 190, 192, 213; delays in implementation following, 6–7, 213; Dorsey's suit and, 261, 263; Fields's libel suit and, 253; First Amendment and, 4, 7–8, 91, 110, 169, 172, 212, 242; freedom of expression today and, 173; Gadsden city officials and, 179; Gertz v. Welch and, 341n58; Gilligan's libel cases and, 224–26; Goldwater v. Ginzburg and, 302–3; Hazel Brannon Smith's libel case compared to, 68, 71; "Heed Their Rising Voices" ad and, 2–3, 82–86, 89–90; James Earl Ray's libel suits and, 14, 267, 277; Kenneth Rowe and Parms, libel suits against, and, 249–50; legal ramifications taking hold, 256, 267–68, 295; Liebowitz's libel suit and, 236–37; Lindsey v. New York Times and, 318n72; Naimaster's libel suit and, 242; Pape's libel suit against Time and, 281–82; police officers' libel suits and, 13–15; Rainey's libel suits and, 13, 198–200, 284–85, 294; Sitton's killed story and, 98; Stanley's libel cases and, 169–73; suit filed by Lester B. Sullivan, 1–3, 78–79, 82, 84–85; trial in Montgomery, Alabama, 86–91; Walker's suit against Hodding Carter and, 160; watchdog reporting and, 304. See also actual malice standard

New York Weekly Journal, 80
Niebuhr, Reinhold, 298–99
Nightline, 284
Nimkoff, Max, 117
NNPA. See Negro Newspaper Publishers Association
Norris, Frank, 161
Northside Reporter, 66, 71

Obama, Barack, 283
O'Doherty, Matt, 33
Ohio, 242–50, 254
Oklahoma City, 81, 125–28
Ole Miss riots (1962), 7, 12–13, 130, 139, 146–57, 298, 319n98
Orion Pictures, 13, 284–86, 288, 290, 294
Outlook, 66
Overstreet, Haldred, 251–52
Owens, Jesse, 157
Oxford, Mississippi, 147, 154–55. See also University of Mississippi (Ole Miss) riots

Page One (WABC-TV), 218–19
Paley, William S., 123
Pape, Frank, 15, 257, 277–83, 295
Parks, Frank, 86, 317n35
Parks, Rosa, 86, 90, 266
Parms, Edwin, 242–44, 247–50
Patrolman's Benevolent Association, 221
Patterson, James, 1
Patterson, Joe, 143
Patterson, John, 82, 84–86
Payne, Jesse James, 36–37
Pearson, Levi, 53
Pearson, Thomas H. (Babe), 137–38, 142–44, 146, 324–25nn53–54, 325n58

Pearson v. County Board of Education, 53
Pellicciotti, Brenda, 273
Pennsylvania, 239, 262–63
Pentagon Papers, 304
Penton, George, 124
Percy, William Alexander, 158
Perry, Matthew J., 168–72
Phenix City, Alabama, 86
Philadelphia, Mississippi, 7, 164, 197, 213, 285–88, 293–94
Phillips High School, Birmingham, Alabama, 108–9
Pierce, D. D., 125, 128
Pierce, Ed, 247–48
Pierce v. Moon, 125–28
Pigee, Vera, 137
Pinkerton Tobacco Company, 197
Pitcher, Sargent, Jr., 132–34, 136
Pittsburgh Courier, 24, 49–50
Plessy v. Ferguson, 7, 52, 57
Poitier, Sidney, 83
police brutality: in Akron, Ohio, 242–50, 254; in Bessemer, Alabama, 96–97; Byrd and, 66–71; with cattle prods, 174–75, 178, 182–85, 187, 189–90, 213; Charlotta Bass and, 18; in Chicago, 277–83, 295; in Clarksdale, Mississippi, 141; in Darlington, South Carolina, 163–68, 170, 173, 212–13; fear of speaking out against, 303; in Ferguson, Missouri, 15, 173, 296–97, 343nn1–2, 344n4; Fourteenth Amendment and, 135; in Gadsden, Alabama, 174–75, 177–78, 182–85, 187, 189–92; Harley and, 75–77; in Holmes County, Mississippi, 66–68; *Mississippi Black Paper* and, 298–99; in Montgomery, Alabama, 82–83; NAACP and, 216, 223, 242–43, 248–50, 252–54, 259, 295; in Neshoba County, Mississippi, 288–89; in Newark, New Jersey, 229–33; in New Iberia, Louisiana, 255–64, 295; in New York City, 214–29, 234–37, 254, 297–98; in Oklahoma City, 81, 125–26; press coverage of, 303–4; protests against, 214; public criticism of, 2–4, 13–16, 66–68, 75–77, 81; in Savannah, Georgia, 75–77, 251–54; SLAPPs and, 254, 295
police culpability, 234–37
police officers: actual malice standard and, 13–15, 226–27, 260, 295, 297; alternatives to libel law and, 256, 295; Fourteenth Amendment and right to criticize, 171, 225; SLAPP suits filed by, 214–54
poll tax, 87
Porter, E. Melvin, 127
Porter, William, 15–16
Powe, Lucas, 319n79
Powell, Annie, 217
Powell, James, 13–14, 215–17, 221–22, 225–26
Presbyterian Church USA, 62
Price, Cecil R., 193–95, 198–99, 286–87, 292–93
Price, G. W., 19, 25–27
Pring, George W., 5–6, 18, 254
Pritchard, William S., 122
Proctor, Angie Grooms, 102
Progressive Democratic Party, 50
Progressive Democrat Institute, 48
Progressive Labor Movement, 223, 226
Progressive Party, 27–28, 308n26
prostitution, 86, 317n35
Providence Watchman, 21–22
Provident Hospital, Fort Lauderdale, Florida, 73
Provost, William, 229–31
Pruitt, Prentice, 71–75, 315n192
Pryor, Ralph, 238–39
Pulitzer, Joseph, 39–40
Purnell, Norman, 248–50
Putnam, Richard J., 261–62

Rabbits' Wedding, The (Williams), 104
Race, Racism, and American Law (Bell), 6
Race Beat, The (Roberts and Klibanoff), 85
racial covenants in real estate, 6, 30–31, 306n15, 309n35
racial segregation. *See* segregation
racism: in Birmingham, 94–95, 99–100, 122; CRT and, 29, 299; Hellman's childhood and, 181–82; Hodding Carter and, 157

institutional, 143, 200, 296, 299; press criticism of, 18, 26, 94–95; *Sullivan* case and, 91. *See also* Ku Klux Klan; white supremacy and white supremacists
radio, black music limited on white stations, 94, 105
Rainey, Lawrence A., 13, 193–200, 213, 257, 284–95, 298
Randle, Henry, 67
Rather, Dan, 273
Ray, James Earl, 14, 256, 264–65, 267–77, 295
Ray, Jerry and John, 268, 276–77
Ray, M. L., 189
Ray, George "Speedy," 272
Reader's Digest, 88
"Ready for Mob Control?" (Boone), 207–8
real estate, racial covenants in, 6, 30–31, 306n15, 309n35
Reconstruction, 87
Red Man tobacco, 197, 286
Red Scare (1919), 72, 228
Red Summer riots (1919), 278
rent strikes, 219, 223
Republican Party, 31, 239
Republican Party (Democratic-Republicans), 79, 81, 315n6
Revolt of Mamie Stover (film), 265
Revolt of Mamie Stover (Huie), 265
Rice, Tamir, 344n4
Rice, William O., 243–48
Richardson, Ruby, 184
right of assembly, 135–36
"Riot Squad in Gadsden, 466 Jailed" (M. L. Ray), 177–78
Rising Sun, Maryland, 238–39
Roberts, Cecil, 88
Roberts, Gene, 85, 98
Robinson, Jackie, 83
Robinson, Shirley, 215–16
Rock Hill, South Carolina, 100
Rodriquez, Francisco, 75
Roosevelt, Eleanor, 83
Roosevelt, Franklin D., 305–6n5
Rosenberg, Norman L., 315n6
Roth, Lillian, 271
Rowe, Gary Thomas, 319n92
Rowe, Kenneth, 242–50
Russell, Jane, 265

Russwurm, John B., 307n30
Rustin, Bayard, 217

Salisbury, Harrison: Bessemer, Alabama, indictments and, 97, 102–3, 319n79; Birmingham Chamber of Commerce and, 96, 104, 318n70; "Fear and Hatred Grip Birmingham," 11–12, 93–98; Graves interview and, 122; libel actions against *Times* and, 1–2, 11–12, 88, 96–98, 101–6, 108–16, 118–20
Sampson, Gary, 243
Sandburg, Carl, 158
Sanders, Harland, 309n50
Saturday Evening Post, 147–48, 151–53, 179, 186–87, 271–72
Savannah, Georgia, 75–77, 251–54
Savannah News-Press, 75–77, 252–53
Savell, Van, 144, 154–57, 324n53
Scarbrough, Tom, 142
Schiffer, George, 236
Schneider, Mark Robert, 34
school desegregation: Boone and, 202, 204–5; Central High School, Little Rock, Arkansas, 153; resistance to, 161; self-interest of whites and, 299–300; in South Carolina, 49, 57–64, 167, 172; University of Texas Law School, 170. See also *Brown v. Board of Education of Topeka;* University of Alabama; University of Mississippi (Ole Miss) riots
school inequality, 51–57
Schwerner, Michael, 13, 193–99, 284, 286–87, 292–94, 298
Scott, Albert E., 125–26
Scott, C. A., 46
Scottsboro Boys, 200
Scott's Branch School, 52–54
Seay, S. S., 82, 84–86, 90
sedition law, 4–5, 79–80, 155, 160, 300. *See also* Alien and Sedition Acts
seditious libel, 3, 15, 34, 80, 92, 316n7
segregation: black press and, 18, 30, 40–41, 49; of buses, 88; civil rights

segregation (*continued*)
  and, 129; courtroom, 91, 133–34; efforts to defend, 68; enforced by violence and threats of violence, 12; housing, 6, 30–31, 127, 278, 306n15, 309n35; of interstate transportation, 6, 129–30; legal resistance to implementation of rulings on, 6–8; of movie theaters, 219; of public beaches, 73–74; of public parks, 102, 319n91; of restaurants, 219; of schools, 18, 41, 66, 71–73, 139, 169–70, 172–73. *See also* desegregation
self-censorship, 92, 212
Sellers, Clyde, 86, 317n35
Sengstacke, John, 46, 48
Sentinel, 28
separate-but-equal doctrine, 41, 52
Seventh Circuit Court of Appeals, 279, 281
sexually transmitted diseases, 65–66
Sharper, H. P., 61
Shaw Air Force Base, 63
Shelton, Robert, 164–65, 207–11, 238, 287–88, 319n92, 333n140
"Shocking Story of Approved Killing in Mississippi, The" (Huie), 266
Shuttlesworth, Fred: Chadwick and, 104; as civil rights leader in Birmingham, 102, 108–9, 122; interracial play ordinance and, 321n159; libel suits against, 82, 84–86, 90, 102
Simon, J. Minos, 258, 260–62
Simpson, James A., 96, 103–7, 109–13, 116–17, 123, 200, 322n165
sit-in movement, 82–84, 107–8, 111, 127, 130–31, 177–78
Sitton, Claude, 93, 98
situation pieces, 93–94
Sixteenth Street Church bombing, 112, 204
slander, 4, 13, 91, 128, 160, 199
SLAPP. *See* Strategic Lawsuits Against Public Participation
slavery, 8–11
Smith, Gerald A., 242
Smith, Hazel Brannon, 11, 64–71, 77, 160–61, 313n149, 314n182
Smith, Howard K., 12, 120–23

Smith, Morgan, 113
Smith, Walter "Smitty," 66
Smolla, Rodney A., 5
social responsibility theory, 92
Somerville, John Alexander, 24–25
"Sophronia's Grandson Goes to Washington" (Hellman), 181–85
South Carolina: McCray and civil rights fight in, 39–51, 77; Perry's work in, 168–72; school desegregation in, 49, 57–64, 167, 172; school inequality in, 51–57, 77. *See also specific cities, towns, and counties*
South Carolina Supreme Court, 59–60
Southern Leadership Conference, 90
Southern University, 130–31
Soviet Russia Today, 28
Sparkman, John, 182–83
Spears, Ellis, 21
Spina, Dominick A., 230–33
Squier, Madline H., 117
Stanford Law Review, 300
Stanley, A. W., 165–68, 170–71, 173
State, The, 51
Steel, Lewis M., 248–50
steel plants, 175
Stefancic, Jean, 300
Stell, L. Scott, Jr., 76
Stevens, J., 227
Stewart, James E., 127–28
Stewart, Potter, 281–82
Stinnett, Caskie, 183
St. Louis, Missouri, 269, 275–77
St. Louis Post-Dispatch, 160, 276
Stone, John, 141
Stoner, J. B., 264–65, 268, 270
"Story of a College Football Fix, The," 179
St. Petersburg Times, 69
Strategic Lawsuits Against Public Participation (SLAPP): civil rights struggle and, 7, 11, 18, 48, 77, 118; definition of, 5–6, 18; financial hardship to media from, 300; government protection against, 303; Grooms and, 118–19; growing trend in United States, 233; legislation against, 300–301; libel-proof doctrine and, 256–57; police brutality cases and, 254,

295; sedition law resurrection and, 300. *See also under* libel law and civil rights struggle
Stutts, Roy D., 48–49
Sullivan, Charlie, 143–44
Sullivan, J. T., 205
Sullivan, Lester B.: bus station beatings and, 124–25; court costs paid by, 92; Dewey Colvard compared to, 185–86; Freedom Riders and, 12; Gilligan compared to, 226; John Patterson and, 86; segregation of public parks and, 319n91; suit filed against *New York Times*, 1–3, 78–79, 82, 84–85. See also *New York Times v. Sullivan*
Summers, Martha, 33
Summerton, South Carolina, 52–56
Sumter County, South Carolina, 57–64
Sumter Daily Item, 57–58
Sumter First Presbyterian Church, 62, 64
Sutton, Claud, 75–76
Sweat v. Painter, 170

Talladega College, 40, 50
Tannehill, Jack, 197
Tappan, Arthur, 10
Taylor, Bill, 75
Taylor, Fred, 105–9
Teel, Leonard Ray, 161
Tennessean, 100
Texas, 87, 170
Texas Court of Civil Appeals, 327n102
"Thame's Line," 105
Thirteenth Amendment, 10
Thomas, Davis, 183, 188
Thomas, Eugene, 334n150
Thornley, Fant H., 104
three-fifths compromise, 81–82, 316n13
Three Lives for Mississippi (Huie), 194, 199
Till, Emmett, 265–66
Time, 14–15, 197–98, 206, 271–75, 280–82
Time, Inc., 196
Times-Picayune, 160
Todd, Francis, 9–10
Tolbert, Willie, 41–45, 47, 51
Topeka Plaindealer, 23

Transit Workers Union (Baltimore), 240–41
Trenholm, H. Councill, 84–85
Tri-Line Offset Company, 223
Troy, Gil, 228
Trump, Donald, 15, 228–29, 301
Tuscaloosa, Alabama, 177, 200, 202–8, 211
Tuscaloosa News, 160–61, 164–65, 201–5, 207–8, 210–12, 238, 288, 333n121
Tutwiler Hotel, Birmingham, Alabama, 94, 97

"Unconscious of a Conservative, The," 302
Union Baptist Church, Gadsden, Alabama, 175
Union Leader, 159
United Klans of America, 164–65, 207, 210, 238. *See also* Ku Klux Klan
United Press International (UPI), 137–38, 144, 265
University of Alabama, 101–2, 177, 179, 203–7, 212
University of Georgia, 179
University of Mississippi (Ole Miss) riots (1962), 7, 12–13, 130, 139, 146–57, 298, 319n98
University of Missouri, 39
University of New Hampshire's Distinguished Lecture Series (1962), 13, 159–60
University of South Carolina, 64
University of Texas Law School, 170
UPI. *See* United Press International
Urofsky, Melvin I., 7
U.S. Commission on Civil Rights, 15, 168, 280–81
U.S. Court of Appeals for the Eighth Circuit, 276–77
U.S. Court of Appeals for the Fifth Circuit, 38, 119–20, 135–36, 142, 152–53, 262–63
U.S. Court of Appeals for the Fourth Circuit, 242
U.S. Court of Appeals for the Second Circuit, 275, 302–3
U.S. Court of Appeals for the Sixth Circuit, 273–75

U.S. Court of Appeals for the Third Circuit, 262–63
U.S. Department of Justice, 275–76, 283, 295, 299–300
U.S. District Court for the Eastern District of Missouri (St. Louis), 276
U.S. District Court for the Northern District of Alabama (Birmingham), 101, 152, 192
U.S. District Court for the Northern District of Georgia (Atlanta), 162
U.S. District Court for the Northern District of Mississippi (Clarksdale), 142
U.S. District Court for the Western District of Louisiana (Lafayette), 260–62
U.S. District Court for the Western District of Tennessee (Memphis), 271
U.S. Marshals Service, 146–51, 154–55
U.S. Post Office, 30, 308–9n33
U.S. Supreme Court: *Boynton v. Virginia*, 6; *Briggs v. Elliott*, 41, 55; *Buchanan v. Warley*, 30–31, 127, 306n15, 309n35; *Cox v. Louisiana*, 130–36; criticism of, 238; *Dorsey v. NAACP* and, 263, 339n19; exoneration of *Time*, 15; First Amendment and, 110, 153, 169, 172, 212, 261; freedom of association and, 209; *Garrison v. Louisiana*, 21; *Gertz v. Welch*, 341n58; *Goldwater v. Ginzburg* and, 302–3; *Henry v. Collins*, 146, 171, 325n58; *Meredith v. Fair*, 319n98; *Monroe v. Pape*, 279–80, 341n72; NAACP grocery boycott and, 251; *NAACP v. Alabama*, 85–86, 88, 170, 209; *Plessy v. Ferguson*, 7, 52, 57. See also *Associated Press v. Walker; Brown v. Board of Education of Topeka; New York Times v. Sullivan*

Vanderbilt University, 161
Vietnam War, 304
Vines, F. A., 105
Virginia, 87, 186, 192–93
voting rights: delays in implementation of, 6; literacy tests and, 127; Mississippi Sovereignty Commission and, 139; poll tax and, 87; voter registration efforts and, 50, 81, 124, 127, 129, 193, 311–12n102; Warley and I. Willis Cole and, 30–31

WABC-TV, 218–19
wade ins, 73–74
Waggoner, J. T. "Jabo": libel suit against CBS, 123, 322n167; libel suit against *Times*, 96; Salisbury article and, 103–4, 106, 112, 114–15, 119
Wagner, Robert, 222
Wagner Junior High School, 215
Walker, Edwin A.: Hodding Carter and, 159–60; McGill and, 161–62; Naimaster compared to, 242; Ole Miss riots and libel suits filed by, 12–13, 130, 153–57, 159–60, 162, 324n53, 327n99; Savell and, 155, 324n53. See also *Associated Press v. Walker*
"Walker Suit Club," 160
Wallace, George, 101–2, 176–77, 192–93, 206–7
"Wanted for Murder" (posters), 221, 223–27, 236–37, 297
Waring, Waties, 56
Warley, William, 29–36, 77
Warner, Oliver, Jr., 196
Warren, Earl, 238, 266
Warren, Leonard, 194–95
Warsham, Hoyt, 174–75
Washington, Booker T., 31, 40
Washington, George, 304
Washington County Circuit Court, Greenville, Mississippi, 160
Washington Post, 271–72, 301, 303–4
Watergate, 304
Watts, California, 19–20, 25–26
WCC Books, 194–95, 331n80
Weaver, Robert H., 70
Webster's New International Dictionary, 77
Wellford, Harry, 275
West, E. Gordon, 132
Western American, 35
Wetli, Joseph I., 247–48

"What a Price for Peace" (Boone), 205, 212
"What Next in Mississippi?" (Massie), 147–48, 151–53
Where Main Street Meets the River (Carter), 158
White, Alicia, 15–16
White, Cal, 43, 44–45
White, John W., 48
White, Victor, III, 295
White, Wingate, 131, 134–35
White Citizens' Councils. *See* Citizens' Councils
Whitehead, Don, 198
whiteness, 81, 138, 147, 157, 162, 208, 264
white supremacy and white supremacists: accusations of, 195, 199; in Birmingham, 100, 107, 118; *Brown* decision and, 59; challenges to, 208, 212, 214; complicity of law in upholding, 6–8; decreasing sympathy for, 267; in federal-court record, 107; interracial sex and, 42, 44, 51; justice system and, 34; legal doctrine shaped by, 299; libel onslaught of, 173; in Mississippi, 138, 147, 153, 157–58; Walter B. Jones and, 86–87; writers targeted by, 162. *See also* Citizens' Councils; Ku Klux Klan; Ray, James Earl

"Who Speaks for Birmingham?" (documentary), 12, 321n155
Who Speaks for Harlem? (NBC News), 222
"Why of Mississippi, The" (Carter), 159–60
Wilkins, Collie, 334n150
Wilkins, Roy, 74–75, 223
Williams, Abraham, 163–68, 170, 173
Williams, Eloise, 163, 165
Williams, Kenneth, 141
Williams, Mildred, 175
Willis, Samuella, 124
Wilson, Darren, 15, 297, 343n2
Wilson, Leonard R., 205, 333n121
Wisdom, John Minor, 135
Woods, William, 327n101
Woodward, Joanne, 174
Woolworth's lunch counter, Greensboro, North Carolina, 82–83
World War II, 27–28, 202, 299
Wright, George C., 32, 36

Xavier University, 138–39

yellow journalism, 39–40
Young, Jack, 143
YouTube, 16

Zenger, John Peter, 80
Zollo, Fred, 13
Zwerg, Jim, 99

www.ingramcontent.com/pod-product-compliance
Lightning Source LLC
Chambersburg PA
CBHW030126240426
43672CB00005B/34